AMILY TREE

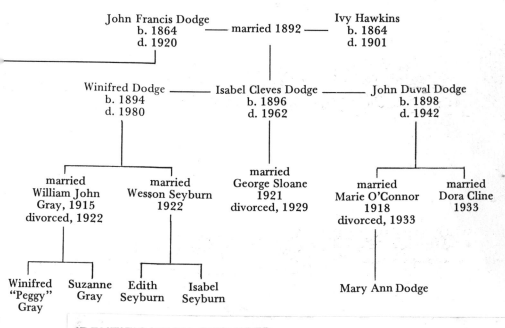

John Francis Dodge
b. 1864
d. 1920
—— married 1892 ——
Ivy Hawkins
b. 1864
d. 1901

Winifred Dodge ——— Isabel Cleves Dodge ——— John Duval Dodge
b. 1894   b. 1896   b. 1898
d. 1980   d. 1962   d. 1942

married   married   married   married   married
William John   Wesson Seyburn   George Sloane   Marie O'Connor   Dora Cline
Gray, 1915   1922   1921   1918   1933
divorced, 1922   divorced, 1929   divorced, 1933

Winifred   Suzanne   Edith   Isabel   Mary Ann Dodge
"Peggy"   Gray   Seyburn   Seyburn
Gray

THE
DODGES

For Anthony and Dean

THE DODGES

The Auto Family
Fortune and Misfortune

Jean Maddern Pitrone and Joan Potter Elwart

Icarus Press
South Bend, Indiana
1981

THE DODGES
Copyright   1981 by Jean Maddern Pitrone and Joan Potter Elwart

Icarus Press, Inc.
Post Office Box 1225
South Bend, Indiana 46624

1 2 3 4 5 6 7 8 9 10 84 83 82 81

Library of Congress Cataloging in Publication Data

Pitrone, Jean Maddern, 1920-
    The Dodges, the auto family fortune & misfortune.
    Includes index.

    1. Dodge family. I. Elwart, Joan Potter. II. Title.
CT274.D62P57   929'.2'0973   81-6684
    ISBN 0-89651-150-2   AACR2

Part I
JOHN & HORACE

1

Nestled into the lush valley of the St. Joseph River, the village of Niles, Michigan, was still the country of pioneers in the 1860s—the decade in which John and Horace Dodge were born. During the years in which Maria Casto Dodge and Daniel Rugg Dodge became the parents of three children—Della in 1863, John Francis the following year, and Horace Elgin in 1868—Niles flourished. The town had two newspapers, seven churches, eight doctors, a clothing store, a hardware store, two carriage-and-wagon shops, and more than thirty other prosperous businesses by the time the Dodge boys started to go to school. But Daniel Rugg Dodge and his two brothers (Edwin and Caleb Dodge, all of whom were descendants of an English pioneer who had come to New England in 1627) found it difficult to support their families out of earnings from their foundry and machine shop near the banks of the St. Joseph River.

Della, John, and Horace were born in a small wooden house on North Fifth Street at the edge of town, a spot ingloriously marked in later years by the town standpipe. With the birth of Maria's three children, there were five youngsters in the Daniel Dodge household, including Laura and Charles, children from the previously widowed Daniel's first marriage. Although barefoot children roamed the Niles countryside in the summertime, the Dodges' children had no shoes even in early winter when Maria sent them to the brick schoolhouse down the road from their home. Still, Maria, of industrious Pennsylvania Dutch and French heritage, never let the family's poverty become an excuse for lack of ambition.

Della was enrolled in school first. When John was almost five years old, he joined his sister and was placed in the class of Miss Ella Tibbets. Miss Tibbets soon discovered that John was a bright student with a fiery temper that matched his red-gold hair and outmatched his scrawny body.

3

Maria's influence evidenced itself in her children's achievements. A book, preserved by the family for nearly a hundred years, indicated John's dogged perseverance:

John Dodge
Union School
Grammar Dept.
Third Year 1877

This book is presented for punctuality. Present every day and every half day for three years and not once tardy.

Mary Manson, Teacher

At an early age, John found his first job, driving a cow three miles a day for fifty cents a month. Later, the boys spent much of their free time puttering around their father's foundry, learning the skills of the forge and machine shop. Since the boats that navigated the St. Joseph River provided the Dodge shop with most of its business, the boys soon became familiar with the intricacies of the marine engines their father and uncles repaired. Horace especially was entranced by the power and speed of the craft on the river. Someday, he vowed as he watched the boats moving down the water, he would own the biggest and most powerful boat of all.

The red-headed, freckle-faced Horace Elgin did not have many friends among his schoolmates. Supersensitive to being teased about his name and concealing this sensitivity with a swaggering belligerence, Horace used his middle name as the lesser of two evils during his schooldays. He was known as Elgin Dodge—a tough character with an explosive temper.

While their poverty made the brothers unacceptable to many of their schoolmates' families, the boys developed strong alliances elsewhere. Although racial distinctions were made in the town of Niles, with black children sent to a separate school, the Dodge boys were drawn to a cheerful, patient black man—Cyrus Bowles—who had come to work in their father's shop. Cyrus made whistles for them, showed them how to fish on the banks of the St. Joe, and entertained them with stories of his childhood in the South.

Six days of the week, the young brothers were admiring listeners as Cyrus spun his stories, but on Sundays the boys' admiration shifted to a man who came from the opposite stratum of Niles society—John S. Tuttle. Tuttle was a school board trustee and superintendent of the Methodist Episcopal Sunday School the boys and Della attended faithfully. Under Tuttle's refining influence, Horace Elgin decided that one of his first gifts to his brother John would be a Bible, which he purchased from his savings of small coins.

Something about the scruffy, eager Dodge boys attracted the personal interest of the Sunday school superintendent, who encouraged the brothers to visit his rambling home—a home that the townspeople pridefully pointed out to visitors as a showplace. And each time the boys walked past the carefully tended flower gardens as they came to visit the Tuttle home, Horace watched for an opportunity to go into the parlor and over to the piano where he would pick out a melody on the keyboard. When the boys left the big house, they would hurry home to share their experiences with their mother. Someday, they boasted to her, they would become as successful as John S. Tuttle, who had made his money dealing in furs and hides. They would build a home as beautiful as Tuttle's for the Dodge family. And he would have a piano too, Horace added firmly.

Maria would nod and smile and then remind the boys and Della that they could take pride in their own pioneer heritage. Maria herself had been only a small child when her parents William and Indie Duval Casto, had left her birthplace in Rising Sun, Indiana. But now she passed on to her own children the stories her parents had told of their trek from Indiana up to the southwestern Michigan settlement. The Niles settlement of those days had centered around a wharf for riverboats and a rope ferry to haul stagecoaches across the river . . . a settlement where Indians, some wearing rings in their noses and flaunting silver breastplates, still mingled with the white residents.

John's seatmate in school was the son of another of Niles' more prosperous families—the Bonines. Occasionally, Fred Bonine was an after-school companion of the Dodge boys. By the time John was in high school, the high-wheeled bicycle came into fashion, and Bonine was the first boy in Niles to own one of the $200 bicycles. John and Horace watched enviously as Bonine pedaled past them on his cycle. Soon the boys were busy steaming a strip of wood and bending it into shape to use for the rim of a high wheel for their own improvised bike. They took a wheel from an old baby carriage to use for the small rear wheel and fashioned a high-wheeled cycle as functional as any purchased in a shop. For two years they rode it proudly, pedaling down Main Street on Saturday afternoons and attracting the attention of shoppers and farmers piling supplies into wagons.

In his teen years, the undersized John suddenly spurted to six-foot stature and was now ready to try to find work more appropriate to his new dimensions. Tom Davis, drayman and the town ashman, agreed to hire John for fifty cents a day to help him carry sacks of bran out of railroad cars. Tom was a familiar figure in Niles, sitting on the high seat of his wagon at the reins of his dirty white team of horses and followed by his mangy dog. Although John was not at all concerned that

Davis was a black man and that ashmen were at the bottom of Niles' social structure, the memory of young Dodge carting the heavy bran sacks for the black ashman apparently left its imprint on the town.

Whenever there was time for anything apart from work and school, Horace would grab his fishing rod and settle along the riverbank, content to dream and to watch the boats for hours. But John quickly tired of this pastime. Instead, he loved to take long walks along the curving country roads, latticed with rows of fruit trees and grape vines twined neatly on barrel hoops mounted on posts. He liked to climb hillsides blooming with yellow daffodils or to tramp through the forests that began where the tidy farms ended, watching for skunk cabbage thrusting purple sheaths through the mud of the swamps in the springtime. Summer brought violets and bloodroot and Dutchman's Britches and hepaticas thick on the south side of the ravine, and John would continue to walk the hillsides until autumn frosts brought the season to an end.

The two brothers shared their family's pride in Della's accomplishments in the summer of 1879 when the sixteen-year-old girl graduated with honors from high school. Although many boys from families in better financial situations than the Dodges were leaving school to help support themselves and their families, John and Horace continued their studies. No trade or vocational subjects were offered in the Niles school. The boys chose their classes from among courses in algebra, geometry, Latin, rhetoric, Greek prose, and astronomy, and in 1882 John was graduated.

The best job he could find as a new graduate was in the old Krick factory for $6.25 a week. Willingly, he turned over his weekly wages to his family because his father's shop was doing poorly. The railroad had developed into a booming new transportation medium in the past few years, and as Niles was emerging as a railroad link of this new industry between Chicago and Detroit, the Dodge business, dependent in great part on the obsolescent river traffic, continually worsened.

When their father's two brothers—and partners—died within the span of one year, the boys found that family ties in Niles were diminished for the Dodges. Shortly after John completed school, but without waiting for Horace to graduate, the family packed its belongings and moved across the state to the growing industrial center in southeastern Michigan.

Settling first in Port Huron, Daniel Dodge started a machine shop specializing in marine motor work. In the confusion of setting up a shop in the busy shipping port situated on Lake Huron at its junction with the St. Clair River, Horace was able to avoid his mother's pressure to enroll in school and finish his high school education. Instead, he joined John in the Dodge shop where the boys helped their father and experimented with the complexities of the internal combustion engine. And as the school year advanced and Horace was still working in the shop, Maria gradually gave up her attempts to influence her younger son to return to school after Daniel boasted of Horace's deftness with machinery.

When machine shop work did not keep them as busy as they had hoped, the boys got jobs at the Upton Manufacturing Company, makers of threshing machines and agricultural implements. With a part of his earnings, Horace bought a second-hand violin and contentedly practiced on the instrument when he came home from work in the evenings.

Soon, however, the Dodge brothers began to wonder if they had made a mistake in settling in the small town of Port Huron when, only sixty miles away, the city of Detroit offered endless business and employment possibilities to the restless and ambitious. And there was the excitement of big-city life in Detroit, the boys pointed out to their undecided father. Horse-drawn cars moved up and down Detroit streets. Woodward Avenue, illuminated by electric arc lights, was paved with cedar blocks, while boardwalks in the shopping areas kept pedestrians' boots out of the mud. Detroit's professional baseball team played in its own stadium; the Detroit Opera House orchestra performed weekly at Belle Isle.

In 1886 when the Dodge family moved to Detroit, the Detroit River was rivaling the Suez Canal in the amount of tonnage passing through its channels. Huge sailing vessels crowded the wharves at the end of Woodward Avenue where tugs, moving in and out, pulled the larger ships from the docks out into the open water, where northern winds filled the ships' great sails and carried them gracefully on to the lakes. Large steamers also swept down the channels, carrying wheat from the West, copper ore for the furnaces at the edge of the river, and iron ore for the city's rolling mills.

The waterfront was lined with businesses catering to the shipping trade. Atwater Street offered an assortment of havens for seamen, including George Rausch's "thirst emporium," the Princess Saloon. Third Street, running uphill from the river, boasted many types of lodgings for sailors lying over between ships or waiting out the winter months. For the indigent, there were the welcome lights of the Salvation Army. For those who had providently laid away a few dollars, there were places such as the Dry Dock Hotel, run by the buxom Margaret Rausch, wife of the scrawny proprietor of the Princess

Saloon. At Margaret's Dry Dock Hotel, a warm clean bed was available for the night or the season. For a quarter, a sailor could fill up with one of Margaret's home-cooked meals that began with hot soup, even in summer, and included beef, mutton, and pork, three kinds of vegetables, bread and butter, and concluded with a slab of pie.

Margaret and George Rausch—later to become in-laws of the Dodges—had come to Detroit from Canada in the hope of molding a more successful future in the flourishing Michigan city. Bringing their small daughter, Matilda, with them, they had settled close to the city's main artery, Woodward Avenue.

Many immigrants trained in the skills of seafaring also settled close to Woodward Avenue and found employment around the wharves at the foot of the central street . . . at the T. W. Noble Company, sailmakers, riggers, and suppliers of cotton duck and awning goods, and just across the avenue, at the J. P. Donaldson Company, ship chandler. Among the immigrant employees of these companies helping to swell Detroit's population in the last quarter of the nineteenth century from 60,000 to 285,000 were the William Thomsons, father and son—who also would become Dodge in-laws.

On the Dodge family's arrival in Detroit, twenty-two-year-old John and eighteen-year-old Horace went to work at Tom Murphy's Boiler Shop. Under the supervision of Murphy, a marine engineer, the boys built boilers and repaired boats—a job requiring strength and endurance that could be supplied only by husky, rugged men such as the Dodge brothers. They worked hard for $18 a week until John, advanced to foreman, was raised to $20 a week.

The Dodge family had settled into a rented home on Porter Street, and as soon as he was working steadily, Horace bought a piano. The move to a new city gave Horace, who was still having identity problems, the chance to rid himself of a name that had embroiled him in a number of fist fights in earlier years. Since births were not yet being officially reported in the state of Michigan at the time the Dodge boys were born, the Dodges, like many of their contemporaries, did not hesitate to adjust names and their spellings without benefit of legalities. As a newcomer to Detroit, Horace Elgin listed himself as Dellie I. Dodge. In Port Huron he had called himself Delbert. From Delbert to Dellie, Horace would be known a little later as Ed, then as H. E., and finally, coming full circle, once again as Horace.

Seeking broader opportunities, the brothers left Tom Murphy's employ after six years to cross the river boundary into Canada to look for work with the Dominion Typography Company in Windsor, only to be told that just one man was needed. "We're brothers, and we always work together," John stated flatly. "If you haven't got room for two of us, neither will start."

Hired at salaries of $150 a month, the Dodges worked with micrometers and calipers at a time when there were few people using such precision tools in machine work. Their employers were surprised and pleased with the accuracy of the machines Horace produced to cut the matrices of the letters. For Horace, intently exploring every possibility for improving a machine part or a pattern and leaving it to John to explain the need for micrometric exactness in the production of interchangeable parts, it was satisfying work.

When typographs were not in demand, the company began to make the Maple Leaf Bicycle, or the E. & D. Machine—the *D* in the symbol indicating Dodge as an associate in its design and making. With an estimated ten million cyclists in the country, Detroit streets were filled with wheelsmen who were called "scorchers" as they raced recklessly through the city.

When the Dodges began experimenting with the designing of an improved bicycle, Horace worked at home on his first mechanical invention—a four-point, dirt-proof, easily adjustable bearing for their machine. The brothers edged their way into the world of mechanical entrepreneurs when they leased the ball-bearing device to the bicycle maker on a royalty basis.

Until this time, the Dodge family had remained together as a unit except for the boys' half-sister Laura, who had married and remained in Niles. Half-brother Charlie Dodge also lived with the family in Detroit for a time. But in February of 1892, Della married Uriah Eschbach, the former superintendent of the Port Huron company where Horace and John had worked. John and Horace witnessed the wedding ceremony of their sister just four days before her twenty-ninth birthday as she became the bride of the forty-seven-year-old Eschbach, Civil War veteran and a widower with a daughter almost as old as Della. Eschbach took his bride from the Dodge home, now on Trumbull Street, to Ann Arbor, where Uriah had gone into the laundry business.

Always ambitious, John had even more reason now to strike out for success in the business world as he courted Ivy Hawkins, a dressmaker who lived with her family only a few blocks west of Trumbull. The pretty, dark-haired Ivy had been born in Canada and had emigrated with her parents, two brothers, and a sister to Detroit, where her father found work as a general laborer and her two brothers as machinists.

When John and Ivy—both twenty-eight—were married in September 1892, they set up housekeeping in John's home on Trumbull while Horace and the rest of the family moved into another comfortable two-story frame house four blocks away on Lincoln Street. The marriage simply widened the family circle slightly. Eighteen months after John married Ivy, their first child, Winifred, was born. In February 1896 a second daughter, Isabel Cleves, was born and named for John's paternal grandmother.

But John and Ivy were distracted from the pleasure they took in their two small daughters by their worry over John's health: he had begun to suffer from a persistent, hacking cough. It was not a smoker's cough, because his strict Methodist upbringing had kept him away from tobacco, and from liquor as well. Apart from the coughing, he felt weak and tired, suffered from cold sweats at night, and experienced intermittent fevers. At thirty-two years of age, and for the first time in his vigorous life, he stayed home from work, the doctor having prescribed bed rest and medicine.

Was it consumption? This was the question that tormented John at a time when tuberculosis was referred to as "consumption," "the wasting disease," or "the white plague." The doctor was hesitant to make such a diagnosis in an era when there were no X-rays to give confirmation. John's mother would speak of her son's illness only in euphemisms, insisting that John "took spells" and "was not too strong."

When John had a violent allergic reaction to the medicine the doctor prescribed, another medication was tried, with similar results. Finally, a Parke-Davis compound that John referred to as *131* was found to be the only medication that he could tolerate. As he began to regain his strength, John always made certain a bottle of his *131* compound was kept at home and another at his work. And he began doctoring his cough with the potent elixir of the turn of the century— whiskey.

Shortly before John became ill, Horace had begun courting the attractive Christina Anna Thomson, known as *Tini* even though Christina thoroughly disliked the nickname. The modishly full-figured Christina—a Scottish girl of medium height, her light brown, naturally curly hair fashionably long—was three years younger than twenty-seven-year-old Horace. But there was more than good looks that attracted Horace to Christina. As a self-taught pianist and violinist, Horace admired Christina's skill as a pianist and was impressed with her formal musical training.

Christina, later to call herself *Anna*, had been born on August 7, 1871, in Dundee, Scotland, to Elizabeth Stevenson and William

Thomson. In Dundee, she had studied music in school at an early age. She continued her piano studies after her mother and father had emmigrated to Detroit in 1880 with their three daughters—May, 18; Catherine, 14; and Christina Anna, 9. A sailmaker by trade, Thomson had no trouble finding work with a ship chandler along the riverfront, and the family settled into the same neighborhood, on Orleans Street.

On Orleans, Christina met a girl who was to become a lifelong friend—Isabelle Smith, daughter of a widowed dressmaker who lived across the street from the Thomsons. Christina and Isabelle were intrigued by the fact that they had been born on the same day of the same month of the same year, and the two girls visited back and forth constantly.

As the child of working-class parents, Christina Anna was expected to be self-supporting as soon as possible. She found her first job at the Morton Baking Company, packing cookies. Three years later, she became a foreman for Morton, then moved on to work as a finisher in a factory. But this kind of job was not attractive to Christina, and in 1896 she began teaching piano students and calling herself *Anna*. Her friendship with Isabelle Smith had flourished over the years to the point where Isabelle often accompanied Anna to the homes of piano students, visiting with the parents while the lessons were being given. Anna was a strict teacher, impatient with those who did not perform according to what she considered to be their potential, and her students knew an unprepared lesson was provocation for a whack over the knuckles.

The Thomson family was favorably impressed with Horace as a suitor for their Anna. His good nature was apparent. And he was a hard worker. What more could they ask for their daugher? Anna's six-year-old niece, Ella McNutt (daughter of May Thomson and Robert McNutt, blacksmith), loved the big red-headed Horace and would artfully wedge herself between her aunt and her genial suitor as they sat on the Thomsons' parlor settee. The man who could be a titian bear in the machine shop became a gentle, tractable victim of the charms of the small niece and of all the warm circle of the Thomson family . . . and, most of all, of Christina Anna.

When Horace, twenty-eight, and Anna, twenty-five, were married in 1896, there was no money for a wedding trip. The young couple could not even justify a day away from work to mark the occasion. Anna and her friend, Isabelle Smith, took the ferry across the river to Windsor, while Horace left the typography shop long enough to pronounce his wedding vows, with John and Isabelle as witnesses. Then Horace went back to the shop and Anna to her piano students.

The newlyweds went to live with Horace's parents in their Lincoln Street home. Determined to finance a belated honeymoon, Anna began putting money aside in a teapot during that first year of marriage, dreaming of a trip to Niagara Falls. But her thoughts flashed immediately to her savings when Horace came home one day, face flushed with excitement. If he and John could scrape up enough money to lease the Dominion Typography Company building and fixtures, he confided to his wife, they could take over the operation of the business. It wasn't fair, Anna thought in dismay, to expect her to give up her plans for a honeymoon trip! But Horace continued to talk, his red hair bristling as if electrified with excitement. It was his and John's chance to go into business for themselves, he explained. Did she have faith in him, or didn't she? Anna decided that she did have faith and that Horace needed a business more than she needed a honeymoon. She removed the lid from her teapot and gave him the $200 she had saved.

Daniel Dodge, the father who shared the years of struggle with his boys, died in July 1897, the year his sons began this first business. Soon after the brothers assumed their own business, their family obligations mounted. In August 1898, John and Ivy had their third child, a son named John for his father and Duval for his great-grandmother. John Duval's arrival was marked with some concern when Ivy began suffering from respiratory problems immediately after his birth, however. And five months later, in January 1899, Anna and Horace had their first child—a daughter named Delphine Ione. The brothers decided to sell their newly acquired business to an Ontario firm, which took over the lease.

When Horace and Anna had their second child—a boy born in 1900—they gave him the name his father had found troublesome for so long. With the same fierce determination that marked his decisions for the rest of his life, Horace resolved that he would make the name Horace Elgin Dodge one that his son and the world would recognize and respect.

The brothers, who had continued to work for the Ontario firm, had expected to receive substantial royalty payments from the buyer for their ball-bearing bicycle invention. But the company, beginning to fail, had reneged on royalty payments. As soon as the Canadian company made plans to dispose of its assets, the Dodge brothers canceled their claims against the firm in exchange for their pick of the machinery in the Windsor plant.

Using the machinery retrieved from the bankrupt business, the brothers decided to make another try for success by setting up their own machine shop on the American side of the river. In spite of the financial risks and an awareness of their own father's repeated failures in machine-shop ventures, they went ahead with their plans. And the plans continued, even though John was apprehensive about Ivy, whose condition continued to deteriorate until she could scarcely care for their three young children.

In September 1902, the brothers leased quarters in the Boydell Building in Detroit and hired twelve men to work for them. Many times, after the employees had gone home to their families, John and Horace locked up their shop, went out for a sandwich, and then returned to work half the night, getting out estimates, designs, and plans for machinery, making tracings, and studying books on mechanics. Although they contracted for any job in the mechanical line, they drew much of their first work from the many stove manufacturers in Detroit.

Just a month after the Dodge Brothers shop had opened, John's personal life collapsed around him upon Ivy's death from tuberculosis. With all his assets invested in the shop, John had to turn to relatives (John's Aunt "Frank" and Aunt "Sate"—sisters of Maria Dodge; the sisters had inherited a small sum of money at the time their younger brother was killed in the Civil War) to borrow enough money to bury his wife in Woodlawn Cemetery, where he purchased a double plot of eight gravesites—four for his own family, four for Horace's family.

Then John rearranged his life to try to provide for his children— Winifred, now nine; Isabel, seven, and the toddler John Duval. Although his mother, Maria, was now an invalid in a wheelchair, she was moved from Horace's home into her older son's home on Trumbull Street to supervise hired help in caring for John's motherless children while John spent most of his time at the shop.

Although opportunities for achievement may have abounded in Detroit at the beginning of the twentieth century, few men dared to gamble for success as heavily as did the Dodge brothers. Few men had the stamina required to manage the demands the brothers' business and personal lives exacted in those early days. Yet Anna, looking back on those years with fondness a few decades later, was to reminisce, "The happiest years of my life were when I was packing Horace's lunch pail."

2

As early as the 1700s, ingenious Frenchmen and Englishmen were building piston and cylinder engines. Through the years, other men continued experimenting with internal combustion engines in hopes of building successful self-propelled land vehicles. In 1894, Charles B. King, builder of marine gas engines, astonished Detroiters by driving through the city's streets in a gasoline-powered car, although Frank Duryea of Massachusetts had driven his car—known as America's first successful gasoline automobile—on the streets of Springfield a year previously.

For the next several years, beautiful, custom-made, and individually crafted motor cars were built and prized by racing buffs. But the public in general, and investors in particular, believed the automobile was not a practical business proposition, viewing it as a rich man's plaything in the same category as the polo pony.

Henry Ford built his first car in 1896. But it was a young man from Lansing, Michigan—Ransom Olds—who organized the first automobile company in Michigan in 1897. Olds then began the manufacture of a small car to sell for $1,250 on the premise that he could mass-produce an automobile that could compete mechanically with custom-made machines and yet be economical enough to attract a broad market. But the car was too complicated in design, Olds lost money, and the company failed.

By 1900, seventy-one American companies were making cars. The companies sprang up at the rate of one a week until 1908 when 502 car manufacturing businesses had been formed. The attrition rate was about 60 percent; most of these companies tried to follow Olds' lead . . . and failed for the same reason. Each attempted to build a car that in theory had parts exactly alike, but all these cars were full of mechanical inaccuracies.

14

When Ransom Olds managed to get financial backing for a second car-manufacturing venture, he produced the famous one-cylinder "curved-dash Olds runabout"—the "merry Oldsmobile." It weighed 700 pounds and sold for $650. It used a tubular frame, chain and sprocket, ball bearings, and pneumatic tires on bicycle-type wheels.

Just when success seemed to be within Olds' reach, the Olds factory burned down. All that was saved was the one completed model of the curved-dash runabout that the timekeeper had managed to push out into the yard. The company had to concentrate all its resources on this model now; even the designs had to be redrawn from the surviving car since the original designs had been burned.

To avoid a production delay that might have meant another business failure, Olds improvised a plan by which the Olds company would act as assembler, having the various parts for the little car produced in other machine shops. Some firms would supply bodies, still others springs and wheels. But Olds wanted the best machinists in Detroit, the Dodge brothers, to make the transmissions.

The brothers took an order from Olds for 3,000 transmissions, a mammoth contract for that era, and went into frantic production, knowing that the profits to be made on the contract could put the Dodge machine shop on a sound financial basis. Olds found a large open building in which he assembled his automobile parts, and once again the little Oldsmobile began wheeling down the streets of Detroit. In 1901, the company turned out 425 cars in a few months. Such quantity mechanical production had never before been known. In 1902, Olds produced 2,500 cars, Michigan was credited with the manufacture of nearly half the motor vehicles in the country, and the horses and wagons on Detroit's streets now shared the roads with 800 motorcars.

With only a small shop and staff, the Dodges kept pace with a tough schedule as their business rose to quick success with the wide acceptance of the Oldsmobile. The brothers worked for fifteen and twenty hours at a stretch, often sleeping on benches in their shop in order to be on the job at 6 A.M. To friends, John Dodge confided that in two years while they occupied the shop in the Boydell Building he spent only six weekday evenings at home.

The physical and emotional pressures of his life at this time took their toll on John's health—his respiratory problems returned. The bottle of *131* was quickly emptied at the shop and replaced with another bottle. And after work, he doctored every cough with swigs of whiskey. Horace, who joined his brother in all activities, joined him also in the whiskey drinking, although both men were careful not to let the drinking interfere with their work. The work, above all, had to continue in the unrelenting pace of turning out transmissions to make their quota and to keep their profits as high as possible without expanding their work force.

Although John did not pamper himself because of his own health problems, he worried incessantly about his small son, since little John Duval also suffered a series of colds and coughs. The father watched the boy carefully for signs of the "white plague." In his fears for the boy's health and his worries over leaving the child to be raised by hired help, John tried to compensate by petting and indulging the boy.

There was little time to spend with the child, though, now that the reputation of the Dodge Brothers for precision machining was attracting the attention of other manufacturers. No longer was it necessary for the brothers to scour the city, searching for work for the shop. In addition to their continuing commitment to Olds, the brothers accepted some of the orders that poured in from other manufacturers. Their shop was too small, they realized, and they continued to turn their profits back into their business with the construction of a three-storied brick building on Monroe and Hastings streets in 1902. They hired additional shopmen and added a bookkeeper to the payroll. Then they placed an advertisement for a stenographer.

Sitting at his large, well-polished mahogany desk with its high roll top, John Dodge studied the tiny applicant who sat opposite him, then checked over the qualifications she had listed: one year at Gorsline Business College—typing, shorthand, bookkeeping . . . presently employed by E. J. Kruce Cracker Company . . . wants to find employment closer to home.

Once more, John's eyes carefully swept over the young woman— an inch or so over five feet, black hair piled carefully on top of her head, snapping brown eyes. Yes, John thought, she would do very nicely. Matilda Rausch would do very nicely, indeed.

Matilda settled quickly into the routine at the Dodge shop. When she returned at night to the Rausch family apartment over her father's saloon, she shared her experiences with her parents and her sister. "Mr. Dodge tells me his wife died last year. Why does he tell me this kind of thing?" she complained to the Rausches soon after she began to work for Dodge Brothers. "What should I care about his personal life?"

John had good reason for indicating his marital eligibility. Shortly after he employed the new secretary, he asked her if she would go with him to a concert at the Detroit Opera House. Soon he became Matilda's regular escort; the two went out together at least once a week. John's Methodist upbringing had prevented him from learning to dance and from playing social card games, but Matilda was not concerned about that, since she did not enjoy these recreations either. She was quite happy to go to the Opera House, where she could observe aristocratic Detroiters in their box seats.

With their shop beginning to succeed financially now, the Dodge brothers made almost daily short treks over to Churchill's Saloon, where anyone connected with automobiles—hard drinker or teetotaler—could be tracked down. It was not unusual for four or five men to carry a heavy piece of machinery into the saloon, place it on the floor or a table, and set the machine in motion.

The young Henry Ford had been trying for a number of years to develop a successful car. He had gained some recognition as an automobile racer, but since he had already failed twice in the automobile business, he was having trouble finding investors. He was seeking money to manufacture the car he had most recently designed with the help of C. Harold Wills after having had problems with the internal combustion engine he was trying to perfect. By 1902, Ford had convinced two associates, coal dealers Alexander Malcomson and James Couzens, to help him in the promotion of his latest car design.

When Ford approached the Dodges with his sketches, the brothers were wary. Their shop was already deluged with orders for parts and with requests for assistance in new automotive ventures. Yet Ford was very convincing with his talk of quantity production and expert promotion by Malcomson and Couzens. As Horace studied the plans, he was intrigued by the engine design. His nod toward John told the older brother that there were good possibilities here, since the Dodge shop, equipped with a variety of machines for a wide range of production, had much of the tooling for the precision manufacturing of a chassis. In contrast, the rudimentary little garage in which Ford had been experimenting had no specialized tools at all.

Horace went to work on the Ford plans. He redesigned the rear axle and worked on the engine to make the mechanism more efficient. Near the end of 1902, the Dodge brothers produced in their machine shop the automobile that was to be the basis for Ford's successful business (see *Michigan Manufacturer and Financial Record*). A 1920 copy of *Automobile Topics* claimed that this automobile was quite different from the creation first submitted to the Dodges on paper.

Ford then asked Dodge Brothers to make 650 chassis—engines, transmissions, and axles—for his business. Because of their personal involvement in the design of the proposed car, the Dodges were excited over the prospect of the Ford automobile becoming a success. But if they accepted Ford's offer, they would have to give up their lucrative contract with Olds. The brothers talked things over, carefully elaborating the risks inherent in giving up their Olds contract at a time when they were beginning to make a large amount of money for the first time in their lives. Then they agreed to do what each of them knew from the beginning he wanted to do—gamble everything they had in the hope of making even bigger profits on the Ford automobile.

On February 28, 1903, Dodge Brothers signed a contract agreeing to supply the 650 chassis for $250 each, to be paid to the Dodges in installments. Since the brothers had to invest their own money in new machinery, tools, and materials in order to turn out the chassis in volume, the payments made by Ford over the first several months would no more than cover the brothers' $60,000 retooling expenses. Their single protection against financial ruin was a contract clause stipulating that Ford assets would revert to the Dodges in case Ford & Malcomson, Ltd., failed to meet the payments.

Ford and Wills were to be responsible only for an assembly job as their part of the automobile's production. The Dodges were to deliver a complete car, except for wheels and body. The Ford partners contracted for the remaining parts—tires at $46 a set from Hartford, wheels for $25 a set from Prudden Wheel, bodies from Wilson Carriage at $52 each, and cushions for $16. The man who rented Malcomson his coal yard was to construct an assembly building to be rented to the new company at $75 a month. Most of these people, including the Dodges, provided their services and materials on faith, because the penniless Ford could find little financial backing.

A dozen men were hired at $1.50 a day to assemble the car, paint it, and test it. Expecting to deliver ten automobiles a day beginning July first, the company planned to have 650 cars finished by October 1903.

The first of many rows and arguments that characterized the Dodge-Ford relationship erupted a few weeks after the brothers signed the contract. In May 1903, Malcomson inserted a two-page advertisement in a trade paper announcing a car to sell for $850. The Dodge Brothers machine shop had been leased by the automobile company, the advertisement stated, and four-fifths of the 650 chassis contracted for had been completed. The Dodges were annoyed because the number of completed chassis had been so exaggerated, and they were enraged at having been made to appear subservient to

Ford when there had been no takeover of the Dodge business. Compelling the publisher to print a correction, John demanded an apology from Malcomson. But the brothers continued to work on the chassis.

When the first $5,000 payment was due the Dodges in mid-March 1903, John and Horace came to Malcomson to collect. Malcomson stalled, then finally had to admit the company did not have the payment money. Reminded of the agreement under which the Dodges had the right to take over all machinery and running-gear if the scheduled payment was not made, Malcomson pleaded for time. The Dodges were firm. Their money was tied up in materials, and they were at the end of their resources. Either Malcomson would get the money, or the brothers would take over the sale of the cars.

Under pressure, Malcomson went to his uncle, banker John Gray, to borrow money. By this time, a second payment of $5,000 was coming due to the Dodges. Gray finally agreed to advance $10,500 on the condition that a corporation would be formed, of which he would be president, and would hold 10.5 percent of the stock. On June 16, 1903, papers of incorporation for the Ford Motor Company were filed, and one thousand shares of stock were issued with a par value of $100 a share. Ford and Malcomson each received 255 shares—a total of 51 percent—for their contribution to the company, although they had invested no money. Gray, as president, received 105 shares. The Dodges each accepted fifty shares of stock in the new company in payment for the first $10,000 owed to them. Couzens could come up with enough money to buy only 25 shares. Wills, the man who had helped Ford with his original plans, had no money for stock, but had to be satisfied with an oral agreement with Ford, who promised to give 10 percent of his personal profits to Wills to keep his associate working with the company. The owner of the assembly building took his year's rent in shares, and five other investors were enticed to take small shares in the new company. Altogether, only $29,500 was paid by stockholders in cash, and the company had to exist on this until the cars were sold.

Entries in the Dodge Brothers black-and-red payroll book noted that each brother received $43.20 in salary for two weeks in July 1903. Once more, after a year and a half of prosperity with Ransom Olds, the brothers were back to minimum salaries, but with the expectation that this time of frugality would be only a brief one. By July, the Dodges began to deliver the chassis on horse-drawn hay ricks from their Monroe shop to the assembly plant. There, the chassis were dumped on the floor and handled in groups of four by three workmen to a car. Motors were tuned up, carburetors adjusted, valves and transmission bands tested, and brakes put in working order. Then, two men picked up the body and bolted it in place while the third man attached the fenders—fenders "so light," one worker said, "you could wear them for earrings." The workers, expected to turn out fifteen automobiles a day, completed the processing of each car with a paint job.

The new Eastern High School had been built just around the corner from the single-story frame assembly plant, with a macadamized road in front of the school. Here, the Ford workers tried out the new cars. Students heckled as the first Fords spun past. Small boys, loitering around the neighborhood slaughterhouse, ran out and stared enviously at the men behind the wheels of the machines.

Couzens, in charge of the company's business office, had established dealers in various states, and following the successful pattern set up by Olds, he insisted that the entire purchase price be collected in advance of delivery. On July 15, the first order for a Ford car arrived with a check for $850 from a doctor who became one of the first of many physicians to make serious use of the automobile early in its history.

This early car, named the *Model A*, weighed only 1,250 pounds. The driver had the steering wheel on the right and could speed up to thirty miles an hour on a good road. There was no door for the driver to get in and no running board, only a small carriage step. It had a two-cylinder engine that developed eight horsepower, and a six-foot base. The transmission had two speeds forward and one in reverse, and the ignition and throttle were adjusted by hand. For an additional $100, the buyer could purchase a tonneau, a backseat arrangement that slipped on and off from the rear.

The first shipment of cars sold immediately, and as the car began to pay its way from profits, stockholders never were required to put up any more cash. By October of that first year, Ford expanded the assembly plant, and the Dodges, who contracted to deliver 755 more chassis in the first five months of 1904, made a personal profit of more than $25,000. With this, in an era when there were no income taxes, the brothers planned to add two more buildings to their Monroe Avenue plant.

Although their business and their 150 factory employees made strenuous demands on the time and energies of the Dodges in 1903, the two brothers always took time for some social life. The high point of Horace's and Anna's week was their visit to the Detroit Opera House. At home, both of them loved to play the piano, although Anna's abilities at the piano were limited ever since she had severed the tendons in one hand.

On the few nights that Horace was not at the shop or with his brother at Charlie Churchill's Saloon, he and Anna discussed their plans to move into a more attractive home. They could afford it, Horace assured Anna, now that they were making good profits from their production of Ford engines and transmissions. Although the cars had begun selling only in the middle of July, the Ford Motor Company paid its first dividend in November—a dividend of $10,000, of which the Dodges collected $1,000. Coming four months after the sale of the first car, the dividend payment augured a bright future for stockholders.

Before the year ended, Anna had found a larger home on nearby Forest Street—a home with stained-glass window inserts in the front door and large bay windows in front and at the side of the house. Shopping trips now were exciting for Anna. She bought curtains and drapes for the windows and extra furniture for the larger rooms. Although she could now afford occasional household help, Anna was concerned about the reliability of hired help for caring for her children when she had to leave the house. But soon after the move to Forest Street, Anna's niece Ella—the same Ella who had tagged after Horace when he had come to the Thomson house to court Anna—came to live with her aunt and uncle while she attended neighboring Central High School. Anna could go shopping then, without worrying about the children. Delphine and Horace Jr. were preschoolers of five and three during the year their father was immersed in perfecting and producing the first Fords, and for Anna, life in the house on Forest was a quiet one. Sometimes she and her niece played cards in the evenings. At other times, Ella read a chapter from the Bible to her aunt, then read other stories while Anna listened and worked on her needlepoint.

As the Dodges' machine shop prospered, both Horace and John spent more time in Detroit saloons. Unlike their teetotaling associates, Olds and Ford, the Dodges visited saloons as much for pleasure as for business, moving from Louis Schneider's bar up the Woodward Avenue row of saloons. They favored Charlie Churchill's place, known as the "gentlemen's place" because it served hors d'oeuvres and displayed a brunette Venus on one wall. John admired the painting of the nude woman so much that he acquired a similar figure to decorate his desk at the shop.

When fortified with alcohol, the high-spirited Dodges lost any inhibitions they might have had, and whether they were in good temper or bad, the consequences for bystanders were much the same— perilous. In the midwestern town at a time when only the strong survived, toughness and aggressiveness were valued qualities of successful men. But even in a city where rough men were no novelty, the boisterous activities of the Dodge brothers were conspicuous.

On Saturday night, the brothers liked to move from the more decorous automotive saloons into the roughest quarter of Detroit, where they would drink until some friend had to take them to their homes. One night, however, as Horace left a saloon and went out to his Model A to drive himself home, a passerby stopped to watch as Horace cranked away at his stubbornly resistant automobile. Thick neck reddening over his collar, he continued to crank away viciously, until the onlooker dared to snicker. Anger etched in every line of his broad, beet-red face, Horace dropped the crank, walked deliberately toward the man and knocked him down with one swing of his powerful arm, and then returned to his cranking.

Ordinarily, though, John's unruly behavior during some of their drinking sprees attracted more attention than that of his brother, which was fortunate, because John did not have an Anna at home to lecture and rebuke him. And so John continued to travel the saloon circuit, getting so fractious one Saturday night that he decided he wanted the saloon proprietor to dance for him. When the proprietor ignored his boozy patron's order, John bridled and pulled out his revolver. The frightened saloon owner promptly climbed up on a table and performed while the triumphant John threw glasses at the bar mirror in applause. Later, a sobered John revisited the saloon and tossed a fistful of bills on the bar to cover the damage.

Still, the sprees were only sporadic. Between such episodes, a gentlemanly John enjoyed the feminine companionship of his stenographer, Matilda Rausch. Even though he detested pretentiousness, he was not averse to acquiring a few of the trappings of success, especially when they might make a favorable impression on Matilda and her family. And the family was impressed when the tall, broad-shouldered John drove up in his new Ford car. Wearing a high silk opera hat, he bounded up the stairs to the apartment over the saloon. Matilda's younger sister, Amelia, watching from her upstairs window as the couple drove away, regretted that John's splendid image was somewhat diminished when he stepped into the automobile. Since the Ford had no top, John had to remove the silk hat from his red hair and set the hat on the back seat of the car while he drove. Amelia watched her sister and her sister's escort disappear down the street in the shiny Ford and thought it all quite romantic, even if Mr. Dodge was so much older than Matilda.

And because of John Dodge's attentiveness to Matilda, the year 1903, which had been such an eventful one for the Dodge brothers, turned out to be rather eventful for the Rausch family too. In January of that year, fifteen-year-old Amelia Rausch graduated from the eighth grade of Detroit's Duffield School. The girl's mother, bulky-figured Margaret Rausch, fussed over her petite daughter as she dressed for the graduation ceremony, helping Amelia brush her freshly washed, shining brown hair that hung almost to her waist when it was free of the tight pigtails she usually wore. Amelia, though, was not fussy about her hair . . . unlike her sister, Matilda, who painstakingly crimped her darker, black hair with a curling iron in the front and pinned the back into braids. And when the hair did not go into place to please her, Matilda's fiery temper erupted.

Both girls had sharp brown eyes and petite figures. Amelia, only one inch above five feet when she stretched her tallest, was unhappily aware that the yards of organdy her mother had sewed into a diaphanous graduation dress with puffed sleeves could not camouflage her slightness. Matilda, an inch taller and with a more developed figure than her sister, was as fussy about her clothes as about her hair. But even Matilda, Amelia thought, was unable to project an image of the 1903 woman of fashion—bosomy and well-rounded.

The tiny Amelia, nicknamed *Melie* by her parents, was as vivacious as Matilda, nicknamed *Tilly*, was reserved. The mother, Margaret Rausch, felt a good deal of gratification that Amelia's vivacity attracted a group of friends who came often to the Rausches' upstairs apartment on the way to or from school. But Margaret had worried about Matilda's lack of close friends in her school days. She wondered if the older girl's social growth had been stunted because of the demands at home, where the girls were expected to help with the housekeeping because their parents spent so much time at their business. The mother knew too that schoolmates frequently taunted the girls about being daughters of a saloonkeeper, and she worried whether Matilda's withdrawal from young people of her own age was a result of embarrassment over her background.

Margaret Rausch had several talks with her older daughter's teachers about Matilda's problems, but their combined efforts did little to change the inhibited social pattern of the girl. At school dances, Uncle Harry Glinz, Margaret's bachelor brother who had been occupying the Rausches' third bedroom in recent years, was pressed into service as his niece's escort.

Matilda's favorite recreation, in her early teen years, was to walk through the fashionable neighborhoods of the wealthy, admiring the large homes and the handsome clothing of the elegant ladies she saw entering or leaving their houses and carriages. Coaxing her younger sister Amelia to accompany her, Matilda loved to walk at night near the home of the Ducharmes, a family made prosperous by ownership of the Michigan Stove Company.

Standing outside the Ducharme home, the sisters watched through the lighted windows as uniformed servants served candlelit dinners to formally dressed men and women. The girls argued over which of the gowns was the most beautiful and twittered with excitement as each course was served, lingering outside until the guests were handed into their carriages and were driven off into the night with a clattering of horses' hooves.

But Matilda's fanciful dreams of elegance never overbalanced her basic practicality. She worked hard at her studies at Gorsline Business College and pleased her family by successfully completing her year's course and going to work, first for the E. J. Kruce Cracker Company and then for Dodge Brothers. It was welcome news to the family when, at Dodge, Matilda found her employers most amiable. And when John Dodge first came calling on Matilda, Margaret Rausch was pleased that Matilda had found herself a gentleman-friend. True, the man was almost old enough to be the girl's father, but his obvious prosperity compensated for his deficiencies in youth.

On the evening of Duffield School's eighth-grade graduation in 1903, Amelia Rausch tossed her diploma in the drawer in which she had saved all her grade-school promotion cards. From the time she had started attending school, she had made a habit of saving reminders of events in her life. Her passion for collecting matched that of Matilda. But while Amelia's collection was a helter-skelter assortment of trivia tossed into a drawer, Matilda's collection was carefully sorted and filed.

On this graduation night, Amelia danced about the Rausch apartment in great excitement. Matilda had promised that she and John Dodge would take Amelia with them tonight to a show, in celebration of the graduation. The younger sister took a final look at her flushed face in the bedroom mirror and hurried out into the parlor.

"Surprise!" The Rausch apartment was full of Amelia's friends, invited by Matilda. Amelia stared at her sister. "But . . . aren't we going to the show?" she asked.

"I told you that to keep you at home," Matilda said, laughing. "John isn't coming tonight at all."

Amelia was touched by her sister's warm gesture. While the younger sister was wary of Matilda's unpredictable temper, she told herself her sister's acts of generosity made up for her occasional angry outbursts. Matilda *was* concerned about her well-being.

In the September following Amelia's eighth-grade graduation, the younger sister followed Matilda's example, choosing not to enter high school but to go to business college instead. She began a nine-month study of shorthand and typing at Miles Business School, and life settled into a routine for both sisters as John Dodge continued to call on Matilda at least once a week. Amelia had hoped that after Matilda was comfortable with the idea of having a male escort, the older sister's circle of beaux would widen. But through the fall of 1903, John Dodge continued to be Matilda's attentive and sole escort.

John's household had begun to function smoothly for the first time since Ivy's death, after he had hired Anna's close friend, Isabelle Smith, as a housekeeper for his children in his Trumbull Street home. John's mother got along well with Isabelle, and John knew that both Horace and Anna were hoping that he might see the practical advantages of marriage to Isabelle. His children would then have a mother, and he would have a wife waiting at home. Isabelle was a responsible woman, a woman reasonably near his own age, the others prodded gently and cautiously. An attractive woman too. Love? He had loved Ivy, and that love was gone. Perhaps he was, as the others obviously thought, a fool for searching for love again.

On December 8, 1903, John impetuously took Isabelle up to the small town of Walkerville, Ontario, where they were quietly married by the Reverend J. H. Kirkland, a minister of the Methodist Church, with Anna and Horace as witnesses. There was no announcement, at John's insistence. None of the Detroit newspapers carried any mention of the wedding. And the woman who had become Mrs. John F. Dodge was referred to publicly by John only as "my housekeeper."

3

While the American public decidedly was ready for the automobile, little else was. Automotive services and accommodations were nonexistent, and motorists could only hope to find a general store that might stock gasoline along with kerosene. When a motorist was fortunate enough to find a few gallons of gasoline and a can for pouring the fuel into the tank, he was often charged as much as $2 per gallon.

After hardware stores and blacksmith shops began stocking gasoline, the first garages for the repair of balking automobiles appeared on the Detroit scene in 1905. These were disreputable-looking structures with surroundings that looked like junkyards littered with old oilcans, gas barrels, and piles of stringed cotton batting that had been used to sop up oil spills.

It would not be until the year 1910 that Detroit would have its first gas station—an old election booth equipped with a large iron tank. Then, the attendant's job was to grapple with the customer's snorting machine to bring it to a stop, after which he had to haul buckets of gasoline from the supply tank to fill the receptacle beneath the car seat. When the owner finally hooked up a garden hose to the supply tank and installed a pump, the attendant could hand-pump the fuel through the hose while the owner held the hose to the automobile's gas container.

Regardless of the lack of accommodations for the automobile, production of the Ford car leaped ahead in 1904, and the paperwork in the Dodge Brothers office increased enough to justify the employment of another stenographer. That summer, Amelia joined her sister Matilda in the Dodge office, operating a small switchboard of one outside line and four inside lines connecting with the shop. Occasionally the stenographers were asked to look after young Horace when Anna

26

wanted to leave the chubby little boy at the office for a couple of hours. And on one occasion an attractive woman came into the office. John introduced her brusquely as "my housekeeper" and promptly escorted her outside. His secret marriage had interrupted his relationship with Matilda for only a few weeks. He was deeply, passionately, in love with his secretary. He realized that now, more than ever before, berating himself for having let himself be led into a marriage of convenience.

Both Dodge brothers, after a lifetime of deprivation, began spending the profits they were accumulating from their sales of engines and transmissions to the Ford Motor Company and from the stock dividends paid by the company. By June 1904, less than one year from the date the company had begun selling its first cars, dividends of 98 percent were paid to its stockholders. The Dodges received $9,800 in dividends on their original $10,000 investment in stock. The Ford Motor Company, however, continued its policy of frugality as far as expenses were concerned. When John Dodge moved, at the November first noontime meeting of the board of directors, that the directors should be paid $25 for each special meeting attended, Henry Ford seconded the motion. When it was voted down by the other directors, Dodge and Ford had to settle for a $3 payment. At the regular weekly Monday meetings, board members were compensated with a payment of $5.

With sales for fiscal year 1904 amounting to $1,162,815.87, the Ford Motor Company still had less than $10,000 of factory equipment and machinery in its assembly plant and had spent only $7,109.66 on factory improvements. This contrasted with the Dodge Brothers' expenditures of more than $60,000 on machinery and equipment purchased specifically for the manufacture of the chassis and transmissions for the early Ford car.

In June 1905, the Dodges received another $10,000 in dividends, plus an additional $10,000 the following month—dividends which were only a faint indication of the millions of dollars they would receive within the next several years. Aware of the rapidly increasing value of their Ford stock, the brothers felt themselves gifted with the touch of Midas.

Flushed with this sense of wealth, Horace talked exuberantly to John of having a steam launch built so they could enjoy navigating the Detroit River. Although John was much less enthusiastic about boating than was Horace, he would not risk dampening his brother's pleasure, knowing that Horace was already setting aside a corner of

his engineering office for his hobby—designing marine engines. And
Horace happily went down to Studer's Boat Works, where Ransom
Olds was having a racing yacht built, to order the construction of a
steam launch for himself.

Employees in the Dodge shop, noticing the closeness of the
brothers as they came together to work in the morning and left
together at night, began referring to their bosses as the "Gold Dust
Twins." But the Gold Dust Twins were not destined to board their
steam launch for a trip down the river because, in June 1904, there
was a gasoline explosion and fire in the boat works. The Dodge
brothers' $1,800 launch, almost completed, was destroyed along with
Olds' boat and several others.

Disappointed, Horace turned back to working with problems in
the shop. In 1905, Ford production increased to twenty-five
automobiles a day, and the Dodges' production demands increased in
the same ratio. Production numbers of this kind meant more than $800
in daily profits for the Dodges, apart from stock dividends and the
value of the stock itself.

Already turning out three models of Fords—the Model B, which
sold for $2,000, the Model F touring car for $1,000; and the Model C
runabout for $800—Ford was now maneuvering to set up a second
company to turn out a still less expensive Model N. This substitute
and temporary company was to be organized for one purpose—to
squeeze out Malcomson from the flourishing Ford Motor Company,
since Malcomson had consistently offered opposition to many of
Ford's ideas. Ford's old associate, Malcomson, was offered no stock in
the new company, incorporated as the Ford Manufacturing Company
on November 22, 1905. But the Dodges each held 350 shares of stock
in the newly formed organization, John Dodge serving as vice-
president and Ford as president.

Next, Ford called a special meeting of the board of directors of the
Ford Motor Company without informing Malcomson of the meeting.
They met on December 6, 1905, at which time they agreed to ask for
Malcomson's resignation. John Dodge, who had never been friendly
with Malcomson, went along with Ford on this, even though he
recognized Ford's deviousness in ridding himself of his early partner.
But Malcomson emphatically refused to resign. Ford was content to
wait until he changed his mind, certain that it would be only a short
time until Malcomson realized that the new company, from which
he'd been excluded, would be siphoning off the profits of the original
company as the Ford Manufacturing Company began to produce the
new and inexpensive Model N.

In John's home on Trumbull, his mother, Maria, was once more supervising hired help in caring for the children, Isabelle Smith Dodge having left the house at John's insistence. She had been unhappy with John's absences from home in the evenings and with his occasional nocturnal drinking sprees in the saloons, but nevertheless had tried to continue to manage the household and to care for Maria. Her pride, however, was wounded by John's continuing insistence that the marriage be kept a secret. When he demanded that she should leave his home and divorce him because the marriage had been a mistake and because he loved another woman, Isabelle finally packed her bags and walked out of the Trumbull home after little more than a year of marriage. She would *not* divorce him, she told him firmly. Instead, she would look forward to his recovery from his infatuation with his much younger secretary and to his public recognition of herself as his wife.

Maria Dodge was upset over the departure of Isabelle, who had given the elderly woman very good care and companionship. John tried to pacify his mother with plans for building a luxurious new home for his family in the Boston Boulevard neighborhood of fashionable houses. At a time when his working-class home on Trumbull might sell for $4,000, his intended quarter-of-a-million-dollar expenditure for a new home was a magnificent sum. The fact that less than four years previously he had had to borrow money to bury his young wife made the success represented by this kind of house all the sweeter to John. He designed special accommodations on the ground floor for his invalid mother, including a bath with gold fixtures. But Maria Dodge, suspecting her son's plans to ensconce a new mistress-of-the-manor in the Boston Boulevard house, insisted she would never live there with John.

With their factory operating successfully, John and Horace found more time for themselves. For Horace, the spare time was an opportunity to get out on the Detroit River in the forty-foot steam launch that he had had rebuilt after the boat-works fire and to race the *Lotus* around Belle Isle in a swell of spray. Although the *Lotus* was the fastest craft on the Detroit River, Horace continued working on other marine engines at the Dodge shop, thrilled with the thought of having an even faster boat. And when the particular craft on which he was working blew up or sank—which was often—he roared with delight, picked up the debris, and went back to the shop to learn from the mishap and to begin working on a more efficient engine. Soon after he began racing the *Lotus*, he built an engine for another forty-foot craft, which he named the *Hornet*, taking pride that these two boats were the first speedboats seen on the Great Lakes. Whenever he had the engine of one

of these boats torn apart for improvements, he drove the other speedboat. And in the winter, he scooted over the ice in an ice-boat equipped with sails.

Feeling a little guilty for spending so much time on his boats and
away from Anna, Horace decided to apply for membership in the
Grosse Pointe Country Club on the river, knowing that his wife would
enjoy the parties and social activities of the club. When his application
was rejected, Horace was angered because of Anna's humiliation and
disappointment. Quickly, he bought a parcel of land adjoining the
club and swore publicly to build a house so palatial that it was going
to make the Grosse Pointe Country Club "look like a shanty." Someday he would use the clubhouse for a garage, he added.

In that same summer of 1906, financial reverses on Wall Street un-
settled the automotive industry. Thousands of customers canceled
their orders for new cars, most of which were at the high end of the
price scale. In the changed market, the economical Model N,
manufactured by the new Ford Manufacturing Company, appeared
to be the only type of car that might survive the crisis.

At this point, Malcomson succumbed to the pressure, seeing that
Ford could manipulate both companies so that the Ford Manufacturing Company would profit while the Ford Motor Company would
languish. Malcomson then agreed to sign over his shares in the
original company to Ford and Couzens for $175,000. Ford had to bor-
row $45,000 of this amount from the Dodges. At the same time, Ford
squeezed out a number of the remaining stockholders in his bid for
control of the company. Before the end of 1906, Ford owned 585
shares of the 1,000 shares of the company, Couzens owned 110 shares,
and the Dodges still had 50 shares each. Because of the death of John
Gray earlier in the year, Ford was now president of the Ford Motor
Company, with John Dodge occupying the vice-presidency. Ford
Motor Company dividends dropped drastically in 1906 to a total of
$10,000 from a high of $200,000 paid out in dividends in 1905. But
this was all part of the plan. Now, having accomplished what he set out
to do, Ford was willing to have the short-lived Ford Manufacturing
Company absorbed into the Ford Motor Company in early 1907.

By the end of 1906, Amelia Rausch was no longer working in the
Dodge Brothers office. She had worked for the Dodges for a little more
than a year when Matilda suddenly told her younger sister that "it
would be better if you worked somewhere else," since Matilda was

also leaving Dodge employ. Following what would become a lifelong pattern in dealing with her strong-willed sister, Amelia did not insist on an explanation from Matilda, but "in order to please my sister," as she told her friends, she meekly followed directions.

Amelia soon found another position with a Dodge supplier, while Matilda took a job as stenographer for the Detroit Lumber Company. Amelia was suspicious that the sisters' move from Dodge was provoked by some sort of quarrel between John and Matilda. But her suspicions were allayed when John's visits to the Rausches to pick up Matilda continued without interruption. The two had been dating for almost four years now.

At home, Amelia overheard heated arguments between her parents and Uncle Harry, the barber, who protested his niece's relationship with John Dodge. Harry Glinz, who had left the Rausch apartment for a home of his own, insisted that Dodge was married and that Matilda had no right to go out with him. Trumbull Street neighbors of John who came into Harry's barbershop declared that the woman who had taken care of the John Dodge children and who had called herself *Mrs. Dodge* had told some of the neighbors she was Dodge's wife. When Matilda's relationship with John continued despite Uncle Harry's protestations, the uncle, who had been an intimate member of the Rausch family, no longer came to the house nor spoke with the Rausches.

Since the matter was considered indelicate for Amelia's young ears, she never heard the conclusions of the arguments. But regardless of any conclusions or judgments of Uncle Harry or her mother or father, Amelia knew they were as likely to change the mind of her determined sister as they were likely to reverse the flow from the beer barrels downstairs.

Matilda did not work long for the lumber company. Instead, she enrolled in a meal-planning class that emphasized not so much the preparation of food as the supervision and organization of an affluent household with servants. She studied elocution with a tutor and learned the graces expected of women functioning in society. She took piano lessons and convinced Amelia to do the same so they could rehearse duets. To help herself retain her French lessons, she practiced writing out phrases that she wished to memorize.

She completed all her lessons painstakingly. A piece of Scripture appealed to the studious Matilda and she copied it in her precise, school-girlish handwriting on notebook paper and filed it away with the French phrases.

Let your light so shine before men, that they may see your good
works, and glorify your Father which is in heaven.

It became obvious to the Rausch family that Matilda was working
very hard to project an image of refinement. Rejecting her nickname,
Tilly, she insisted on being addressed by everyone as Matilda. Amelia
wanted to please her sister, as always. Yet she could not bring herself
to use the formal name because she knew the Rausches' old friends
thought the change was pretentious. They would, she knew, accuse
Amelia of putting on airs like her sister. So to offend no one, she began
her lifelong practice of referring to Matilda as *my sister.*

And while Matilda worked at projecting a new image, Horace
went along with his plans to build what the newspapers called his
"spite" home in Grosse Pointe. In the meantime, John moved his
family into his luxurious new three-storied home at 33 East Boston
Boulevard. Located several miles north of the working-class
neighborhood where the Dodge family had previously lived, the huge
brick house had a broad expanse of lawns and such a wide westerly
stretch of grass toward Woodward Avenue that John planned to put
in a putting green to practice his golf. But much to John's disappointment, his mother was stubbornly resolved not to move into her son's
new mansion; she could not be swayed by talk of the great open staircase or the library or the third-floor billiard room. And she ignored
John's coaxing reminders of the special ground-floor bedroom and
bath adjoining with a wide door for the easy maneuvering of her
wheelchair. Maria would not go to Boston Boulevard, even though
there were live-in servants, one of whom would be assigned to her
care. Instead, Maria Dodge insisted on being taken west to Decatur,
Michigan, to stay with her two sisters, the aunts who had loaned John
the money for a gravesite at the time of his first wife's death.

On August 7 of that year, 1907, Maria died in her sisters' home
and was buried in Niles, beside her husband. At John's request, his
sister Della and her husband left their business in Ann Arbor and
came to live with John and his children to oversee the house.

Like her brother Horace, Della had not been satisfied with her
name and had long since graced herself with the more fashionable
Delphine. Nor was she satisfied with her husband's name. Uriah
Eschbach, under Della's prodding, had now become *Rie Ashbaugh.*
And the elegant Ashbaughs settled into John's magnificent Boston
Boulevard home as if they had been born into riches.

Soon after John had moved into his new home, he asked Amelia
Rausch to "come back to Dodge," and Amelia, with Matilda's per-

mission, moved back to the Monroe Avenue office. With this latest job switch, Amelia was convinced that her sister and John Dodge must have come to some agreement about resolving their five-year courtship. But Matilda's air of detachment allowed no questions from Amelia, and the younger girl continued in her confusion when the Rausches also changed their way of life by giving up the saloon that had provided them with a comfortable living and home for most of the girls' lives. The family went into the grocery business instead, buying a store on Kercheval Street and moving into the apartment upstairs.

While the Rausches settled into their grocery store apartment, John Dodge also was trying very hard to make a change in his life. He took Isabelle Smith Dodge, the woman he had secretly married in 1903, up north to the Dodges' cottage to try to talk her into a divorce by promising her a generous private financial settlement that would take care of her for the rest of her life. Finally acknowledging the impossibility of reconciliation between John and Isabelle and knowing how desperately John wanted to marry Matilda, Horace joined John as they begged and coaxed, begged and prodded, begged and bullied, and then begged some more until Isabelle agreed to the divorce.

Both John and Isabelle wanted the divorce to be kept a secret. Isabelle was concerned that, as a divorcée, she would be scorned. John was even more concerned about news of the divorce leaking out to newspapers. He knew that Matilda would never marry him if there was public knowledge of his divorce.

When Isabelle filed divorce papers in a small Michigan town a couple hundred miles from Detroit, the charge was desertion, which— like adultery—was one of the few charges on which a divorce could be based. The unpublicized suit was settled on October 29, 1907, with payment to Isabelle of $2,000 as far as anything official was concerned. Privately, however, there were other generous arrangements through which Isabelle was made independent for life. Anna and her sisters were loyal to their friend and determined to remain close to Isabelle in spite of John's problems. Isabelle quietly resumed the use of her maiden name, and there was no publicity about either the marriage or the divorce.

At noon on December 10, 1907, John burst into Amelia's office. "You can take the afternoon off," he said with some excitement. "I'll be out of the office and won't need you." He paused a moment and added, "Your sister and I are going to be married this afternoon."

Surprised and hurt because Matilda had not mentioned her plans, Amelia mulled over the news as she went home. Now that she was almost twenty-one years old, she suspected that a lack of maturity on her part was no longer an excuse for her sister's reticence with her. She was afraid to question Matilda, fearing her violent temper. But the questions still whirled around in Amelia's head. Five years was a very long courtship. After Matilda had obviously decided last year to marry John, why didn't they marry immediately? Amelia knew that patience had no part in John's character. He made up his mind and acted in the same instant; he deferred no pleasure but satisfied all impulses instantly, no matter who disapproved. Why couldn't her sister have done her "studying" after the marriage? Why get married now, in the middle of winter with no honeymoon trip? Why no engagement notices? no ceremony? no invitations? no friends?

Few of her questions were answered when she arrived home. Her father's thin face was set and angry. The only thing her parents knew was that Matilda said she and John planned "to go before the minister with just Horace and Anna as witnesses." Margaret and George were not to share this important moment with their daughter. And none of the Rausches were invited to the family dinner to be served afterwards at John's fine new Boston Boulevard home, where Matilda would meet the three Dodge children for the first time.

As her parents and sister watched in bewilderment, Matilda rushed around the apartment, getting into the winterish street dress she had chosen in place of the traditional wedding gown. She took special care in piling her dark hair into its bouffant styling. Soon the door closed behind her, and her tiny feet beat a staccato sound on the stairs.

Margaret Rausch, straight hair pulled back severely from her plain, square face, stood looking out the window. Behind her round, steel-framed eyeglasses, her eyes betrayed their amazement and misgivings as this first daughter hurried away to marry the prosperous John Dodge.

At four o'clock that afternoon, Matilda Rausch, twenty-four, and John F. Dodge, forty-two, were married by the Reverend C. S. Allen in the minister's Detroit home. The marriage record listed only one previous marriage for John.

When Matilda moved into the Boston Boulevard home in the last few weeks of 1907, she found herself the mistress of one of the largest and most elegant houses in Detroit, with a staff of servants to manage as well as a house full of family. John's oldest daughter Winifred was now fourteen years of age, Isabel was two years younger, and John Duval was an active nine-year-old. During the past years that John's sister Della and her husband Uriah Eschbach had lived at the Dodge home, the brother-in-law's suspicious respiratory problem had confined him to his room. But family loyalty had overcome John's fear of tuberculosis, and the Eschbachs continued to live there even after John's marriage to Matilda.

Language tutors and cooking instructors notwithstanding, Matilda was not yet equipped to handle all the duties turned over to her by her sister-in-law Della, who plunged into club and social work now that John's generosity gave her the leisure for these inclinations.

Having chosen Matilda to suit himself, John was forthright now in his intention of establishing her as head of his family. He began calling her *Mother* and insisted the children do the same. The girls, who had accommodated themselves to a number of "mothers" in their brief lifetimes—Ivy, Grandmother Maria Dodge, Isabelle Smith Dodge, and Della Eschbach—adapted themselves to the new presence with a minimum of discomfort. The two sisters were accustomed to turning to each other for closeness and companionship. There was little they needed or wanted from a new "mother."

In the mornings, the sisters put on their Liggett School uniforms—blue serge dresses with pique collars and cuffs, dark stockings, and Antioch oxfords—ate breakfast with the family and then were gone for the day. After dinner at night, the two excused themselves and spent the evening in their bedroom suite, doing homework and sharing girl talk. While many wealthy families sent their daughters to boarding school, John had decided on the day school—the most elite private school in Detroit. Founded by two sisters and their Congregational minister father, Liggett School was ultraconservative in everything from decorations (classrooms were always gray, pictures black and white) to decorum. Its headmistress emphasized: "We still talk about manners. My theory is to correct a girl the instant she falters. I point out, 'This is not the way Liggett girls behave.' "

Matilda found that little John Duval, or *Junior*, was a lonely child, overindulged by the string of maids and mother substitutes who had paraded through his life since infancy. None of these people, in the absence of his father, was willing or able to assume the responsibility of establishing a strong personal relationship with the child. His physical needs had been cared for, and beyond that he was pacified. His sisters, in youthful thoughtlessness, closed him out of their company. Matilda determined to organize her schedule to provide time for the boy. She arranged violin lessons for him and took instructions on the instrument herself so that she could help him with his music lessons. She read to him often from Kingsley's *Water Babies* and other classics and tried to instill in the child her own appreciation of books.

The first Christmas she was in the family, Matilda asked John to buy a piano for the girls. But the sisters had a tendency to argue over possessions, and John decided to give the large Steinway to Matilda so that she could referee its disposition.

Eager to prove herself an efficient mistress of the manor, Matilda took stock of the elaborate household. Her staff consisted of a cook, kitchen girl, upstairs maid, parlor maid, a girl in the dining room, a houseman or two, and a laundress. In addition to the main floor rooms, the home included three bedrooms for live-in help, a suite shared by Winifred and Isabel, rooms for the Eschbachs, John and Matilda's master bedroom, and John Duval's room, which shared a bath with the guest room. A large third floor, including the billiard room, was used for storage. While the move from the upstairs apartment to the many-bathroomed, gold-fixtured house on the boulevard would have confounded most mature and experienced housekeepers, Matilda found it a satisfying outlet for her pleasure in organizing and administration.

She began setting up files for household and personal accounts. Each Christmas card that arrived that first Christmas was carefully filed away, the beginning of a collection that was to include every card received over the next sixty years. Grocery bills were filed, recipes filed. Cupboards and drawers were numbered, and a storage "table of contents" informed her instantly of the location of any item in the spacious house.

But in spite of her compulsion for saving everything, Matilda decided to clear away some of Ivy's things. The washerwoman was the recipient of the first Mrs. Dodge's dining room table. A few days later, John noticed the table had disappeared. "What the hell happened to the table?" he demanded of Matilda. His wife took one look at his glowering face and knew, even though the Dodges' relationship with the Hawkins family had been completely severed, that she had misjudged John's attachment to his first wife's memory. She fumbled for an explanation, but John interrupted her with a curt order, "Get it back!" and stalked out of the room.

Matilda had no choice but to go down to the laundry room the next day and bargain, with some embarrassment, for the return of the table in exchange for a new one of the laundress' choice.

In the spring of 1908, John discussed with Matilda his plans to look for a place in the country—a place where John Duval could run freely and where they all could relax in an informal setting. For John too it would be a fulfillment of his early love of the outdoors.

He could afford to indulge this love of the outdoors with the purchase of a country place now. Beginning April 1908, the Ford Motor Company began making a series of monthly dividend payments of $100,000—$10,000 of which went to the Dodges each month. By November 1908, the Dodges had collected $60,000 in yearly dividends, capped by a November stock split of twenty-to-one.

Ever since the recession of 1906 had turned into deeper economic troubles in 1907, John and Horace had begun reassessing their association with Ford. Although the inexpensive Ford Model N had sold very well all through the recession, Ford's own shop had been making the engines and components for this inexpensive car after the dummy company was formed to rid the Ford Motor Company of Malcomson. Now that Malcomson had withdrawn from the company and the Ford Motor Company had absorbed the secondary enterprise, the Model N components were being made in the Ford factory. Dodge Brothers were manufacturing parts for the more expensive Ford car, the Model K—its selling price listed in 1907 at $2,800. To increase lagging Model K sales, Ford notified his dealers that those who would not take Model K's would not get the popular Model N's either. Each dealer was allotted one Model K for every ten Model N's and was asked for a minimum deposit of $200 for each of the Model K's delivered.

The squeeze play that had forced Malcomson—along with some other minor original stockholders—out of the company had demonstrated to the Dodges that Ford had no loyalty to those whose money and labor had brought him success. For the past several years, Horace and John had restricted their business exclusively to products for the Ford Motor Company. They realized now the dangers in having only one customer for their large plant in the event Ford's company should decline or, as was much more likely, would also ultimately manufacture the components the Dodges were producing for the more expensive Ford cars.

In discussing plans for their future, the brothers were concerned with more than personal profits. "There are the boys we've got with us," John pointed out. "We got them to go in with us, and we've got to see them through. And our name means a lot to us. We've worked hard for all that name stands for."

Attuned to each other's thinking processes and emotions, the brothers were already in agreement on making plans for a new focus for their business—plans to build a bigger factory and to manufacture a car bearing their own name. "I am tired of being carried around in Henry Ford's vest pocket," John Dodge insisted. And the plans for a new automobile intrigued Horace, whose job it would be to design the car and to pattern the machinery for producing their own car. But for now, they decided, it was to their best interests to help the Ford Motor Company stay in a healthy financial condition since, as holders of Ford stock, they shared in the profits of that company.

Even while the Model N continued its success throughout the recession, the Ford Motor Company placed a new and better small model, the Model T, on its drawing boards, a car planned to sell at prices beginning at $825. The Model T's body was high above the road, its entire power plant and transmission were enclosed, and its four-cylinder engine generated twenty horsepower.

Introduced in 1908, the Model T—with its heavier wheels and springs and its magneto built into the motor to replace the dry batteries of earlier models—was an instant success. But looking to the future, Ford determined to restrict dividends and retain profits to reinvest in the business.

With Ford car sales zooming to record heights of more than 10,000 sold in the 1908-9 season and more than 18,000 sold in the 1909-10 season, the Dodge brothers were unsatisfied with the dividends of $180,000 paid to them during 1909 and the $200,000 in dividends they acquired in 1910. According to the profits accumulated by the company, dividends should be considerably higher, the Dodges believed.

At every meeting with Ford, John objected vigorously to Ford's tight grasp on the company's profits. But arguments were useless. Ford was adamant, as always. The Dodges were just as resolute about their plan to build their own car, plans they kept to themselves for the present.

John put aside his problems with Ford, though, as he began looking at farms in the beautifully wooded hills north of Detroit, hills that resembled his boyhood haunts. His purchase of a $50,000, 320-acre farm a few miles from Rochester, Michigan, was the first of nine farms he would eventually buy to make up his Meadow Brook estate.

John's enthusiasm for his farm was infectious. The house was ideal for his family—eighteen rooms rimmed with comfortable sleeping porches and windows that looked out from the highest point of the rolling countryside to a magnificent view across the meadows and woods. A twenty-four-foot spring, Meadow Brook, ran through the land. Besides the house, the farm had two big barns plus a dairy barn, a pig shelter, chicken coop, well enclosure, and a shop.

When John and Matilda asked Matilda's parents to oversee the estate, the Rausches sold their business, gave up their apartment, and moved out to the country. Now that her parents had moved north of Detroit, Amelia moved into the guest room in the Boston Boulevard household, and the third floor was remodeled for an apartment for the Eschbachs.

To the relief of Mrs. Rausch, John Dodge began extensive remodeling of the farmhouse soon after the move to Meadow Brook— the family would no longer have to line up by an outside privy whenever the Dodges visited there. Margaret Rausch had water carried from the backyard well enclosure to the bedrooms for washing up in the mornings. She worked in the dim light of kerosene lamps and cooked on a wood stove until John began the remodeling, which enlarged the kitchen and added more rooms and conveniences.

With George Rausch, John worked out his plans for the farm. There were to be dairy and beef cattle. Sheep. Poultry. Garden crops. Even bees and honey. Together, John and his father-in-law laid out the orchards—pears, apples, peaches—which George Rausch was to plant and tend.

Margaret Rausch did not have to be told what John wanted from her—baked beans, always, for breakfast the days he came from town. She started baking them in the wood stove at ten o'clock the previous night and stayed up to feed the fire until the small hours of the morning. And after the ten-pound bean crock was emptied, Margaret served soused mackerel, swimming in spicy tomato sauces, for John's breakfast.

The cooking was only a part of Margaret's day-to-day life at the farm. Live-in help was hard to get and keep: no one wanted to live so far from town. So Margaret considered herself fortunate when she could have one woman to help her on a permanent basis with the cleaning of the twelve bedrooms with their wide sleeping porches, and the washing of linens for twenty-six beds, usually full with family, friends, and employees. The oak floor in the dining room had to washed—and "freshened" between times with a skimmed-milk rinse.

Busy with the cooking and serving of meals, Mother Rausch could not sit to eat with the family. And Matilda made it clear that Father Rausch, in his work clothes, was not an appropriate figure at the

Dodge dining-room table. The two parents took their meals with the eight or more farm hands in the dining room for the help. Like the rest of the help, the Rausches were paid a salary by John.

At both the farmhouse and the Boston Boulevard home, John's tastes dominated everything, even to the kind of records selected for the walnut phonograph that Amelia often hand-cranked for his entertainment in the evenings. No popular records were allowed in the house—only the classics, and an occasional recording by Harry Lauder.

For the first time in her life, Matilda brought her quick temper under control. Faced with a husband capable of thunderous, violent rages that could be triggered by minor provocation, Matilda did not provoke him with impunity. Her strong will to organize and run things, quickly gave way under John's forcefulness. When Della Eschbach objected to Matilda's caterwauling violin, John gave one explosive order, and the violin was permanently shelved. Nor did Matilda object when John, ignoring his wife's penchant for neatness, made a habit of tossing his coat on the massive teakwood chair that stood in the foyer. And while everyone else had quickly adapted to the use of the name Matilda, John never felt any necessity to discontinue the use of *Tilly* on the few occasions when he did not refer to his young wife as "Mother." There was only one other person who persisted in the use of the detested *Tilly*. Anna Dodge never felt it incumbent on her to indulge her husband's former secretary in her bid for a more dignified form of address, even though Anna, personally, detested nicknames.

During the week the John Dodge family did not spend much time together. They usually had breakfast as a family unit at eight o'clock. Then John drove himself and Amelia to the factory offices, unless it happened to be the morning after one of John's evenings out, when Amelia took the streetcar to work while her employer slept late. John and Matilda had reached an agreement that if his nightly visit, with Horace, to Charlie Churchill's or Schneider's saloon kept him past 6:30, the family would have its evening meal without him. She could not keep placating the cook, Matilda carefully reminded her husband, when dinners were delayed.

When John was at home for dinner, he usually spent a few minutes with the children after the meal and then expected everyone to retire to his or her own room. Apart from his occasional late evenings at a saloon, John was in the habit of going to bed by ten o'clock. The only two not totally resigned to this quiet family routine in the evenings were the lively young John Duval and Amelia, whose shouts sometimes were heard coming up from the basement as they zipped between the clothes baskets in the laundry room on their roller skates.

But John and Horace had fewer late evenings together in their favorite saloons after Horace and Anna moved in 1909 out to the property they had bought in Grosse Pointe. They lived temporarily in the white cottage already on the property while their red sandstone mansion—under the direction of a young Detroit architect, Albert Kahn—was being built. An enterprising salesman of organs, hearing that Horace Dodge planned to install a great pipe organ in his mansion, tried to find a way to bring his organ to Dodge's attention. Knowing that Horace was an avid yachtsman who subscribed to leading boating magazines, the salesman ran a four-page advertisement for his organ in one of these magazines. His acumen paid off when Horace Dodge saw the advertisement and ordered the pipe organ for his home.

In 1910, the Horace Dodge house was ready for occupancy, its wide-pillared portico and the large spindle-posted porch above the portico giving an air of elegance to the Jefferson Avenue front view of the house. Inside, the rooms were larger than those in John's Boston Boulevard home, the paneled walls richer with carvings, the ceilings more ornate with latticed wood designs, the fireplaces gleaming with white marble. Anna had furnished the house with Tiffany lamps and urns, tapestried chairs, massive carved tables, and thick rugs of brilliant patterns. At the rear, south side of the house, formal rose gardens were terraced down toward the Detroit River where it emptied into Lake St. Clair. The Horace Dodges' choice for a name for their home—Rose Terrace—was thus a fitting one.

At the bottom of the formal rose gardens Horace had constructed docks where he sat by the hour, watching the lake traffic—freighters and pleasure boats plying the busy waters of Lake St. Clair. He soon knew every flag that flew over every mast that sailed past the foot of his terrace of roses.

On the first Christmas Horace and Anna spent in their new home, they hosted both their families, the Thomson sisters and the John Dodges and Amelia Rausch, for a holiday dinner. At two in the afternoon, the family gathered around the long table in the dining room where, attended by several uniformed servants, they enjoyed a five-course meal that lasted until 5 P.M. Anna was pleased that the dinner was a success, since she hoped it would be the first of many formal dinner parties to be given at Rose Terrace.

Although Horace enjoyed his beautiful home, he was not enthralled with the idea of formal dinner parties. He enjoyed, instead, going over to the Harmonie Club in Detroit, where a number of his and John's German friends liked to congregate in a spirit of *Gemutlichkeit*. A heavy, broad-chested man, only slightly less portly than his older brother, Horace ate the hearty German food served at the Harmonie Club with gusto, washing it down with German beer.

At this same time, Horace began dabbling in real estate—buying properties, constructing buildings on them, and then renting them out or selling them. He coaxed John to join him in this enterprise, forming the Dodge Realty Company.

Anna had no interest in any kind of business and, unlike Matilda, was happy to delegate the details of running her home to competent help. She had enrolled her daughter, Delphine Ione, in the best private school in her Grosse Pointe neighborhood, the Catholic School of the Convent of the Sacred Heart. Although Catholic faith and practices were completely foreign to Anna, she set aside her reservations to follow the lead of other wealthy families of the area, Catholic and non-Catholic, in entering her daughter into the convent's day school.

Like her Uncle John's girls, Delphine Ione dressed in the subdued uniform of the institution—a navy-blue serge dress with a stand-up collar, long sleeves, and full pleated skirt. And even though the family fortune was being made in gasoline-powered automobiles, Anna drove Delphine to school in an "electric." A gasoline automobile required a strong and courageous driver with its need for frequent, energetic cranking, and various mechanical adjustments. The electrics were simple to drive. Young ladies of only twelve years drove themselves around the village of Grosse Pointe in the machines. Some of Delphine Ione's classmates, who had whispered about the Dodges being refused membership in the country club, democratically accepted Anna's offer of a ride to school when she stopped the electric beside them as they walked toward the convent.

Of average height and slender to the point of being thin, Delphine Ione, in her early teenage years, had thick chestnut hair that glinted with red lights—the legacy of her father. She was not interested in school athletics, and classmates were not quickly attracted to become friends with the withdrawn and moody girl. Lacking the power of intense concentration that characterized her father, she was not a particularly good student except for her special interest in the piano, on which her mother had personally given her instructions. At the convent, Delphine studied music and piano with the nuns, as did all the girls at the school. When the nuns recognized Delphine's special talent, they encouraged her to have concert artist aspirations, much to Anna's and Horace's delight.

Young Horace was a chunky boy with a temperament that consisted of only one mood—exuberant, buoyant good-humor. To the doting Anna, it was only natural that her son should be the center of interest, even when he took a perverse joy in shocking people to call attention to himself. As the children grew, Anna fondly made plans for their future. She would send them to schools steeped in the traditions of social decorum and refinement—Manlius Institute in New York for Horace and Springside School in Chestnut Hill, Pennsylvania, for Delphine Ione. In these schools, the brother and sister could mingle with the children of the best families in the country, acquiring whatever graces and contacts might be necessary to gain them acceptance to the social circles that were closed to Anna.

While Anna happily charted her children's future, Horace had more than the completion of Rose Terrace to interest him in 1910. Albert Kahn had done such a fine job building Rose Terrace that the Dodge brothers commissioned the young man to build their new Dodge plant on acreage the brothers had purchased in Hamtramck. John Dodge recorded the highlights of the plant construction in his diary:

> Tuesday, April 16, 1910: Gave Albert Kahn the sketches for new factory in Hamtramck.
>
> June 1, 1910, Thursday: Started to dig foundation of forge plant; bad weather, could not do much.
>
> Nov. 16, 1910, Saturday: Started furnaces and blowers in forge plant for first time. Used Edison current.
>
> Dec. 5, 1910, Monday: Turned on steam in forge plant, had about a dozen hammers working. Expect to make forgings tomorrow. All piping is about finished, will blow out engines in morning.
>
> Dec. 7, 1910, Wednesday: Turned over Ball engine—worked fine. Blowed out an Allis engine. Started to make sample forgings under hammers.

As John's diary chronicled the history of Dodge Brothers' expansion in 1910, the city of Detroit recorded a parallel growth for the first decade of the 1900s, with Detroit becoming the eighth largest city in the United States. Detroit newspapers printed countless stories of expansion and mergers among automotive companies during this decade. By 1910, automotive writers rated the Monroe Street plant of the Dodges as the largest and best-equipped machine plant in Detroit. But the Dodges' new plant in Hamtramck was to be even bigger and better equipped, having a 5.1 million square-foot assembly plant that would eventually become the Dodge Division of Chrysler Corporation.

On moving day, Dodge office employees were driven, in a Ford, from the Monroe office to Hamtramck—right into the new building and onto the elevator. Then the Ford rolled down the second floor of the administration building, distributing the employees to their offices, beginning with the Dodge brothers.

John's and Horace's routines changed slightly as they settled into their new offices at opposite ends of the second floor. Their favorite meeting places—Churchill's, Schneider's—were not as accessible now, and Horace's Grosse Pointe home was too far away for convenience, so the brothers decided to take their noon meal at John's Boston Boulevard home. Matilda, who had begun working in volunteer activities, now found her schedule interrupted, as she felt she had to be home to hostess the noon meal. The cook grumbled because she had to make "two soups" every day, and the maids were still testy over Della Eschbach's insistence that they should climb up to her third-floor apartment to announce dinner. When the maids threatened to quit if they had to climb the extra flight of stairs, John settled the matter by installing a bell. Matilda was pleased that John had resolved the issue in a way other than that demanded by Della.

The efficiency with which John administered his domestic and business affairs was applied with equal resourcefulness to the political appointment to the Detroit Water Board he had accepted from Mayor Codd. During the five years John served as a water commissioner, Detroiters' complaints about a lack of water pressure were silenced, due to John's efforts in overseeing the building of a new pumping station. When he left the Dodge plant during the day, he often went out to supervise personally the installation of new machinery or new mains and pipes. Seized with impatience as he watched a workman tamping dirt in a trench on one occasion, John jumped down into the ditch, grabbed the ram, and showed the astonished laborer how the job should be done. To John, work was work, and he relished doing a job properly, whether it was packing dirt in a ditch or managing a million-dollar deal at his desk. When he stepped down from the water commission at the end of 1910, the city's water rates were among the lowest in the country and its plant one of the most modern in the world.

After long hours at business and city affairs, John's trips out to Meadow Brook were welcome respites. He liked to leave for the farm on Saturday mornings, often driving out with the family in the car or, in the wintertime, in a horse-drawn sleigh. Sometimes Isabel and

Winifred brought along girl friends for the weekend, and they coasted on the ice-covered hills and went jingling through the snowy woods in the sleigh.

John Duval, now at school in Gainsville, Georgia, missed the winter weekends at the farm. But he wrote frequently to Matilda, in evenly spaced, neat script:

> Dear Mother,
>   This is just a few lines to show how much I have improved in my handwriting, and I hope that you think so, too, and will be able hereafter to read all of my letters, and not only those when I ask for something. I can also spell better, and also try to speak more correctly.
>
>   Your loving son,
>   John.

In spite of the reassuring letters, Matilda fretted over the boy as she and his father received reports that John Duval was not doing well in school.

Horace and many of the Dodges' friends in business and city government were frequent guests at the farm. And just as Horace shared John's recreations at the farm, so John encouraged Horace in the younger brother's obsession with boating. In 1910, the brothers took delivery on still another of the fast, beautiful boats that Horace loved. That summer, Winifred christened the *Hornet II*, a 100-foot diesel steam yacht that Horace had designed. The steam yacht's two bright brass stacks winked a challenge at every other boat on the river as its two 1,000-horsepower engines drove the cruiser at thirty knots—to the delight of Horace, who boasted that the next fastest boat on the Detroit River could make only half that speed.

With the sudden growth of Detroit after 1900, there were many other Detroiters who also had the wealth and time to indulge their tastes for the finer things of life. When a group of Detroit women formed plans for a new symphony orchestra for the city, Anna Dodge was among the promoters who made $1,000 contributions. So began a bittersweet relationship between the Dodges and the Detroit Symphony Orchestra that was to span the next half century.

Anna's preoccupation with culture in the promotion of the Detroit Symphony had only begun when headlines in January 1911 newspapers astonished even those Detroiters who knew of John Dodge's recklessness when he was drinking.

> *Crippled Attorney Kicked and Beaten*
> *by John Dodge and Bob Oakman*
> *in Schneider's Saloon*

The story sifted down to Detroiters from the disclosures of the attorney, thirty-year-old Thomas J. Mahon, as he talked to reporters. John Dodge and his friend, Oakman, made no public comments on the affair.

Mahon, who walked on two wooden lower legs with the aid of a cane, talked freely, giving the details of how he had come into Schneider's bar with an attorney friend on January 3, after closing his law office for the evening. As Mahon and his friend, Frenchman Edmund Joncas, were introduced to Dodge and Oakman, the two attorneys observed that the other men had been drinking heavily. The four men talked together only briefly when John Dodge suddenly became belligerent. "You're one of those damned foreigners, aren't you?" he demanded of Joncas.

The Frenchman looked at him in surprise. "My ancestors were pioneers in Detroit," Joncas countered. Then, quoting from several pioneer histories, he began to document his genealogy.

"College talk!" the glowering Oakman shouted. In an attempt to demonstrate his own erudition, Oakman began spouting a garbled account of Greek mythology and history.

Mahon's reaction was patronizing. "Just exactly what is your thesis?" he asked.

Even drunk, Oakman and Dodge could not miss the sarcasm in Mahon's question. They responded with a torrent of curses and threats. Mahon's offer to buy cigars for everyone did not placate them. They knocked the cigars to the floor.

Unintimidated, Mahon coolly warned that he had known of Oakman's reputation for some time. Oakman reacted instantly. He grabbed the attorney by the throat and shoved him against the bar. "What have you heard about me?" he roared. Striking the younger man in the face, he knocked him to the floor and kicked him.

In the same instant, John Dodge moved in on the French attorney whose accent had annoyed him. Mahon, sprawled on the floor and unable to get up, saw Oakman turn to swing his fist at Joncas, who was already trying to protect himself from Dodge. Stretching out on the floor to reach his cane, Mahon just managed to grasp the cane when Dodge turned and grabbed it from him. The man on the floor cringed as Dodge struck him with the cane, then kicked at him.

Mahon's face was bruised and bleeding now from a cut beneath the eye. Both Dodge and Oakman moved back when they saw this, making room for the attorney to struggle to his feet while Joncas seized the opportunity to retreat.

Apprehensive over Mahon's condition, Oakman was apologetic, insisting he did not realize they had hurt him and offering to call a cab for him.

"Get away from me, you brute!" Mahon yelled.

Frustrated by the crippled attorney's refusal of help, Oakman grabbed at the younger man again, held him by the throat and pressed him against the bar a second time.

"Damn you . . . I'll make you," he threatened.

"I don't care if you have only two wooden legs," the terrified attorney heard John Dodge shout. "I have a damn good mind to beat you up again."

In spite of their renewed blusterings, Dodge and Oakman were frightened by what they had done. The barkeeper too was apprehensive. He hadn't wanted to provoke his good customers—Dodge and Oakman—by interfering when they became argumentative, which was not unusual for them. Nor had he really believed they would attack a crippled man. Then everything had happened so quickly. Now he was concerned only that Mahon should get out of the saloon, fast, before there was any more trouble. He watched as Mahon hobbled painfully out of the saloon and waited in a doorway on Woodward Avenue until a cab arrived.

The escapades of the Dodges, which had been looked on by some with an admiring tolerance, were suddenly viewed differently. Mahon was a young, respected attorney, with his entry in *The Book of Detroiters*, a listing of prominent people in the city, rating four times the space of John Dodge's listing. Added to this was the fact that Dodge and Oakman had ganged up on a crippled man in a vicious, unprovoked attack.

More than two weeks later, the *Detroit Times* reported, "Attorney Thomas J. Mahon is still confined to his bed in his home, 20 National Avenue, as a result of the beating and kicking he received in Louis Schneider's saloon at the hands of Robert Oakman, real estate agent of the D. R. R., and Water Commissioner John F. Dodge."

Arrested on a warrant sworn out by Mahon as he filed a damage suit for $25,000, Dodge and Oakman were released on bail of $2,500 each. A shroud of silence engulfed the Dodges' Boston Boulevard home. Matilda would not discuss the matter with her sister, Amelia, who assumed that a large financial settlement from John had put an end to the suit, which was subsequently dropped. But John Dodge never again entered Schneider's saloon, blaming Schneider for not having subdued and protected him against his own passions.

Amelia said nothing to her sister, but she clipped the newspaper stories and tossed them into her drawer, while echoes of the provocative stories reverberated through the city. Students at Liggett School overheard the usually well-modulated voice of Ella Liggett warning John Dodge that " . . . if this kind of thing continues, I won't keep your girls in school."

At Rose Terrace, Anna complained to Horace about his brother's outrageous behavior. Ordinarily, she did not dare criticize John, because Horace's face would redden with anger as he defended his brother. Although Horace did not become enraged as quickly as did John, the younger brother's rages, when they did occur, were intense for a short time, then they fizzled into a kind of moody sulkiness that lasted for a much longer time. Anna had always found the moodiness as difficult to bear as the temper spasms, so she had learned not to try to discuss John's shortcomings with her husband. But the notoriety attached to John's latest escapade had ruffled Anna to the point where she could no longer silently swallow her resentment. And as Anna complained, the blood rushed to Horace's face. But this time he could find no words to defend his brother, so he did what he usually did when he wished to avoid confrontations with Anna: he headed for one of his haunts to be with the friends whose company he found so convivial—the Oakman brothers, the Stein brothers, Oscar Marx, Rudolph Grandt, and others of the gang who crowded into the Harmonie Club or Charlie Churchill's or the Pontchartrain Hotel to talk politics or play cribbage. Although Horace visited the homes of these friends on occasion, most of his cronies had never entered the doors of Rose Terrace. Nor did they have expectations of visiting that palatial home, which Anna reserved for more suitable guests. Rudolph Grandt worked in the Dodge shop, and Horace, completely unmindful of the usual employer-employee relationship, was a loyal friend and comrade to Grandt. Some others of Horace's friends were looked on as grubby small-time politicians by Anna. They were no more welcome at Rose Terrace than was Grandt.

When Horace wanted to entertain a few of his friends somewhere apart from the saloons or the Harmonie Club, he took them out on his cruiser, where they spent the evening singing and harmonizing . . . and drinking together. Like John, Horace had no intentions of changing his manner of living to suit his wife's ambitions.

Both brothers freely admitted their preference for the company of ordinary people. When Fred Lamborn, known as a "tramp machinist" because he moved from job to job, joined the Dodge work force, the Dodges and Lamborn got along so well that Lamborn set down his tool box and made a career with the brothers. Quickly moved into a supervisory position, Lamborn observed that the working relationship between Ford and the Dodges did not look promising. "Henry would load up with axles, transmissions, and other stuff that we made," he recalled later. "Then he'd cut prices on his cars and come to us and want a price cut on parts. Since he was loaded up, he wouldn't take the stuff until we cut the price."

Horace and John refused to try to slice overhead costs by resorting to penny-pinching methods where their employees were concerned. Free beer and sandwiches were served in the Dodge forge and foundry at 9 A.M. and 3 P.M. And the Dodge brothers' instinctive concern for their men prompted them to initiate, informally, practices other employers adopted only after persistent and violence-ridden strikes. In building the Hamtramck plant, John and Horace included a well-equipped hospital, complete with a welfare department with matrons and visiting nurses to look after women employees as well as the wives and families of male employees. The brothers insisted on seeing the report of each medical case so they could determine whether the employee was being treated fairly.

When eighteen-year-old John Brandt came to work for the Dodges, he was pleased with his new job, since the brothers paid better than average wages and had a reputation for treating their men well. As the boy worked at his machine one day, an office clerk came up to him and handed him a piece of paper, which turned out to be a garnishment of wages for nonpayment of a clothing bill. Brandt protested that he had never bought a single item in that store—that, in fact, he had never been inside the store. But he was told by the other workers that it was not uncommon for merchants to take advantage of factory workers, some of whom were illiterate. Worse yet, standard procedure for most employers, when faced with garnishment notices for an employee, was to fire him.

Brandt worried about the garnishment until he was called into the office, where the Dodge brothers came up with a plan. How about firing Brandt, they suggested, then providing the assistance of Dodge attorneys to sue the store for $25,000 damages. And after the store had been sufficiently impressed with the dangers of taking advantage of a Dodge employee, Brandt would be hired back at the plant.

Although the garnishment was subsequently dropped by the store, Brandt was devoted to the Dodges after this incident. Like young Brandt, many other plant workers had an admiration for their employers that was undiminished by stories of bar-smashing and drinking on the part of the Dodge brothers. In some ways, these

stories contributed an earthy character to their employers' reputa-
tions that the men savored. In regard to the publicity about John
Dodge and the crippled Mahon, Brandt and many other of the
workers shared the belief that John Dodge must have been badly
provoked and that the whole story had not been revealed. The
brothers were hard-working and productive men who were entitled to
let off some excess energy once in a while, as far as Dodge employees
were concerned.

4

The $200,500 of Ford dividends received by the Dodges in 1911 more than doubled in 1912 when the Dodge share of Ford dividends was greater than a half-million dollars. Since the beginning of 1911, the new Kahn-designed Ford plant—referred to as the "Crystal Palace" because of its four-storied, many-windowed areas—had been manufacturing many of its own engines, transmissions, and axles, while various feeder plants were vying with each other for Ford accounts. These factors were squeezing the Dodges in their manufacture of transmissions, rear axles, drive-shaft assemblies, and drop forgings for Ford, since the Dodge brothers had to negotiate yearly with Ford for new contracts. Chafing under these pressures, the Dodges began quietly working at building their top level of personnel in preparation for the future manufacture of their own car.

The influx of top personnel began as the brothers induced an old friend of their Canadian bicycle-building days to come to work for them. The Dodges had tried to recruit their friend, Fredrick J. Haynes, back in 1903 to help staff the Ford Motor Company when Ford needed the help of experts. But Haynes had refused, saying to John and Horace, "If it were your business, or if you wanted me to come with you, I'd do it. But not with Ford." In 1912, though, Haynes came to Dodge, as did several other key men. And in the meantime, the Dodges continued to manufacture transmissions for Ford, while carefully guarding their future plans from any kind of publicity.

The bad publicity surrounding the Mahon-Dodge affair had faded by the time Winifred graduated from Liggett School in May of 1912. Barring any more unfortunate incidents, Isabel would graduate the following year.

Neither the publicity nor the plans for expansion of their plant to produce a Dodge automobile pushed aside the brothers' political interests at this time, however. For the past few years, the closest friends

51

of Horace and John had been men with political ambitions. The inseparable Dodge brothers, along with two other sets of brothers—the Steins (Edward and Christopher) and the Oakmans (Robert and Milton)—had become the nucleus of a group of energetic men desirous of acquiring city or county political offices. Although both John and Horace disavowed any such personal desires, both enjoyed the feeling of power they received from promoting their friends' ambitions. The Dodges had been mildly active in the Detroit mayoralty campaigns of 1908 and 1910. And when their German friend Oscar Marx entered the 1912 mayoral contest, the Dodge brothers donated money freely to the Marx campaign. With no tax credits for such donations at that time, the Dodges asked nothing in return for their lavish contributions. For Horace and John, it was enough to have their generosity appreciated by their best friends and to savor their "kingmakers" image.

As the Marx campaign progressed, the brothers met often with their colleagues aboard the *Hornet*, well stocked with food and liquor. When Horace, who joyously skippered the craft around Lake St. Clair, was eventually persuaded by land-lubbing John to moor the boat, the favorite tie-up pier was on the Canadian shore near Wolf's roadhouse, where the men talked heatedly of politics as they drank and partied. Business deals too were arranged; Horace and John were persuaded by Bob Oakman to join Wolf and himself in financing the purchase of Canadian shoreline properties for subdivision and resale.

When Marx won the 1912 election and became mayor of Detroit, John accepted an appointment to the newly created Board of Street Railway Commissioners. Here, John felt, his experience in the area of transportation could be of service to the city.

While the men were engrossed with politics, the Dodge women tried to build a place for themselves in the social structure of the city. Matilda joined Anna in her support of the Detroit Symphony Orchestra as one of its earliest patrons. In the environs of the symphony, Matilda found herself in the company of many Detroiters of importance, including the Ducharmes—owners of the large home in the Rausch family's former neighborhood. The Ducharmes could not possibly have known that, only fifteen years ago, the Rausch sisters had stood in the shadows outside the Ducharme home and looked enviously into the lighted windows. But Matilda knew, and her small-boned, erect figure became just a bit more erect each time she encountered any of the Ducharmes or Jerome Remick, president of the symphony organization and the man for whom her father had once worked as a coachman. The Kruces—owners of the cracker company where Matilda had worked before going into the Dodge office— were also among those into whose midst Matilda moved determinedly.

With the same drive that characterized John and Horace, their sister Della plunged into social work with all the fervor of her passionate Dodge nature. Intelligent and aesthetic-minded, the childless Della—whose polish and poise came to surpass the finesse of many women of Detroit's upper stratum—marshaled some of the city's prominent women into support of a Salvation Army refuge for girls who had been orphaned or deserted, and she served as the first president of the Women's Auxiliary to the Salvation Army Rescue Home. Proud of the recognition given his sister, John Dodge became the major financial backer of Della's pet project—the building of a modern hospital—and both John and Della basked in the pleasant publicity when Evangeline Booth came to Detroit to dedicate the new facility.

Overshadowing both Matilda and Anna, Della was elected president of the Detroit Federation of Women's Clubs to lead its campaign of social and civic reforms. She also founded and edited the official magazine for the associated women's clubs and was acclaimed locally for her more creative writings—poetry.

Whatever expenses Della incurred, in her political and charitable work, were simply billed to the brother with whom she lived—John Dodge. Horace and Anna were equally generous with Anna's family—the Thomsons, as the Horace Dodges helped with the purchase of homes and furnishings for Anna's sisters and parents and financed their travels, as well as paying for music lessons and college expenses for nieces and nephews.

Matilda's parents, George and Margaret Rausch, contrasting their hard-working roles at Meadow Brook farm with the comfortable lives of Anna's relatives, decided to leave the farm in favor of an easier life. Keenly disappointed at the Rausches' move, John Dodge prevailed on his half-sister Laura and her daughter and son-in-law to take over management of the farm. But it was not long until the new caretakers decided that, with all the work involved in farming and in processing the produce, it was too demanding to get everything ready for the John Dodge family and their friends to come out every weekend. Family visits to Meadow Brook soon became a rarity.

Unhappy at the cessation of weekends spent at his farm, John agreed to take a cruise with Horace in their jointly owned *Hornet.* Should they go to Georgian Bay or cruise around Lake Michigan to

Chicago? Elbows resting on the bar in Churchill's saloon, the brothers ordered new rounds of drinks as they talked over their destination. The discussion started reasonably enough, then flared into shouts and fist-pounding that were ignored by the bartender. He had heard the brothers argue before and knew that even their amicable disagreements were loud. "Flip a coin," someone finally suggested. Responding to it, the brothers agreed that whoever won the toss would assume sole ownership of the boat. A silver coin made an arc into the air, then clinked down on the bar. Heads! Horace had won the toss and was the sole owner of the *Hornet II*. He grinned. Now that John was to be his guest, it would be the *older* brother's privilege to choose the destination of the cruise, Horace offered magnanimously. The two men left the saloon happily—together.

As 1912 was moving into 1913, John decided this was a good time for a lengthier boat trip—a trip to Europe on an ocean liner with his family. Horace and Anna had visited in Europe, but this would be the first ocean trip for John and Matilda. The only threat to the smoothly functioning operation of the Dodge plant at this time was the infiltration of union organizers. This promised to become a long-continuing threat. But apart from union organizing pressures, 1913 was a bustling, prosperous, and exuberant year for Detroiters—the last before the outbreak of World War I. At night, people thronged the downtown streets, where the electric signs of the Detroit Opera House advertised a popular novelty—Kinemacolor process motion pictures—with the debut of *The Making of the Panama Canal*. *Zena, the 20th Century Psychic Wonder* flashed from another theatre's marquee while the Casino, the Bijou, and the Royale were jammed with customers clamoring to see Detroit's first nickelodeon movies.

The city was beginning to move to a new tempo. Skyscrapers of more than ten stories were being built, and Detroit women were teetering on four-inch French heels and hobbling around in tight skirts. Because these fashions created problems, an ordinance was prepared requiring the steps of streetcars to be lowered. "Their height causes exposure of hosiery when women are boarding the cars in modern tight skirts" was the explanation.

In a new mood of pleasure-seeking, joyriders "borrowed" cars left on the streets, driving them until they ran out of gas and then abandoning them. It had been sufficient precaution, previously, for a motorist to take his spark key with him when he left his auto. But spark keys were generally available now to anyone. So Detroiters tried other devices—chaining the front and back wheels together or padlocking the spark and gas levers together, chaining the crank to the car or taking the crank away with them. Still, padlocks were picked, levers bent, chains broken, and in hot weather, cars often could be started without the cranks.

John Dodge moved away from these and other problems of the industry when he sailed on the *Mauretania* with Matilda, John Duval, and with Matilda's sister, Amelia, on April 23rd. Matilda carefully saved the bon-voyage cards from the family—sentimental messages from Anna and the John Dodge daughters, and a more jaunty message, via telegram from Horace. "Have one on me . . . cheer up and come back safe."

In Manchester, England, John looked over mail he received from his trusted assistant, Fred Haynes. Haynes had enclosed some reports of secret agents, hired by the Dodges as informers, to investigate the activities of organizers for the Industrial Workers of the World.

In one of the reports, Agent #105 told of the I.W.W. meeting he had attended the night of May 13th. Twenty new members joined the organization, he related. While the organizers had spoken about sabotage, the I.W.W. leader announced he was going to try to get a permit to speak in front of the Dodge plant. "Have this fixed," John wrote at the bottom of the report, determining that no union organizer would flaunt his subversive concepts near Dodge property. Workers at Dodge were satisfied workers, he was sure, because he and Horace had a policy of fair treatment for their men. They were not willing to stand by idly while unionists convinced the men to be dissatisfied.

By the time John returned from his trip abroad, Mayor Marx was having problems in Detroit. Among the most serious charges against the mayor, and involving the Dodge brothers, was the accusation that many of Mayor Marx's political appointees—including the police commissioner, parks commissioner, city controller and other influential appointees—were personal friends of the Dodges, appointed to please the mayor's financial backers.

John's own appointment to the Detroit Street Railway Commission pushed him further into the controversy. Any breakdown of the privately owned, profit-oriented street car system resulted in paralysis of the city's business life because, even in the automotive capital, great masses of the city's population were still dependent on street cars for transportation. There was trouble over ownership of the street car lines—whether the city or private industry could operate the lines more efficiently . . . trouble over fare reductions ordered by the commission . . . trouble over a threatened strike by streetcar workers and threatened seizure of the cars by the police commissioner when the company operating the streetcars, the DUR, instructed its conductors to refuse the reduced 3¢ fare when riders tried to pay it. Newspaper headlines predicted there would be rioting in the streets on August 7th when the reduced fare was to take effect.

John Dodge, who hated to compromise, evidenced control of his explosive temper this time as he and fellow commissioner James Couzens offered the city the use of a thousand automobiles to substitute for streetcars, and the DUR, frightened by this proposal, agreed to a compromise fare of seven rides for 25¢.

While the political battling over the streetcars continued, John and Horace finally conceded in July 1913 that it was time to break away from Ford. The separation from Ford would not affect the more than $1 million in dividends that the Dodges would receive from their Ford stock in 1913, and these dividends could be used for the manufacturing of their own car. Ford would not be pleased with that kind of competition, the brothers happily reminded each other. But their arrangement with the dictatorial Ford had never really pleased the independent Dodges, either, even though during the past ten years they had furnished the Ford Motor Company with engines and parts valued at $100 million.

According to the terms of their Ford contract, a one-year's notice from either Ford or the Dodges could terminate the agreement. In July 1913, Horace and John officially notified Ford of the cancellation of their contract. By July 1914, they would no longer be making parts for the Ford car. Their own plans for the new Dodge automobile, quietly in the making for a long time, were given a new momentum now, in view of the termination of the Ford agreement. Horace began buying new machinery, planning new layouts, and designing special tools and equipment. In the meantime, the brothers stopped in occasionally at the Ford factory to observe the making of the parts for the Ford and to see if there was infringement on any of the Dodge patents.

After the streetcar dispute was settled in August, John and Horace drove back to Niles on one of their annual pilgrimages to visit the graves of their parents in Silver Brook Cemetery. They still felt a strong attachment to Niles, and they liked to renew associations with old friends such as John Tuttle, their former Sunday school teacher. A few years previously, when the brothers learned that Tuttle had heavily mortgaged his home in an effort to meet pressing financial obligations, the Dodges offered financial help. But this year, Horace and John agreed, it would be nice to do something for the whole town. It was hardly appropriate, they thought, that the little green cottage of their births, standing next to a towering standpipe now, should be the only mark the Dodges left on Niles..By the time they arrived in Niles, they had decided to present the townspeople with something that would inspire the same warm memories for the Dodges that the Dodges felt for the town.

The next day the Niles paper carried the brothers' announcement that they would make a gift to the town of $100,000 for a park, or.for whatever useful project the town might want.

As usual, John was the spokesman for the brothers. "The amount sounds big," he pontificated for the edification of local reporters, "but really it is nothing to us now. H. E. and myself are worth fifty million dollars. We want to do something for Niles right away, and while I have suggested a donation of a hundred-thousand dollars, we will double this amount if your citizens will advance a judicial manner by which it can be spent."

The Dodge brothers' expectations of their gift being received with gratitude were dashed when Niles remained unimpressed. Letters deluged the Dodges, criticizing the proposed gift. Some complained that a park was more of a burden than a benefit because it would cost money to maintain. When told that the Dodges intended to create a perpetual fund for maintenance, the complainers added that the park, or any project of that kind, would increase property values, and the townspeople's taxes would go higher.

John and Horace pushed aside their disappointment and insisted their offer would remain open in the future. Since there were no income tax laws at this time with deductions to inspire the wealthy to make civic gifts, the only reason for the Dodges' offer was the brothers' love for Niles. But the contention among Niles citizens continued, and the scorning of the brothers' offer seemed, to Horace and John, to be another rejection of themselves, as adults, just as they had been rejected in their childhood.

In the same August of the Niles gift proposal, John announced his resignation as director and vice-president of the Ford Motor Company. And if Niles had failed to heed the Dodges' pronouncements, certainly the entire automotive world was startled by the public statement the brothers made to the press on August 17, 1913. They would manufacture a car, they said, beginning the next year, while gradually discontinuing the manufacture of parts for Ford Motor Company.

In one month's time during 1913, Dodge Brothers produced 10,213 transmissions, 8,388 rear axles, 11,891 steering gears, and 9,545 drive shafts for Ford. The cessation of the Ford contract and the changeover to the production of their own car was a gamble for the brothers—a gamble that was appreciated by newsmen who asked for more details.

For the past two years, the newsmen were told, the Dodges had been buying property adjacent to their Hamtramck plant, and now they planned to double the size of that plant. Moreover, the new business would be built and the manufacturing processes begun with the Dodges' own capital. They would borrow no money to produce the car on which they had been experimenting for the past two years—a car with four cylinders, more than twenty-five horsepower, priced from $550 to $700.

Matilda's opinions and Anna's opinions were not sought by their husbands in regard to business matters. This was not a source of concern, however, even to Matilda—who liked to think of herself as an efficient manager, for both women had learned to have great faith in their husbands' industrial competence. But both women shared a secret anxiety that their men might get themselves into an unsavory situation—quite apart from their business—that would bring humiliation to their wives and families.

When Anna, later that summer, thrust the *Detroit Journal* at Horace as he came into the house, he knew that she had seen the headlines broadcasting his brother John's latest bit of recklessness. "Marx and Dodge Auto Hits Woman, Then Speeds Forward Without Stop, Policeman Says." The article told of a motorcycle policeman observing a Hupmobile traveling eastward on Jefferson Avenue and crossing to the left side of the road where the street was under construction. At the same time, a heavy car traveling some forty-five miles an hour came from the opposite direction in disregard of the twenty-five-miles-per-hour speed limit. The big car smashed into the left side of the Hupmobile, then roared away from the scene of the accident, the motorcycle policeman in pursuit. When the officer caught up with the car, he found the driver was John Dodge, his companion Mayor Marx. "That'll teach them to keep to the right!" Dodge insisted as he was questioned by the policeman.

Although a complaint was filed by the slightly injured occupants of the Hupmobile, neither Dodge nor Marx was arrested. When reporters descended on the mayor's office the next day to question him about the incident, the mayor was belligerently defensive of Dodge. In the expletive-deleted style of the early 1900s, the newspaper quoted the mayor for the edification of Detroit citizens. "John Dodge could buy your blankety-blank old paper and turn your plant into a machine shop!" Marx had snarled.

After a warrant charging John Dodge with reckless driving was finally issued, the justice of Grosse Pointe Village conducted a private "trial" at his home. "Dodge's friends had the affair hushed up," the *Journal* claimed. Other newspapers carried editorials criticizing special treatment for the rich.

The affair did not compare with the ugly Mahon incident, but both Anna and Matilda were embarrassed by the notoriety. Matilda went on, however, with her planning for a debut for her beautiful eldest step-daughter, Winifred.

Hoping the elegance of the debut party would persuade Detroit society to overlook John's past indiscretions, Matilda made arrangements to present Winifred at a dinner dance at the Pontchartrain Hotel on December 19. In an English garden setting complete with box hedges and shrubbery, vines wreathing the ceiling, and songbirds hidden in the greenery, John Dodge—his thick-muscled body encased in the stiff accouterment necessary for hosting polite society—stood with his wife and daughter to receive the felicitations of their guests. Matilda was satisfied with the party when she leafed through the pages of Detroit's society paper, *Detroit Saturday Night*, to find a complimentary coverage of the debut.

Early in December Anna was equally satisfied to find that Horace was socially acceptable to some exclusive circles, if not to the Grosse Pointe Country Club, as he became Commodore of the Detroit Boat Club. The Dodges' tailor, never conceiving the possibility of either brother acting independently of the other, automatically made up two commodore uniforms and sent one to Horace and one to John.

The Commodore title and uniform were appropriate, now, as Horace awaited the readying of a beautiful new yacht he had ordered built. The day following Winifred's debut party, Horace and his daughter, Delphine Ione, stood at the Robins Drydock in Brooklyn to watch the large yacht slide into the waters as Delphine christened it the *Nokomis*. One-hundred and eighty-feet from bow to stern, the steam yacht had a top speed of nineteen knots, boasted a kitchen as complete as that of a hotel and had a dining room furnished with thick rugs and shimmering chandeliers. Another of Horace's boyhood dreams had reached fruition.

5

The Dodges had gradually cut back their production for Ford in 1913 as their contract with Ford Motor Company drew nearer its termination. Consequently, the number of Ford Motor Company's own employees rose spectacularly from 5,710 in 1912 to 13,198 in 1913. In Dodge Brothers' Hamtramck office, John and Horace busied themselves with a myriad of details for their expansion from a one-customer business. More design and testing offices were needed, plus a sales organization to set up dealerships, and advertising and public relations departments.

In the midst of the expansion and remodeling of their two-storied administration building into a four-storied structure, the gruff and quick-tempered John became even more testy. His secretarial sister-in-law, Amelia, was a convenient target for many of these blustery outbursts. Horace also became provoked with increasing frequency at this time. Although his drafting office was at the opposite end of the shop from John's business office, Horace's oaths frequently echoed the length of the shop.

Both men cursed freely as, obsessed with their own plans for expanding their plant and producing their car, they read daily accounts in the newspapers of Henry Ford's latest pronouncements in regard to 1,000 acres of land Ford had purchased near the Rouge River in Dearborn. He was going to expand his company and manufacture the materials for his cars, including his own steel and glass. To finance this expansion, Ford planned to use much of the $58 million the company had accumulated in profits, instead of distributing it to stockholders.

Ford was not going to get away with these dictatorial policies this time, John and Horace decided. Distribution of profits to stockholders would provide the brothers with extra capital to invest in the production of their own automobile—extra capital they were determined to have. Confronting Ford, they insisted that Ford should buy out those stockholders who dissented from his policies if he wanted 100 percent control of the company. Ford was completely negative to this demand. His 58½ percent of the shares was enough to guarantee his command of the company, and he had no reason to accommodate the Dodges. Goaded into action by Ford's arrogance, John and Horace began conferring with their lawyers over legal strategy to contest Ford.

The brothers also involved themselves in another court action in March 1914. As a result of the federal government's having levied a tax on income for the first time in 1913, the Dodge brothers felt the new tax system discriminated against companies owned by individuals and families as contrasted with those owned by corporations.

"The Dodges do not object to income or surtaxes because they are graduated," their lawyer explained, "but they do object to paying heavy surtaxes when corporations engaged in the same business and competing with them, are not required to do so, and they also object to the provision permitting corporations to withhold from taxation a reasonably necessary portion of their income for purposes of the business, while individuals and partnerships are not allowed the same privileges."

Near the end of May, the suit was decided adversely, and the Dodge bill of complaint was dismissed. But John and Horace had no time to brood over the court decision. They had already turned their attention to appraising their chances for success with their own automobile at a time when they would have to meet heavy competition from Henry Ford—and from the 146 different new cars going into production in 1914. They concluded that they should be able to market successfully a low to middle-priced car, light-weight but rugged, a car that could be easily and inexpensively repaired. Rejecting the usual idea of yearly models, they decided on an innovative approach—whenever an improvement was adopted, it should be included in the production line at any time of the year. They determined to put out a car that, even as it aged, could inexpensively incorporate the latest Dodge improvements with the installation of factory parts produced for that purpose. This would make the Dodge car a good investment for the buyer and would maintain a high resale value for the automobile.

In order to build a gasoline-powered car that women drivers could manage, Horace experimented with various self-starter systems before adopting a 12-volt silent starter that functioned through a chain drive. Built by the North East Electric Company of New York, the starter was activated by a push of the foot. The Dodge engine could not stall, for when the armature voltage fell below the battery voltage, starter cranking would resume automatically, making the Dodge car the ideal vehicle for a woman driver.

While working on the car or on the design for the machinery to produce the car, Horace frequently went into isolation for several days at a time in a cottage on the Meadow Brook property while John handled the day-to-day business dealings of the plant. A peculiarity of these business dealings was the refusal to respond to mail addressed to Dodge Brothers if the writer did not capitalize the *B* in the word *Brothers*. This capitalization, the brothers felt, stressed the permanence and closeness of their alliance.

In the rush of design and production preparations, there was little time for visiting at the farm, but still John's beloved Meadow Brook was there, waiting for his return. George and Margaret Rausch had finally come back to the farm after John's repeated requests. But this year, the usually energetic George Rausch had not been feeling well. On June 15th he died quietly at age sixty-six, attended by Amelia and Margaret in his room off the back hall reserved for the hired help. His body was brought from the farmhouse to Woodlawn Cemetery. Horace and John had built a magnificent mausoleum in Woodlawn into which John had moved the body of his first wife, Ivy, from the plot where she had been buried. John then sold the smaller eight-grave plot to Margaret Rausch, his mother-in-law. It was here that her husband was buried.

Amelia decided to take a short leave from the Dodge office and to spend a few weeks with her mother at Meadow Brook to help the mother adjust to her loss. She would stay, she announced, until her mother made up her mind about any changes in her life. Matilda and John, becoming concerned again about the possibility of Margaret Rausch wanting to leave the farm, promptly asked Amelia to give up her job in the city and to stay out at the farm permanently with her mother. She could be of value on the farm, they pointed out—paying the help, taking care of the books, and keeping inventory of all the equipment and produce.

Raised as a city girl, Amelia loved the excitement and convenience of Detroit and was not at all sure she wanted to leave her city friends for the lonely, quiet life on the farm. But, as she explained to her friends, "to please my sister," she cleaned out her drawers at her office at Dodge Brothers and moved her belongings into the farmhouse.

John was in an extremely expansive mood at this time. Not only was the Dodge car nearly ready for production, he and Matilda—after seven years of marriage—were also expecting their first child. He would be fifty years old when the child was born; Matilda would be thirty-one. Matilda's responses puzzled him, however. She seemed very happy about the expected baby; yet she delayed confiding in her mother and her sister, as if she were embarrassed by her pregnancy, while John found it difficult to restrain his ebullience. Deciding to take matters into his own hands, he walked into the farmhouse kitchen one day and announced to Margaret Rausch that she would become a grandmother soon.

The excitement that Margaret and Amelia Rausch shared over this news faded, in part, as they talked it over after John had left the farmhouse. Why, they wondered, had not Matilda confided in them earlier—why, at least, had she not joined them in this moment of intimacy?

As Matilda awaited the birth of her first child that summer, she often heard the roaring and chugging of prototype models of the new Dodge car. John and Horace took the models out to the privacy of Meadow Brook and drove them up and down and around the undulating Rochester hills. This was just one of the procedures the men devised for testing their automobile and its accessories. They tested tires by rolling them off the roof of their four-storied building in Hamtramck, and when the U.S. Chain Tread tire stood up under this trial, Horace said emphatically, "That's the tire for us." Then, over the protests of watching employees, John impulsively jumped into one of the prototype models, gripped the wheel with his large hands, and accelerated the car to more than fifteen miles an hour . . . straight into a brick wall. "I might as well," he explained as he and Horace inspected the damaged radiator, "because someone else is going to do it when these cars get on the road."

The car that evolved from this testing weighed 2,200 pounds, stood six-feet-nine-inches tall, and had a sturdy, unpretentious appearance to its black, all-steel body that earned for it the affectionate title "Old Betsy." But the dependability of the Dodges' "plain-Jane" models was based on the L-head, four-cylinder engine, which produced an abundance of energy to drive the 100-inch-wheelbase touring car over the highways and unimproved roads of 1914. This Dodge engine was the culmination of a lifetime of tinkering by Horace, and it would prove to be so efficient that it was the only engine used in Dodge cars for a number of years.

Once again, the brothers were working long hours, seven days a week, in the final preparations for the mass production of their car as a conveyor system was installed in their 70-foot by 876-foot assembly room, which housed $300,000 worth of machinery. With the new, modern conveyor system installed, Horace invented a universal stand for holding engines on the assembly line, then searched for an improved process for baking enamels on the bodies of cars. When he finally hit upon the idea of researching the field of refrigeration, he found materials being used as insulators that were superior to any materials currently used in enameling ovens. The new enameling ovens designed by Horace for the Dodge factory reduced heat loss from more than 40 percent to only 4 percent. Horace also directed the purchase and installation of the new equipment, sending some of the machinery back to its manufacturers with directions on how to improve its design or function.

Expecting to face the usual problems in getting business people and car dealers interested in an untried business venture, both John and Horace were gratified to find that, without a single piece of advertising literature having been sent out, applications for sales agencies came, in volume, into John's business office from all parts of the country. None of these potential dealers knew, as yet, what kind of car the brothers were planning, the price range, or any other details. But everyone connected with the automobile industry was aware of the role the brothers had played in Ford's success with their expert machining skills.

Although less had been written about the Dodge Brothers plant up until this time than about any other great manufacturing institution in the country, automobile trade magazines now began publicizing the Dodges. *Michigan Manufacturer and Financial Record* claimed in August 1914 that "the Dodge brothers are the two best mechanics in Michigan. . . . Into the Ford cars," the magazine continued, "have gone Dodge motors, rear axles, all important assemblies, and many other parts. In fact, during the past decade over 60% of the Ford car has been produced in the Dodge factory. . . . To a great extent, the splendid work of the Dodge Brothers, their quality production, has been the silent compelling factor behind the record-breaking sales of Ford."

As a result of the outside publicity, John was not convinced of the necessity for advertising. To him, marketing their product was simply a matter of making a good car and selling it at a reasonable price— expected to be a little higher than the price of the Model T Ford. "Horace and I go into the factory and sweat blood to save a tenth of a cent," he complained to advertising people, "and you fellows turn right around and throw away ten percent."

Despite his complaints, there was one early advertisement placed in which both brothers took a wicked pleasure in irritating Henry

Ford. The ad read: "Think of all the Ford owners who would like to own an automobile."

The advertising that finally appeared was innovative at a time when most advertising copy was verbose and exaggerated. First, two words appeared on billboards: *Dodge Brothers.* After the public's curiosity was aroused, two more words were added: *Motor Car.* Single words came next: *reliable, dependable, sound.*

The formal announcement of the car was made in a half-page advertisement published in the August 19, 1914 *Saturday Evening Post.* "Dodge Brothers, Detroit, who have manufactured the vital parts for more than 500,000 motor cars, will this fall market a car bearing their own name." The only illustration was the Dodge emblem.

A month earlier—on July 15—Dodge Brothers had made their last Ford part, and two days later the brothers had incorporated their business with a capitalization of $5 million of their own money and had begun the final changeover of their factory to produce their own car, John serving as president, Horace as vice-president. Their expectations were high, but they had no idea that these expectations would be surpassed, nor that the company, within a dozen years, would be worth $170 million.

While a quarter-mile of new factory was being built, the Dodges transformed and reequipped what would shortly become one of the largest manufacturing plants in the country. With payrolls to be met for a beginning force of 5,000 employees and with mounting business and family expenses of day-to-day life, the brothers applied their 1914 Ford stock dividends of $1,220,000 to their own business. There was no leeway for mistakes, they realized. Because of the huge capacity of their plant and the mass scale of their production, a multiplying of mistakes at such a pace would incur serious financial losses.

The Dodge plant, ready to manufacture its own cars in 1914, was described by the *Michigan Manufacturer and Financial Record* in detail: "The foundry with its long line of molding machinery, its battery of core ovens, its monorail and double traveling crane system, its cupolas, its locomotive crane ... its eleven rapid-fire brass and aluminum furnaces melt 150,000 pounds of gray iron each day as well as 25 tons of brass. Again, the two forge plants ... make possible the shaping of 300,000 pounds of steel every day. The screw machine automatics turn out 87,830 parts a day, the gear department cuts 30,000 gears daily, while in the lathe department over 122,000 parts are machined every twenty-four hours.

"The fly-wheel department drills 6,000 differential gears a day, and more hubs than any other factory in the world." The article went on to detail prodigious numbers of brass bushings, steering columns, fenders, splash guards, hoods, radiators, and other parts being turned out for the new car in the Dodge plant, where a complete laboratory and a quarter-mile test track were being installed.

The magazine predicted a ready acceptance by the public of the new Dodge car when it first came off the assembly line because, it said of Dodge Brothers, "there is no operation in their own shop from drop forging to machining, from tool-making to micrometric measurement that they can't do with their own hands."

On November 10, 1914, a lifetime of driving ambition and dreaming and hard work was highlighted for John and Horace when the wide-shouldered, red-headed brothers, both wearing black overcoats and bowlers, rode out of their Hamtramck plant in the rear compartment of the first Dodge automobile and proudly posed for a photographer in front of John's Boston Boulevard home.

Two and one-half weeks later, Matilda gave birth to her first child, a daughter named Frances. Although both the Dodge wives attended church regularly, Horace accompanied Anna to church only occasionally, while John accompanied Matilda even less often. It was decided that the minister should come to the Dodge home to perform the baptismal ceremony, with Horace serving as the child's godfather. The minister, who had not expected any evidence of sentimentality on the part of the brothers, whose reputation for toughness was well known, observed with some surprise that both men became misty-eyed as the baptismal ritual took place.

In the factory, though, as the first Dodge cars came off their production line, the brothers were dynamos of energy, and John found it necessary to ration out the supply of automobiles to impatient dealers with lists of prospective customers. And while the plant worked at capacity, new facilities were being constructed and a foreign sales organization was developed.

By March 1915, factory production was flowing smoothly enough that Horace could take Anna for a trip west to visit the California exposition. But since management problems required John's presence at the plant, he decided to add to Meadow Brook's recreational facilities—not so much because of his love of sports as because of his liking for male camaraderie. He knew his friends would appreciate the new golf clubhouse with an indoor pool that he'd ordered constructed near his nine-hole golf links.

In the city, John and Horace liked to meet their friends in the new $2 million clubhouse of the Detroit Athletic Club, in which the brothers had memberships. Founded by Packard Motor Company President Henry P. Joy as a place for men of the automotive industry to meet apart from the saloons of Woodward Avenue, the DAC became a mecca for automotive people, with membership as important as a Dun and Bradstreet rating.

In the late spring of 1915, John and Matilda announced the engagement of Winifred, now twenty-one years old, to William Gray, Jr. The alliance was an eminently satisfactory one to Matilda, since the senior Gray was a prominent banker and a fellow member of the DAC.

The following month, Della Eschbach's husband, Uriah, died of tuberculosis in the Eschbachs' third-floor rooms of the John Dodge home. Obituary notices referred to him as *Rie Ashbaugh*, the name Della had chosen for him shortly after their marriage. For some years previously, Della had been a follower of a religious movement that investigated and experimented with various psychic phenomena and extrasensory perception—an interest she shared with her sister-in-law Anna, but not with Matilda. Now, after her husband's death, Della invited a friend, Helen Bovee, who shared her psychic interests to come to live with her as her companion in the Boston Boulevard home. Matilda was concerned that the psychic interests of the two women might disturb or influence the children in ways that contradicted her own beliefs, but John was unresponsive to his wife's complaints. So Matilda was forced to conceal her fury at having to accommodate not only her sister-in-law, but also her sister-in-law's friend—a woman about whose presence she had not even been consulted. Della airily ignored Matilda's disapproval, feeling that her brother's house was her house too.

Matilda was aware that Della had reason to feel secure in John's supportiveness. His attachment and sense of duty to his sister had been strong enough to overcome his dread of tuberculosis in having permitted the ailing Uriah Eschbach to continue living in the third-floor quarters of the Dodge home to which the older man had been confined for so long. And John had clearly evidenced his pleasure in Della's accomplishments when she was invited to address the Michigan Women's Press Association and then was elected as that organization's delegate to the National Council of Women. Della had also prevailed upon John to donate a new clubhouse (costing $100,000 and located at Hancock and Second Avenue) for the Detroit Federation of Women's Clubs during Della's reign as president of the statewide federation of that organization. The solidarity of the Dodge family was a matter of pride to John, Horace, and Della—no one realized that more than Matilda and Anna.

By the time Horace had returned from his trip to California with Anna, new employees swelled the Dodge payroll. At the end of May, car production had reached a total of 10,000 automobiles. And it was rising rapidly, day by day, as the company's modern white-tiled power plant, with its two huge compound engines and its generators, created 1,850 kilowatts of electrical energy to operate the factory's machines, presses, cranes, magnets, and elevators. Pleased with these records and with the way their car had been received by the public, the Dodges would have been even more pleased if they could have known of a letter that Henry Ford received, in Februrary 1915, from one of his major dealers—Miller Brothers Automobile and Supply House. The letter informed Ford that "one of our sub-dealers" had requested permission to handle the Dodge car.

With production increasing so smoothly, Horace came out to Meadow Brook often with young Horace that summer, although his daughter, Delphine Ione, found country life not to her taste. The fires in Margaret Rausch's favorite wood-burning stove were lighted from early morning through dark as she prepared three sets of meals for three separate sets of people—the children; the family and its friends; and the help and the guests' chauffeurs. Hungry caddies also needed to be fed. It was Amelia's job to see that the caddies were paid their daily $2 fee and to make certain that the new clubhouse was well stocked with some 150 brands of wine and liquor. In her usual conscientious way, she kept the supplies under lock and key, protected from any pilfering on the part of the hired help.

Apart from the golfing, John and Horace liked to play an improvised game they referred to as "polo." Using automobiles instead of horses as mounts, the two tore around the hills, trying to butt a four-foot ball past two goals set up in the fields.

John's favorite recreation, still, was tramping over his hills. Walking always seemed to revive his spirits—he walked until his companions tired and then tramped on alone. When he went out after dark on the farm, however, he always carried a rifle with him. All the factories had labor troubles brought about by union organizers, and most employers received intermittent threats from disgruntled employees or former employees. The threats angered John and Horace, who felt that their paternalistic dealings with their employees should have insulated them from such problems. Although they had used the piecework incentive, they had never pressured their employees by establishing abnormally high quotas. They had inaugurated beer breaks for the men workers and had equipped a comfortable lounge for their women workers, with prearranged rest breaks. Their medical-clinic services had expanded right along with their plant, and both Horace and John took a personal interest in any employee who came to them with a family problem or financial problem. The brothers had arranged for monthly payments of small sums of money to several widows of former employees. They would take care of their own people, they determined, and would keep the union out of the Dodge factory.

Still, the threats not only angered them, but frightened them. They were especially frightening to John, who, as president of Dodge Brothers and the one responsible for business dealings, received most of the menacing letters. He had always felt comfortable with guns—as had Horace, who loved to hunt and fish. But John had always feared the darkness. That and his uneasy apprehension of a cough or a cold were the two chinks in his armor of invulnerability. Now, as he walked the grounds of his farm at dusk, his rifle gave him courage.

He worried too about the Rausch women left alone at the farm, so he bought a pistol for the tiny Amelia and taught her how to use it, despite her fear of guns. But he knew that a car, rather than a gun, would relieve her sense of isolation. With a car, she could drive the three-and-a-half miles into neighboring Rochester to shop and to attend church and to begin a new social life for herself. While in Detroit, Amelia had previously driven an electric automobile that had belonged to Matilda. The electric's disadvantage was that it ran out of "juice" and often stranded the driver. After Matilda had been inconvenienced a few times, John had hired a chauffeur to drive a gasoline-powered limousine for his wife. Amelia had then used the cast-off electric, but she simply abandoned it when it balked, taking the streetcar home. Now that the Dodge cars were equipped with a dependable "silent starter," however, Amelia did not have to worry about running out of power or about cranking the car. When John sent the new Dodge out to the farm for her, Amelia affectionately dubbed the car "Pauline" because of its predictable habit of triumphing over their perilous highway adventures.

When John and Matilda had come out to the farm that summer and installed their new baby, Frances, and her nursemaid into a front bedroom at the farmhouse, John began building guest houses on the grounds, so that the farmhouse could be reserved for the family and its maids. And shortly, it was time to prepare the farm for the winter. As the bushels of red and golden apples, purple plums, and pears and the sacks of potatoes, squash and tomatoes were stored in a root cellar with double doors large enough to allow a team of horses and a wagon to enter, John pridefully supervised the harvesting of the bounty of his land. Cider and vinegar were made from the apples, cupboards were stacked with jars of tomatoes and fruits canned by Margaret, animal carcasses were hung on hooks in the "keeping room" for butchering, hams and bacon were cured in the smokehouse, sausage was made and stuffed into skins.

As much as John enjoyed his country-squire role, the Dodge family observed Thanksgiving Day in their home in the city. Amelia, who had come into Detroit to take care of some farm business, decided to start back to the Rochester farm in spite of the threatening weather because she did not like to leave her mother there alone for the holiday. A heavy, unseasonable snow had begun to fall as Amelia drove north from Detroit, and the trip, which ordinarily took an hour and a half, became an ordeal. Her Dodge was not prepared for a snowfall, and the windshield soon became clogged with snow. Amelia had to stop the car every half-mile to wipe the windshield with a cloth, then drove the greater part of the way with her head stuck out the side of the open touring car to find her way through the blizzard.

Matilda came out to the farm less often that winter. She was busy with her baby and with plans for Winifred's wedding and Isabel's debut. Most of the farm help moved on to other seasonal work, and the tempo of life at Meadow Brook slowed. Since "Pauline" was no match for the snow-packed country roads around Meadow Brook, Amelia filled up the long wintry days by sorting and packing away the many things Matilda sent out for storage—letters, clothing, newspaper clippings, photos.

Winter or summer, John arrived regularly at the farm on Saturday, leaving on Monday morning. Enjoying the peace of the wintery countryside, he tramped the hills in drifts up to his waist. The multipaned windows in the sleeping porches frosted in icy patterns, but the south windows on the porch adjoining the living room were protected from the worst of winter, and John sat near them by the hour, looking over the frozen landscape and reviewing the successful year the Dodge car had had.

The brothers' first two-passenger roadster had been brought out in late summer and was now selling well at the same price as their touring car, $785. Both Horace and John had looked with satisfaction on their records of the car's production and acceptance by the public as the Dodge automobile celebrated its first anniversary. The public had bought more than $35-million worth of their cars this first year. And their plant had not yet succeeded in keeping up with the public demand. The brothers were especially concerned with keeping the promises that had been made to dealers for certain quotas of cars to be delivered, wanting to prove that a Dodge brother's word was his bond. In New York, one of the largest car dealers in the country had been promised a delivery of 500 cars that first year. When the dealer received only 350 cars and still requested a consignment of 1,500 cars for the next year, Horace and John personally handed the dealer their check for the total commission the dealer would have made on the 150 cars he did not get by the end of the first year.

For the Dodge family, year 1915 ended in a flurry of parties. On October 30, Winifred became Mrs. William John Gray, Jr. The twenty-one-year-old brunette daughter of John and his first wife, Ivy, was attended at her marriage by her sister Isabel, her brother John Duval, and her friend and neighbor, Josephine Clay, who was later to become Mrs. Edsel Ford. And on December 28, Isabel was introduced to Detroit society at a dinner-dance at the Pontchartrain Hotel.

Although the John Dodge daughters of his first marriage were now adults, Matilda found the job of managing the Boston Boulevard home more, rather than less, demanding. The newly married couple, after a wedding trip to the East, returned to live at the John Dodge home until a new home planned for them by John was completed. It seemed to Matilda that the big house on the boulevard was bursting at the seams with family.

6

By 1916, Dodge automobiles had enough innovations to rate lengthy descriptions by automotive writers: "tonneau carpeted and fitted with nickled foot and robe rails . . . electric lighting and starting . . . a sixty-mile-an-hour speedometer . . . a grease cup on the floorboard through which the clutch throw-out yoke may be given attention without raising the board . . . horn can be sounded either by hand or by a side-swing of the knee . . . wheel far enough forward to admit the driver without compressing his waistcoat unduly."

Like other enterprising businessmen, the Dodges sought and acquired government orders in 1916. Three olive drab Dodge cars and fifteen men under the command of Lieutenant George Patton, Jr., took part in the first mechanized cavalry charge in United States history when Brigadier General John J. Pershing sent them across the border on reprisal raids against Pancho Villa in Mexico. The Dodge cars swayed and lurched along in low gear, belching steam and grinding their way through the sand so successfully that, less than three months later, Pershing requested another 250 Dodges from the War Department, putting out an order that only Dodges would be used by his staff in Mexico's rugged territory.

While the affairs of their own business could not have been better, the Dodges' involvement in Ford's business was continually worsening. The previous October, Horace and John had not been surprised at Couzens' resignation as vice-president, treasurer, and general manager of Ford Motor Company. Ford, intolerant of any role except that of dictator, seemed to be deliberately provoking divisions with his old business associates. Now, the fact that the Dodges had successfully put a car on the market to compete with his—financed, as he viewed it, with *his* profits—infuriated Ford. He would simply stop paying dividends on the bulk of the company's profits, Ford decided—profits accumulating to nearly $60 million by the end of July 1916. And he announced a cut of $80 in the price of his car.

The Dodges were incensed. They wanted their dividends from Ford for use in expansion of their own business. And they thought the price cut was not only unnecessary, since Ford was already selling cars as fast as he could produce them at the present price, but the reduction was also a threat to their own prices. In a letter dated September 23, 1916, the Dodge brothers demanded of Ford that he distribute no less than 50 percent of the accumulated cash surplus. When Ford refused this demand, they confronted him personally. If he wanted total control of the business, he should buy them out, they insisted, offering to sell him their stock for $35 million. When Ford refused, the brothers ordered their lawyers to bring suit to compel Ford to distribute profits.

Leaving his lawyer's office, John headed for the DAC. Going into the grill and ordering his dinner, he picked up the latest copy of the *Detroit Times* and leafed through its pages, looking for any choice items concerning Ford's latest pronouncements. Instead, he saw his own name heading another article critical of him and one of his political cronies. With an oath, John crumpled the paper with his big fist, then signaled for the waiter and told him to hold his dinner. The startled waiter watched as the hefty, broad-shouldered Dodge sprinted with surprising agility for the door and into his car. Driving out to the home of James Schermerhorn, owner of the *Times*, John braked his car to a quick stop, ran up the steps and leaned on the doorbell until a maid opened the door. Rushing past the maid toward Schermerhorn, John grabbed the man by the necktie and jerked the astonished publisher toward him. One blow to the jaw knocked Schermerhorn to the floor. But John was not yet satisfied. He grabbed Schermerhorn a second time and landed another blow. "The next time you print any lies about my friend, I'll come up and hit you again!" he threatened. He left the house as quickly as he had come, drove back to the DAC, went back to his steak, and ate it with gusto.

John and Horace felt that their interest in politics and in the causes of their friends in politics was as paternalistic as their concern for their factory employees, and they took offense at any criticism of this paternalism. That summer the brothers attended the Republican National Convention in Chicago, with John serving as a delegate while discouraging the attempts of his friends to induce him to run for the Senate. Knowing that his friends admired his leadership and speaking abilities, John was aware of his own lack of the kind of scholarly knowledge of American history that he thought national political figures should have. Deciding to remedy this, he began a con-centrated study of an early-American figure he particularly admired—Alexander Hamilton. In typical John Dodge fashion, he continued with his studies of Hamilton until he became an authority on the statesman.

Horace's interests were more closely allied with city and county politics. Marx was still mayor of Detroit, and others of Horace's close circle of friends were running for the offices of county treasurer and sheriff. Night after night, Horace met with his friends as political strategies were set up, and both Horace and John contributed freely toward the campaigns of these men.

In the autumn of 1916, the Dodges looked forward to the prospect of the upcoming public fight with Ford in the courts as much as they looked forward to the seizing of public office by their friends. On November 2, John and Horace secured a court order enjoining Ford from proceeding with his planned Rouge River plant expansion and demanding division of Ford's surplus profits. The trial made public, for the first time, the enormous fortunes Ford and the Dodges had made in just a few years. Ford was ordered to temporarily discontinue building blast furnaces and foundries at the Rouge, and the automotive world waited expectantly for public hearings scheduled for the following year.

That fall Dodge Brothers turned out car number 100,000. Already fourth in volume of business in the industry, they established a new record by turning out this number of cars in less than two years.

While John and Horace were absorbed with their business problems that fall, their two sons added further complications to their lives. Both boys, always more interested in pursuing pleasure than studies, had gone off to New York City for an unscheduled spree and had failed to report to school. Horace and Anna, on being notified of the problem by the administration at Manlius, went to New York, where they spoke with school authorities and made the necessary arrangements for young Horace to return to school.

John Duval's education had already included a series of expulsions, with his father scrambling about to find a new school to take him on each occasion. This time John Duval was simply sent home with his baggage—no notification to his parents, no conferences, no compromises. When the efforts of Matilda and John failed to get the school to readmit John Duval, the father was furious with the boy. He decided that since there was talk of war and conscription, he would put John Duval to work in the factory to keep him from going overseas.

Although the Dodge brothers were making plans to add three new models to their line of automobiles, Horace took time to celebrate two important occasions. The first celebration was on December 30, 1916, when his friend Ed Stein resigned as county treasurer to become county sheriff and immediately appointed twenty-five new deputies and named Horace E. Dodge as undersheriff. Although the appointment was considered a complimentary one, paying a thousand dollars a year which Horace gave to Anna's favorite charity, Horace was pleased with it and made up his mind to be of real assistance to Stein.

The second occasion occurred shortly after the new year arrived, when the Horace Dodges took a party of friends to Wilmington, Delaware, for the launching of still another, and larger, steam yacht that Horace had ordered built by naval architects Gielow and Orr. Christened the *Nokomis II* by Anna, the craft was the biggest private yacht on the Great Lakes—243 feet in length, with a 32-foot beam. Electrically lighted and with a thermo-fan heating system, the yacht had two galleys—one for the crew, the other for the owners. Aboard the craft, Horace and Anna could relax in luxury in the owners' comfortable staterooms, or could entertain guests in the large living or dining room, fitted with buffet and sideboard. But this launching was nearly the end of civilian frivolity for the Dodges as the United States moved closer to a declaration of war against Germany.

April 1917—the month in which the United States entered the war—brought an increase of $50 on the Dodges' cost per car, since steel and other basic materials were being diverted into the manufacture of munitions. Still, the brothers continued expanding their line, as planned, with the production of a touring model with a nonfolding top and a glass enclosure that permitted controlled ventilation, which sold for $165 more than the standard touring Dodge. They also produced a convertible coupe and a convertible sedan with removable side-window and center-post pillars that could be stored in a compartment in back of the rear-seat cushion.

But the war was making itself felt, both in the Dodges' private and business lives. In May, Horace bid a sentimental goodbye, with a commemorative ceremony, to his yacht, *Nokomis I*, which he had volunteered to the government as a submarine chaser. Each guest present at the ceremony was presented with a booklet containing a picture of the *Nokomis* and the Dodge brothers, plus a sentimental poem written for the occasion by Della.

Also in May, the main case in the Ford-Dodge suit finally came up for a public hearing. As people fought for space in the small courtroom, trying to get a glimpse of the powerful Ford and the Dodges, the county guard had to be called to control the crowd. The Dodges' chief counsel had one central goal—to wring from Henry Ford the story of his early association with the Dodges and to document the Dodges' role in Ford's success. Reluctant to make such admissions, the tall, lean, stern-looking Ford was brought back to the witness stand day after day in the contest of wills. Little by little, lawyer Elliott Stevenson dragged one concession after another from Ford as Stevenson established that the Ford company, at the beginning, was almost exclusively an assembling operation with the Dodges actually producing Ford's car.

"Dodge Brothers spent $60,000 to $75,000 to re-equip their plant to do the work—to retool," Stevenson reminded Ford, as the lawyer probed the Ford Motor Company's origin. "They jeopardized everything they had."

"I don't know that," Ford answered evasively.

"Well, *you* didn't have any risk, did you?" Stevenson pressed.

Ford denied this. He had given up his drawings for his car to be manufactured, he pointed out. But Stevenson reminded him that other testimony had indicated that Ford's original designs were for a car that did not function properly until Horace Dodge began tinkering with it.

"And the Dodges," Stevenson continued, "gambled with their business to undertake the manufacture of an undeveloped car, didn't they?"

Ford squirmed in the witness chair, then replied that he had forgotten quite a bit about his company's beginnings.

"You haven't forgotten that they produced the cars that brought the money to make you a success!" Stevenson exclaimed. "There isn't any doubt of it, is there?"

"No," Ford acknowledged quietly.

As the continuing trial revealed the huge profits Ford Motor Company had made in recent years, union organizers, who had been pressuring both Ford and the Dodges, now found public sentiment on their side when they demanded unionization of Ford's plants.

Hoping to redeem his tarnished image, Ford, with the help of his lawyer, tried to establish his motives as altruistic in cutting prices of cars and withholding profits from stockholders. If his company had not been organized for profits, Stevenson demanded, why had it been organized? Ford's response was pious. "Organized to do as much good as we can everywhere for everyone concerned." Then he added, "It has been my policy to force the price of the car down as fast as increased production would permit."

Stevenson seized on this. "Then your conscience would not let you sell cars at the price you did last year and make such awful profits. That is what you said, isn't it?"

"I don't know that my conscience had anything to do with the case," Ford snapped.

Stevenson smiled silkily. "Why did you say it wasn't right to get such awful profits if it wasn't your conscience?"

"It wasn't good business for the institution," Ford admitted.

The circuit court rulings sustained the Dodges' position. Ford had already acquired capital assets far beyond the legal limit, the court declared, and no further accumulations could be made. The Ford Highland Park plant expansion was enjoined, and the planned blast furnaces and foundries at River Rouge could not be built. Moreover, $19 million was to be distributed at once to the stockholders, and future earnings were also to be distributed. The case was to be kept in court so that the company's conduct could be supervised.

The battle was not yet finished, Ford vowed. Reluctant as he was to continue the public circus surrounding the case, he was even more reluctant to abandon his plans, to distribute surplus dividends, and to surrender his control of the company to the court's discretion. Ford appealed the ruling to the Michigan Supreme Court, and hearings were scheduled for the following year.

Competitive as ever, John and Horace were intent, after that, to beat Ford on the production line as well as in the courts. They kept careful notation of the number of cars shipped out of Detroit in a small black notebook. In May 1917, John's jottings indicated that 7,888 cars had been shipped out of Detroit for the month. Dodge led all Detroit companies with 2,112 cars shipped; Ford was next with 1,634.

The pride John felt in the affirmative decision by the court and in the flourishing Dodge factory was matched by his pride and happiness when a second child—a son—was born to Matilda on July 23, 1917. The boy was named Daniel George Dodge for his two grandfathers.

At this time in the changing wartime economy, the United States government notified Dodge Brothers that it would take advantage of the offer John and Horace had made to assist in the Allied cause, which was being hindered, the brothers were told, by an insufficient supply of the type of French guns desperately needed for Allied forces. Factories that built the 155-millimeter French-type howitzers and the French 75 were unable to produce more than five guns a day because of a recoil mechanism so delicate it had to be made by hand. The recoil apparatus prevented the gun from tearing itself to pieces as it fired. With the gun placed at a 45° angle, this recuperating apparatus, made from a solid billet of steel, would return the barrel to its original position in a little less than thirteen seconds.

After the Allies had begged United States Secretary of War Newton Baker to find American handcraftsmen who could assist in the production of the recoil mechanism, two American companies attempted to build the gun parts and failed. Then, at a conference in Washington, it was suggested that if anyone could make the mechanism, the Dodge brothers could.

Called to Washington by the secretary of war, John Dodge met with a French delegation, which promised to send skilled craftsmen to Detroit to show his workers how to hand-tool the delicate mechanism. John brushed off the suggestion in his usual unceremonious way. "Give us a blueprint," he said. "We can make all you want of anything if we have a blueprint."

The French delegates all spoke at once, volubly, in their own language. This American was a madman, they assured each other. Couldn't he understand this was not a production job?

John waited, frown lines deepening in his wide forehead as the French-English dialogue continued among the foreign delegates and war-department officials. Then John spoke out loudly—earthily. Did they want the mechanisms manufactured, or didn't they?

"Look here, Mr. Dodge," the secretary of war protested. "I'm not accustomed to being spoken to in that kind of language."

Veins swelled in John's neck. "The war would be a hell of a lot better off if you were!" he responded angrily.

After the conferees' civility returned, John offered to take a model of the mechanism back to Detroit so he could discuss production possibilities with Horace. The older brother was confident of Horace's ability to decide quickly whether the recoil mechanism could be machine produced. And, if such production was possible, Horace would be the one to figure out the way to do it successfully.

A few days later, John returned to Washington. He had just one question. "How many do you want?" he asked.

The Dodge brothers' promise to make fifty recoil mechanisms a day, beginning in only four months, was regarded with skepticism by the French representatives. U.S. government officials were skeptical for a different reason—John and Horace did not want the government to build the plant nor to supply the machinery for the mechanism. The Dodges would finance the entire undertaking, John asserted, and would take no profit. But they insisted on doing the work in their own way, with no government interference.

At first, John's proposal was considered preposterous by a government that had saturated every munitions plant in the country with military and government officials and supervisors. No important military materials were permitted to be handled without intimate government control. But there was a need for the guns and, seemingly, no alternative for the government except to accede to the stipulations of the independent Dodges.

On Saturday, October 27, 1917, word of the government's acceptance of the Dodges' proposal, on Dodge terms, was received in Detroit, but Dodge Brothers' machinery had already been set in motion without waiting for official word. On that same Saturday, the Detroit Water Department, Public Works Department, and the gas and electric companies came out to the Dodges' property where the new plant was to be built. By Sunday, dirt was being dug for the foundations. By the next Tuesday, sewer systems and water mains were being installed. Carloads of materials arrived on a newly laid spur of the Detroit Terminal Railway, and cement mixers, cranes, steam shovels, and switch engines moved over the unplowed field. Within five days after the signing of the governmental contract, steel was arriving from Bethlehem Steel Company.

To keep the work going constantly, as 1,800 men worked on the construction of the plant, John and Horace built a sleeping place for themselves at the site. As in the days of their beginnings, they ate and slept on the job site for weeks at a time, eager to prove their frequent boast that a Dodge brother's word was his bond.

Although John had no time for Meadow Brook now, he made arrangements to substitute for Margaret Rausch's hearty home cooking of his favorite foods by ordering the cook at his Boston Boulevard home to prepare great crocks of beans. He had the crocks carted down to the Dodge foundry, where the beans could be heated and cooked for a day or more before being served to the workers. John and Horace ate their meals quickly, then moved about the project, overseeing everything. As they supervised a group of workers straining to push a great timber into position, the brothers pulled off their coats and added their considerable weight to that of the day laborers as they pushed with their shoulders against the timber and moved it into place.

Four months, they reminded themselves, for Horace to finish designing and building the special machinery that would make possible the quantity production of the mechanism for the great gun. Four months for John to complete the building of the plant and the installation of the machinery.

By the end of November, the foundation had been completed on the eleven-acre site, and the steel structure was rising for the 600-by-800 foot munitions plant that would cost the Dodge brothers $10 million when completed and equipped. In their final arrangements with the government, the Dodges had agreed to take a 10-percent profit on their actual expenses—a profit that would allow for the payment of various taxes. As independent businessmen and owners of all the stock in their own company, the brothers could sign the kind of agreement that would not have been acceptable to most stockholders.

John and Horace had always boasted of their independence. But they were proud too of their patriotism, frequently referring to themselves as "all-American" because they could trace their ancestry back to New England before the time of the Revolutionary War. John's interest in genealogy had intensified as he had delved into his studies of the life of Alexander Hamilton. He was pleased when his collections of Hamilton materials led to a meeting and discussion with Arthur H. Vandenberg, later to become a U.S. senator, who was collecting information for a book. Vandenberg used some of John's contributions in the two Hamilton books he eventually had published.

Inside the Dodge Brothers plant, in 1917, flags and bunting were draped over recruiting posters and Liberty Loan placards. Many employees had left for military duty, and replacements had been hired, but John Duval continued to work for his father. In his greatest personal patriotic sacrifice, Horace resigned himself to the idea of having his beautiful new *Nokomis II* sent into governmental service in the spring.

But Horace could not brood over the anticipated loss of his yacht—each of his days was filled with plans for the building and installing of 129 pieces of specially designed machinery, devised by Horace, including a delicate lapping machine that was Horace's special pride and invention. And he worked too at small improvements in the recoil mechanism itself.

As December closed in that winter, cold and blustery, zero temperatures froze the ground and the concrete and the workers' fingers. Workers stomped their feet and thawed their fingers over fires in open drums, and the work continued.

The Dodge touring car, with a durable khaki canvas-duck top, was adopted, that year, by the government as a standard army-type vehicle, without any modifications—its value already proven in the Pershing expedition into Mexico. Dodge cars now chugged right through some of the biggest battles on the European continent—Chateau-Thierry, Meuse-Argonne, Marne.

Civilians became more aware of war's realities when Detroiters were given sugar rations and as more young men, registered for the selective service since the previous April, boarded trains for army camps. "U-Boat Sinks American Destroyer, 60 Tars Missing," newspapers announced as Detroiters tried to forget their troubles and thronged to the popular bars and places of entertainment. Prohibition would take effect in Michigan in May 1918. But the Metropole, the Pontchartrain, the Griswold, and the College Inn were patronized as if Detroiters were drinking up to prepare for the dry years ahead.

7

In January 1918, steel-helmeted doughboys from Camp Custer marched down Woodward Avenue, preparing to "go over." It was a depressing month of wartime fuel shortages and continued cold weather, including a blizzard that limited attendance at a Detroit Symphony concert to a few people—Horace and Anna among those who braved the weather to attend. After the concert, the Dodges met with the orchestra's manager at the popular Pontchartrain, where the manager confided his problems to a sympathetic Horace. Concert attendance was poor because of the war . . . some pledges of financial support had failed to materialize . . . visiting conductors were not a satisfactory arrangement. The manager eyed Horace reflectively. Would Mr. Dodge, he asked, like to *buy* the orchestra?

Horace grinned. His own symphony! Well, why not? Still, he felt this was a matter he should discuss, first, with John. But when John reasonably pointed out that Horace certainly had no need for his own orchestra, Horace had to agree. Still, determined not to let the orchestra flounder, he financed the search for a skilled conductor—a search that narrowed down to Victor Herbert and Ossip Salomonowitsch Gabrilowitsch, the brilliant Russian pianist and son-in-law of Mark Twain. The symphony president liked the pretentiousness of the long name, and Anna and Horace were partial to pianists, so "Gabby" became the symphony's new conductor.

By March first, the new munitions plant the Dodges had built was ready for production. And as the last of the machinery was installed—just four months from ground-breaking day—the brothers were in an exhilarated mood, congratulating each other and everyone who had assisted them. Once more, they exulted, the Dodge brothers had proved the validity of their word. They had promised production beginning in four months. Now they proudly wired Washington the news that their plant would go into operation at the promised date.

Army Ordnance experts watched with interest as the first mechanisms came off the machine line. They took the mechanisms and studied them skeptically, then pronounced the results as perfection. As the only plant in the country to manufacture the recoil mechanisms, the Dodges' factory reached a peak production of thirty mechanisms a day—never close enough to the brothers' projected figure of fifty a day to please Horace and John. Still, thirty was six times the number being hand-manufactured in any French munitions factory, and Horace and John had to be satisfied with this.

In their own automobile plant, the brothers also began producing a screened express truck mounted with extra heavy springs on their regular passenger-car chassis, and the government immediately placed orders for the trucks for its Army Ordnance and Quartermaster corps. The truck weighed 2,600 pounds and had a 1,500-pound capacity. Immediately after this first truck was in production, the Dodges began the manufacture of a closed, panel-side delivery truck with windowed rear-cargo doors. More orders came in from the government as these trucks were used for ambulances.

For the past year, the Dodge automobile plant had been in fourth position in volume of production of American cars.

Their factory covered seventy-five acres of land, including its own trim shop, where 8,000 pounds of mohair and over 625 full-sized hides were required each day for the making of the tops, side-curtains, and upholstering for the cars. Its drop-forge department was equipped with 54 steam hammers and consumed 225,000 pounds of steel and 15,000 gallons of crude oil each day. Eighteen thousand employees worked in the plant, which had been mechanized as fully as modern methods and Horace's ingenuity permitted—with moving chain assemblies, cranes, interplant railroads and monorail systems, chutes and elevators, and a unique torsion machine for testing drive shafts and other vital automobile parts. The machine was the second of its kind ever built, the first one having been made for the Japanese government, and it was capable of exerting a torsion strain of 230,000 inch-pounds.

The Dodges were continuing to introduce improvements into their cars at any time during the year, rejecting the idea of yearly models. By 1918, their automobiles had a lengthened wheelbase of 114 inches, a multiple-disk clutch and spiral bevel gears.

In spite of the noninterference promises by the government, the Dodge plants and offices were a network of government "supervisors" and informers. Government agents accused the brothers of giving them no information or providing them with blind information. When one of the officers—a Captain Jeffords—reported to Washington that he thought the Dodge brothers "were running things pretty high-handed . . ." and protested to the Dodges about their brick and lumber orders, John and Horace demanded the officer's removal.

In spite of the army's surveillance, a large portfolio of high security mechanical drawings appeared in Matilda's collection of papers at Meadow Brook, including the blueprints, tracings, preliminary sketches, and other details of the guns on which the Allies depended.

In the privacy of their offices, John and Horace raged over the intrusions into their business. When one of their foreign-born employees was arrested by federal officials on suspicion of sabotage after the $100,000 piece of machinery the employee operated had malfunctioned, John and Horace insisted on conducting their own investigation before the government sent in more officials to probe the workings of the plant. For hours, the brothers disassembled parts and examined the machine. Eventually, they discovered a screw was missing, and the shop superintendent himself confessed to having removed the screw in an attempt to facilitate the operation of the machine.

But some of the government's suspicions were not unfounded. In April, John received a letter demanding increased wages and threatening the lives of his family and brother. Security tightened. Government detectives were assigned to guard the two men and their families. Always conscious of these dangers to her family, Matilda made a practice of never going farther than two hours' distance from her young Frances and Daniel. And Winifred, still living at the family home, now had an infant daughter—Peggy—of her own to be guarded from kidnappers.

The spring sunshine that year was especially welcome after the dreary winter with its coal shortages and heatless Mondays. John planned on planting every inch of ground on the farm to increase crops for the war effort. His sister Della traveled over the state raising money for Liberty Bonds and chairing various committees for the Red Cross and War Victory Commission.

Neither Della nor John and Matilda were at the Boston Boulevard home on the warm April weekend when the Detroit newspapers headlined stories of a young John Duval Dodge's secret marriage, at age nineteen, to an eighteen-year-old Detroit girl. Enjoying a brief golfing vacation at French Lick, Indiana, John and Matilda read in amazement of their son's elopement with Marie O'Connor—an elopement that had taken place two weeks previously. Since that time, the youthful bride had been living at home with her parents. But when

Marie had become ill with pneumonia, she had told her parents of the marriage, and John moved into the O'Connor home to be with his wife.

Now that the secret was exposed, John Duval had no reluctance to discuss the marriage with reporters. He was working as a captain in the ordnance department of his father's factory, he told them. "Father and I never got along very well together," he added, explaining that he did not intend to make any of his future plans public, "except that I expect to start in business myself," he declared.

Secret marriage! His own business! John Dodge's face flamed with rage. Hadn't he given this son of his every opportunity to make something of himself? And wasn't the boy deliberately now trying to humiliate his father publicly and show contempt for his family?

Workers at the Dodge plant read of John Duval's plans and joked among themselves at the pretentiousness of the young man's declarations. While reports of the occasional transgressions of John or Horace were excused, and even enjoyed, by the shopmen, the same excesses were condemned in John Duval because they were not balanced by the brothers' human compassion and productivity. John Duval—whom the workers frequently referred to as "John Devil Dodge"—had not concealed his lack of interest in the business and had spent little time at the factory. Still, there were those among the plant supervisors who felt that both John and Horace were evidencing some short-sightedness in keeping their sons at the fringe of the business and not personally preparing them for futures within the plant. In their fierce individualism, the brothers kept personal control of their empire from the boardroom down to the greasy mechanical operations. They either were oblivious to the needs of their sons or were intolerant of the thought of sharing any of their empire, even with their children.

John now angrily stated his intentions to disown his son. Nor was there any softening of his attitude with the wearing off of the initial shock. John Duval had flouted his father's authority for the last time, John Dodge determined, as he called his lawyer and ordered the changing of his will.

Long before the signing of the Armistice that November, John Duval, faced with the implacable disdain of his father, left Detroit to make a new life for himself and his young wife in Texas. And with the signing of the Armistice, happy Detroiters thronged the downtown streets, passing by the Pontchartrain and the former saloons along Woodward to celebrate in the "beer flats" set up in apartment houses. Grosse Pointers did their drinking and celebrating in the more elegant

"2156," an imposing East Jefferson mansion supplied with liquor by the rum runners, who moved back and forth across the mile-wide river separating Detroit from Windsor.

Horace comforted himself on the loss of his convivial drinking places with the brilliant new symphony season now commencing. Conductor Gabrilowitsch insisted, with the war ended, that the orchestra should have its own auditorium with suitable acoustics. Horace assumed the project as his own and attracted the support of affluent music lovers in Detroit for the new Orchestra Hall.

As Christmas of 1918 approached, Horace did some special planning for a gift for his close friend, Sheriff Ed Stein, who would be turning over his post at the year's end to a newly elected sheriff. Ever since the election, which Stein had lost by a margin of only 500 votes, Horace had shared his friend's disappointment over the defeat. If only he had called in his foremen and superintendents at the factory and passed the word down the line that the sheriff should be reelected, Horace told Stein regretfully. But he hadn't done this because he had not believed that Stein was in any danger of losing the election.

Stein's loss meant that Horace would no longer be undersheriff, and Horace was regretful about that too. In the past two years, he had relished the excitement of going along with Stein on official business, investigations, and on raids and roundups of criminals. He had made regular and frequent visits to the county jail, where he talked with prisoners and made friends with many of them, trying to motivate them to try to keep out of trouble once they had served their jail terms. For some of the released prisoners, whose sincerity impressed Horace, he provided jobs at the Dodge factory and saw to it that trades were taught to his protégés.

For the two years in which the undersheriff appointment had become a kind of favorite recreation for Horace, he had occasionally felt some guilt about spending so much time on county business instead of with his wife and family. On these occasions, he merely donated a few thousand dollars to one of Anna's favorite charities in support of some of the interests that provided hobbies for her, including a $30,000 donation to the Protestant Orphan Asylum, of whose administrative board Anna was a member.

When sheriff-department people were needed to help with the transfer of several prisoners from the Wayne County Jail up to the prison in Marquette, Michigan—some 500 miles to the north— Horace happily volunteered for the trip. Then he and Robert Oakman rolled dice to see who would pay for a private railroad car for the group of friends to travel in style, with their meals served by special waiters. Horace cheerfully paid the bill, and when the train was marooned in a snowstorm, he was just as cheerful to be in the company of the friends he enjoyed for an extra day. As far as he was concerned, Anna could have her new friends. She could fill their mansion with her new associates if she chose—he had no objections to flaunting his success to these people. But for his personal pleasure, he clung to his friends of many years.

Horace had begun the custom of going over to the jail at Christmastime and distributing several hundred dollars in gold to the prisoners, while passing out boxes of cigars to the deputies. But he had been surprised and touched when he was presented with a small gift box from Stein and the "boys at the jail." Inside was a gold sheriff's badge. Afterwards, Horace proudly wore the badge, centered with a diamond, whenever he came to the jail or accompanied Stein on county business.

Early on Christmas morning of 1918, Horace headed for the jail and distributed his gold pieces, then asked Stein to accompany him on an errand. Driving out to West Grand Boulevard, Horace stopped the car in front of a large home and handed Stein the key to the house, saying that it was a Christmas present for the Stein family. Later that day, Horace spent some time at the home, celebrating with Stein and his friends before returning to Rose Terrace and the Christmas dinner awaiting him there.

Although Anna was under the impression that Horace was offering the home to Stein, rent free, on a temporary basis, the Stein family moved into the $21,000 home with the understanding that the house was theirs—permanently. Horace's generosity became too much for Ed Stein's wife to accept, though, when he had several thick Oriental rugs sent out to the new Stein residence. Mrs. Stein regretfully sent the rugs back to the store.

On the same day that Stein surrendered his post to the new sheriff, there was a surprising announcement from Henry Ford. The announcement dealt with his sudden resignation from the Ford Motor Company and the appointment of his twenty-five-year-old son, Edsel, as company president. The Dodges were not misled by Ford's announcement, suspecting it had something to do with his strategy for the upcoming suit in the Michigan Supreme Court and quite sure that their old associate still intended to dictate company policy, in spite of his publicized plan to go away for a long rest.

On February 1, 1919, the Dodges emerged triumphant from the Michigan Supreme Court. The justices' opinion, which acknowledged the possibility of Ford's altruistic motives in running the company for the benefit of the workers and the buying public, affirmed the fact that "a business corporation is organized and carried on primarily for the profit of the stockholders." While upholding Ford's plans for expansion, the court curbed his power to control the company, and it defined the rights of the minority stockholders—ordering Ford to distribute $19.3 million from the company's surplus holdings to its stockholders.

Seven stockholders divided the $19.3 million of surplus profits from the year 1916. The Dodge brothers received a little more than $1.9 million in addition to their other dividends for that year.

Ford was now determined to regain control of the company, and the only way to do this was to buy out the other investors.

While being questioned by the Dodges' attorney in one of his recent court appearances, Ford had snapped, "If you sit there until you are petrified, I wouldn't buy the Dodge brothers' stock, if that is what you are talking about!" But the court decision had changed Ford's attitude, and he was ready with a plan to persuade the other stockholders to sell. In March, he announced from California his plans to form a new automobile company that was going to build a car still cheaper than the present Ford—a car to sell at $250. He indicated he intended to allow the original company to wither from lack of attention while shifting all his energy and resources to building up a business to compete with his original organization. When asked what his plans were for his old company, Ford disclaimed further interest in it, saying, "I don't know what will become of that."

That was the same strategy he had used to squeeze out Malcomson years before. And even though John and Horace recognized the strategy, they were wary of Ford and knowledgeable of his shrewdness in business dealings.

When Ford commissioned trust-company representatives from Boston to approach the minority stockholders to buy them out, the Dodges quickly sold their shares for $25 million, which supplied them with the fresh supply of cash they wanted to invest in their own business so they could give Ford even greater competition in selling cars. The rest of Ford's stockholders, intimidated by Henry's threats, sold their interests at similar profits except for Couzens, who held out for a little more per share before selling.

That winter, Horace and John decided to expand their truck production by manufacturing their own engines and transmissions for trucks produced in association with Graham Brothers Truck Company. Marketing the trucks under the Graham name but through Dodge dealers exclusively, Horace and John proved their projections correct as truck output climbed—accounting for 20 percent of their total volume within five years.

Shortly after their new models of automobiles went into production in early 1919, the John Dodge and Horace Dodge clan journeyed south for a Palm Beach holiday. It was John's first visit to Florida. In the fashionable resort city, the John Dodges spent their time quietly in their rented beachhouse in Royal Park, where the women went out on the beach with their blankets and sat in the sunshine, watching John and Horace fish.

Anna and Horace stayed at the Breakers Hotel, as in previous winters. Within the limitations her husband's casual way of life had imposed on her, Anna had reared her daughter Delphine like a princess. She had supervised her daughter's friends carefully while looking for opportunities to launch Delphine and herself into more exclusive circles. Palm Beach was the ideal place, she thought, for this opportunity. And that winter, she bided her time and watched the young people divert themselves with golf and bathing and dancing. Horace Jr., especially, created a sensation as he dashed down Lake Worth at terrific speeds in the Dodges' speedboat, its nose bounding several feet above the water.

Delphine's piano playing attracted an attentive audience as she entertained the younger set with her bright Chopin and racy jazz. But the winter of 1919 was not yet Anna's year, and when the family left for Detroit in April, in spite of the attractiveness of the young people, none of the Dodges had really penetrated into the exclusive center of Palm Beach.

With the millions from the sale of their Ford stock about to be distributed, both Dodge families embarked on an orgy of spending. While Horace had faced the resistance of Grosse Pointe society a dozen years earlier and had gruffly elbowed his way in, John and Matilda had been satisfied with their Boston Boulevard address. But now, with a growing family (Matilda was expecting a third child in June), John decided to follow his brother into Grosse Pointe.

He would build a home so palatial, he decided, it would eclipse anything ever built in Michigan and rival any structure in the world. If money was the index of success, he was going to display his success to the proud "elite."

Hiring the best of architects and artisans, he had 350 workmen begin the construction of the home, expected to cost between $3 and $4 million, which would include 110 rooms and 24 baths. Two acres of floor space were to be comprised by two floors and the ground level, with a great center hall the size of twenty ordinary rooms, a huge ballroom and swimming pool, and 6,000 square feet of space for a servants' wing.

To John, the grounds were even more important than the building. He planned vegetable and flower gardens, a dairy barn, and a poultry run, plus a tremendous greenhouse that was to be divided into eleven compartments, each with a different climate, for plants native to any part of the world.

The planning for the new home did not prevent John from making his annual visit, with Horace, to the graves of their mother and father in Niles that year. While they were in the little town, the brothers learned that the Michigan Central Railway was moving its freight yard and engine terminal to Niles, with an influx of 550 workers and their families. Four hundred homes were needed to house them. Harboring no grudges for the refusal of the town to accept their gift offer several years previously, the brothers immediately advanced a half-million dollars to set up a building-and-loan association for loans to the townspeople for homes.

The brothers had already returned to Detroit from Niles when they learned that Cyrus Bowles, the black man who had worked for their father so many years ago, was paralyzed from a stroke. John wrote to his former schoolmate, Fred Bonine—now mayor of Niles—to inquire about Bowles. "I wish you would have someone investigate and get for him anything he needs," he wrote. "If he should die, I wish you would see to it that he receives a fitting service and a proper funeral. And send the bill to me."

The aged black man did not die, however, and each month thereafter, a check arrived at his home, sent by John and Horace. On a larger scale, John was generous enough to try to help out his friend Robert Oakman, who had been unable to obtain a much-needed loan of a quarter-million dollars from his bank. The bank had not only been unwilling to advance Oakman the money, but had decided he was a bad risk and called in his previous loans. Leaving the bank, a despairing Oakman took his troubles to John Dodge.

Within an hour, John strode into the bank and demanded to see the bank president. Was the Dodge name worth anything? he asked loudly. The president tried to soothe him with assurances that Mr. Dodge could have any amount of money he wanted. Either give Oakman the money he requested, John declared, or he, John Dodge, would withdraw everything he had in the bank.

The bank president was just as determined as John, however. Oakman was a bad risk, he explained. And if Mr. Dodge was so certain of his friend's integrity, why didn't he just sign his own name for Oakman's loan?

Even in anger, John recognized a reasonable question. And it sounded like a dare. With a flourish of his fountain pen, John scrawled his signature, leaving the amount open for his friend to fill in the blank later with a quarter-million-dollar figure—not even requiring Oakman to sign a note for the amount.

Horace had already made a lavish investment in the Detroit Symphony Orchestra after its conductor had insisted that the orchestra should have its own auditorium. When the orchestra debuted at beautiful new Orchestra Hall in October 1919, every box in the golden horseshoe was filled with the elite of Detroit, resplendent in opening-night finery. Gabrilowitsch bounded on stage, wearing his trademark—a 2½-inch-high white collar—and mounted the podium before his ninety-piece orchestra and an audience of 2,200 people, who applauded for five minutes. Among the most enthusiastic people in the audience were the occupants of Box W—Horace Dodge with Anna, Delphine, and Horace, Jr., and John and Matilda.

Even Horace's hunting expeditions with friends were secondary to the symphony concerts. During one hunting expedition to his lodge in northern Michigan that fall, Horace fretted at missing the orchestra's performance of a favorite concerto. Impulsively, he chartered a special train back to Detroit, arriving at Orchestra Hall a half-hour before the program was to begin. He sat at the back of the auditorium this time, instead of in his box—a brawny, russet-haired man in hunting boots and breeches, completely immersed in the music; then returned to his train and his friends up north.

Although as many as a dozen changes had been made in the Dodge car in 1919, including the production of the company's first four-door sedan with velvet upholstery, the factory's production was increasing so rapidly and smoothly that both Dodge brothers had more leisure time than ever before. But when John was in his administrative office, he watched carefully from the windowed wall of the office over factory procedures.

He was watching the day that a new, eighteen-year-old employee jumped into one of the cars sitting around the shop, turned the starter, and pressed the accelerator. The car leaped ahead and bumped into a barrier, where it continued to roar as the boy frantically searched for a way to shut off the machine.

"What the hell are you doing!" John shouted, cursing as he rushed out of his office. Too shaken to give any explanation but the truth, the boy admitted that he'd had an uncontrollable urge to learn how to drive a car. Nearby workers pretended to bend closely over their work as John's words thundered over the noise of their machines. "No wonder there's never any gas in the cars around here!" he fumed finally as he stomped away.

The boy, regretting that he'd succumbed to the razzings of the other workers about not being able to drive a car, returned to his machine with some dismay, worrying that John Dodge might order his discharge. But a short time later, the boy was amazed to see John Dodge walk down the aisle to his machine and to hear the factory-owner's words of apology for losing his temper.

Although John Dodge was not known to offer many apologies, older shop workers were not too surprised at his actions. They knew of their employer's empathy for young men eager to learn a trade. But John Dodge's own son, John Duval, still remained an outcast from the family—even though the father lavished generous gifts on others of the family members. When, just before Christmas of 1919, the Ford financial settlement was paid, John promptly gifted Matilda—now the mother of a third child, six-month-old Anna Margaret—with a check for a million dollars. And although Matilda had never dared protest John's generosity with his own relatives, including his sister Della, she did feel free to protest her husband's extravagance in his purchase of a $5,000 ring for Matilda's younger sister, Amelia.

Matilda had been relieved when Della and her companion had moved out of the Dodge home the previous March, at which time Della had taken the position of superintendent for the Michigan Industrial Home for Girls. John's oldest daughter, Winifred, and her husband and small daughter had also moved out of the Boston Boulevard home and into the elegant house that John had built for them in the prestigious Indian Village section of Detroit.

December was an eventful month for Anna Dodge too. She planned to present her daughter Delphine Ione to Detroit society with the completion of the girl's schooling at Springside School in Pennsylvania. Anna decided on a December party, transforming the ballroom of the Statler Hotel into a series of dazzling gardens. Her slender, dainty daughter was every inch a princess, Anna thought fondly, as she watched the delicately boned girl in the blue silk-brocaded gown whirl around the dance floor. Delphine danced with one partner after another until the morning hours when the young people had a breakfast of sausages and flapjacks before heading for home.

Both Horace and John were looking forward to attending the January automobile show in New York after the holidays had ended. With their court victory over Henry Ford still freshly savored, the brothers anticipated a triumphant arrival at the convention and into the society about which the two men cared the most—the automotive community. But each brother had a few matters to take care of before leaving for New York. Horace was financing a new building for his old Jefferson Avenue Presbyterian Church, and John donated a quarter-million dollars to Matilda's First Presbyterian Church and endorsed a $135,000 check for the Salvation Army.

Then, the entire Dodge clan and its friends gathered at the John Dodges' Boston Boulevard home on New Year's Eve to celebrate. But at midnight, even the presence of their families and close friends was an intrusion into the special closeness between the two brothers. They walked into the library, closed the door behind them, and—in complete privacy—toasted each other and the arrival of 1920, the year that John Dodge expected to move his family into the great stone mansion being built for him in Grosse Pointe.

As the brothers walked out of the library and rejoined the others, John said quietly, "This is the last time my brother and I will ever greet the New Year in this house." No one, including John, was aware of the ominous portent of his prophecy.

8

On Friday, January 2, John and Horace joined three of their friends—Milton Oakman, Oscar Marx, and Ed Fitzgerald—at the Michigan Central Station for their trip to New York City for the 1920 National Automobile Show. With a hissing of steam and a slow grinding of wheels, the train jerked away from the depot, and the Dodges and their friends settled back on the red plush seats, carefully pouring jiggers of smuggled Canadian whiskey from a flask. A faint haze of cigar smoke floated lazily around the broad face of Horace Dodge. John, who did not smoke because of his fear of respiratory troubles, brushed away the smoke with one beefy hand and looked out at the bleak January landscape framed fleetingly in the soot-streaked windows as the train roared its way toward New York.

It had not been easy to get away from their wives. Both Matilda and Anna had wanted to accompany their men to the convention. But John had said "no," and Matilda was accustomed to accepting his ultimatums. Horace, however, had never mastered the art of issuing ultimatums to Anna, his wife of twenty-six years. He was relieved when Anna finally decided not to go along so that he, like his brother, could throw off the restraining influences of womenfolk to join in the boisterous gatherings of friends and conventioneers.

The presence of their three friends on the train enlivened the lengthy Detroit-to-New-York trip for the brothers. With their arrival in New York on Saturday morning, the five men checked into the Ritz-Carlton Hotel. That afternoon, they went over to the automobile exhibition at Grand Central Palace.

Within an hour of the 2 P.M. exhibition opening, crowds of people thronged the great-domed Palace, clustering around the lustrous black Buicks and a half-dozen Chevrolets—some black, others olive green—in display spaces near the entrance. John and Horace walked past the Buicks and Chevrolets to Space A-20 and stood near their latest automobile model—Dodge Brothers' first enclosed four-door

94

sedan. Their full, almost square, faces beamed with pleasure at the comments the sturdy four-cylinder black sedan evoked from onlookers. They had not made a mistake, they agreed, in sticking with their dependable "Plain Jane" Dodge Four series after the war, the monogram *D B* stamped in aluminum on the hub caps, even though six-cylinder models now represented 55.8 percent of the industry.

From their main-floor display space, the brothers could see nearby the new lighter-weight Studebaker, less than 2,500 pounds, with a detachable aluminum motor head and fitted with cord tires as standard equipment. Beyond the Studebaker models, a Mitchell six-cylinder roadster, in an attractive light blue finish, boasted a slanting radiator and sloping rear end very different in design from the usual angular, high-hooded models. A powerful twelve-cylinder Packard, neighboring Dodge Brothers cars, also drew admiring observers. But the trend in 1920 automobiles was toward the practical car—lighter in weight with the use of aluminum, economical in fuel consumption with manifolding improvements allowing for more efficient heating of fuel mixtures, and simplicity of operating devices.

Horace and John felt that the Dodge car, as the essence of practicality, needed no gimmicks to build its sales volume. In the summer of 1919, their factory had produced 500 cars each day and still ran behind the volume of orders received from dealers. As pleased as the brothers were now with their sedan, their open touring car with its leatherette wrap-around top, and their sporty open roadster with slant-type windshield and pleated leather upholstery, they retained a subdued tone in National Automobile Show advertisements. They preferred to rely on name value for prestige. The entwined *D B* monogram represented two words that "are an advertisement in themselves," the ads stated, because of the brothers' "integrity in manufacturing and business methods."

The splashy gimmicks of some other manufacturers, however, attracted much attention from the general public and from the 3,000 car dealers attending the convention. In the lobby of the Commodore Hotel, the Marmon car manufacturers had stationed two mechanics to tear down a Marmon motor and completely rebuild it in one hour and forty-five minutes, in performances scheduled three times each day. Nearly half the eighty-four exhibitors, showing some 350 different models at the Palace, had a stripped-down chassis on display. All the cars displayed were gasoline models except for the Milburn electric and the Stanley steam car, which still was reasonably popular.

Later that afternoon, the Dodge brothers shouldered their way through the crowds surrounding the automobile-accessories exhibits—wire wheels, lamps, horns, lenses, baggage carriers—and went on to the motor-truck display over at the Artillery Armory in the Bronx. In the Armory, Dodge trucks were on view along with sixty-eight other manufacturers' commercial vehicles ranging from light half-ton delivery trucks to five- and seven-ton motor transports. The attention-grabber here was the Helomido, referred to by its Indiana Truck manufacturer as a "hotel-on-wheels" or a "house truck." Its long angular, bus-like body, mounted on an Indiana truck chassis, contained sleeping compartments, an ice box, and the rudimentary necessities of household living. Literature at the Helomido display told of a trip the president of the Indiana Truck Corporation had recently made in the Helomido from Marion, Indiana, to San Francisco and on to Los Angeles—3,279 miles over "desert sands and mountain passes." The only big truck ever to have made this trip without a convoy, the Helomido had compiled 235 hours of running time, with an average speed of fourteen miles an hour.

If there were to be a time in the near future for truck transportation to realize its potential and for "house-trucks" to become popular, the first step had to be improvement of the country's highway system. Dodge Brothers and *all* truck manufacturers were concerned about this. A conference scheduled for this first evening of the automobile exhibition was to deal with motor transportation, with regular afternoon sessions at the armory for discussions of the needs for improved roads.

John and Horace had a choice of sessions to attend each afternoon and evening—each session dealing with one or more of the many problems growing from a swiftly expanding automobile industry. The brothers had already spent some time wrestling with a major problem in the automotive field—that of car theft. Horace had produced a steering wheel the automobile owner could detach from its steering post and take with him on leaving the car. But with 5,000 cars stolen in the last six months in various parts of the country, the Dodges now joined a group of manufacturers looking for a more effective theft deterrent than anything yet on the market.

At speakers' predictions of two million cars to be produced in 1920, Horace and John leaned back in their chairs and exchanged expansive smiles. Nine million automobiles in use by the end of the year! Each brother knew the other was relishing the thoughts that their company had become the fourth largest manufacturer of automobiles in the nation and that they could look ahead to even greater production.

Americans generally were in an anticipatory mood after the war's end. The imaginations of laboring men were fired by Horatio Alger-type stories that included the saga of the swift rise to wealth of the grease-stained mechanics from Niles, Michigan—the Dodge brothers. For the first time, some of the luxuries of life seemed to be within the reach of the ordinary wager earner. Even the relentless January cold could not chill the exhilaration of a people looking forward to peace and prosperity—and new cars. The only shadow cast over New Yorkers' high-spirited mood was early January news from Chicago reporting the spread of influenza in Illinois. After more than a half-million Americans had died in the epidemic of 1918, the word *influenza* was a terrifying one.

The Dodges had arranged to host a luncheon on Thursday noon, January 8, at the Ritz-Carlton. But on the day before the luncheon, a doctor hurried to the brothers' adjoining hotel rooms and pronounced both men to be suffering from the "grippe."

Within a matter of hours, Horace was the sicker of the two. John, only mildly ill, attempted to go into Horace's room in spite of his chronic fear of respiratory ailments. The doctor barred his entry, however, and John had to be content with sitting in a chair just outside Horace's door where their friends always found him keeping his vigil during the next few days.

As conventioneers smuggled liquor into the hotel for their various gatherings, Horace, his influenza rapidly worsening into pneumonia, and John, who refused to leave his post at his brother's door, were unmindful of the ebb and flow of hotel life around them. All that was important now was the ebb and flow of each rasping breath drawn by the sick man and the heave of his great chest as he fought for air.

The best of New York medical specialists trekked up to the Dodges' Ritz-Carlton suite, and John also insisted on calling their personal physician from Detroit. Horace's wife, Anna, left for New York on Friday with John's wife, Matilda, accompanying her. On the same Friday night, with Anna out of town, Delphine Ione gave a "Leap Year" party in the Rose Terrace ballroom. With free access to her father's liquor cache, Delphine Ione was a lavish hostess to her young guests, and the party turned into a wild bash.

When the train bringing Anna and Matilda to New York arrived in that city on the Saturday morning of January 10, the women were greeted with the news that John too had finally surrendered to his own aching limbs and permitted himself to be ordered to bed. Horace passed the crisis of his illness on that same day, with Anna nearby, but John's condition worsened. Two days later, when his doctor said his illness was critical, John's two eldest daughters, Winifred and Isabel, left Detroit for New York, even though Winifred was expecting her second child in a few months.

Barrel-chested men such as the Dodges, it was said, were particularly susceptible to the ravages of influenza and pneumonia. But these were strong, tough men, Oakman and Marx and Fitzgerald reminded themselves as they waited helplessly at the hotel after the automobile show ended on January 10 . . . waiting for John to make it through the crisis.

Back at the Dodge plant in Detroit, workers who had always swapped tales of the legendary escapades and drinking bouts of their employers now picked up rumors that were circulating, connecting the brothers' illnesses with drinking poisonous bootleg whiskey at the convention. And in spite of official reports to the contrary and in spite of the good health of the brothers' friends who had shared the same bootleg supply of liquor in New York, the rumors persisted.

At the Ritz-Carlton suite of the brothers, several doctors hovered over John's bedside. Nurses bathed the feverish patient with tepid water and administered quinine. John, lapsing into unconsciousness, became unable to recognize his wife and daughters, his tuberculosis-damaged lungs filling with fluid.

The Thursday death announcement headlined: *John F. Dodge Dead in East.* Feature stories told of the rags-to-riches saga of the Dodge brothers, culminating in the death of the fifty-five-year-old John on January 14 in New York's Ritz-Carlton at 10:30 P.M.

The family could not keep the news from Horace in spite of fears about his reaction to the shock. Horace was aware, now, of what was going on around him. And he had been asking constantly about John, so he had to be told of John's death. Still too weak to leave his bed, Horace could only turn his head away and try to hide his tears. While Anna attempted to console her ailing and grieving husband, the casket bearing the body of John Dodge was placed aboard a baggage car draped in black cloth for the return trip to Detroit via the *Wolverine*. Accompanied by the family physician, a nurse, and the three men who had come to New York with the brothers, Matilda Dodge and her two stepdaughters were helped aboard the Commonwealth—a private railroad car that had been leased previously by the John Dodges for a very different purpose. The Commonwealth was to have taken the John Dodge family to Florida for the remainder of the winter season, but it was sent on to New York when the unexpected death occurred. Saturday, January 17, was to have been the departure day for Florida. Now it would be the day of John F. Dodge's funeral.

With the private car protecting the widow from the stares of the curious, the *Wolverine*, slowed by snowstorms and drifts, plowed its way through the blustery night toward Detroit. For the Dodge widow, her shock and grief compounded by the onset of the first stages of influenza, the train trip through the blizzard was a slow, agonizing death procession.

The ordeal aboard the train ended when the *Wolverine* steamed into the depot Friday afternoon, four hours overdue. While a hearse waited nearby, sixteen muscular shopmen from the Dodge factory lifted the coffin from the baggage car, walking between lines of plant workers standing with heads bared to the chill of the January day. The heavily veiled Matilda Dodge and her two stepdaughters were escorted to a limousine by the pastor of the First Presbyterian Church. As the hearse was driven off in the direction of the funeral parlor, the limousine moved off in the north-Woodward direction of the stately homes lining Boston Boulevard. At 33 East Boston, the Dodges' three youngsters—Frances, Daniel, and the baby Anna Margaret—awaited their mother's return.

As early as 7 A.M. on Saturday, a line of people began to form outside the Boston Boulevard home. The line grew longer while a steady procession of people moved into the large home and passed the coffin, covered with a glass because of people's fear of flu contamination. Wealthy and influential Detroiters mingled with a stream of factory workers who talked among themselves of their affection for the employer whose fair-mindedness and camaraderie had gained their respect in spite of his notoriously short-fused temper. John F. Dodge, they said, was a man who spoke to, not at, the shop worker on a man-to-man basis. Standing in line with the factory workers were many women, wives of former Dodge employees, who were receiving monthly checks from Dodge Brothers. The money came from the private $5-million fund the brothers had set up for faithful, needy employees—and this in an era when companies felt very little responsibility for the well-being of their workers.

The great front doors were closed to the line of people only once. The people waiting outside were told that the closing of the doors was to allow the furnace to heat the house. The real reason, however, was to protect the privacy of Matilda, who insisted on being taken from her bedroom down the stairway to the front-entrance hall to see her husband for the last time. Making a seat with their crossed hands, the family chauffeur and another employee carried the widow, ravaged by influenza and heavily sedated, down the stairs to the side of the coffin, then slowly returned her to her room. A maid tucked the blankets around her mistress as Matilda wearily lay back against the pillow—a small, limp, childlike figure enveloped in the massiveness of the bed.

At 1 P.M., the Presbyterian minister gave the eulogy for John Francis Dodge in the Boston Boulevard home, speaking of Dodge's honesty and his concern for the welfare of the factory workers.

> John Dodge had a marvelous virility in his big red-blooded body, and he had a will indomitable, which opposition stimulated instead of discouraged," the Reverend Vance told the mourners. "His great executive ability was natal like the big body it tenanted. These things do not come to a man by education. . . . Many of you knew John Dodge only as a great lusty man who with ripping oath could break into a crowd and get his way . . . but John Dodge had a wonderful, a beautiful love for his family and his home. He was red-blooded, but no woman could lure him from fidelity to the woman he made his wife, and all his plans grouped about his wife and his children.

John Dodge's sister Della moved uneasily in her chair as the minister spoke of her brother's undying fidelity. The minister did not know, of course, of John's secret marriage to Isabelle at the same time he was regularly dating Matilda. Few people *did* know—and those who knew had always protected John's privacy. Just the same, Della was relieved that Anna was still in New York with Horace so that Anna did not hear the minister's words. Anna was loyal, of course, which was fortunate for Matilda, since Matilda was even more fiercely protective of the secret John-Isabel marriage and divorce than John himself had been. Even supposing the secret were made public, the one to suffer the most humiliation would be Matilda, because of her fear of being known as a woman who consorted with a married man and became the wife of a divorced man—tantamount, in Matilda's puritanical mind, with being forced to wear a scarlet letter. Even at this sad moment, however, Della could not bring herself to regret any humiliation that might be visited on Matilda.

Tears filled Della's eyes as the pallbearers moved in to remove the body of her brother, who had been so generous to her all his life. The sixteen shopmen had been requested by John himself as active pall-bearers. And then there were the honorary pallbearers—107 prominent men, mayors and ex-governors, state and national representatives, including Henry Ford and James Couzens, now mayor of Detroit. Although the two sets of men were of two distinct worlds, both were the worlds of John Dodge.

Neighborhood children, standing behind the board fence at the back edge of the Dodge family's property, pressed their noses to the boards and stared through the cracks as the pallbearers placed the heavy casket, covered with a blanket of blue violets, into the hearse for the trip out Woodward Avenue to Woodlawn Cemetery. Among the mourners, three family members were conspicuously absent. Matilda was too ill to attend her husband's funeral service. Nor was the brother Horace strong enough to make the trip back to Detroit as yet. The casket would remain unsealed, it was decided, until he could return and view the body. And John Duval, the youngest child of John Dodge and his first wife, Ivy, had not yet arrived from El Paso, Texas, although he had wired that he was on his way north.

The services at the cemetery were brief on the bleak January afternoon. On the same day, the *New York Times* predicted the return of an influenza epidemic. In other large cities, influenza already had reached epidemic proportions. There were 379 cases of the flu reported in Detroit on January 22, and another 760 cases the following day. In New York, extra police aid was provided to help in the crisis, but police too became flu victims. City courts and offices closed, and there was a shortage of nurses. By the end of January, the ineffectiveness of ordinary emergency measures was compelling desperate city officials to resort to such futilities as fining citizens for spitting on the sidewalks. By February 10, however, the epidemic had begun to wane.

After slowly recovering from her own illness, Matilda had begun nursing little Anna Margaret when the baby became ill with influenza. When Anna Margaret too recovered, Matilda could no longer avoid the necessity of sorting out her life. Accompanied by her sister, Amelia, she went shopping for the black mourning accessories that any respectable widow wore for a two-year period after the death of a husband—black veils and gloves and handbags from the J. L. Hudson store to accompany the complete wardrobe of black dresses and coats that her personal dressmaker was preparing. At Hudson's, Matilda glanced at the smart new styles, even though she would never buy anything off a department-store rack. She stopped to admire the triple-flounced skirts worn with pointy-toed boots that laced up the front—and then resolutely made her way to the mourning department. Still only a youthful and slim thirty-six years of age, she was required by custom to eschew the frivolities normal to women of her age. She was, after all, a widow now, with three young children, and the responsibility weighed heavily on her mind. Horace would, of course, take care of the business at the factory, but she would have to take care of the business of her young family.

She began taking care of the responsibilities by making a journey, with Amelia, to John's office at the factory to remove his personal belongings. His large roll-top desk and his heavy tool chest were sent to be stored at Meadow Brook. But Matilda was perplexed when she could not find the statue that John had kept on top of his desk—the statue of a female cloaked in a cape with an opening that displayed buxom nudity. She had not approved the statue, and now she was particularly concerned that it be taken from John's office. She decided not to inquire about it, however, because she found the matter embarrassing. Besides, she confided to Amelia, it was likely that Horace had taken it.

Horace, who had returned to Detroit after the first week of February, had immediately made the pilgrimage out to Woodlawn Cemetery with fourteen friends. At 4 P.M. on February 10, the fifteen men went up the stone steps and into the vault, while Horace looked upon his brother for the last time. There was no religious ceremony of any kind. The men stood quietly while cemetery officials sealed the casket and placed it in its niche within the vault.

The winter of 1920 wore on relentlessly, its blustery cold unusual even for Michigan. Every afternoon as the icy tombstones and sepulchres of Woodlawn Cemetery were shrouded in the shadows of the swiftly approaching darkness, two private watchmen drove a car to the Dodge mausoleum and took up a lonely vigil there until daylight. Matilda had found that no watchman was willing to stay alone at the mausoleum to guard the body of John Francis Dodge resting beside his first wife, Ivy Hawkins Dodge.

Riches had made possible the building of the great white stone mausoleum, its two sphinxes overlooking the several steps leading up to the pillared entrance. But Matilda found that riches also made it necessary to have men hired to guard the dead inhabiting the cold, hollow edifice. She did not want to risk having herself and her family upset by the grave-robbing practices of the 1920s, when bodies of the wealthy were stolen from their coffins and held for ransom from the bereaved families.

Matilda Rausch Dodge, daughter of a saloonkeeper, had become very much aware of the power and privileges and prestige that money could command. She had discovered too how charitable people of wealth could afford to be. But now, as a wealthy widow with multimillions in her possession, she was to discover that money could also break the bonds of affection holding a family together . . . could breed suspicion, weakness, and heartbreak.

9

Anna and the family doctor decided that Florida sunshine would be good medicine for Horace, who, in the aftermath of influenza, remained in a very weakened condition. Hoping that the move away from Detroit might distract her husband from his sharp grief over the loss of his brother, Anna made arrangements to leave Michigan's wintry climate in February.

Nineteen-year-old Horace Elgin, Jr., came from New York's Manlius Institute to Palm Beach at Easter to be with his family. Since the health of Horace, Sr., was the focus of Anna's attention at this time, the chubby young Horace, temporarily free of his mother's relentless proddings to apply himself to his studies, applied himself instead to other and more entertaining pastimes. The young Dodge scion was unconcerned about failing his courses, trusting that he'd muddle through somehow. After all, his parents had made a generous donation to the school's building fund. Beach parties and boating occupied the young man's time, along with the pleasant pursuit of Palm Beach flappers in their daring, just-below-the-knee skirts and rolled stockings.

His sister, twenty-one-year-old Delphine Ione, had been swept up into the Palm Beach social swing before the Easter holiday. Daily, she joined the throng of bobbed-haired young women and girls on the sandy beaches, their one-piece bathing suits—little different from the men's suits except for the skirts modestly draping the mid-thigh-length trunks—exposing tanned arms and sheer-stockinged legs. At night, the same sun-and-surf bathers, red-lipped and cheeks brightly rouged, crowded the dance floors of posh boatclubs or private villas. Between swigs from hip-pocket flasks of bootlegged gin or Scotch, the couples danced the fox-trot and the tango—dances recently banned by the Archbishop of Paris because, he pronounced, they could not "be danced decorously."

Discouraged over her husband's periods of deep depression and his continued brooding over John's death in the midst of all the Florida sun and pleasures, Anna's spirits soared when Delphine Ione was able to penetrate the almost impregnable portals of the exclusive Everglades Club. At a costume ball held at the Everglades, the vivacious, lissome Delphine Ione, wearing a fluffy green ballet costume, attracted a number of eager partners from among the eminently eligible young men in the stag line. Repeatedly, Valentino-like James H. R. Cromwell—son of the undisputed leader of the Palm Beach social set—claimed the effervescent girl from the Midwest for his dancing partner.

Still, at the conclusion of the costume ball, there were certain amenities to be observed if James H. R. wanted to call on Delphine Ione at the Breakers Hotel suite of the Dodges. So tenuous were the Dodges' social connections in Palm Beach at this time that Cromwell had to search for a mutual friend to present him officially to Delphine Ione and her parents.

Immediately, Jimmy Cromwell became the girl's constant companion. The sight of the darkly handsome Cromwell towering over the slim, golden-tanned Delphine attracted the attention of even the most jaded Floridians. Here was youth, energy, good looks. And, of course, money . . . always the money.

Anna was wildly enthusiastic over the match. She knew from experience that money alone could not buy total acceptance of the nouveau riche by those in the social register. Now here was James H. R. Cromwell—son of mainliner Philadelphian Mrs. Edward Stotesbury and stepson of Edward T. Stotesbury, wealthy banking financier—in obvious pursuit of Delphine Ione and aspiring to charm Anna with his easy grace and Eastern accent.

In her desire to impress the Stotesburys, Anna was pleased with Horace's announcement to newspapermen at the beginning of April of his arrangements to build a mammoth and luxurious steam-powered yacht in which he and his wife planned a trip around the world. On its completion in a year's time, the new luxury vessel would be one of the largest privately owned yachts in the world. Anna had encouraged her husband to plan this new and elaborate boat, knowing there was no other kind of project that had as much chance of rousing him from depression. It was a project that would certainly impress even the lofty Stotesburys, she was sure.

Both Horace and Anna were delighted to find that Cromwell shared their children's obsession with boating and motorboat racing. Even though Anna herself was not an avid sailor, her ancestry was that of a seafaring family in Scotland. Horace's passion for boats was, of course, a lifelong one. The fact that Jimmy Cromwell's deceased father, Oliver Eaton Cromwell, had been a noted yachtsman seemed a good omen.

Horace's gift of $50,000 to Good Samaritan Hospital in Palm Beach also attracted favorable publicity to the Dodges in early April. Given in gratitude to the Palm Beach doctor who had been treating Horace, the money provided for an isolation building for patients with contagious diseases—a building to be named the Delphine Dodge Hospital, after the donor's daughter.

The next announcement that Horace was asked to make became a matter of contention in the family, with Anna and Delphine Ione combining forces to bend Horace to their will. Delphine Ione and Jimmy Cromwell were planning marriage. The engagement should be announced immediately, the mother and daughter insisted, because the wedding date was set for June 16.

Horace was aghast. June 16—barely six months after his brother's death. It was too soon for the celebration of a wedding within the immediate family. Delphine Ione and her young man had known each other for only a month—he did not want his daughter to rush into marriage.

Anna swept aside his objections. Did he not realize that Delphine's young man was not just *any* young man, but a man of culture and breeding . . . definitely the eligible young man of the year and just returned to the social scene after service in the navy? Did he not want the best for his daughter? Did he want Delphine to risk losing her opportunity to marry into a family with such outstanding social connections? Did he realize that Edward T. Stotesbury was a business affiliate of J. P. Morgan? And that Lucretia (also known as Eva) Stotesbury was the widow of well-known yachtsman Oliver Eaton Cromwell?

Horace tried to brush off Anna's arguments. Stotesbury, he pointed out, was a self-made man, like himself, who had started out as a grocery clerk, with nothing but his brains and aggressiveness as assets. And if he was in business now with J. P. Morgan—fine. But that was no reason to look on the Stotesburys as any better than the Dodges. And Oliver Eaton Cromwell? Just a playboy who had left a widow and children with very little money. Good thing the widow had managed to find herself a hard-working, moneyed widower like Stotesbury. There was absolutely no reason for Anna or any of the Dodges to think their little Delphine Ione was so fortunate in gaining the favor of any Cromwells or Stotesburys.

But Anna was relentless. Did he realize that Jimmy Cromwell had been scheduled to go on a world tour and that he had given it up because he had fallen in love with Delphine Ione . . . that even now he was planning to reschedule the world tour as a honeymoon for his bride and himself? Did Horace want to risk postponing the wedding and separating the young couple while Cromwell went off, alone, on his tour?

Horace, still too weak to carry his protest further, did no more to delay his daughter's wedding. In mid-April, the *Detroit Journal* ran the following item under a picture of piquant-faced Delphine, her chestnut hair worn in a short, fluffy bob:

> *Michigan Beauty Who Will Wed Former Resident of Washington*
>
> Mr. and Mrs. Horace Dodge announced the engagement of their only daughter, Miss Delphine Dodge, to Mr. James H. R. Cromwell of Philadelphia, son of Mrs. E. T. Stotesbury by her first marriage, and of the late Oliver Cromwell of Washington. Mr. Cromwell served in the navy in the war and will enter the firm of Drexel and Company, bankers, in Philadelphia after the honeymoon.

Anna's family had no reluctance to voice their reservations to Horace about the romance. The sisters, Catherine and May, who had been wintering in Florida near Lake Worth, had openly discussed their doubts as to whether Delphine would be accepted into the strata of society of which the Stotesburys were a part. Although Horace found no pleasure in Anna's social manipulations, he was supportive of his wife and daughter now that the Dodge-Stotesbury commitment had been made. "They may not accept us, but they *will* accept our children," he insisted.

Although Anna was too caught up in her own affairs to visit her sisters at Lake Worth that season, Horace found the Lake Worth cottage and the company of his in-laws much to his liking. Since Horace had provided Anna's family, the Thomsons, with their home in Florida, he had asked the Thomsons to store the Dodge liquor cache at their cottage, the hotel accommodations being too public and inadequate for storage of a bootlegged supply sufficient for their needs. Although Mother Thomson had died the previous year, Anna's two sisters had continued to winter in Florida at the cottage where Horace was a regular visitor, coming to play cards with his sisters-in-law.

Anna's oldest sister, Catherine, had brought her small grandson, Robert, with her from Detroit that winter to recuperate from a seige of pneumonia. Horace, who had a fishing outfit for the child, spent hours fishing with him. The big, gentle Horace, his thinning red hair now subdued with gray, enjoyed the chatter of the seven-year-old boy, and the man and boy often walked over to the ferry dock and sat together in the passengers' waiting area. There, through the long afternoons, the two sat on the benches under the roofed enclosure with latticed sides that fractured the sunshine into small geometric patterns that glowed on the ground. Then, in the shadows of the late afternoon, Horace and the boy walked back to the Thomson cottage for their evening meal.

Because the "season" at Palm Beach was expiring by the time the Dodge-Cromwell engagement took place, Horace was gratified that, at least, there were no plans for a formal engagement party. Anna, nervously aflutter at meeting the Stotesburys for the first time, was relieved to find them pleasant-mannered, friendly people—Mr. Stotesbury a lively, white-haired man who was a little shorter than his plump, bosomy wife. There was no opportunity for Anna to benefit socially just yet from this liaison because the Stotesburys, like other Palm Beach residents, were closing up their Spanish palace—El Mirasol—to return to Philadelphia, where they were building a new 145-room mansion.

Returning from Palm Beach to Detroit, Anna was totally preoccupied with plans for the June wedding. It had to be an elaborate one, she determined—a wedding befitting her princess-daughter Delphine Ione and Delphine's prince-charming, James H. R. She wanted the nuptials to be the most lavish and glittering affair ever witnessed in Detroit.

With the wedding less than two months away, the guest list was a prime concern to Anna, since it was only in recent years that the Dodges had been included in Detroit's *Blue Book* listing of prominent families. She knew that this meant conferring with Sara Burnham, the frosty mentor of Detroit society and arbiter of the *Blue Book*, who could make or break social status with a flourish of her pen. Nervously, Anna approached the redoubtable Miss Burnham. Her words tumbling one over the other in her eagerness, Anna assured the other woman that the wedding would be as fine as money could make it, that the Stotesbury family and its guests from the East would be attending, that the Detroit Symphony Orchestra would provide music for the reception, and that the Dodges were prepared to pay handsomely for Miss Burnham's services. Anna was relieved when Miss Burnham nodded. Yes, she would begin to assemble lists of prospective wedding guests for the Dodges.

In early May, Anna and Horace boarded a train to New York, where they visited Cartiers for the purchase of two pearl necklaces.

For Anna, a five-strand pearl necklace—reportedly costing $1.5 million—that had belonged to Catherine II, former empress of Russia. For Delphine Ione, a $100,000 necklace. According to legend, the Russian empress' pearls had brought misfortune to each owner of the gems. But the practical Anna ignored the legend and preferred to think instead of the comfortable feeling she would enjoy with the strands of perfectly matched royal pearls around her neck, when, at the wedding, she would stand in the receiving line next to that regal east coast society leader and Palm Beach queen, Mrs. E. T. Stotesbury. Anna ran her hands over the smooth pearls and smiled. "Pearls are a lady's gem," she declared. "Always correct."

The plans for the June wedding swept Anna along in a delightful kind of excitement while she tried to ignore her husband's frequent periods of moodiness when his blue eyes took on a saddened, hazy look. As if on command, Detroit's *Blue Book* aristocracy, mesmerized by recent accounts of the Dodge fortune and by the glitter of the Stotesbury connections, returned their acceptances to Anna's invitations. The widowed Matilda, however, looked at her invitation and resisted the desire to tear it into bits. Did Anna and Delphine have any real feeling for John, she wondered, when they could within six months overlook his passing and plan wedding festivities? And how could they expect her—John's widow—to join in the wedding celebration!

Matilda's sister, Amelia Rausch, was probably the only person in Detroit to decline Anna's wedding invitation. And to make sure her motives of loyalty to John were correctly interpreted, she omitted sending the couple a wedding gift. But Matilda finally decided to put in an appearance at the wedding to avoid an open breach in the family.

Thursday, June 16, dawned clear and bright. As guests arrived at the Jefferson Avenue Presbyterian Church, they walked under a canopy supported by standards showered with peonies and through a corridor banked solidly with the blooms. Inside the church, walls and windows were screened with pink and white flowers and trailing ferns. Mrs. Stotesbury, resplendent in an apricot gown and a wide hat trimmed with aigrettes, carried an apricot taffeta parasol. Then Anna, wearing mauve taffeta draped with lace and a matching hat boasting a lavender ostrich plume, swept down the aisle.

On cue, a thinner and paler Horace Dodge walked down the white carpet with his only daughter, her eyes large and luminous beneath a Normandy cap of lace, her slim figure graceful in its designer gown of satin and Belgian lace with a rose-pointe lace surplice cascading over the train. A police lieutenant, hired to guard the bride's sapphire bracelet—a gift from the groom—and her pearl necklace, tried to be inconspicuous as movie cameras whirred while Horace Dodge kissed his daughter and then joined Anna in the armchairs that replaced the removed front pews of the church.

Quietly, the vows were spoken, the newly married couple embraced, and the organ pealed out the triumphant wedding recessional as the smiling couple came back down the aisle. Then, police guards trailed the motorcade of shiny automobiles that roared down Jefferson Avenue toward Rose Terrace.

Although hundreds of the *Blue Book* guests had never met Anna and Horace, they attended in numbers from 2,000 to 3,300, depending on which newspaper Detroiters preferred to believe. The mother of the bride headed the Rose Terrace reception line, her Empress Catherine pearls moving gently across the mauve taffeta bosom as Anna reached out for the hand of Michigan's Governor Sleeper. Murmuring gracious responses near Anna was Lucretia Stotesbury. In her determination not to be overshadowed by any display of splendor by newly rich midwesterners, Lucretia wore her own valuable pearl necklace, plus a diamond collar (supposed to have been Marie Antoinette's) encircling her neck, and diamond and pearl earrings from Queen Isabella's jewel collection.

While an organist played Rose Terrace's great pipe organ, guests wandered through the mansion and up to the third floor where wedding gifts were displayed—an autographed photograph of General Pershing, a complete silver dinner service from the Stotesburys, a huge chest of flat silver and a silver table service from the Dodges. Horace and Anna had also promised to give the newlyweds a townhouse of their choice, complete with furnishings, in Philadelphia.

Many of the wedding guests strolled out of the mansion to the brick-walled rose terrace where they began dancing to the music of a 100-piece band on a pavilion just below the terrace near the water's edge. Others chose to go to the adjoining lawn, where the Detroit Symphony Orchestra was performing a series of special numbers in deference to Horace Dodge, its benefactor. And as police, hired for the occasion, guarded the expensive gifts and jewelry, liquor bootlegged across the river from Canada was served lavishly. In the midst of the celebrating guests and the dancers, Matilda Dodge, dressed in black, moved about—a somber figure.

As the rays of the setting sun tinged the sky a rosy pink, the crowd moved toward the pier at the foot of the estate where the Dodge yacht—the former *Nokomis II*, renamed the *Delphine* after its return at the war's end—was anchored. There was a flurry of excitement as the bride tossed her bouquet from the yacht's deck and the bridesmaids scrambled for it. Then, as a cornetist serenaded the couple with the strains of "Farewell, My Own True Love," the white and gold *Delphine*, pennants flying in the evening breeze, steamed away from the pier to the booming of a seventeen-gun salute.

The newlyweds' plans were to take the *Delphine* to the east coast, where they would later board an ocean liner for their trip around the world. Anna too was now looking forward to a lengthy, relaxing cruise when the new yacht, the *Delphine II*, would be completed the following spring. The cruise, she hoped, would help her husband regain the robust health he had enjoyed until pneumonia and the shock of his brother's death had drained him of both physical and mental vitality. If ever Anna had been jealous of the close affection between the two brothers, she had more reason for jealousy now that John was dead and Horace had sunk into a melancholy that was lifted only occasionally. Often, now, Anna had to remind her husband to change his shirt or to put on a tie, although he owned an extensive wardrobe and had, up until very recently, dressed immaculately—unlike John who had ordered new clothes only because Horace had ordered something new.

Occasionally Horace went into the plant. But here, among the 18,000 Dodge employees and the machines he loved, the void left by John was even more gaping. Although he was president and treasurer of the company, Horace left most of the business affairs to his trusted assistants who had been groomed personally by the Dodge brothers. And soon after the young Cromwells left on their honeymoon, Horace made a brief trip to Chicago with friends to attend the National Republican Convention, but retreated to his bed after his return home.

It was only later in the summer, as Horace seemed to brighten again, that Anna could begin to plan for another winter in Palm Beach. Now that she had impressed the Stotesburys and their friends with the wedding, she wanted to make an impression on Delphine's eastern in-laws with the purchase of an elegant Palm Beach home for the following winter. It was no longer fashionable to stay in the great wooden hotels that had been built to house the wealthy who vacationed there during the early 1900s. According to the *New York Times:* "Mostly curious people from the midwest come to the hotels and imagine it is 'the thing' to live at the largest hotel. . . . Though they could get into the hotels, they could no more penetrate the social circle in Palm Beach than on Park Avenue or Rittenhouse Square."

Nor was it Anna's idea of elegance to live in one of the larger cottages near the ocean—not while the Stotesburys were living in El Mirasol, their palatial Spanish-type mansion with wide ocean frontage and with neighbors such as the Astors and Vanderbilts. Most of these stone and stucco villas, lining the ocean front for almost eight miles, had been built or remodeled by the popular architect Addison Mizner, who had restructured and enlarged the Stotesbury place with a Spanish motif and made it the largest of the villas. Although the seventy-year-old Edward T. Stotesbury made regular appearances at the Beach Club and the Everglades Club, his aristocratic wife was rarely seen at either club. Instead, she entertained sumptuously at El Mirasol, which had become a mecca for Palm Beach socialites. An invitation to the sprawling El Mirasol was the magic key for acceptance by the "400" set. And now that Anna was anticipating such invitations during the coming winter season, she wanted a comparable villa in which she could offer hospitality, in turn, with equal grace and lavishness.

Once again, Anna was heartened by her husband's progress when, throughout the late summer and early fall, Horace began going into the plant again. Occasionally too he visited the shipyards where the *Delphine II* was under construction. When Anna learned that one of the large Spanish villas along the Palm Beach ocean front was for sale, she pressed Horace to buy it. The home—Villa Marina—was the property of Charles E. Dillingham, New York theatrical magnate who had frequently entertained large parties of friends in the rambling stucco structure. Convinced that the villa would be perfect for the expanding social life she contemplated in Palm Beach, Anna persuaded Horace to make the purchase.

In November, both Anna and Horace were pleased when their son, Horace, Jr., became engaged to Lois Knowlson of Detroit. Although the girl's parents, the Albert Knowlsons, certainly couldn't be compared socially with the Stotesburys, they were respected and prominent Detroiters, and Anna was grateful that young Horace, whose whims were unpredictable, had chosen a sweet and attractive girl of good family.

Horace, Sr., attended the couple's engagement party at the Statler Hotel in November but became very ill again shortly afterwards—so ill this time that Anna cabled Delphine Ione the news of her father's condition. The Cromwells, now in Japan, canceled the rest of their trip and made arrangements to return home. Conferring with her doctor, who agreed that the Florida climate would be beneficial to her husband, Anna renewed plans to travel south to their new villa.

Because Horace was too ill to attend the symphony orchestra concerts, Conductor Gabrilowitsch brought his musicians to Rose Terrace to play a concert just for Horace, previous to his departure for Palm Beach. And in spite of his weakness, Horace called his attorney to his home on November 27, 1920, the day before leaving for Palm Beach, to draw up a brief will. He signed the will, then paid a visit to the tomb of his brother. The next day, he and Anna and their doctor boarded a private coach for the train trip to Palm Beach.

When Horace gained some strength after his arrival at Marina Villa, the doctor who had accompanied the Dodges returned to Detroit, giving his patient permission to take short walks and to drive his automobile. But on Thursday, December 7, Horace unexpectedly began hemorrhaging. New York specialists, hastily summoned by Anna, boarded a Florida-bound train, but the fifty-two-year-old Horace died on Sunday evening with his wife and son at his side. The death certificate cited the hemorrhaging as a secondary cause of death from atrophic hepatic cirrhosis. The Dodge brothers, inseparable in life, had joined one another in death within a year.

A distraught Anna and young Horace left Florida by special train—a train bearing the coffin and body of Horace Elgin Dodge. Horace's friend Oscar Marx, his attorney, and his vice president at the plant, Fred Haynes, left Detroit to meet the train at Atlanta, to accompany the body back home.

When the funeral train—engine, baggage car, diner, and Dodge private car—arrived in Detroit, several hundred people were waiting there, lining the track. As the funeral cars stopped on an elevated siding at the left of the station, Lucretia Stotesbury quickly went over to the private car to be with Anna Dodge. But the distraught Anna seemed hardly aware of Lucretia's presence.

Relatives, friends, and acquaintances watched as Anna was carried from the Michigan Central Depot trainsheds to her waiting automobile. Then pallbearers—veteran employees from the Dodge factory—lifted the flower-covered casket from the baggage car and placed it in a hearse. Motor police led the hearse to Blake Chapel on Peterboro Street. The body, Anna had decided, would remain at the chapel overnight so that Dodge employees would be able to pay their last respects to their employer at the chapel without making the long trip out to Rose Terrace.

An honor guard of workmen kept watch over the body that night as some 23,000 employees and business associates of Dodge Brothers filed through the chapel "to look upon the face of their dead chief," one newspaper reported.

The next morning, the heavy bronze coffin was removed from the chapel and taken out to Rose Terrace, where it was placed on a bier in the music room and surrounded by roses. Della Eschbach, arriving from her home in California where she had been living since shortly after John's death, was a comfort to Anna in their shared grief. Because the house was filled with family and friends, the strain between Della and Matilda, who arrived later with Amelia, was not apparent to others. But Matilda felt uncomfortable, and Amelia was glad to be asked to do something for Anna—to stretch out a pair of new black kid gloves so that Anna could wear them to the funeral—so she could forget about the tension between her sister and Della.

To both Della and Amelia, Horace's funeral was like an eerie replay of John's recent funeral . . . so many of the same faces . . . the presence of the same dignitaries . . . and, soon, the same trip out to the same stone mausoleum. Anna, of course, had been in New York at the time of John's funeral, and Matilda had been up in her bedroom, too ill to attend, so they were not so much aware of this macabre sense of taking part in a well-rehearsed drama.

On Wednesday afternoon, the day of the funeral, the huge Dodge plant slowed to a halt. The machines stopped whirring and employees emptied the building for the solemn hours of the services at Rose Terrace. In the great home on Jefferson Avenue, an organist, brought from New York City, played Horace's favorite hymns on the huge pipe organ until the pastor of the Jefferson Avenue Presbyterian Church arrived to begin the eulogy for Horace Elgin Dodge . . . a man with a passion for music . . . a mechanic with the soul of a poet.

When the Reverend Forrer had finished his eulogy, Detroit Symphony Orchestra members played a dirge. Then the pallbearers lifted the bronze casket and carried it slowly out the massive doors. As the funeral procession came down the long curved driveway, a police escort led the line of cars down Jefferson Avenue, turning north and driving past the silent factory—Dodge Brothers, and on to Woodlawn Cemetery. At the cemetery, there was another brief ceremony in the cold December air before the coffin was placed behind the heavy door of the Dodge vault and Horace was, once more, beside his brother John.

The date was December 15, 1920. The Cromwells were still aboard an ocean liner, moving across the waters toward the United States, and were not expected to land until January 3. Anna Dodge had only young Horace on whom to lean. She, like John's widow, was now in control of a great fortune ... the immigrant Scotch music teacher was now a multimillionairess.

Part II
MATILDA

10

After the sudden death of John Dodge in January 1920, there was little respite from local newspaper publicity for his youthful widow, Matilda. Immediately following the filing of the will, the estrangement between John Dodge and his son, John Duval, was publicized once more. *Dodge's Will Cuts Off Son*, newspaper headlines announced. Young John Duval was to receive only $150 a month for life from the multi-million-dollar estate.

Reporters, questioning the family lawyer, were told emphatically that Dodge's attitude toward his eldest son had been unchanged at the time of the father's death. He *had* intended altering his will to include his youngest child, baby Anna Margaret, but death had cut short those plans. In reinforcement of his intentions toward his son, John Duval, however, he had included the statement, within the will, that no one should accuse the wife or children of John Dodge of having influenced him in reference to the provisions he had made for John Duval.

By terms of the will, some of the relatives who had been subsisting largely or partly on John's and Horace's financial support, could now enjoy independence. His sister, Della Eschbach, was granted a $5,000 legacy plus $6,000 a year for the rest of her life. Della had left many of her possessions at the John Dodge home after she had moved to Adrian, Michigan, in March 1919 to superintend the Michigan Industrial Home for Girls in that city. As Matilda went about the organizing of her life after John's death, she was not pleased to have many of her sister-in-law's belongings still occupying the third-floor rooms into which Della had brought her companion to live after the death of Uriah Eshbach. Deciding to write to Della at the Adrian home for girls, Matilda politely but firmly reminded her to remove her belongings from Boston Boulevard. The proud Della immediately complied, and the breach between the two was now an open one.

At the Adrian home where Della had ensconced her companion-friend, Helen Bovee, as her personal secretary, the idealistic Della found herself depressed and fragmented as she was exposed to the pitiful life stories of the 450 "wayward" girl occupants of the home. Indelibly influenced by memories of her own deprived childhood and her own yearnings for the beautiful and aesthetic, Della set out to restructure the entire school program—inaugurating French classes and fine-arts courses, ordering repairs for buildings and the purchase of new materials, abolishing the severe punishments of solitary confinements, bread-and-water diets, hair clippings, and spankings. By July 1920, under censure by the home's board of guardians for her large expenditures and impractical management, Della left Michigan for California, accompanied by her companion.

To his mother-in-law, Margaret Rausch, and his sister-in-law, Amelia, John Dodge had left bequests of $5,000 each plus $1,000 yearly to Mrs. Rausch and $2,500 yearly to her daughter. When Matilda learned of this, she considered it generous enough that she decided to promptly discontinue paying her mother and sister the monthly salary that John Dodge had paid them ever since they had moved into the Meadow Brook farmhouse.

Amelia was unhappy at having the salary discontinued. Reliable help for the farm was hard to get and retain, and Margaret Rausch was working harder than she should have been working in her late years. There was the milking, churning of butter, feeding of chickens and pigs, and the gathering of eggs that had to be done, whether help was available or not. There was the preparing for the weekend company from Detroit—baking a ham, popping popcorn, and stocking a supply of gingerale at the clubhouse.

Amelia never had been a housewifely person. And even more distasteful to her than the work was the isolation of farm life. When she voiced her discontent to her mother, Margaret Rausch nervously reminded her daughter that they had a comfortable place to live and the use of the Dodge car that John had given Amelia. She could drive into Rochester and even into Detroit to visit her friends. But to Amelia, life on the farm could not compare with living in town. Soon, she determined, when the will was settled, she would be able to make her own decision about where she would live.

The two aunts, sisters of Maria Dodge, who had loaned their nephew John their small savings to bury his first wife in the days when he was starting out in business, were remembered with annuities, as was the half brother, Charles.

There was no question of the ownership of the Boston Boulevard home, the Rochester farm, and the mansion under construction in Grosse Pointe. Since these were held jointly by John and Matilda, they became the widow's property. But the income from the bulk of the estate—most of it in Dodge company stock—was to be divided among Matilda, Winifred, Isabel, Frances, and Daniel . . . and now, Anna Margaret, as provided for by state law.

The strong-willed John had imposed an uneasy peace on his household while he lived. With his death, repressed animosities surfaced, beginning with Della's departure from Detroit. In the autumn of 1920, John's second-eldest daughter, Isabel, told Matilda of her intention to marry George Sloane. Although Matilda had no objections to the girl's choice of a prospective husband, she definitely had objections to any public plans for a marriage or even an engagement while the family was still in mourning. Regardless of Matilda's opposition, Isabel accepted a ring from Sloane; to maintain appearances of family harmony, Matilda made the engagement announcement on Thanksgiving Day of 1920. Although Sloane, a Princeton graduate and a successful New York broker, was an eminently acceptable son-in-law, with the added recommendation of being a son of Mrs. Stanley Cozzens and a member of an old, conservative New York family, Matilda was unhappy. Isabel had known George Sloane for only a few months, and the proper two-year period of official mourning for her father was not yet completed.

Still, Isabel went ahead with her plans for a wedding the following February. The society weekly, *Detroit Saturday Night*, reported, "Miss Dodge and her sister, Winifred, have been inseparable from their childhood and it is a pretty sentiment which prompted Mrs. Gray to give the wedding for her sister."

However nicely the society weekly had phrased it, Matilda, still wearing dark clothing and a long mourning veil attached to her hat, would not have Isabel married from the Dodge family home. However, she did consent to give the bride away; dressed in an embroidered black chiffon gown, she solemnly performed this duty at the late-afternoon wedding in the living room of the Grays' home.

As Isabel left on a three-month European honeymoon, her brother, John Duval, began his trek from one lawyer to another, looking for a way to break his father's will and to acquire his share of the fortune he considered his birthright., At the same time, Winifred and Isabel sought legally to block completion of the huge Grosse Pointe mansion begun by John; $2.5 million already had been invested in the half-finished mansion. It was conceivable to Matilda's stepdaughters that the widow could spend millions more in completing the building and in collecting art treasures to furnish it, since the will had specified payment of all Matilda's expenses in completing and furnishing the home in addition to Matilda's share of the estate.

The widow retreated at the girls' opposition. Without her aggressive husband beside her to bull his way into Grosse Pointe, she was unsure of her reception in the tight society of the town, knowing that each new resident's social acceptance was "passed" or "blackballed" by certain Grosse Pointers of top priority. Matilda temporized, ordering work on the estate discontinued while she considered her position.

She did order the greenhouse completed, though. There was no reason, she thought, why she could not sell flowers to her prospective neighbors in Grosse Pointe to help defray some of the expenses of the huge estate. While Anna's passion was fashionable society, Matilda envisioned herself in the role of the astute businesswoman, managing her multi-million-dollar fortune with aplomb.

Although she had had money for any comfort, accessory, or luxury she desired in the years she had been married to John Dodge, all the power had been held firmly by her husband. Now, the power had been passed on to her like a shining torch. Never again would she be known as little "Tilly" Rausch, awkward, introverted daughter of a scrawny saloon-keeper and a big-boned hefty mother who also worked in the saloon. These childhood days were far behind her now. She would speak of them to no one, she determined, as if they had never existed.

Her father, George Rausch, had come to Detroit from Germany at age twenty-three in 1871. He had worked there as a coachman, then had gone to Walkerton, Ontario, where he and his brother, Christian, had set up a cigar factory. In 1881, George married Margaret Glinz, daughter of neighboring German immigrants. Two years later, on October 19, 1883, when George was thirty-five and Margaret twenty-five, their first child, Matilda, was born. The following year the Rausch brothers gave up their cigar business and moved back to Detroit.

Deciding that saloon and hotel businesses should do well in Detroit, George opened the Princess Saloon and Margaret the Drydock Hotel in 1884. But shortly after moving with their small daughter to the apartment over their Atwater Street saloon, the

Rausches called the doctor to the bedside of the year-old Matilda. Diphtheria—just as the parents had feared. As the baby's air passages blocked and the feverish Matilda struggled to breathe, an emergency tracheotomy was performed by Dr. Jennings, after whom Jennings Memorial Hospital was named. Then the parents began a day-and-night vigil with the child, clearing the breathing tube periodically with a feather.

Slowly, under the solicitous eyes of her mother and father, Matilda recovered from the illness while the Rausches tried to keep up with the work in the saloon and hotel. Margaret was relieved that her small daughter had, apparently, fully recovered from the diphtheria only to worry again when Matilda began having "spells." The mother watched in horror as the little girl stopped breathing, fell to the floor, and turned blue. But Margaret's distress changed to irritation when it became obvious that the spells were self-induced temper spasms. Mother Rausch's cure was a no-nonsense hand applied forcefully to the child's buttocks. While the breath-holding episodes were cured, the electric temper was not, and the family soon came to recognize it as a permanent part of Matilda's makeup.

By 1886, Margaret was pregnant with her second child. Matilda was only three and still required a great deal of attention while the hotel's relentless demands continued. The wood-burning cookstove heated the kitchen unbearably in the summer, and when Margaret tried to lighten her work by eliminating the soup course from her twenty-five-cent meal, customer complaints forced her to return it to the menu. Finally, the work became too much. Margaret gave up her hotel business to help her husband in the saloon.

On March 22, 1887, the Rausches' second daughter was born in the bedroom over the riverfront saloon that was to be the family's home for three more years. For the first two of these years, the little girl was known only as "Baby Rausch," when the parents failed to decide on a name. They finally agreed on Amelia, a name they thought had the same aristocratic aura as did the name Matilda. Rarely were the names used, though, much to Matilda's distress, since she detested her nickname of "Tilly" although her younger sister did not seem to mind being known as "Melie."

With the purchase of a new saloon on St. Aubin Street, the family moved into a more comfortable apartment above the new place of business. Here there were three bedrooms and "inside" facilities that were an improvement over most of the accommodations offered in Detroit housing. The family enjoyed the luxury of running water, a flush toilet, and a zinc tub with a wooden frame. There was no furnace, so wood and coal had to be carried up the stairs to feed the stove.

Within a year, the business became so prosperous that George and Margaret planned a trip to Germany to visit George's parents. Leasing their business for a year, the couple took their two daughters to live in Walkerton, Ontario, with Margaret's parents. Matilda attended school briefly while she was there, then went back to Duffield School in Detroit when the family returned to its business.

The child's very first school, though, had been a German seminary where the classes were taught in German. Although the parents wanted their girls to be Americanized, they also wanted each to acquire some knowledge of her German heritage first. So, after giving Matilda brief contact with her German culture, they moved her into the public school. When Amelia was old enough to begin school, she too was enrolled in the German seminary.

At Duffield School, each sister had to repeat the early grades already completed in the German school in order to relearn everything in English. This put the Rausch girls in classes with children younger than themselves.

At home, George and Margaret insisted that English be spoken, except to the grandparents. They felt their customers and friends became uneasy and suspicious when German was spoken in their presence. So the German learned at the seminary was soon forgotten, and communication with the maternal grandparents deteriorated into a kind of English-German pidgin exchange.

Because their parents put in so many hours in the saloon, each sister had several jobs to do at home. Amelia's job was the endless chore of keeping the stove supplied with wood or coal in winter. Saturdays she cleaned the back stairs and bathroom and tried to skip off with her friends before the relentless Matilda pressed her into further service. Matilda, being older, helped with the cooking during the week and cleaned the apartment on Saturday. She had no patience with Amelia's flighty way of trying to avoid housework. To Matilda, there was great satisfaction in bringing order out of disorder, in having floors freshly washed, curtains newly laundered, and furniture polished to a shining finish.

In school, however, there were no such pleasures for Matilda. When she or Amelia wore a new dress to school, it was not unusual for them to hear a classmate whispering about saloonkeepers' daughters wearing new clothing bought with money that had come from fathers of families in need of food. The emotional Amelia showed her hurt at these taunts, but Matilda obstinately held her head higher, even though the taunts made her feel sick inside. After school, while Amelia walked home happily with friends, Matilda would often walk through the alleys to avoid possible rebuffs from classmates and, especially, to avoid any teasing from boys.

Matilda's girlish dreams were of a life very different from the one she lived in the St. Aubin apartment over the saloon. An immigrant cousin of the Rausch girls, who worked for the J. L. Hudson family, entertained Matilda and Amelia with stories of the life of the affluent and with details of the fine dinners served in the homes of the wealthy.

Meals at the Rausch house were served with no ceremony. The only time the family could sit down to eat together was on Sunday. All week, George Rausch worked downstairs during the supper hour, while Margaret and the girls ate. Then George came upstairs for his meal, while Margaret went down to tend bar. The girls, though, were never permitted to help in the saloon. The parents wanted better lives for their daughters.

Matilda had achieved this better life for herself with marriage to John Dodge. Now that he was gone, her future, and that of her children, was hers to mold. The past was permanently behind her, she determined. While Horace lived, even though he was ill and rarely went into the Dodge plant in his last year of life, Matilda had not often gone into the factory. But with Horace's sudden death, she took a new interest in the business.

The half-million production mark had been reached for Dodge cars in July 1920 as a glistening new roadster was driven off the assembly line just sixty-seven months after the assembling of the first Dodge car—an achievement that set a new high for the automotive industry. But after Horace's death, the factory had remained locked and idle, and the company was reorganized during a period of economic recession. On March 17, 1921, nearly 4,000 men went back to work under the direction of the new president, Frederick J. Haynes, named personally by Horace only days before his death.

Haynes planned to add more workers to the payroll, he now informed Matilda, until the plant was back to normal production with some 20,000 workers. Periodically, Matilda appeared at the factory to keep Haynes and the other supervisors mindful of her interest in company operations. Anna came much less often, and then only to keep observers mindful that Mrs. Horace Elgin Dodge was, after all, the first, only, and long-time wife of one of the Dodge brothers.

Long before the end of 1921, both the John and Horace Dodge heirs were benefitting financially from the upswing into full production at the plant. By mid-July, Haynes was directing the production of 600 cars a day.

In that same month of July, John Duval started suit to break his father's will. The family hoped to avoid an open breach and to settle the matter without publicity. But according to Michigan state law, the intentions of a deceased citizen, as stated in his will, could not be circumvented by any agreement among the heirs—the purpose of the law being to rule out possibilities of collusion or intimidation. The Dodge family put its lawyers to work at getting the state's inheritance law changed. After the lawyers conferred with legislators, action was fast in the legislature. Before the end of 1921, a new Michigan law, legalizing out-of-court settlements of inheritance disputes, was approved and became known as the "Dodge Law."

The passage of the "Dodge Law" enabled the family to settle its dispute over the fortune, subject to the approval of the Probate Court. With John Duval's two older sisters backing a substantial settlement for him, John Duval was awarded $1.6 million on condition that he would not seek any greater share of the estate. Matilda then elected to take control of her share of the monies rather than leave her millions in the John Dodge trust fund and to live on the resulting interest. And if John Duval was to get this kind of settlement from the principal, Matilda and the two stepdaughters reasoned that there was no reason why each of the other children should not have a million dollars out of the principal. The million dollars for each of the three minor children would be held for each child until his or her twenty-first birthday, when the child would receive the million dollars plus accrued interest. At twenty-five years of age, that child would receive his accrued income from the remaining principle of the estate still held in trust. The trust—which approached $40 million—would remain intact until the death of the last of the Dodge children, at which time it would be divided evenly and distributed to the Dodge children's heirs.

Shortly after becoming a millionaire with settlement of the will dispute, twenty-two-year-old John Duval, who had been working sporadically in the Dodge plant since his father's death, left the workaday world behind and took his young wife on a tour of Europe.

To John Duval's wife, a trip to Europe, with first-class accommodations on ship and in hotels, was the beginning of a thrilling new way of life. To her husband, who had been accustomed to private schools, automobiles, and plenty of money until he had been estranged from his father, there was a new kind of thrill in having money at his disposal with no one to try to dominate him with warnings of what he should or should not do. To Matilda, the money settlement was well worth its cost if it would bring some stability into her stepson's life.

Ever since Winifred and Isabel had contested Matilda's plans to complete the Grosse Pointe mansion, Matilda had disliked Winifred's husband, William J. Gray. It was Gray, she felt, who had prompted her stepdaughters to protest the withdrawal of funds from the estate to complete the mansion. Still, when she heard rumors of trouble between Winifred and her husband, she hoped the marriage would not fall apart. A divorce within the family was unthinkable. The Grays and the Wesson Seyburns—leaders of the young-married set in their exclusive Indian Village neighborhood—had made a handsome quartet at various functions of socialites. Now there was talk of an impending marriage between the classic-featured, bobbed-haired Winifred Gray and the suave and handsome Wesson Seyburn. The rumors intensified as Winifred—charging Gray with cruelty—filed suit for divorce and as it became known that Seyburn was no longer living with his wife and child.

When Gray did not contest his wife's divorce suit, Winifred was given custody of their two small daughters. Immediately after the decree was granted in March 1922, Winifred and her Aunt Anna boarded a ship for a Mediterranean trip. But long before Winifred returned from her cruise, the sensation created by her divorce from Gray had paled in comparison with the notoriety brought to the family by John Duval.

Returning from their European trip, John Duval and his wife settled into a Grosse Pointe apartment where they enjoyed a high style of living that John's money settlement had made possible. Like his father before him, John Duval gloried in getting behind the wheel of a shiny new automobile and accelerating the machine down the road. Arrested by Detroit police in March for speeding thirty-two miles an hour on Jefferson Avenue, John had not yet come into the courtroom to face the speeding charge when he got into much more serious trouble.

Cruising around the Kalamazoo area on a Saturday night at the wheel of a high-powered, four-passenger sports car, John Duval and a companion offered three Kalamazoo College girls a ride home when the girls came out of a dance hall. The three girls got into the back of the car, and John Duval zipped past their boarding house and out to the paved highway, where he opened up the throttle and sped along the darkened road. Huddled together in the tonneau of the open touring car, the girls pushed away the flask of whiskey offered them from the front seat. Then, as John Duval braked the car for a railroad crossing, one of the girls in the back pushed open the door and jumped from the sports car as it bobbed over the tracks.

The screams of the two girls still sitting in the tonneau were lost in the roar of the motor and the rushing wind. Six miles out of town, the driver turned off into a side road. Seeing that the two girls were hysterical with fear, John Duval, suddenly apprehensive, turned the car around and drove carefully back toward town while the others searched the side of the road with a flashlight, but found no trace of the girl who had leaped out the door.

With the arrest of the two men as they returned the girls to their boarding house, the story was headlined in the next day's newspapers. The injured girl was now in a Kalamazoo hospital where she had been taken by a passing motorist, who had sighted her lying on the roadside. John Duval and his friend were locked up in the Kalamazoo jail.

Mother of Girl Will Sue Him, headlines expounded. "From what I hear, Mr. Dodge has been up to such things before and it is time someone stopped him," the mother of the girl stated.

Neither the mother's threat nor his weekend in jail had any humbling effect on John Duval; he rejected the food at the jail as "too coarse" and reminded his jailers that he was a deputy sheriff. Released on bond on Monday afternoon, he was met by his blue-eyed, dark-haired wife, attractive in gold-fringed Russian boots and a short-skirted black velvet dress draped with a fur coat. All these details were dutifully published in the papers, and Matilda read them with rising indignation, wondering where and when the notoriety would end. Her husband, she had thought at one time, had been hard on his young son in cutting him out of the will. Now she could see that her husband had been right to disown the boy who brought so much scandal on his name.

But the rush of stories and pictures had only begun, Matilda discovered, as John Duval was sentenced to five days in the Detroit House of Correction along with twenty-two other Detroit speedsters. The picture accompanying this story was of a tearful Mrs. Dodge who sat on the bottom step of the iron stairway leading up to the cells, her sable coat dragging on the dirty floor, her necklace glimmering in the pale light of an overhead bulb. "They can't do this thing," she was quoted as saying. "He hasn't done anything. He is just unlucky."

Out of impoundage the next day, and out of gray prison garb, to be taken to the county courthouse for a petition by his lawyers to the state supreme court for his release and a new hearing, John Duval again posed for newspaper pictures as he sat in the sheriff's office, smoking a cigarette and propping his feet up on a table. "I ought to run for president after all that publicity," he joked to newspapermen. But when the new petition was denied, John Duval was returned to the house of correction, to prison clothing, and to a shovel and the coal pile. At his release at the conclusion of the five days, the only trace of John Duval left at the prison was a sterling silver corkscrew.

The very next day, however, he had to face the first of two charges confronting him in Kalamazoo—that of driving while intoxicated. The girl who had jumped from his car, now ready for hospital release with no permanent injuries except a cut over one eye that had required a number of stitches, did not appear on the witness stand. Newspapers had already run a story quoting the girl as having said she expected a settlement from Dodge. But the prosecuting attorney, who told the jury that "gin was driving the car that night," drew admissions from the other two girls that Dodge had made "improper advances" when he finally stopped the car. The judge sustained the defense's objection to this. Clearly, the trial was concerned only with drunk driving.

Newspapers also spelled out the dramatic fifty-minute plea made by John Duval's lawyer. "On that night, several people saw him who said he was not drunk," he pointed out. "They are not people who would say he was drunk simply because he has a naturally bloodshot eye," his argument continued. "The three girls didn't think he was drunk—they got in the car." In concluding, the lawyer asked for the same consideration for Dodge "that a poor boy would receive," arguing that the only offense of which Dodge was guilty was speeding.

When the jury brought in its "not guilty" verdict, John Duval was bound over to circuit court for a later hearing on the charge of possessing, transporting, and distributing liquor. This second case was tried in April, and the circumstances surrounding the case attracted as much attention as the trial itself. With one woman selected to serve on the jury with eleven men, prominent citizens of Kalamazoo protested the jury selection as a blot on the honor of their city. "Just think of the long night vigil the twelve may have to make—eleven men and one woman locked up in one room," Kalamazoo's first woman city commissioner declared. A spokesman for the Kalamazoo County War Mothers charged the jury selection as "unfortunate . . . it seems to me like unnecessarily inviting talk of an unpleasant nature," she told reporters.

The woman minister of the Kalamazoo People's Church was more positive. The only good that could come of such a move, she stated, would be to pave the way to better accommodations for jurors in the future. "It is like the thorny path of the suffrage pioneers," she said.

"If it were not for them, voting might still be conducted in the rear rooms of barber shops."

Matilda herself, an ardent proponent of women's rights, could not have agreed more fully with the minister. But she wished that this test case, with its attendant publicity, had not coincided with her stepson's trial.

The girl who had jumped from the car was in court for this second trial, to testify that both defendants, Dodge and his companion, had offered liquor to the girls. Found guilty this time, John Duval was lectured briefly by the sentencing judge: "those interested in you claim you have been handicapped first by the death of your mother at an early age, second by the death of your father before you were twenty-one, and third by being thrown into undesirable company . . . but you are both now over twenty-one, and society expects you to conduct yourselves as men."

Always sensitive to criticism, Matilda was indignant at what she felt was the judge's criticism of her role as stepmother. She had tried to be a good stepmother to all three of John's children by his first wife, and especially to the youngest, John Duval. Now she felt as though they were in collusion against her.

The judge placed both men on a year's probation, ordering them to abstain from intoxicating liquors and to report monthly to a probation officer, with a special probationary provision that John Duval should find a job in Detroit. His two sisters were, as always, supportive of their younger brother. Isabel—a close friend of the young Mrs. Edsel Ford, who had been one of Isabel's attendants at her wedding—managed to wring a concession from Henry Ford to agree to serve as young Dodge's custodian and to give the young man a job in his factory.

Isabel was equally supportive of her sister Winifred, offering her Long Island country home for Winifred's September marriage to Wesson Seyburn. Matilda did not have to make the decision of whether or not to attend the wedding because she left Detroit in August 1922 for a European trip with her three children. Accompanying them on the *Aquitania* were two maids, a nurse for the children, and a French governess. By the time of Winifred's marriage, Matilda and her party had traveled through parts of France, Germany, and Switzerland and were heading for Nice where Matilda had taken a year's lease on a fashionable villa.

Leaving with the bitter taste of notoriety brought on the family name, Matilda was in Europe by the time September newspapers carried much more favorable publicity. This was a series of accounts of the presentation by Dodge Brothers, Inc., of eleven park sites, comprising 627 acres, to be given to the State of Michigan as a memorial to the company's founders. The chairman of Dodge Brothers' board of directors explained the gift and its purpose:

> As the motor car has enlarged the range of pleasure travel for the public, it has also put the public in the position of having almost no place to go where it is really welcome. Auto picnic parties have invaded farms, fields, and private orchards only to be driven out by indignant owners. They have camped on highways along the lakes of Oakland County in such numbers that Oakland County has been compelled to pass an ordinance in its own defense to prohibit such camping. . . .
>
> Both Dodge Brothers were lovers of the great outdoors. . . . The board of directors feels that it can establish no finer memorial for these two men than to provide a system of parks which will give health and happiness for all time to thousands of workmen from Detroit and vicinity in whom Dodge Brothers were so intensely interested, and to whose welfare they always devoted so much of their time and resources.

A half-century later, these same parklands would still be offering sanctuary to the people of the Wayne and Oakland County areas.

11

Settled into her *Villa Lesfalaises* in Nice, Matilda sent for her mother and her sister Amelia to join her in December at the villa. For the children's sakes, she wanted to have the Christmas holiday season a time of family gathering. Before the Rausches' return to Meadow Brook in April, Matilda took her sister with her on a tour of Italy. They were with a tour group in the Vatican when the unexpected occurred—the sight of Anna Dodge and Della Eschbach approaching with a guide.

"Don't let them see us—duck!" Matilda ordered Amelia. Quickly the two women concealed themselves behind a pillar, and Anna and Della passed and moved out of view.

Matilda stayed on, with her children and servants, in the villa until the late autumn of 1923, when she returned to Detroit and moved out of the Boston Boulevard home with all its memories. The purchase of the home into which she moved had been arranged before she had left for Europe—a home on Lincoln Road in Grosse Pointe. In this comfortable house, she anticipated putting down new roots. Here her family could grow up in the kind of environment that would be the most advantageous for them.

Although this Lincoln Road residence was not far from the partly finished mansion that John Dodge had been building on Grosse Pointe's lakeshore at the time of his death, Matilda still had made no decision about the unfinished structure. Buttercups and weeds flourished on the grounds where formal gardens were to have been tended. Rainwater and leaves lay in the bottom of the fountain-pool. Inside the 100-room mansion, pieces of scaffolding collected dust under the vaulted ceilings. Only the greenhouses, with 8,000 square feet of floor space and costing one-quarter-million dollars to build, were in operation now, providing fresh flowers and tropical blooms for Matilda's tables and for her church's altars.

As the winter wore on in the house on Lincoln Road, the two youngest children became ill—Anna Margaret with a severe case of measles, Daniel with a milder case. For a time, the children and their nurse were quarantined in their rooms. But when the children's Aunt Amelia and Grandmother Rausch came in from the farm to visit on a Sunday in March, the nurse brought the youngsters outside for the first time. The four-year-old Anna Margaret looked as if she had not yet recovered from her illness. Her blue eyes—a Dodge heritage—looked all the bluer in her very pale face framed with blonde hair. The little girl was cross. Even in good health, this youngest daughter of Matilda's had a robust temper that seemed to be a combined heritage from both her father and mother. The brown-eyed, dark-haired Daniel was the favorite of his Aunt Amelia and his grandmother. "The only one who looks like a Rausch," they often remarked.

On Friday, April 11, one of the Meadow Brook employees made his regular trip to Grosse Pointe to bring cottage cheese, eggs, and butter to the Lincoln Road house. When he returned to the farm, he brought bad news. Little Anna Margaret had been taken to Harper Hospital on Tuesday. Amelia and her mother exchanged surprised glances. Why, they wondered, hadn't Matilda let them know? Why had she left it to a servant to give them the news?

Inquiries to the Dodge home were responded to, guardedly, by servants. Matilda was constantly at the hospital, near her baby's bed as the child suffered and weakened. A doctor tried to prepare Matilda for the worst. Inflammation, likely resulting from the measles, he told her, had spread through the child's body. An emergency operation might save her life.

The operation was performed, but the child could not be saved. The inflammation had gone into the intestines and body tissues. Anna Margaret died the following Sunday—Palm Sunday 1924. At this tragedy in Matilda's life, Anna Dodge and her son Horace rallied to her side as the quiet funeral took place and as the coffin was taken out to the Dodge mausoleum to be placed near that of the little girl's father.

Although prepared to continue offering sympathetic support and companionship to her sister-in-law, Anna withdrew at Matilda's resistance to her small attempts to be helpful. Externally, Matilda appeared to be totally self-sufficient and controlled.

The hiding of personal hurt and grief had always been a part of Matilda's makeup. The deeper the hurt, the more difficult it was for her to discuss it. Her relatives considered there was no further need for solicitude as the bereaved mother forced herself to move back into the normal routine of her busy life after the child's death. With the blonde Frances holding tightly to her hand, Matilda appeared again at her church and Salvation Army Auxiliary meetings, accepting the presidency of the auxiliary and the leadership of its 600 members in their work with orphans.

There were other commitments to keep her occupied too. She was vice-president of the Detroit Historic Memorials Society, a trustee of Alma College, and was prominent in the League of Women Voters, apart from her forays into the business affairs of Dodge Brothers. And in October 1924, another important appointment came her way. With women-suffrage legislation in force nationally since August 1920 and women's groups demanding representation, officials of the Fidelity Trust Company in Detroit had announced it would appoint an outstanding woman to its board. Its choice was Matilda Dodge.

Matilda's business and charitable affairs filled the days . . . the weeks . . . the months, covering the emptiness after the death of her youngest child. Each day's routine gradually became less mechanical, though, when the brittle shell of her defense began to crumble as one of Detroit's most eligible bachelors singled out Matilda Dodge for his attentions. The man was Alfred G. Wilson—a tall and distinguished-appearing man in his early forties and of considerable prominence in the First Presbyterian Church where Matilda too was very active. The son of a retired Presbyterian minister, Wilson was both a deacon of the church and a bass singer in the choir.

At church affairs, the John Dodge widow and the bachelor Wilson were seen arriving, then leaving, together. At the Dodge home, Alfred Wilson became a frequent visitor, although the couple was rarely seen in public places other than the church. Still, the couple's quiet and circumspect alliance began to attract some notice. Rumors circulated among Detroit socialites.

There were rumors also that the two Dodge widows had decided to sell the Dodge automobile corporation. In 1924, the corporation had boosted its sales by 35.6 percent, shipping out 225,104 motor cars and reaching a sales peak of $216,841,380. This was a record year for Dodge, although the automobile industry as a whole showed a production decrease.

Anna had realized, by this time, that her son Horace did not aspire to any position of management in his father's business. Matilda, visualizing success in her own right, unshadowed by the overpowering image of her late husband, felt the sale of the business would release her capital for projects of her own choosing.

At the end of March 1925, a deal was arranged that was the biggest single cash transaction that had ever taken place in United States private business circles until that time. Dillon, Read and Company, New York investment bankers, made a bid of $146 million for the Dodge Brothers Company. Fifty million dollars of this purchase price was solely for goodwill—a tribute to the Dodge Brothers and their business skills. This goodwill value had not been estimated at the time of the evaluating of the Dodges' estate when the brothers had died. And the value of the stock, held by the families, also had appreciated considerably.

Eight days after the sale was announced, the new Dodge Company securities were offered for sale to the public. The new owner of the company made a profit of $28 million on the sale of Dodge stock as the public bought up all the available securities. The *New York Post* reported that "never before in the financial history of the country has so wide a response been given a public offering." Anna, herself, bought 60,000 shares.

Coinciding with the Dodge sale negotiations, the name of John Duval popped back into the news as he started probate court proceedings to establish his claim to one-fifth of the estate of his young half-sister, Anna Margaret. In connection with the suit, accounts of the brief life and tragic death of Anna Margaret were featured again in newspapers, bringing fresh reminders of grief to Matilda. The usually self-reliant woman found herself leaning on Alfred Wilson for support and solace. And when the ten-year-old Frances caught her hand in the washing-machine wringer, it was the sympathetic Wilson who consoled Matilda and tried to amuse the injured child as she recovered from the accident.

After the doctor recommended horseback riding to exercise the child's damaged muscles of the hand, Matilda began thinking seriously of a new mode of life . . . of moving out to the farm in Rochester . . . of marrying Alfred Wilson and providing a father for her young children. The most important reason, of course, was that she had fallen very much in love with Wilson.

On the afternoon of April 15, 1925, Matilda arranged for her chauffeured limousine to be sent out to Meadow Brook to pick up her mother so that Mrs. Rausch could take Frances and Daniel to the theatre. After the grandmother and the children had left for the theatre, the telephone rang at the farmhouse. "Is Mother there?" Matilda asked when Amelia came to the telephone. Assured that her mother had left the house, Matilda said hurriedly, "When she gets back, tell her to look at tonight's newspaper." That evening's paper

carried the report of Matilda Rausch Dodge's engagement to Alfred
G. Wilson.

Once the engagement was announced and Matilda wore publicly
the six-carat blue-white diamond ring Alfred gave her, she was caught
up in the swift tempo of pre-wedding details. "Mother, you won't love
me anymore," her young daughter Frances protested.

Matilda took time from her conferences with Sara Burnham on
wedding plans to reassure her daughter, promising she would take
both Frances and Daniel to Hot Springs, Virginia, the next month.
They would have a lovely vacation together—just the three of them,
she rhapsodized.

While Matilda vacationed with the children, Alfred Wilson quietly
slipped into the probate courtroom where John Duval was being
heard in his suit for division of Anna Margaret's estate among the
children of John Dodge. When his presence was noticed, Wilson left
as quietly as he entered—but not before he had heard John Duval's
attorneys say that their client was anxious to get a share of his half-
sister's estate to use for the production of a new automobile.

The outcome of the suit was still undetermined on June 29, 1925—
the date of the Dodge-Wilson nuptials. Sara Burnham came to the
Lincoln Road home to direct affairs, even though the wedding was a
small one to which family members had been invited by telephone.
The six-foot, broad-shouldered but slim-figured Wilson—thick dark
hair tinged with silver at the temples—towered over his five-foot-two-
inch slender bride who wore a cream chiffon, lace-paneled dress with
matching hat.

As the couple exchanged vows, Matilda's sister Amelia and the
groom's brother Donald were the only attendants. Matilda surely was
marrying for love this time, Amelia was certain as she observed the
soft and pensive look in her older sister's usually brilliant dark eyes
while she stood with Alfred in front of the officiating Presbyterian
minister, who was assisted by Alfred's father. The John Duvals were
not present, nor were Anna and her children, who had left for a cruise
on Lake Huron. But the stepdaughters, Winifred and Isabel, and their
husbands, witnessed the ceremony along with the blond-curled, blue-
eyed Frances and the handsome dark-eyed Daniel in his blue coat,
short white linen pants, and knee-socks.

The couple's wedding trip to England, via the *Aquitania*, was a first
visit to that country for Alfred, a self-made man who co-owned a
lumber company with his brother. For seasoned traveler Matilda, the
trip was to be not only a romantic honeymoon but also an opportunity
for study of the gracious Tudor homes of England. Matilda was plan-

ning a new home now—a Tudor mansion to grace the rolling acres at Meadow Brook . . . a home that someday would belong to young Daniel Dodge as he carried on the Dodge name and heritage.

Plans for the new Meadow Brook mansion were drawn up as soon as Matilda and Alfred returned from their honeymoon to the Lincoln Road house. A short distance away was the new home built on the lake shore by Matilda's oldest stepdaughter, Winifred, and her husband, Wesson Seyburn, now the parents of a two-year-old daughter, Edith. The Seyburn home was the scene of lavish entertaining when Winifred was there, although she spent much of the winter season in Palm Beach, the summer season in the East or in world travels. Like other wealthy young Grosse Pointe matrons, Winifred dallied with Junior League activities as a service to the underprivileged of her hometown, Detroit.

Matilda, who had never accepted the role of the dilettante, renewed her active promotion of educational and public-health reforms in her work with the National Council of Women. Chosen to be a speaker at the council's October 1925 convention, Matilda stressed her belief in the capabilities of women as reformers, activists, and upholders of moral standards.

Her stepson, John Duval, was no less earnest in his attempts to achieve the goal he had set for himself—succeeding as a manufacturer of a new automobile. Now in his late twenties, John Duval introduced the prototype of his Dodgeson to the public at the January 1926 automobile show in New York. He distributed brochures emblazoned with the brown-gold Dodgeson emblem, explaining the operating principles of his eight-cylinder rotary valve engine actuated by a vertical shaft from the main crankshaft. *Designed and engineered by John Duval Dodge, son of John F. Dodge*, the brochure boasted, even though John Duval had hired a very experienced engineer to plan the new engine.

Hoping to attract potential investors through automobile-show promotion, John Duval had everything else prepared for manufacturing his car. Parts suppliers were ready to start turning out the various Dodgeson components. But millions of dollars were required for actual production, so the future of the Dodgeson depended on acquiring financial backers and winning a share of the estate of Anna Margaret Dodge.

When his court petition was given a hearing in January 1926, the judge ruled that the child's mother should be the recipient of Anna Margaret's $7.5 million. John Duval immediately filed an appeal, joined by his sister Winifred. His sister Isabel Sloane also filed suit in federal court, asking that the five remaining children of John F. Dodge share equally in the child's estate.

Matilda retaliated by asking for dismissal of the suit. When the judge refused her request, she braced herself for the barrage of publicity that began with *Mrs. Wilson Balked in Huge Will Fight*.

John Duval's earlier settlement of $1.6 million had already been depleted. Salesmen and entrepreneurs who had pursued the new millionaire with investment schemes had been joined by bill collectors trying to exact payment for purchases of jewelry and other luxuries. Fines, gambling debts, and out-of-court suit settlements had taken their toll of his inheritance.

Although Isabel was involved in the will dispute, her marriage into the New York Sloane family had separated her from Detroit and from the local gossip over Dodge affairs. While there was speculation among the tightly knit members of eastern society that the Sloane-Dodge marriage was not as unruffled as it appeared to be, the young Sloanes continued to entertain frequently at their handsome estate, Brookmeade, on Long Island and at Palm Beach in the winter season. In August 1926, George and Isabel were the center of a gala crowd at the daily horse races in Saratoga, where the sights and sounds of horses' streaking around the track gripped Isabel with a glowing excitement that was to stimulate her for the rest of her life. Buying a yearling for $21,500 at the Saratoga sales, Isabel shipped it back to Brookmeade—the start of her stables there.

In May of that same year, Matilda had been surprised to learn that her sister-in-law, Anna Dodge, was also going to be married. Somehow, Anna had managed to keep her plans a complete secret until only days before the informal ceremony at the home of her son, Horace. Matilda and Alfred attended the ceremony as Anna became Mrs. Hugh Dillman in early May, but it was to be one of the last functions of the Horace Dodge relatives at which Matilda would appear. Because of the increasing notoriety given to what she termed "the other side" of the family, she determined to separate herself from Anna and her children.

Preoccupied with her own children, her new husband, and plans for the new home at Meadow Brook, Matilda was both surprised and annoyed when she learned that Amelia was having a home built in Rochester, the town neighboring the Meadow Brook estate. Since 1924, when the workload at the farm had become too great for Margaret Rausch, Matilda had hired a new housekeeper to take her mother's place at the main house, and Margaret and Amelia had moved into a smaller tenant house on the grounds. Soon after moving into the tenant house, Amelia had made her first thrust for independence. Margaret Rausch had nervously demurred when Amelia told her of her plans to build a house in Rochester. What would Matilda say? Margaret asked. But when the house was ready for occupancy, Margaret Rausch moved into town with her younger daughter in spite of Matilda's unconcealed irritation at the fact that it was the John Dodge annuities that had given her sister and mother independence.

But it was also the John Dodge money that made it possible for Matilda and Alfred to plan their new country home on the Meadow Brook acreage. With the Rausches no longer at the farm to supervise affairs, Matilda was sure the place could be operated more efficiently if she herself could oversee the management. And both children loved to be out at the farm where they could ride their horses and explore the farmlands and wooded areas.

Deciding to sell the Lincoln Road home, Matilda still was unable to determine what to do about the deteriorating stone shell of the Grosse Pointe mansion. Leaving its fate once more undecided, Matilda, Alfred, and the two children moved out to the rambling old farmhouse at Meadow Brook, where the sounds of tinkling cowbells and creaking windmills mingled with the clang of carpenters' hammers and the whine of their saws. Stonecutters and masons worked month after month, from 1926 until 1929, on the three-storied Meadow Brook Hall as the L-shaped English baronial mansion shadowed the raw earth with its 410-foot length of stone and oak.

Soon after the construction of the Tudor mansion was begun, Matilda spent $10,000 to build a playhouse for Frances. "Not only that Frances might have a place to play," Matilda explained, "but that she might learn from first-hand experience early in life the art of being a housekeeper."

The playhouse provided a lavish setting for a child's experimentation with homemaking. The five-room, English-style, miniature home was built with made-to-order window casements, door frames, and special brick—all cut to three-quarter size. Heated by its own furnace, the playhouse contained a small sink, refrigerator, electic stove, and cupboards in the kitchen; a tiled bath; and exquisite diminutive furnishings and a fireplace with tiny andirons in the living room.

Frances celebrated her twelfth birthday with a party for twelve friends in her playhouse. "Grandpa" Wilson, Alfred's father, wrote a poem for the occasion:

> In a beautiful cottage on the slope of a hill
> In miniature form she works with a will.
>
> Her curtains to hang, her rugs put in place
> And pictures on wall and mantel to grace.

The Wilson family's efforts to win the affections of a stubbornly resistant Frances and the more tractable and younger Daniel endeared her in-laws to Matilda. She gave her two children every material possession that might brighten their lives. For Daniel, she ordered a workshop built, equipped with a lathe, tools, and machines sized for a young boy's hands. From the casement windows of the small shop, Daniel could look up the grassy knoll toward the big farmhouse or down the lane to the wide expanse of acreage where the thick columns and walls of Meadow Brook Hall were beginning to rise.

From the time the family had moved into the old Dodge farmhouse, Frances' passion for horses became an obsession. She entered her first horse show, with her mother, in the summer of 1927. Matilda's jumper took a first in the Touch and Out event. Twelve-year-old Frances took third place in the Children's Horsemanship class, as she rode her own horse, Jewel.

The girlish figure of Frances Dodge, riding crop in hand, became a familiar sight to Rochester-area people as the girl rode Jewel along the country roads. Long blonde curls flying from beneath her wide-brimmed hat, Frances loved to ride, alone, across the rolling hills of Meadow Brook. On occasion, she allowed her little brother Daniel to follow on his horse.

Alfred Wilson, retiring from the lumber business, settled into the life of a country gentleman, overseeing the farm and building operations even though Matilda was the final authority. For Alfred, a proud man, it was not an easy thing to find his accomplishments obscured by the tremendous Dodge wealth and achievements. But when Matilda left, late in the summer of 1927, for a European trip with the children, Alfred determined to prove himself a successful manager of Meadow Brook farm. The Belgian draft horses, hackney ponies, and the Guernseys that Matilda kept for show purposes would remain his wife's responsibility. But the pigs, the Herefords, the sheep, and all the rest of the farming operations would be his responsibility, he insisted. Husband and wife were to keep their financial operations separate—this was the way Alfred wanted it and the way that he and Matilda finally decided their business affairs should be conducted.

Meadow Brook Hall still had not been completed when Matilda began planning another project—the building of a theatre in downtown Detroit. In the boom years of the late twenties, a legitimate theatre was destined for success, she was certain, observing that middle-class people, with money for luxuries, were emulating the wealthier set in search of first-class entertainment. Matilda purchased the theatre site, commissioned the building, and invested $3 million to establish herself as an independent businesswoman.

While the construction of the manor house and the theatre continued, life for Matilda in those early years of permanent residence at the farm was busy and happy. Deeply in love with her tall, handsome husband in spite of her compulsion to bend his will to her own, she was hopeful that Frances and Daniel would respond to Alfred's efforts to be friends with them even though they would not permit him to become a father to them. Although Daniel had been too young at the time of John Dodge's death to have many memories of his father, Frances could remember John's enjoyment of Meadow Brook.

Detroit's "400" set trickled back into the city in the autumn of 1927 and inaugurated the new social season by appearing at the symphony opening at Orchestra Hall, where boxholders met and exchanged gossip. Women wearing brocaded shoes and velvet dresses glittering with crystals and sequins, eyed other women draped in richly furred and heavily embroidered shoulder wraps. Bobbed heads were seen in the crowd, but most of the fashion-conscious women were letting their hair grow again, swirling it close to their heads where jeweled pins held it in place. Matilda Wilson's luxuriant dark hair was as carefully coiffed as usual as she sat next to her husband in the Wilson box, a kolinsky-trimmed crimson wrap draped over the shoulders of her black velvet gown. The Wilsons, it was rumored, would soon have their manor house completed. Its opening, the women whispered, would unveil a magnificence that was supposed to overshadow that of any mansion on this side of the Atlantic.

12

While the banking firm of Dillon, Read & Co. was in control of Dodge Brothers, the automobile company lost money for the first time, in 1927, as the new management brought out a six-cylinder car aimed at a higher-priced market. In 1928, the banking firm sold Dodge Brothers to Walter Chrysler, who increased the physical size of Chrysler Corporation five times by his purchase of Dodge in a stock-exchange merger for $170 million. Chrysler assumed the liability for $59 million in Dodge bonds and issued stock in his own company for the remainder of the money.

Dodge heirs, with substantial sums still invested in Dodge stocks, continued to live in luxury from the income on their investments. In the spring of 1928, three years of legal battles ended with a court decision that awarded the $7.5 million estate of Anna Margaret Dodge to her mother, Matilda. The decision smashed John Duval's hopes of acquiring enough money to market his own car and marked the dissolution of his Dodgeson Motor Company's Lafayette Building headquarters.

In that same spring of 1928, Margaret Rausch, who had been in failing health for the past few years, died at Amelia's Rochester home. Matilda was surprised and hurt that her mother's modest estate was willed entirely to Amelia, except for a few personal items willed to other relatives and a bequest of $1,000 to John Cline, farm manager at Meadow Brook. Matilda was aware that Cline had become very friendly with her mother and sister during the years the Rausches had lived at Meadow Brook. She knew too that Cline had continued to visit them after their move to Rochester, and she had felt it her duty to warn her mother and sister that they *did* have a family obligation not to embarrass her by socializing with farm employees or low-status working-class people. If Amelia thought now that her mother's bequest had put the Rausch seal of approval on the farm manager, Matilda determined to talk the matter over with her sister.

Both Matilda's stepdaughters had risen to the uppermost social strata—Isabel with her marriage into the prominent Sloane family; Winifred with her penetration of exclusive circles that were honored, on occasion, with the presence of such dignitaries as Edward, Prince of Wales, or the Infante Don Alphonse and the Infanta Dona Beatrix of Spain. Such family connections demanded complete loyalty on the part of Amelia Rausch to her older sister, Matilda reasoned.

Matilda's own code of loyalty to the Republican party occupied her that summer and autumn, as she worked for the advancement of women within the political scene. *Vox Republica* printed a photograph of Matilda, a fur around her shoulders and her dark wavy hair framing the edges of her cloche, as a delegate-at-large to the National Republican Convention—one of ten women among Michigan's sixty-six delegates.

At home on the Meadow Brooke estate, the Wilsons projected an image of fashionable country gentry. Regally erect in the saddle as she rode Lady Avon accompanied by Frances riding the girl's favorite white horse, Victor Gray, Matilda was as happy as her young daughter to win the parent-and-child-class cup at a Detroit horse show in September. Alfred and Daniel took second place in the same class.

In these early teen years of her life, Frances became so absorbed in training and riding horses that even her choice of boarding schools was determined by the convenience of keeping one of her horses with her. From the local private school, Cranbrook, Frances took Victor Gray with her to the Ward Belmont School in Nashville, Tennessee.

By this time Frances' half sister, Isabel Dodge Sloane, was making an impression on the national racing scene. Her string of flat racers and jumpers, from her Brookmeade Stable, had made its racing debut at Saratoga in 1927. By 1929, Isabel was investing a great deal of money in the purchase of yearlings. In that same year, she divorced her husband, George Sloane. Her married life, she confided to friends, had been marred right from the time of her honeymoon by Sloane's abusive temper. But Matilda was not one of Isabel's confidantes, and the divorce separated them still further.

The Wilsons' move out to Meadow Brook, however, had not separated Matilda from her many interests in Detroit. Each time the Salvation Army held a bazaar at Detroit's Leland Hotel, Matilda's chauffeur drove the Wilson automobile up to the hotel, where the car was unloaded of tablecloths and silver from Meadow Brook and flowers from the Wilson greenhouse. Matilda worked tirelessly with cash register and adding machine at these affairs. When suppers were served at her church, she would tie an apron around her waist and go to work in the kitchen.

Matilda discarded her apron for furs and velvet, though, when her new theatre opened in a blaze of lights on Detroit's Madison Avenue on December 10, 1928. Watching the crowds from her box seat as the first-nighters thronged inside to see Marilyn Miller star in *Rosalie*, Matilda felt the sellout of standing-room tickets augured a successful future for the Wilson Theater (later known as Detroit's Music Hall).

The opening of the newly completed Meadow Brook Hall on November 28, 1929, was an even more impressive occasion for the Wilsons. Invited guests, driving into the grounds, could see fourteen chimneys, each distinctive in design as it rose from the tiled roof, accentuating the roofline in Hampton Court style. Visitors entered, first, the massively proportioned Great Hall with its lofty oak-beamed ceiling, then moved on into the red velvet carpeted drawing room, a copy of the Bromley Room in London's Kensington Museum, with Sir Joshua Reynold's painting, *The Strawberry Girl*, hanging over the stone fireplace.

In the oaken library, the faces of poets, writers, and philosophers, carved into the paneling, looked over the visitors' heads. And near the Great Hall and the library, guests could see the pipe-organ console that boasted an echo organ on the third floor and an extra console for playing rolls.

The third floor was off-limits to the visitors. It was here that Matilda had stored the bedroom furniture taken from the John Dodge Boston Boulevard home to which she had been brought as a bride. Here too was John Dodge's desk . . . pictures . . . mementoes. But Alfred Wilson did not have to go up to the third floor to see reminders of his predecessor. A chair with carved dragon legs and arms—the chair on which Dodge customarily had tossed his coat and hat when he came home to Boston Boulevard—stood in a prominent place in the entrance hall. In the living room were two green overstuffed chairs in which John and Horace had relaxed when they came home for lunch from the factory. And the intricately carved, oriental teakwood table that commanded attention in the center of the living room had been a gift to John Dodge from the owner of Churchill's Bar.

How much was sentiment on Matilda's part and how much was her natural penchant for saving things, Alfred never could be sure. He reminded himself that Matilda saved every Christmas card she received—saved postcards, napkins, and doilies commemorating any occasion, banquet menus, letters, and trivia of all kinds. In her abhorrence of wastefulness, she had ordered the motto "Waste not, want not" imprinted in blue lettering on the floor-to-ceiling tiled walls of the hotel-type kitchen.

Matilda's aversion for waste did not limit her expenditures for the finest of furnishings, paintings, and decor for Meadow Brook Hall. Friends who were taken up to the second-floor bedroom suites viewed the lushness of gold-plated bathroom fixtures, sheets monogrammed in silver, and porcelain doorknobs with delicate roses painted on them in the English room, the Italian room, the Adams room, the French room . . . Then there was Matilda's Louis XIV room with its carved marble fireplace, elegant chaise lounge, and its canopied rounded bed standing on a carpeted dais, and Alfred's adjoining room with its special seven-foot bed and his shower room with large round gold knobs like those of a ship's engine room. A secret stairway, circular stone steps winding in Tower-of-London style, led from a door concealed in the wall-paneling of Alfred's first-floor study to the second-floor hall and on up to the third floor.

In planning the lavish 100-room Meadow Brook Hall, Matilda had not overlooked the children's needs and desires. When Frances learned her stepfather was to have a hidden stairway, she demanded a secret staircase of her own, so a similar one was installed for Frances to climb from her Early American bedroom suite to a third-floor private hobby room. In Daniel's wing of the house, a concealed pull-down ladder enabled him to climb from his bedroom up to his third-floor playroom, fitted with a basket for practicing basketball, a punching bag, and a camouflaged peephole from which he could spy into his bedroom.

The quiet Daniel rode horseback occasionally but was not fascinated by horses as was Frances. He liked to tinker with engines and mechanical gadgets in his workshop or to explore the fields for unusual rocks to add to his collection. When Matilda was occupied with guests or secretaries, Daniel kept out of sight in his workshop or up in his bedroom or playroom. But Matilda often thought that Daniel had a sixth sense that alerted him to those times when his mother was, occasionally, alone. At such time, he would quietly come into the breakfast room when his mother was there or into her upstairs sitting room or into the study that Matilda liked to call her "morning room." There was none of the brashness of John Dodge about this slender brown-eyed Dodge heir, Matilda realized, treasuring the infrequent quiet moments with her son at her side, sharing an occasional confidence with her.

For a time, shortly after the family moved into the Tudor mansion, Matilda had more opportunity for these reflective intervals with her son as she recovered from a miscarriage. When her strength did not return as quickly as she expected after the miscarriage, Matilda temporarily discontinued some of her excursions into Detroit and concentrated, instead, on the daily operation of her huge household and its staff.

Much of her management planning was done in her paneled "morning room," copied from a Kensington Museum design, where Tiffany leaded windows overlooked the south lawns of the house and the formal gardens. Dispensing with a housekeeper after an unsatisfactory trial period, Matilda found it more to her liking to have complete control of Meadow Brook. No detail was too insignificant to escape her notice as, sitting at her desk under a sparkling Waterford crystal chandelier, she supervised menu-planning, inventory, and replacement of linens, towels, and household supplies, and the recording of expenses for utilities.

Matilda's firm hand reigned not only over the manor house, but over the large farm, the gardens, the stables. Alfred Wilson's directives to the staff often were countermanded by his wife. Alfred usually tried to placate Matilda with "Now, Dearie," as she displayed a temper that she had never dared demonstrate when she had been married to the tempestuous John Dodge. Now, she was in the dominant position, and much as she loved Alfred, she enjoyed the power that the Dodge millions had given her.

Alfred's resultant frustrations were sometimes vented on Meadow Brook employees. John Cline, employed at the farm since 1910 and farm manager since George Rausch's death in 1914, was one of the employees summarily fired by Wilson, then reinstated by Matilda. Yet when Matilda *did* want to fire someone, she dispatched Alfred to give the orders.

Matilda and Alfred left Meadow Brook in March of 1930 for a five-week visit to Miami, then sailed for Europe, returning in early summer. That same autumn, John Duval went to Europe for an indefinite stay, much to Matilda's relief when she heard of it. Her stepson had been the cause of occasional spasms of notoriety—another arrest for drunk driving, with charges dismissed when the policeman admitted he had made the arrest because of Dodge's arrogance rather than his driving . . . news stories of John Duval being pursued by process servers and constables with summons for unpaid bills. When Matilda was told, in December, that John Duval had opened a real-estate office on the Riviera, she fervently hoped his business venture would be successful enough to keep him across the Atlantic.

Settled back at Meadow Brook after her own European trip, Matilda had no excuse for avoiding further discussion with Alfred about adopting children. Now in her mid-forties, she realized that trying to bear a child at her age was risky. Yet she understood Alfred's desire for children—for namesakes. And his arguments were reasonable enough—the care of the children should not be too demanding . . . a nurse and a governess could be hired as they'd been hired for Frances and Daniel . . . the adoption would be a philanthropic gesture. And the children would be Wilsons—not Dodges.

Reluctantly, Matilda agreed. She did love Alfred and recognized that namesakes and heirs were something he wanted very much. Shortly before the end of 1930, Matilda and Alfred went to a Chicago orphanage, the Cradle, and brought home to Meadow Brook an eighteen-month-old child . . . a little dark-eyed boy, Richard. In an era when it was not fashionable to adopt children who were less than perfect, the Wilsons chose to give the young child, suffering the effects of malnutrition, the opportunity for a healthy, privileged life. Then, so that the sixteen-year-old Frances would feel more personally involved, the Wilsons took the girl with them to Chicago on their second visit to help select another child—a blue-eyed baby girl named Barbara. Matilda installed the two children with a nurse in a second-floor nursery suite that had a fully equipped kitchen across the hall so that the nursery unit could be operated independently of the rest of the house.

With the adopted children well cared for in their own quarters, Matilda was free to turn her attention back to her other affairs. In April 1931, she was elected by popular vote to the State Board of Agriculture, which controlled Michigan State University. And although the nation's economy was so depressed that entertainment businesses, such as the Wilson Theater, were foundering, Matilda did not hesitate to accept a directorate of the Graham Automobile Company that year. The Grahams, whose alliance with Dodge Brothers extended back over the years, had expanded their truck manufacturing to include the production of automobiles.

Matilda's litany of achievements peaked when, on June 1, she was elected president of the board of directors of the Fidelity Bank and Trust Company—the first woman in the country to head the directors

of a major bank. Her days took on a patterned sequence as she rose at
6:30 A.M., then exercised by going out for a half-hour canter on her
favorite horse, Potiphur, before coming in to breakfast with the
children. She worked, after that, until 8:45 at personal business in her
morning room before having her chauffeur drive her to downtown
Detroit and to the Fidelity Bank building. The look of fragility about
Matilda's slender figure as she sat behind the board president's desk
was dispelled as her small hands wrote directives and her sharp brown
eyes quickly read through the papers stacked on her desk.

In her first days as board president, Matilda prepared herself for
the barrage of questions posed by reporters who visited the office of
the woman who was attracting national attention in financial circles.
"My heart is really in the business world," the papers quoted her.

> For the last two or three years, I have devoted myself to our home in
> Rochester and to the children. I planned the gardens, the farms, the
> barns, the landscaping—all the details involved in building a
> country home. The place is now running smoothly, and what was I
> to do with my time? I enjoy bridge, horseback riding, dancing—but
> I could not spend all my time at these pursuits! I have handled my
> own estate and those of my children, but I realize my job here is of a
> different kind. I am responsible now for the money of others. There
> is an obligation to our depositors and to our stockholders. I hate
> waste of all kinds. No one has any right to waste other people's
> money. It makes me furious to have people waste mine. I cannot, by
> unwise judgment, waste other people's. My friends have asked me
> frequently during the last two weeks why I have taken this post. I
> have only one answer: Because I enjoy it.

Weekdays, Matilda was fortunate if she was able to return to
Meadow Brook from downtown Detroit early enough to enjoy another
ride on Potiphur before dinner time. When time permitted, she rode
down through the marsh and the woods, noting whether there was a
fence in need of repair, coming back near the grain fields to see how
last fall's wheat planting was coming along.

But Matilda felt the jar of disruption of her orderly and satisfying
life as the summer of 1931 neared its end. Her sister suddenly announced her intention to get married. Matilda was amazed. How
could Amelia be planning marriage when she had not been keeping
company with any men ... no one, that is, except John Cline,
Meadow Brook's farm manager, who sometimes visited the Rausch
home in Rochester. Amelia nodded her head. Yes, John Cline was the
man she was going to marry.

Matilda's eyes sparked fury. What was Amelia thinking of? she
demanded. Didn't she realize that Cline was only a farm employee?
That he was a drinking man?

As Matilda raged, Amelia remained silent, not daring to voice her defenses. But the younger sister, who had always been so pliable except for the time she'd moved her mother and herself away from Meadow Brook, was now adamant in her determination to live her own life in her own way. Hadn't Matilda's fortune and status come from John Dodge—a working-class man and a hard drinker? And as far as her own moral code was concerned, Amelia reflected, she was not taking *her* man away from a former wife.

Amelia finally found the courage to point out to her sister that John Cline was not trying to intrude into the Wilsons' lives. He knew his "place" and his station in life, she insisted, just as she herself had known her place for the many years that she had lived on the fringes of her married sister's life.

But Matilda was equally adamant in her insistence that Amelia must not marry John Cline. During the years of Matilda's spiraling power, Amelia had become increasingly aware of her sister's strong aversion to anyone opposing her will. There was no doubt in Amelia's mind that by marrying John Cline she was alienating her sister. Amelia could only hope, at the time of her September marriage and the immediate firing of farm manager Cline from Meadow Brook, that her estrangement from her sister would be healed in time.

Just one month after the sisters were alienated, the Fidelity Bank and Trust Company closed its doors, and the bank was taken over by the state banking department. Although Fidelity had been organized as a trust company in 1923, it had received its banking charter only six months previous to the closing, with Matilda Wilson appointed president of its board of directors only four months before the closing.

The words Matilda had spoken so confidently at the time of her appointment—of her responsibilities and obligations to depositors and her abhorrence of wasting people's money—came back to haunt her now. The day after the public announcement of the bank's failure, Matilda struggled for composure as she told reporters that she would place her personal fortune back of Fidelity's saving accounts to guarantee payment in full of $6.5 million in savings accounts so that, although the stockholders would lose money, the savings account depositors would be reimbursed.

Her impulsive decision that she would reimburse depositors was weakened, though, with her dawning realization that she too had been victimized. First of all, her loss, as a major stockholder, was a heavy one. Clearly she had been duped, she realized in humiliation. How gullible she had been when, as Fidelity's assets were being depleted, she had been convinced by other directors to purchase bank stock as it was dumped on the market. She had kept buying stock in good faith until, after the bank's collapse, she discovered that other directors had been selling their stock for her to buy. It was humiliating too for her to realize that her selection as bank president four months earlier had been based on something besides the admiration of businessmen for her executive abilities. She wished now that she had not been so quick to say she would repay savings depositors. It was doubly humiliating to have to renege on that promise. But bankers from other institutions talked with her and persuaded her that this would be a poor banking precedent for her to set.

There were a few people in Rochester—old friends of the Rausches—who had invested their small savings in Fidelity because of Matilda Wilson's connection with the bank and because of their faith in her reputation as a financial wizard. When the bank suddenly closed, these people came to Amelia, asking her to intercede for them with her wealthy sister, protesting that they could not afford to lose their investments. But there was nothing Amelia could do for them. Matilda had cut her younger sister completely out of her life. Still, Amelia realized, from her own knowledge of her sister's pride and from the reports that reached her, that Matilda was suffering emotionally and physically from the blow to her prestige.

Matilda's daily trips into Detroit ceased. Once more, her life centered almost totally around the farm and the horses. When Frances returned home from school for holidays and summer vacation, Matilda encouraged her daughter to enter her horses in local and out-of-town events. On the June opening day of the Detroit Riding and Hunt Club's horse show, Frances took her place astride her saddle horse. To Frances, the applause from the spectators was exhilarating. So, too, was the feel of the lift from the saddle as her mount gracefully cleared the barriers. After that, she began to accumulate ribbons and trophies, with a number of wins in 1933. She drove her dapple-grey Shetlands in tandem and drove her powerful bay hackney team in various shows. Equally at ease on horseback or sitting in a four-wheeled buggy behind the glistening rumps of a pair of hackney ponies or Shetlands, Frances brought more and more wins to her hackney and saddle-horse stables at Meadow Brook.

Graduating from Washington's Mt. Vernon Seminary in June 1933, Frances left Meadow Brook to go on a tour of horse shows in Atlantic City, Syracuse, Toronto, Chicago, and other cities, where her horses took awards in the five-gaited, three-gaited, pony tandems, and other classes. By the end of the year, she was acclaimed in sports pages as the most active girl rider in the country.

While Frances was on tour with her horses, a grim-faced Matilda read newspaper reports of another divorce within the family. John

Duval, recently returned to Detroit, had been sued for divorce by the wife he had deserted. The divorce decree granted Mrs. Dodge a property settlement of $325,000 plus a trust fund of $108,000 for the couple's nine-year-old daughter. John Duval immediately remarried, bringing his wife from her home in Indiana up to Grosse Pointe, Michigan. His business on the Riviera had failed, and now he entered a new business partnership in Detroit—the manufacture of oil burners.

It was not a promising time for new businesses as the depression continued. Out in Rochester, Michigan, school teachers were being paid in scrip, and rumors were circulating that the school system's kindergartens might be discontinued. Young kindergarten teacher Marion Gray, hearing that Mrs. Alfred Wilson needed a governess for the two adopted children, applied for the job. No, she had never been a governess, Marion admitted to Matilda, but she thought her training and experience as a kindergarten teacher would qualify her for the job.

"But a governess," Matilda reminded her, "must know how to deal with servants."

"I'm sure I'll be able to manage that," Marion replied.

Matilda hesitated. "Then there's Miss Frances," she added reluctantly. "Miss Frances is . . well, she's going through that difficult stage."

It was finally agreed that Marion would move into Meadow Brook Hall to care for Richard and Barbara. Settling into her own room in the nursery suite, with its chaise lounge and gold-plated bathroom fixtures, Marion adjusted to the routine of life at Meadow Brook. Her life there was made up of caring for the children's needs—dressing them immaculately and making finger-curls daily in Barbara's blonde curly hair, shopping for them, entertaining them, bringing them down to breakfast in the mornings when they would eat with any of the family members who happened to be there. Sixteen-year-old Daniel, thin and looking even younger than his years, often joined them at breakfast and joked with the children.

Although Daniel enjoyed the children's company when he was home from boarding school, nineteen-year-old Frances avoided both Marion and the children—which was not difficult to do since the children came down to the main part of the house only for breakfast. When the governess happened to meet Frances, Marion answered pleasantly on the rare occasions that Frances spoke to her. The children were never permitted to go into Knole House, Frances' playhouse, even though Richard and Barbara were fascinated by the miniature house. An invitation to bring the eager children to tea at

Knole House was extended only once in the year and a half that Marion worked at Meadow Brook. Although Matilda had built the elaborate playhouse so that Frances might learn the housekeeping arts, it did not occur to the mother that her daughter should also learn to share her possessions with others.

Aware of the little children's loneliness in their isolation from any playmates and concerned over the constant adult supervision she was obliged to give them in their play, Marion sometimes sat, out of sight, behind a tree so that Barbara and Dick would not be inhibited in their sandbox play by her presence. Alfred Wilson regularly stopped in at the nursery in late afternoon or early evening, but Matilda came up there infrequently. Compton—the guard and chauffeur who had been with the family since the John Dodge days—was quick to excuse his mistress' apparent indifference to the adopted children by commenting that Mrs. Wilson had already raised two sets of children.

All Meadow Brook employees shared a respect for their mistress' highly disciplined work habits. If she was not clattering away at her typewriter, she was planning menus, arranging special decorations for entertaining, or conducting her yearly inventory of household and personal effects on a huge table set up in the ballroom—the silver one year, the linens another, the china . . .

Marion Gray was impressed by the way this woman of wealth worked harder at keeping and improving her fortune than ordinary people did at accumulating small savings. But as much as Marion was impressed by the Wilson home and as much as she had become attached to the two young children, she chafed at the confinement. At night, when the children were asleep, she looked out her third-floor window to lonely Adams Road below where only an occasional automobile passed.

By December, though, there was a new tempo of excitement at Meadow Brook as Matilda and Frances planned for Frances' debut with the help of Sara Burnham. The debutante, who wanted, above all, to be distinctive in everything she did, determined that her party at the Book Cadillac Hotel would be the talk of Detroit. The women had the hotel's ballroom floor transformed, for the December affair, into a glittering black and silver ice palace. The ballroom was illuminated by crystal chandeliers tied with metallic gauze, by lights in the black wall panels covered by grapelike bunches of silver balloons, and by a revolving silver ball casting colored lights over the 700 guests as they danced. Even the tables were covered in black with silver borders, and on the supper table, a life-sized silver colt served as a centerpiece.

Matilda, who had worn black to many other social affairs because she had been in mourning, now wore black velvet studded with tiny brilliants to match the black-and-silver theme. Frances' dress was of silver lamé, low at the neckline and hanging straight to the knees where it was tiered to form a slight train in back. Under a tiera of tightly curled black feathers set on her blonde hair, Frances had pencilled thinly arched eyebrows above her blue eyes—eyebrows drawn out to an Oriental hairline curl at the ends.

A single black orchid gave the final dramatic touch to the debutante's costume—an accessory that captured the attention of society reporters so that for years afterwards, the mention of Frances Dodge in the newspapers was accompanied by the reference to her black orchids. In reality, the so-called glamorous display of black orchids was a kind of small disaster—a single orchid dyed black by a maid in the Wilson household as a last desperate measure when the florist's promised black orchid failed to arrive. The dye refused to dry, and Frances had to hold the orchid carefully away from her dress. Even so, some of the black dye smeared the silver gown.

The Wilsons had planned another big party for New Year's Eve, in their clubhouse. So Marion Gray was asked to remain at Meadow Brook even on that gala occasion. "But you are welcome to have your friends come in for the evening," Matilda told her.

As Marion and her friends celebrated the New Year at Meadow Brook, they saw employees taking cases of champagne from the storage room over to the elaborate clubhouse that John Dodge had built. Although Mrs. Wilson drank only an occasional glass of Duff Gordon's Sherry before dinner, Alfred Wilson had a well-stocked bar adjoining his office. When Matilda was watching, however, he drank only a predinner martini or did a moderate amount of imbibing at social affairs.

Matilda was decidedly unhappy that Frances both smoked and drank. Daniel, still immature and schoolboyish-looking with hexagon glasses conspicuous on his pale, thin face, posed no such problems for his mother; he avoided parties and social events.

Compton, the chauffeur, was both a companion and friend to the boy during his middle-teen years. On a couple of occasions, Compton had driven Marion, Daniel, and the two little children to the Detroit Boat Club to give Dan the chance to take them out for a run on the river in his motorboat. The children laughed as arcs of spray fanned out across the water on those balmy summer afternoons when Dan whipped the boat through the water, unaware of the tragedy that this same boat would bring to the Wilsons within a few years.

Concerned that the boating excursions and a trip to the circus provided the only opportunities the children had to mix with other people, Marion asked Mrs. Wilson if she might take Dick and Barbara to see a children's movie playing in Rochester. "Good idea," Matilda agreed. "We'll arrange to get the movie out here and show it." So instead of sitting among a group of noisy children eating popcorn, Dick and Barbara viewed the film in their usual splendid isolation at Meadow Brook.

Soon after the New Year's Eve party at Meadow Brook, Frances, accompanied by Alfred and Matilda, left the country for a six months' world tour. The trip had been planned completely by Frances, who took her mother and stepfather as her guests. Leaving on an Italian liner for a Mediterranean cruise, Frances and the Wilsons were scheduled to motor through Spain, then to Morocco, Egypt, the Holy Land, India, and into South Africa, where they would travel overland through big-game country. May and June were to be spent in England at the horse shows, polo matches, and the Epsom Downs Derby.

While the Wilsons were away, Meadow Brook Hall was closed, and young Dick and Barbara, along with a reduced staff of servants, moved up into the old Dodge farmhouse. Now was her opportunity, the children's governess thought, to try to do something about initiating normal relationships for Dick and Barbara with their peers. Their one continuing association with other children was in their Sunday school classes at the First Congregational Church in Rochester. Here, Marion left her two charges in the primary class with other small-town children while the governess attended an adult class. And on May 15—the day observed as Dick's and Barbara's birthday— Marion invited the primary Sunday School class out to Meadow Brook farmhouse for a party for five-year-old Dick and three-year-old Barbara.

Mostly, though, Dick and Barbara had to depend on each other for companionship. They missed Daniel, who was away at Choate School.

At Choate, Dan's abilities in English class could not compete with his interests and abilities in mechanics and nature lore. In one of his English compositions, graded C, he dealt with rigors of getting out of bed in a school dormitory on a cold wintry morning. It would be a good idea, Dan wrote, to attach a string from his bed to the window so the window could be pulled shut from its open position before he got out of bed. In another composition entitled "Dogs" Dan commented: "I don't care for the two-penny tricks that dogs are taught, because I think that their intelligence is capable of a great deal more development than this."

When Frances and her mother and stepfather returned to Meadow Brook in late July 1934, a retinue of live imports, including dogs, followed them—blooded horses from England, silky-maned Arabian horses, zebras and donkeys, and seven English-bred dogs, including two rare white Pekinese, the only ones in the United States. The dogs came complete with an English kennelmaid to care for them.

Frances spent a month at home on the farm before leaving to take up interior decorating studies at Marian Coates Graves School in New York. When she came home for a few days in November, she had plans drawn for the building of an elaborate kennel to house the precious Pekinese. At the completion of the large T-shaped building, one newspaper commented on the Tudor styled kennel, designed by Frances, describing its green and silver drawing room and its "snowy white bathroom where each dog has his own towel." The paper's reference to Ruby Watson, kennelmaid, as "the girl who answers the phone and opens the door" drew an irate letter from Mrs. Watson.

"And it has taken me twenty years to reach my present state of efficiency," she wrote. "I have graduated as a trainer and handler, also a nurse (canine) with two years of veterinary work."

The kennelmaid's conditioning to being caught in the reflection of the Dodge limelight had begun quickly after her arrival at Meadow Brook. Frances did not bother to pen a letter of protest to the same paper's claim that the Wilsons had taken Frances to the other side of the world to find a real, live sheik for her.

From the school in New York, Frances traveled on weekends to Detroit, Atlantic City, and Newark, showing her horses and exhibiting her Pekinese. Her chic costumes attracted as much attention as did her dogs when she appeared at the Detroit show wearing a three-quarter length taffeta coat over her fashionably long dress that ended a few inches above her ankles. Underneath her curly bangs, the thinly penciled eyebrows and heavy-lidded eyes did not quite balance the long face with its sulky look that was relieved only when Frances flashed her rare wide smile.

At twenty-one years of age, Frances owned some eighty horses, including the newly purchased King of the Plains, bought in Chicago for $20,000. And she planned another trip to England in the spring to add to her stables.

Rochester townspeople had become accustomed to seeing large cattle cars drawn up on the railroad siding near the small depot and hearing the clatter of hoofs as the Dodge horses thumped up the ramps leading into the cars. A retinue of grooms accompanied the animals to the horse shows—as many as eleven attendants with twenty-six horses in two express cars, plus a third car carrying equipment—to see that the horses were fed and watered, manicured, clipped, and braided. Landaus, built by the most artistic carriage makers, and the finest of saddles and silver-encrusted harnesses also had to be transported, along with gray and maroon canvasses to drape Frances' box stalls and yards of maroon velvet to curtain the Dodge tack room.

Slim and serious in her beautifully tailored riding habit, Frances showed her saddle horses in five-gaited and three-gaited competitions. Then, changing into a suit and fur, and with her Pekinese mascot sitting beside her on the carriage seat, she drove her English show ponies around the ring.

The collection of trophies and ribbons was a costly honor. By year's end, the expense of maintaining the Dodge Stables at Meadow Brook amounted to $100,000 for 1935. The quarter-million dollars that Frances had spent during the year included $25,000 toward upkeep of Meadow Brook Hall. In the aftermath of her personal financial loss in the Fidelity Bank failure and with much of her investments tied up in stocks, Matilda was being cautious while the country slowly recovered from the depression. She had reopened Meadow Brook Hall on her return from the world tour only when Frances underwrote part of the maintenance.

Frances had spent another $33,000 on the construction and upkeep of the dog kennel. In her passion for original and distinctive clothes—Frances wore the first coq-feather boa seen on an evening dress in Detroit—another $25,000 had been spent. The total quarter-million-dollar expenditure in a depression year of low prices came out of the $300,000 income that her share of the John Dodge estate, held in trust for her, earned during 1935. When the principal of her trust monies—amounting now to more than $7.5 million—was paid to her on her twenty-fifth birthday, Frances Dodge would be one of the wealthiest young women in the country.

13

When the thoroughbreds from Isabel Dodge Sloane's Brookmeade Stables finished third among the country's money-winners in 1932 and 1933, Isabel reinvested the winnings in more horses and new stables at Upperville, Virginia. By 1934, when the cost of supporting a race horse was approximately $3,600 a year, Brookmeade had 140 horses ready to race. The outstanding horse among the 140 turned out to be a three-year-old brown colt Isabel had purchased for a bargain $1,200. In the last week of April, the three-year-old Cavalcade won both the Shenandoah Purse and the Chesapeake Stakes.

On Saturday, May 5, 7,000 people jammed Churchill Downs to see the Kentucky Derby. Isabel arrived with a party of friends in her private railway car, *The Pioneer*, to find downtown Louisville choked with traffic and the racetrack gates thronged with people buying tickets and purchasing camp chairs, stools, and small stepladders from hucksters. Before post time, the standing room between the seats and the stretch rail was packed so solidly with spectators that people found it difficult to get to the ticket windows to place bets.

Isabel's jockey held Cavalcade to the inside rail as the thoroughbreds pounded around the track. Coming into the stretch, Cavalcade moved up fast from ninth to seventh, then to fifth and third . . . The announcer's voice, rapidly repositioning the racers, was lost in the roar from the crowd as Cavalcade surged past the lead horse and over the finish line.

Matilda Wilson, whose interest in horses paralleled Isabel's, scanned the newspaper photos of her stepdaughter taking possession of the prized gold trophy for Brookmeade. Other photos and articles followed in quick succession. Less than a month later, Cavalcade broke the American Derby record in Chicago by running the 1½ miles in 2:04, then won a race in Detroit for $19,000—boosting his year's winnings to $97,165.

Although another of Isabel's horses, High Quest, won the Preakness that same year, it was Cavalcade who had captured racing fans' imaginations when Brookmeade finished the year as the nation's leading stable with $253,986 in prize monies. When a foot injury prevented Cavalcade from competing in the Santa Anita Handicap, Brookmeade Stables were flooded with inquiries. During February 1935, Cavalcade received more mail daily than President Roosevelt, according to his trainer, who found a minimum of 500 letters coming in each day, with a peak 1,800 letters on a single day.

Although Isabel's colt, Psychic Bid, won the Scarsdale Handicap in 1935, Brookmeade's earnings declined that year. In May 1935, Isabel had decided to enter Cavalcade in the Belmont Park Suburban Handicap. But the big, brown horse stumbled at the start of the race, pitching his jockey, and continued to gallop riderless around the track.

There would be no more debacles for the gallant exchampion, Isabel decided, ordering the horse retired to her farm in Virginia while she busied herself with her usual social affairs at her Palm Beach home, Concha Marina. At Concha Marina, a perpetual open-house policy brought sixty to seventy people to the Sloane pool each after-noon for cocktails, while professional masseurs provided rubdowns and facials to tone up the guests' tired and sagging muscles. Titled Europeans, freeloading now that their finances had been decimated by the depression years, circulated among the guests whether Isabel was at home or whether she was following the race track circuit.

On the Palm Beach scene, the slim blue-eyed Isabel was among the first to introduce the latest fashions, appearing on Palm Beach Boulevard that winter season in navy blue culottes and bright neckscarf, a wide-brimmed Schiaparelli fishnet hat covering her short dark hair. She and her sister Winifred remained very close, spending time together in Florida and in the East. But their associations with their stepmother were limited.

The depression had exacted heavy losses in Matilda's business ventures. After the state takeover of the bank of which she was president, and with her ornate Wilson Theater darkened more often than lighted since its opening, Matilda decided to focus on charitable affairs. There was no chance of failure when you were in the business of giving money away. And it was pleasant to have her work efforts and her administrative abilities recognized by such organizations as the Women's Auxiliary of the Salvation Army, of which she was chosen to be the president once again.

John Dodge and Horace Dodge, left to right.

The first Dodge. Horace Dodge, left rear, and John Dodge, right rear, take delivery of their first Dodge car—November 14, 1914—from the production department of the Dodge Assembly Plant in Hamtramck. This photo was taken in front of the John Dodge home, 75 East Boston Boulevard, Detroit. Courtesy of Dodge Public Relations.

DODGE BROS., DETROIT

Time Record for Two Weeks ending Thursday, *Dec 3* 190*3*

No.	NAME	F	S	M	T	W	T	F	S	M	T	W	T	Total Hours Day Work	Total Hours Piece Work	RATE PER HOUR DAY WORK	AMOUNT DAY WORK	AMOUNT PIECE WORK	TOTAL AMOUNT
	Jno F Dodge	10	5	10	10	10	–	10	5	10	10	10	10	100		40	40 00		
	H L Dodge	10	5	10	10	10	–	10	5	10	10	10	10	100		40	40 00		80 00
	Wm Turn	10	5	10	10	10	–	10	5	10	10	10	10	100		25	25 00		
1	*J Chapman*	10	5	10	10	10	–	10	5	10	10	10	–	90		5½	5 25		
2	*A Vocell*	10	5	10	10	10	–	10	5	10	10	10	10	100		32½	32 50		
3	*O Graul*	10	5	10	10	10		10	5	10	10	10	10	100		30	30 00		
4	*C Burtney*	10	5	10	10	10		10	5	10	10	10	10	100		22½	22 50		
5	*Chas Wright*	10	5	10	10			10	5	8	10	10	10	98		12½	12 25		
6	*Walter Lathrop*	10	5	10	9½	10	–	10	5	10	10	10	10	99½		17½	17 41		
7	*Fred Bertram*	10	5	10	9½	10		10	5	10	10	9½	10	99		15	14 85		
8	*H Graul*	10	5	10	10	10	–	10	5	10	10	10	10	100		15	15 00		
9	*D Nocker*	10	5	10	10	10	–	10	5	10	10	10	10	100		10	10 00		
10	*H Merrill*	10	5	10	10	10		10	5	10	10	10	10	100		12½	12 50		
11	*J Devar*	10	5	10	10		10	5	10	10	10	10	100		12½	12 50			
12	*J Dena*	10	5	10	10	10		6	5	10	10	10	10	100		10	10 00		
13	*W Fetter*	10	5	10	10	10		10	5	10	10	10	10	100		6 7/3	6 67		
14	*A Armspreing*	10	5	10	11	10		10	5	10	10	10	10	100		7½	7 00		

1903 time and pay record, including John and Horace Dodge. Courtesy of Chrysler Corporation Historical Library.

Three generations. Matilda Rausch Dodge at right, her mother sitting in the chair, and Matilda's baby, Frances Dodge on grandmother's lap.

Production at Dodge Main, circa 1915. Courtesy of Chrysler Corporation Historical Library.

Dodge Main test track, 1915. Courtesy of Chrysler Corporation Historical Library.

Matilda (Mrs. John F.) Dodge and her three step-children. John Duval Dodge at left, Isabel Dodge in middle, and Winifred Dodge at right. Taken around 1910.

Matilda (Mrs. John F.) Dodge and her three children—Anna Margaret on her lap, Daniel standing at left, and Frances.

Mrs. Horace Elgin Dodge, Anna Thomson, by Gerald Festus Kelly. Photo courtesy of Detroit Institute of Art. Portrait donated by grandchildren of Horace and Anna Dodge.

The Boston Boulevard home of John F. Dodge.

The original Rose Terrace, built for Horace Dodge by the Albert Kahn architectural firm. Photo courtesy of Albert Kahn Associates, Inc., Architects and Engineers.

Matilda and her children at Nice, France, after the death of John Dodge.
They participated in a local festival and parade at a cost of some $20,000.
The horses' reins were wrapped in satin ribbons, and Matilda threw violets
to the crowd.

Meadow Brook Hall

Rose Terrace

The Sun Room of Rose Terrace

A milling machine in the Dodge Brothers plant. Courtesy of Meadow Brook Hall.

Production at Dodge Main, circa 1915. Courtesy of Chrysler Corporation Historical Library.

John Dodge and Frances

The Delphine II—Horace E. Dodge's yacht. Courtesy of Dossin Great Lakes Museum.

Dodge general offices. The topcoats suggest it was Armistice Day. Courtesy of Meadow Brook Hall.

An early photo of the Dodge Brothers plant. Courtesy of Meadow Brook Hall.

The 1916 touring car used by General Pershing to chase Pancho Villa back across the Texas border. Pancho Villa later bought one of his own. The car is on display at the West Point Military Museum. It was one of the earliest vehicles used by the U.S. Army.

DODGE BROTHERS
MARCH

Music By
VICTOR HERBERT

Lyric By
MAXWELL I. PITKIN

Dedicated by Mr. Herbert to Mr. Horace E. Dodge
in respectful appreciation of his efforts toward
the advancement of American Music

Published especially for Dodge Brothers
by
JEROME H. REMICK & CO.
DETROIT   NEW YORK

After the death of the Dodge brothers, Victor Herbert wrote a march dedicated to Horace E. Dodge. The march was recorded and distributed to Dodge dealers.

Anna Dodge Dillman, seated on chair at left, and her husband, Hugh Dillman, seated in front of her, visit the Dillman family home in Columbus, Ohio.

A planing machine designed by the Dodges to build a recoil mechanism for the World War I 155 mm. howitzer. Courtesy of Meadow Brook Hall.

Left to right: Matilda Dodge, Anna Dodge, Miss McKay (nursemaid for Matilda's baby, Frances) and Horace Dodge Jr. aboard the Nakomis yacht in 1915.

Horace Dodge, left, and John Dodge, right, and a friend at their hunting lodge near Sault Ste. Marie, Michigan.

Matilda's daughter Frances made the rounds of the horse shows and dog shows with all the fervor and flair of her stepsister, Isabel Sloane, at race tracks. At Madison Square Garden, her Padboy of Albuquerque took the blue ribbon for Pekinese weighing no more than six pounds. Frances now had eighteen Pekinese, many of them white, from the foundation stock acquired in England. She had sold only a few of the fluffy white offspring of her original pair—one of them to Clark Gable. Another of the tiny white Pekinese, Ming, was a family pet at Meadow Brook Hall.

In the midst of the family's comings and goings at Meadow Brook Hall, the young adopted children, Richard and Barbara, stayed mostly in their own upstairs quarters in their after-school hours. They ate their dinner at six with their governess, Richard wearing shirt, coat, and tie and Barbara in a fresh dress. Not until he was twelve years old was Richard permitted general use of the main floor of the great house.

Christmas Day was one of the few occasions when both children joined the rest of the family on the main floor for the festivities. Eager to go into the drawing room to find their presents under the towering tree, the youngsters were reminded that the family must have its Christmas-morning breakfast first. When they had finished breakfast, Frances had not yet come downstairs. Richard and Barbara must wait, Matilda told them, until Frances made her appearance so everyone could share in the exchange of presents. The children suffered through the waiting until Frances came down at 10:30. Now it was time to throw open the drawing-room doors and to gaze upon the holiday decorations that Matilda and her staff of servants, secretaries, and florists had spent weeks in planning. But as the door was opened, the little Pekinese, Ming, dashed past the excited children and promptly urinated on the gorgeous red rug—the special seamless rug designed to fit the huge room. Matilda screamed. Her beautiful rug! Why hadn't someone taken care of the dog! Alfred's soothing "Now, Dearie," seemed to inflame his wife even more. The children watched silently, eyes wide with anxiety, as everyone's attention centered on the maid who was summoned to remove the offensive damp spot from the rug while Matilda fussed, then sulked for hours afterwards. Eventually, the children were told to open their beautifully wrapped gifts. Richard and Barbara carefully removed the wrappings and thanked their parents for the presents in quiet little voices.

Before the middle of May 1938, Walter Winchell's column contained a prediction that Frances Dodge soon would announce her engagement to James Johnson of New Jersey. The thirty-two-year-old Johnson had joined the Essex Cavalry unit of the National Guard right after high-school graduation, had become interested in horses, then went into horse show promotion. After Frances and Jimmy met at the 1933 National Horse Show in New York, they began dating. In recent months, though, Jimmy had become more intrigued by swing music than by horses. Now he was eager to put out a magazine entitled *Cat's Meow*, to be written in "hep cat" jargon and to feature stories of swing musicians and jam sessions. Putting out a magazine was an expensive venture, but expense was no problem for Frances Dodge.

Frances' twenty-year-old brother, Daniel, was in Harper Hospital recovering from a mastoid operation when Frances hostessed a "swing" party in the trophy rooms up over the indoor riding ring where she trained her horses at Meadow Brook. Stacks of the first issue of *Cat's Meow* were displayed on the bar, in the ladies' and the men's lounges, and in every prominent spot when guests arrived. Frances announced to her guests that she would personally accept subscriptions to the twenty-page magazine, which had a cover photo of Tommy Dorsey.

Jimmy Johnson had come to Detroit two months earlier to begin turning out the magazine in editorial offices hastily set up in a corner of the Fisher Building offices of the Wilsons in Detroit. While Frances brought in new items on bands, Jimmy wrote the articles and edited the magazine under its new title, *Swing*.

While Daniel was still hospitalized, rumors circulated that he too was planning marriage—to an eighteen-year-old girl from a small Canadian island community. For the past three years, Manitoulin Island's Gore Bay had been the center of Daniel's hunting and fishing expeditions into Canada's northern Ontario. The society whirl had even less appeal for Dan than did his sister's horses. Working with his hands, tinkering with valves and gears, struggling with oily mechanisms—these were the things that intrigued Dan. His latest interest was experimenting with the development of a diesel engine. In his fascination for motorboats, automobiles, and airplanes, he had purchased a Sikorsky amphibian plane, named *Osa's Ark*, formerly owned by the Martin Johnsons, famous explorers. The twin-engined, zebra-striped *Ark* could make the 250-mile trip up to Gore Bay in less than three hours.

At the time Dan had bought his hunting lodge on Manitoulin Island in 1935, he chose the island for its natural, unspoiled beauty and its remote and isolated locale. Only a few intimates were invited from Detroit to the lodge. Dan had no telephone to disturb the quiet. For any necessary calls, he went into Gore Bay, twenty miles away.

When Dan walked into the small building that housed the Gore Bay telephone office to make a call one evening, the young, blue-eyed and clear-complexioned Laurine MacDonald was on duty there, a telephone headset on her auburn hair as she transmitted calls to the busy outside world. But Dan did not meet the girl until sometime later when he was looking for a place to stay right in Gore Bay and was directed to the MacDonald home—a small, saltbox of a house with weather-beaten siding.

"It might not be quite what you've been used to," he was told.

"Fine. That's just the place I'm looking for," Dan answered. For Daniel, the plain surroundings of the tugboat captain's house and the earthy people of the community seemed to evoke a feeling of ease that elaborate Meadow Brook had never offered. After that, Dan Dodge was seen regularly on the streets of Gore Bay—even when he was living out at his log-cabin lodge. Dressed in comfortable fishing clothes, he was able to forget some of his shyness as he stopped and talked with young people of the bay community. Soon after he began dating Laurine, he frequently gave her his car to drive around the island. Because the tall, slender Laurine loved to dance, Dan escorted her to Gore Bay dances although he would not even attempt to get out on the dance floor. Instead, he was content to watch Laurine whirl around the floor with other partners, then to escort her home.

Responsive to each other's sensitive and quiet natures, Daniel and the athletic and vigorous Laurine both enjoyed hiking through the woods and swimming, boating, or fishing in Georgian Bay waters. The people of Gore Bay, accustomed to thinking of Laurine as Dan Dodge's girl, were neither surprised nor inquisitive when, in the autumn of 1937, a beautiful diamond sparkled on the fourth finger, left hand of the $15-a-week telephone operator as she worked the switchboard.

When rumors of the engagement sifted into the Detroit area and no public announcement was offered by the Wilsons, reporters trekked up to Gore Bay to question a reticent Laurine and to send messages back to Detroit via the telephone switchboard presided over by the calm and pleasant daughter of a Gore Bay tugboat captain. When a reporter finally managed to get Laurine to admit her diamond ring was a gift from Dan Dodge, the telephone operator was quoted in the *Detroit News:*

> Our affair is just like any other love affair between a boy and a girl. He's just an ordinary boy and I'm his girl friend, and we never even discuss his money. We're too busy discussing ourselves.

> Anyone who knows Danny knows that ten-million dollars doesn't mean so much to him. Dan's not fast or anything, and he doesn't like people who act fast or sophisticated. He doesn't even dance.

On a Sunday afternoon near the end of May, a group of Frances' and Daniel's acquaintances was invited out to Meadow Brook. There the visitors were greeted by Matilda and Frances with Laurine Mac-Donald at their side. The curious guests noticed that Frances' black street-length dress was just like Laurine's except for color—Laurine's dress was beige. Dan, still wrapped in bandages from his mastoid operation, and Jimmy Johnson grinned happily at the guests as they entered the dining room for a buffet supper. Glass bowls with the etched initials of Jimmy and Frances, Dan and Laurine, decorated the table. At last the engagements had been made public. The next morning, Frances left Detoit for an out-of-town horse show, Jimmy got busy at his typewriter in the Wilson offices, and Laurine remained at Meadow Brook to be with Dan during his recuperation.

Since no wedding dates had been announced on the night of the engagement party, friends had not anticipated Dodge-Johnson nuptials taking place only five weeks later. But on Friday evening, July 1, Meadow Brook Hall's red carpeted drawing room was the setting for the marriage of debonair Jimmy Johnson and Frances Dodge, her slim figure draped in gleaming ice-blue satin, Grecian styled. The wedding procession, headed by Matilda and Alfred, came down the winding great staircase as the huge organ thundered the wedding processional. On the arm of her brother Dan, the bride came slowly down the stairs following her attendants, a long scalloped train trailing behind her.

Matilda had told friends that she had designed Meadow Brook's magnificent stairway in anticipation of seeing her daughter Frances someday sweep down its length on her wedding day. That wedding day was here, now, and Matilda was not as ecstatic as she had envisioned. Frances had passed over Alfred for the usual role performed by the father. And there were Matilda's misgivings about Jimmy Johnson, who came from a background far different from Frances' background of wealth. She repressed her misgivings, though, in the hope that this affable young man would supply the supportive strength the shy, insecure Frances needed to blossom in the knowledge that she was loved for herself, not for her money . . . that a happy marriage might change the manner of life that Matilda found worrisome and that seemed to pattern itself increasingly after that of Frances' father—John Dodge.

As the bridal couple exchanged vows, 100 of the 900 guests filled the drawing room, while the others remained in the huge reception hall. From outside the drawing room's opened casement windows, uniformed maids, chauffeurs, policemen, waitresses, and gardeners watched as "Miss Frances" became Mrs. James Johnson.

Under Sara Burnham's direction, the receiving line formed in the oak-paneled library where the bride stood in a bay windowed recess banked with white flowers and facing a large oil portrait of her father, John F. Dodge. Dozens of servants shouldered trays, moving among the guests, carrying a twelve-pound French salmon on a silver platter, lobster salads, steaming scallop casseroles, and jellied meats. A distressed Laurine fussed over champagne spilled on her dress by a hurrying guest while nearby, Frances cut her four-foot-high wedding cake.

The young Wilson children—nine-year-old Richard, sturdy and handsome in navy flannel jacket and short white pants, and seven-year-old Barbara, blonde curled and dainty in an embroidered frock—sat on the stairway long past their bedtime hour to watch the proceedings with their governess. Below them, Henry Ford in white linen suit and Anna Dodge Dillman in white satin and orchids, were among the society people who moved in and out of the manorhouse to and from the pavilion set up in the east gardens.

Individual packets of organdy-wrapped rose petals were opened by the guests at midnight and the bride and groom were showered with the fragrant petals as they left for New York and a honeymoon in England. The old Dodge white frame farmhouse near the Meadow Brook greenhouses at the crest of the hill was to be the Johnson residence upon the couple's return.

Less than two weeks after the Johnsons sailed for England, newspapers were carrying reports that Dan Dodge would marry Laurine MacDonald on August 14. Questioned by reporters who came to Meadow Brook, Matilda Wilson disclaimed any knowledge of her son's wedding plans. The couple, she said curtly, had left for Gore Bay, and any wedding arrangements would be made by Miss MacDonald's family.

In spite of Matilda's disclaimers, Dan and Laurine returned to Meadow Brook, where they were married quietly on Tuesday, August 2. Although Matilda had remained detached from the festivities of the nuptial-planning, she saw to it, as administrator of Daniel's inheritance, that a prenuptial agreement was signed that was protective of her twenty-one-year-old son's fortune. With this done, the eighteen-year-old telephone operator, in a full-skirted lace gown of pale wheat shade, walked down the wide stairway into a $10 million marriage to the strains of the wedding march ground out by the mechanical player attachment to the organ. In the red-carpeted drawing room where Frances had been married a month previously while some 900 people tried to view the ceremony, Laurine and Daniel exchanged their vows in front of the minister and seven witnesses, including the matron-of-honor and the best man, Laurine's sister and brother-in-law.

The Johnsons were still on their honeymoon, and Laurine's parents were not present, it was announced to the papers later, because of the illness of Mrs. MacDonald. Following the ceremony, Laurine changed her gown and matching wide-brimmed mohair hat for a black crepe traveling dress with rose crepe bolero. The newlyweds headed north in Dan's roadster, pulling a trailer.

Stopping at Sault Ste. Marie first, the couple left a few days later for Dan's Manitoulin Island lodge. Here was the one Dodge home to which Laurine needed to make no adjustment. The woods, the choppy bay waters, and the isolation were familiar parts of her life. A young caretaker and his wife—the Lloyd Bryants—and another twenty-year-old camp employee, Frank Valiquette, were on the premises, and the relationship among the five young people was a friendly one.

On the Monday after their arrival at Gore Bay, the newlyweds got into Dan's speedboat and cut across the bay waters to Little Current for provisions. But Laurine, who swam regularly in the clear water near her island home, was relieved when Dan docked the motorboat at Little Current. She had not shared her husband's zest for riding his bounding speedboat through the roughened waters.

Finishing their shopping for enough supplies to last them for the few days they planned to stay at the lodge before going back to Meadow Brook, they returned to the motorboat for the ride back to the lodge. At the lodge, Mrs. Bryant began preparing an early dinner while Laurine got out the ironing board to press some of her clothes before the trip back to Detroit, where the couple planned to move into a home across the road from Meadow Brook hall.

It was nearly 4 P.M. when Dan wandered outside the lodge to the garage where he had been working on a marine motor, joining Lloyd Bryant and Frank Valiquette. But this afternoon he did not work on the motor. Instead, he and Valiquette went into the brush and opened an old piano box in which dynamite had been stored after the land had been cleared of stumps and rocks eight years previously. The thin-faced, scholarly looking Dodge stared intently at the sticks of dynamite through his silver-rimmed glasses. The former caretaker had warned him often not to tamper with the dynamite. But for a year now, he had wanted to try to set it off. After all, he was the owner of this place . . . a married man now too . . . old enough to make his own decisions. And he was certain the explosive was too old to make much of a blast.

As Dan and Valiquette carried the dynamite into the garage and placed it on the window sill, then fitted one stick with a fuse, Laurine shut off her iron and stepped outside to call her husband for dinner. Walking up to the garage, she looked through the window to see Dan holding a stick of dynamite in his hand while Valiquette touched the end of the fourteen-inch fuse with his cigarette lighter.

A fuse of fourteen inches should burn for three minutes, the men had figured. Still, Dan pivoted sharply on the ball of his foot as soon as the fuse sputtered and tossed the stick of dynamite in the direction of the door. As the dynamite stick made an arc past the window, sparks trailed down to the sill and to the remaining dynamite sticks and caps placed there.

A shattering crash brought Bryant's wife running from the house in time to see Valiquette climbing out the window of the wrecked garage. Her husband, covered in blood, stumbled out the garage door and collapsed on the ground. "Get a doctor . . . I'm done for!" he muttered. At the same time, Laurine ran toward the house, feeling as if she were aflame. She turned on the faucet and doused herself with water.

With one arm throbbing painfully, her face and legs cut and bleeding from splinters of wood and glass, Laurine ran back to the garage where she and Mrs. Bryant half dragged and half carried the stunned Daniel out of the wreckage. First Laurine rushed to her car, planning to drive to Gore Bay for a doctor. But it would take an hour to drive the twenty miles of twisting narrow road to Gore Bay to bring help to the injured men. The only alternative was to take everyone across the bay to Little Current in the speedboat, Laurine decided. Everyone could fit into the boat, and the trip would be twenty minutes shorter.

The women and Valiquette got the two more seriously injured men into the car. Laurine drove the car down to the wharf where they carried Dan, his face and head bleeding and his arm mangled, to the boat and placed him on cushions on the floor of the rear cockpit. Then they carried Bryant to the boat and placed him next to Dan. Valiquette crawled in beside the others and began bandaging Dan's arm to stop the flow of blood. Bryant's wife rode in back with the three men while Laurine got behind the wheel of the speedboat.

For ten miles, the bleeding Laurine gripped the wheel with her one strong arm and one broken arm, clinging tenaciously to the wheel while a strong wind, coming from behind, whipped up four-foot-high waves that battered and buffeted the boat from the rear while Laurine kept the speed at twenty knots. The boat was nearing Rabbit Island when Laurine called out sharply for Valiquette to help. The burned and cut Valiquette forced himself to crawl to the front of the boat and took the wheel from the exhausted Laurine. My God, he thought as he gripped the wheel, this would tear the arms off a strong man!

From the rear cockpit, Bryant's terrified wife held her unconscious husband in her lap and watched as Laurine weakly released the wheel to Valiquette. As if he might have dimly heard Laurine's pleas for help at the wheel, Dan began to thrash about, then suddenly lurched to his feet. He tottered momentarily, then plunged over the side of the boat into the water. Mrs. Bryant's scream was almost lost in the roar of the motor and the pounding waves, but Laurine had heard the scream and looked up just in time to see Dan fall into the churning water.

Valiquette cut the boat's speed and, for ten minutes, circled in the rough waters as Laurine, frantic with anxiety and pain, tried to catch sight of Dan. There had been just one brief glimpse of him in the water as the boat had turned back the first time, then he had disappeared. Finally giving up the hopeless search, Valiquette headed through the seven miles of Georgian Bay waters separating them from Little Current.

As the boat docked, Laurine stumbled out onto the wharf and ran for help. Dr. Young of Little Current gave first aid to Laurine, Bryant, and Valiquette, then sent them inland to the Red Cross Hospital at Mindemoya while a search party set out in the direction of Rabbit Island. But the search was useless—Laurine knew that. As she recovered from her ordeal in the Mindemoya hospital, the bride of thirteen days could scarcely comprehend, as yet, the new kind of life ahead of her as a young widow and an heiress.

At Meadow Brook Hall, a stunned and sleepless Matilda, under the care of physicians, tried to understand what had happened to her only son. Frances and Jimmy Johnson boarded a plane in New York for a hurried flight back to Meadow Brook as Alfred Wilson prepared to fly up to Little Current in Daniel's amphibian plane. He took with him a nurse, two men from the Detroit police Harbormaster's Division, and a supply of ropes, hooks, and diving equipment to search for the body of Daniel George Dodge.

Two weeks after the accident, Daniel's young widow was released from the hospital and brought by plane to Meadow Brook Hall to await, with her mother-in-law, the finding of the body of the husband and son. Matilda now could ask the questions that troubled her . . . could hear the details of the tragedy that had taken her son from her. Neither woman, though, permitted herself to weep in the presence of the other, and strained awkwardness and wariness lay between them as the search for Daniel's body continued.

Right after Laurine's arrival, Amelia Rausch Cline also came to Meadow Brook to offer what comfort she could to her older sister. Amelia had been vacationing with her husband when she had read a newspaper account of the death of her nephew. Immediately, the Clines returned to Rochester. Although Matilda had not spoken to Amelia since the younger sister's marriage to John Cline six years previously and had made no attempt now to notify her of Dan's death, Amelia drove alone out to the estate where she had lived for twenty years. She murmured her condolences to Frances and to Matilda, was introduced briefly to Laurine, and then found herself driving back to Rochester. Matilda's perfunctory responses indicated that even in these days of torment, the older sister was not ready to forgive the younger for her disobedience.

Each day's mail brought more distress to Matilda as she opened letters with proposals from opportunists soliciting payments for supposed information or for ideas or equipment that would locate the body of her son, and from cranks and seers professing prophetic knowledge. Reinforced by years of habit, Matilda filed the macabre letters along with the agonizingly detailed newspaper accounts of Daniel's last moments.

Reminders of Daniel were everywhere—the piles of unopened wedding presents; the newspaper conjectures as to how much of the Daniel Dodge fortune his bride would inherit and whether she had really done all she could to rescue him; the empty honeymoon house across Adams Road . . . the house Daniel had ordered remodeled with a sunken living room, eight bedrooms, a three-car garage with servants' quarters—all for Laurine and himself.

The fruitless search for the body continued. Six fishing boats had made the first efforts to locate the body by dragging the choppy, white-capped waters of Georgian Bay's north channel, attempting to sink their gill nets nearly one-hundred feet deep to the channel bed. The diving equipment, brought by Alfred Wilson in Dan's plane, could not be used effectively until the site of the drowning was located. With the body still not found, a diving bell, rigged with 5,000-watt undersea lamps, was overhauled in Connecticut to be shipped to Little Current. Towed by a tug, the diving bell was to be the first ever used in the Great Lakes. It would be accompanied on its search by a second tug outfitted with air compressors and various power equipment.

On September 7, the diving bell was being readied to be towed out to the treacherous waters where Daniel had disappeared when two Little Current fishermen started out on a fishing trip at dawn. While the rough bay waters swirled around the fishing boat, the men heard the screaming of gulls and noticed birds circling and swooping over the water. Heading their boat toward the gulls, the men sighted a dark object moving in the water midway between Rabbit Island and the mainland. As they came closer they could see that the object tossing in the water was a man's body—a body covered in mud, indicating it had only recently risen to the surface. Tying the body to their boat, the two fishermen returned to Little Current to claim the $1,500 reward offered by the Wilsons. After a postmortem examination by a coroner's jury, the body was placed in Daniel's own plane and returned to Detroit, accompanied by Alfred Wilson.

At 2:30 Friday afternoon, 250 people attended brief funeral services at Meadow Brook Hall where Dan's casket, covered with rosebuds, was placed at the foot of the great staircase in the reception hall. As the family sat at the staircase landing, Dr. Vance spoke briefly about Daniel's short life, a quartet sang "Beautiful Isle of Somewhere," and the funeral procession left the manor house to the organ strains of "Onward Christian Soldiers." Like a soldier, Matilda endured the ride behind the hearse from Meadow Brook to Woodlawn Cemetery. It was a longer and more agonizing ride for Matilda than any previous trek to the Dodges' marble mausoleum had been. The body of her son was interred beside his father and his young sister, his father's first wife, and his Uncle Horace.

Unrelenting in her ostracism of those who opposed her will, Matilda appeared to most people to be equally unbending in the face of great personal tragedy. Only Alfred and Frances, young Richard and Barbara, and some of the servants knew that, at her son's death, Matilda turned the key in the lock of Dan's room. She permitted no one to enter the room for many years, reserving for herself solitary pilgrimages into the suite that looked as if it awaited its owner's return. There, among the wall carvings of King Arthur's Court, the lamps made from an old flintlock pistol and a brass sword hilt, the Choate pennants and the pictures—one of John Dodge's boat and another of Daniel himself—Matilda relived the memories of her "quiet times" with her son.

Even before Daniel's body had been found, varying accounts and conjectures as to the disposition of the late Dodge heir's fortune had occupied newspaper space. With the filing of the will in September, the ante-nuptial agreement was made public in which Annie Laurine MacDonald was to limit her claim on the estate to a quarter-of-a-million dollars. In addition, Dan had willed the Manitoulin Island estate to Laurine, $100,000 to his sister Frances, $25,000 each to his adoptive brother and sister, Richard and Barbara, $25,000 to Compton the chauffeur, and the remainder to his mother, named as executrix.

Leaving Meadow Brook shortly after the funeral, Laurine hired a lawyer who stated that unless a satisfactory settlement was offered the widow, the will would be contested. "We consider the settlement given to her in the will inadequate and unfair," the attorney announced, ". . . in view of the estate being in excess of ten million dollars."

When the settlement was not made within the next few weeks, the contesting of the will began, coinciding with the inquest into the drowning death of Daniel. In Little Current's combined courtroom, town hall, and library, where only 25 people could be seated, the doctor who had performed the autopsy on the body testified that Dodge's injuries, though painful, would not have proved fatal. The former caretaker of the lodge testified that the motorboat from which Daniel had fallen was equipped with lifebelts. A constable demonstrated to a nervous jury how a piece of dynamite fuse sputters for a few minutes before burning as he applied a match to a fuse. But the inquest was adjourned for two weeks, at which time Laurine, the Bryants, and Frank Valiquette would give testimony.

When Laurine, dressed in black, appeared before the jury two weeks later, it took the jurors only ten minutes to rule that young Dodge's death had been an accident and to bring the investigation to an end. But the will contest was only beginning. Even before the inquest had ended, Laurine's lawyer was charging concealment of assets by Matilda Dodge Wilson in an accounting of her guardianship of Daniel until he had reached the age of twenty-one the previous July.

By the end of 1938, Laurine's lawyer had petitioned for a widow's allowance of $33,000 monthly until the estate was settled, claiming that his client was entitled to a scale of living commensurate with the life the young married couple had planned and "in keeping with the Dodge fortune and family tradition." A $5,000 monthly allowance was granted.

A year-end appraiser's report set the value of the Daniel Dodge estate at nearly $1.7 million in personal holdings plus his Canadian property and the trust fund, now amounting to $10 million, set up by his father. Matilda resigned herself to the unpleasant expectation that the litigations over the money would continue for at least another year. And recalling her own successful battle to win her widow's share of John Dodge's will, as guaranteed under Michigan law, she was not optimistic about the outcome of the legal battle for Daniel's millions.

14

When the Probate Court finally made its ruling, Daniel Dodge's estate was awarded to his mother and to his widow. Matilda's share was to be $3,750,000, Laurine's was to be $1,250,000, and the remaining $6 million would go to the state and federal governments in inheritance taxes.

The two half sisters, Winifred Seyburn and Isabel Sloane, and Daniel's sister, Frances Dodge Johnson, immediately filed appeals. If they could have Daniel's money divided among the sisters, no inheritance taxes would have to be paid, since an inheritance tax had already been paid on bequests made in the original John F. Dodge will. The sisters' lawyers argued that Daniel's estate should be distributed according to John F. Dodge's provision that, in the event of the death of any of his children without issue, the deceased child's share of the income should be divided among the surviving children, excepting the disinherited John Duval. Only at the death of the last of the children was the trust to be divided and then distributed among the children's heirs.

But the decision on the sisters' suit was delayed as John Duval suddenly made a third attempt to share in the Dodge millions. He filed suit to have his father's multi-million-dollar estate divided just as though there had been no will. The legality on which the suit was based was his lawyer's claim that the Dodge trust funds violated the Michigan law prohibiting the establishment of estates in perpetuity.

"I believe I'm entitled to a fair share of my father's fortune," John Duval declared. "I want to be square, but I am John Dodge's only living son."

A new and larger share of the estate would help John Duval to keep his latest business venture from failure. Backed financially by his sisters Isabel and Winifred, he had been trying to market a new type of machine for homogenizing milk. But his sisters would not invest more money in his Dodge Emulsor Corporation in spite of John

Duval's convictions that the milk homogenizing machines would be profitable if he could keep the company functioning for a few more years. As much as the two sisters wanted their brother to succeed, they remembered that his attempt to manufacture the revolutionary eight-cylinder inline automobile had failed, his real-estate venture in France had fizzled, his attempt to set up night clubs in Detroit had resulted in a flurry of lawsuits over unpaid bills.

While awaiting the final disposition of Daniel's estate, which was increasing by more than $1 million each year, the widowed Laurine rented a handsome brick house in Gore Bay and moved her parents from their old house near the waterfront to the rented house in the community's better residential section. In September 1939, Laurine settled into a dormitory at Alma College, Ontario, and began commercial and business studies. Apart from having her big car on campus, Laurine became a typical coed as she wore the Alma navy serge tunic uniform with its short black bloomers and black stockings.

To avoid the expense of more lawsuits and appeals, the disputing Dodge women agreed to a settlement in July 1940. Awarded $2.5 million by the settlement, Laurine decided to give up her Alma College studies and live in Detroit. Nearly half the estate was awarded to the three sisters, while Matilda received the remainder. But distribution of the money could not be made until February 1942, when John Duval's suit resulted in a negative decision as a higher court upheld the previous arrangements. By this time, Daniel's estate had swelled to $13 million.

During the time the litigations had continued in the courts, Matilda had tried to go on with a normal family life. Accompanied by the adopted children, Richard and Barbara, Matilda and Alfred took a trip up to Montreal and sailed from there to Labrador in the late summer of 1939. On their return, Matilda planned a party for Frances' twenty-fifth birthday in November—the date when she became eligible to receive the accumulated income, $9.5 million, from her share of the John Dodge trust-fund income. As Frances and her guests sat at the birthday table in the walnut-paneled dining room of Meadow Brook Hall, the sound of trombone and orchestra drifted up through the gallery from the entertainment room below. Matilda had brought Tommy Dorsey and his orchestra as surprise performers for Frances' party.

Marriage to Jimmy Johnson did not circumvent Frances' preoccupation with dog shows and horse shows: she rode her eight-year-old gelding, Greyhound, to score her greatest triumph in Lexington on September 28, 1940. Leaning forward in the saddle, Frances rode

Greyhound around the track to set a mile record of 2.01 3/4 for trotters under saddle. Horesemen, knowledgeable in the difficulties of riding a trotter at top speed, predicted the record would never be beaten—thirty years later, the figure still stood as a world record.

Less than two months after Frances' record ride on Greyhound, Matilda had more news items to place in the family's scrapbooks as she herself was appointed Michigan's first woman lieutenant governor. The state's eighty-one-year-old Governor Dickinson had risen to his position from that of lieutenant governor on the death of the elected governor the previous March. At a ruling by the attorney general that there was no vacancy in the lieutenant governorship and that Dickinson was both lieutenant governor and acting governor, Dickinson appointed Matilda Wilson to his former post as a test of the ruling. The appointment would run until January 1, 1941, when the newly elected Governor Van Wagoner would take office.

Designating Dickinson's action as "silly and foolish," the attorney general went even further. "Should Governor Dickinson now die or become incapacitated, we would be in a fine mess," he deplored.

Matilda's calm and poise remained unruffled by the political clamor. "I will carry out whatever duties devolve upon me from my appointment," she announced. "I feel it is a symbol of Governor Dickinson's belief in the place of women in public life, not a compliment to me, but to the women of Michigan."

State officials saw little of their new lieutenant governor until an administrative board meeting was held early in December. Then, the men stood stiffly in the meeting room as Governor Dickinson escorted Matilda Wilson into the assembly and introduced the petite woman with the silver-fox fur around her shoulders as the new lieutenant governor. Matilda listened coolly and attentively as a report on tax compromises was read, then voted her approval of the report. When no one questioned her right to vote, it was apparent her appointment was being tolerated.

In the same month that Matilda's short role as lieutenant governor ended, Daniel's widow, Laurine, married a Detroit plastic surgeon who had treated her for the facial scars she had suffered in the dynamite explosion on Manitoulin Island. Although Laurine and her mother-in-law had not maintained their family relationship, Matilda was troubled by the fact that Laurine's new husband had been married previously. Matilda did not mention this divorce to her young adopted children, Richard and Barbara, but she continued to remind them periodically that she chose to keep aloof from "the other side of the family—the Horace Dodges—with all their terrible divorces."

Now that her daughter Frances was expecting a baby, Matilda looked forward to the arrival of summer and the birth of this first grandchild. It was a quiet summer at Meadow Brook. The Guernsey cows and Belgian draft horses took prizes at livestock shows in various cities, and Matilda hostessed one social event—a benefit Chinese Garden Party for the United Chinese Relief. On July 1, 1941, Frances gave birth to a baby girl named Judith Frances—and Matilda was a grandmother.

Several years previously, Matilda finally had given the order for the sale of the castle-like home that her first husband, John F. Dodge, had begun to build in Grosse Pointe. Now, as no buyer had been found for the great mansion, still unfinished after a $2.5 million expenditure, Matilda reluctantly commissioned a wrecking crew to tear down the brush-surrounded structure, so the property could be cleared and the land sold. With the wrecking of the home planned by Dodge to be a showplace, one of Matilda's few remaining links with the past was severed.

Still, she was to learn that the past, constantly stalking its victims, could reach out at any time to claim its pawns. By this time, Matilda had been a Wilson for so long and had worked so hard at glossing the Wilson image, many people were scarcely aware she had ever been a Dodge. But they were reminded when on August 12, 1942, John Duval was back in the newspapers as he lay, unconscious and near death, in an oxygen tent in Detroit's Receiving Hospital. For days, details of his latest, sordid escapade filled the papers.

It had begun on August 11 when John Duval, on a bar hopping jaunt, failed to return home for dinner. Moving on from the Fort Shelby Cocktail Lounge to the Tiger Bar near Detroit's baseball stadium, he argued with other bar patrons and insisted on displaying his prowess at Indian wrestling. Later, a taxi deposited him at Van Dyke Place, where friends of John Duval and his wife Dora lived in two neighboring homes. Dora was visiting at one home—the Tuckers. John Duval walked up on the porch of the neighboring home and yelled, "Extra, Extra," until he was admitted to the house by thirty-three-year-old Mignon Fontaine, who roomed there and was alone in the home in the absence of the owners.

Once inside the house, John Duval declined to leave. The young woman finally went into the kitchen with him when he promised to leave after he had drunk one more nightcap. When a knock sounded at the kitchen door, Mignon opened the door to find that John Duval's wife had come over from the Tuckers' neighboring house, carrying a glass bowl and asking to borrow ice cubes. But as soon as Dora Dodge entered the kitchen, she and her husband began arguing. Dora had been spying on him, John accused. Suddenly, he struck her face. Dora fell to the floor; her husband tottered and fell on top of her.

Mignon, who had left the kitchen when the Dodges had begun to argue, rushed back into the room at the sound of a crash to find Dora lying on the floor, blood under her head, and the glass bowl shattered. As she washed the blood from Dora's face and head with a wet towel, John Duval angrily stomped out of the house.

After Dora was taken back to her own apartment by her friends, John Duval came back into the house, complaining of dizziness. Mignon left him lying on a cot downstairs while she went upstairs to her bedroom and locked her door.

As she tried to sleep, she heard footsteps on the stairs. Mignon lay perfectly still as she heard the doorknob rattle several times, followed by the sound of someone thudding against the door.

Knowing the owners of the home were out of town, John Duval went on into the next empty bedroom and stumbled around inside the room. Then he clambered out to the upstairs dust-porch and made his way over to the window leading into Mignon Fontaine's bedroom. Hearing the scraping sound of her screen being removed from the window, Mignon grabbed her robe and unlocked her door, ran down the stairs, out of the house, and across the street. Stumbling up to a neighbor's porch, she rang the doorbell repeatedly, but got no response.

While she was still on the porch, lights flashed down the street and a police car drove up Van Dyke Place in response to a call from another neighbor who had seen a man on the dust porch and thought a prowler was getting into the house. As the barefooted Mignon saw the lights of the approaching police car, she hid in the bushes fronting the neighbor's house. The time was 3:05 A.M.

The officers got out of the police car and went up to the front door of the Lange house where Mignon rented her room. As the door opened, John Duval stood framed in the doorway. What were they doing, going around with flashlights at such an hour, bothering people, he demanded. Asked to identify himself, John Duval refused. Asked who owned the house, he became belligerent. But the policemen were able to get him into the police car without using force.

By the time John Duval arrived at the McClellan Police Station, however, he had become obstreperous and noisy. Ordered to go into a smaller side room, he grabbed the top of the lieutenant's desk and refused to be moved. The lieutenant would find himself transferred, John Duval threatened, because he was dealing with someone bigger than he thought! As a stocky, muscular patrolman tried to drag the resisting Dodge from the room, the two men struggled. When the officer finally managed to force Dodge into a sitting position on the terrazzo floor, standard procedure in handling drunks, John Duval violently threw himself backwards. His head hit the terrazzo floor with a sound like a watermelon hitting the ground.

The police picked up the unconscious man from the floor and rushed him to Receiving Hospital. At Receiving, doctors examined him. Then they ordered the patient given the routine treatment for drunks, which meant placing him in a bed in the psychopathic ward.

By the time Dora and her physician arrived at the hospital just before 6 A.M., it had become obvious that the patient, who was breathing with difficulty, needed more intensive care. He was transferred to another room and provided with an oxygen tent and tube feeding.

John Duval died without regaining consciousness at 10:18 the following night. A postmortem examination revealed the cause of death as a cerebral hemorrhage precipitated by a ten-inch basal skull fracture. Dodge's skull was eggshell thin, the medical examiner reported.

In the next week, the story of John Duval's life and the inquest into his death were subjects of nationwide interest. There was conflicting testimony on the manner in which Dodge had sustained his head injury. Two observers claimed the police officer had dragged Dodge backwards, then dropped him. But the bulk of the testimony supported the policeman's account of Dodge throwing himself backwards from a sitting position.

Although Matilda could separate herself from the affairs of "the other side of the family," she could not completely isolate herself from occurrences within the John Dodge family. On the death of John Duval, Winifred and Isabel conferred with Matilda for permission to have their brother's body placed in the Dodge mausoleum with his father and mother. The request posed a dilemma for Matilda. Her deliberations could not be entirely unbiased as she thought back over the disgrace her stepson had brought so frequently to the name of Dodge. But she tried to be fair. Would John Dodge have wanted the son he rejected in life to be returned to him in death? she wondered. And there were Winifred's and Isabel's rights to be considered. Matilda pondered the question, then acquiesced to her stepdaughters' wishes.

A ten-minute service was held for John Duval at a funeral chapel on August 17. While police kept crowds of onlookers in order outside the chapel, Isabel and Winifred joined John Duval's first wife and daughter—the latter now starting college—in the front seats facing the bronze casket. The widowed Dora remained in a private sideroom. Floral tributes from John Duval's Aunt Anna Dodge Dillman and his cousins, Delphine Ione and Horace, were among the many flowers banked near the coffin. But the stepmother, Matilda, was not among the mourners at the funeral of this last son of John F. Dodge.

Less than a year after John Duval's death, Daniel Dodge's widow, Laurine, divorced her second husband on charges of cruelty. In the two years of their marriage, Laurine was quoted in newspapers, the doctor had not been able to rid himself of the idea that his friends considered him a fortune hunter. Ten days after the June 1943 divorce, Matilda was embittered to read that Laurine had remarried. Her choice of husband was a captain stationed with the Army Ordnance Department in Detroit—a man who shared a love of sports, especially skiing, with the blue-eyed girl who had learned in her childhood to traverse the deep snows of a Manitoulin Island winter on a pair of barrel staves.

Because of the wartime shortage of oil for heating, Matilda had closed Meadow Brook Hall's west wing. Her daughter Frances and granddaughter Judy were living near her in the Dodge farmhouse while Frances' husband, Jimmy Johnson, served in the Army Air Corps. Little Judy spent much of her time with her grandmother at the manor house, following Matilda around the huge tiled kitchen on Wednesdays—maids' day off—when Matilda enjoyed experimenting with her favorite recipes.

Since the Wilson children, Richard and Barbara, were older than Frances' daughter, Judy had to find her own amusements. None of these included going into her mother's elaborate playhouse, however. That miniature manor remained Frances' private, though unused, domain—its use forbidden to her own daughter as it had been to Richard and Barbara. But Judy swam in the pool in the summertime, skated down near the deer park in the wintertime, and rode around the farm with her mother in a cart pulled by a donkey. She watched with interest as weights were affixed to the hoofs of show ponies so that the ponies would learn to lift their feet high. And she especially liked to lean on the fence and watch Richard as he practiced with the three-gaited horses and the hackney ponies for competition.

The high-spirited Richard occasionally incurred Matilda's displeasure with his pranks. At such times, Matilda insisted it was Alfred's duty to be the disciplinarian. At age thirteen, Richard had taken a cigarette and some gingerale from the private bar opening off Alfred's office. As a punishment, Dick was told to drop his trousers while Alfred hit him across the legs with a whittle stick.

Although the boy was occasionally disciplined with the switch, the Wilsons were kind adoptive parents, indulgent with material things to make the children's lives happier. The children were too young to realize, as yet, that their parents' personal lack of involvement in their lives was more because of the age difference than because of indifference. Both Dick and Barbara were aware, though, that they were expected to meet the high standards set for them by the elder Wilsons. And their mother made it clear to them, as soon as they were old enough to begin to understand the extent of the family's wealth, that both children would be given the best of opportunities in their youth, but they were not to expect the parents to subsidize them in any way in adult life.

A man could accomplish in life whatever he was willing to work for, Alfred often reminded his son—reminding him too that as the son of an impoverished minister, Alfred himself had worked his way through Beloit College and built up a thriving lumber business. The father was fond of relating his early-life experiences to Dick, often repeating his favorite tale of how he had yearned to play tennis as a youth and had had to use a roof shingle for a racquet. Now, he pointed out, he could afford to build his own tennis court if he wished. Young as they were, the children realized, vaguely, that because their father's accomplishments had been minimized by his marriage into the Dodge multimillions, he felt compelled to prove himself a successful manager of Meadow Brook farm and a man who did not need to walk in his wealthy wife's shadow.

Hard work—this was the theme when Dick accompanied Alfred Wilson on any of his jaunts to order new farm machinery or livestock. Usually, though, Alfred would go alone, wearing old clothes and driving an aging car so he could make a good deal on a farmer-to-farmer basis in his purchase of Herefords or pigs.

Regardless of the publicity endowing Matilda with the attributes of a skillful farm manager, the responsibilities of running the farm were Alfred's, and he enjoyed even the small details of management. The Wilsons required farm employees to keep accurate records so that each department of the farm could be audited regularly. The audits determined that the sheep were profitable, but the farm lost money on the pigs, while the Herefords, Belgians, and hackneys, kept only for show purposes, were not expected to show a profit.

The meticulous accounting of the farming was a reflection of the recordkeeping done for every expenditure at Meadow Brook, even those of the children. Every telephone call had to be notated in the proper category in the Wilson fetish for detail.

Switchboard operator Thelma Banta had begun her work at Meadow Brook in 1938, the year Daniel drowned and the year of Frances' marriage to Jimmy Johnson. Thelma had worked first for "Miss Frances" at the indoor riding ring where her employer trained her horses and kept her carriages and rigs. In her late teens when she came to Meadow Brook, the youthful Thelma had liked "Miss Frances" right from the start, even though she had been warned that Frances was haughty and unfriendly. But Thelma was an easy conversationalist and an outgoing person whose congeniality dissolved Frances' customary reserve—a reserve, Thelma believed, that stemmed from Frances' insecurity and her suspicions that people were her friends only because of her wealth. Since most people did not have Thelma's pleasantly extroverted personality, Frances' customary reserve could be dissolved, in their company, only by the glow of Scotch on the rocks.

Going to work for Matilda Wilson at the switchboard in the big house in 1942, Thelma had only one problem—that of Alfred Wilson's penchant for making telephone calls at night and not always indicating under what expense category the call should be filed. When this happened several evenings, Thelma recorded the calls on his personal expense account. Shortly after the month's accounting had been turned in, she saw Wilson approaching the switchboard, glowering fiercely. Why, he demanded, had she charged his personal account with calls that should have been listed under the Guernsey accounting?

Thelma's heart pounded, but she kept her voice steady as she told him she would be pleased to place the calls in the proper category if he would kindly inform her as to which category when he made the calls. Recognizing the reasonableness of her response, Alfred Wilson said no more, and never failed to tell her how his calls should be filed after that.

The switchboard operator found that Matilda Wilson was not only reasonable in her demands but that she was friendly to those of the employees she liked, although she was stern with those she thought shirked their responsibilities. At Christmastime, both Matilda and Frances did their own shopping for individual gifts for employees, keeping records of past gifts so there would be no duplications and saving notations of special interests or preferences. Then, they personally wrapped the gifts. Thelma's gift, her first Christmas at Meadow Brook, was a blue eiderdown comforter similar to one she had admired in the Wilson home.

Life at Meadow Brook was an educational experience to the youthful switchboard operator as she was exposed to Gainsborough and Van Dyck paintings, Sevres vases, Georgian silver pots and trays, Tiffany lamps, antique needlework draperies and Flemish tapestries. Most of all, Thelma was impressed by Mrs. Wilson's imported china with figures of cherubs inscribed in such exquisite detail that "you can even see the fingernails," the girl told her family when she returned home on her free day.

With the passing of time, the switchboard operator grew even more fond of her employer because of Matilda's thoughtfulness. When Thelma's parents celebrated a wedding anniversary, Matilda insisted on sending over her silver punch bowl and serving pieces for the occasion. On the death of Thelma's only sister, Matilda sent a beautiful floral arrangement from her greenhouse. Thelma returned to work after the funeral and slipped quietly into her switchboard office when the butler came into the small room. "Mrs. Wilson wants you to shut off the switchboard and come into the breakfast room," he said. In the Chinese breakfast room flooded with morning sunlight, the two women sat at the table and, over coffee, the older woman tried to comfort the younger one. "There is only one solution to personal tragedy," Matilda said finally. "Work—keep yourself so occupied that you will be so very tired when you go to bed at night that there is no alternative but to go right to sleep."

The advice was the philosophy Matilda had followed ever since Daniel's death as she studied books on self-improvement— *Parliamentary Usage, Minute-A-Day English for Busy People, The Toastmaster's Handbook*, foreign language textbooks, books on horticulture . . . on horses . . . on Bible studies . . . And she immersed herself in work for the Salvation Army, her church, the U.S.O., and other societies.

Travels to other parts of the country and the world kept Alfred and Matilda away from Meadow Brook at intervals, with Alfred's brother and sister-in-law sometimes overseeing the farm and the children. The Don Wilsons were in charge during such an absence when the teenaged Barbara arrived home from her eastern boarding school with two school friends. Eager to show off the beautiful riding horses, Barbara asked whether she and her friends could go riding late that afternoon. When the uncle refused permission, the girls were determined to go anyway. They sneaked down to the riding stables at dusk and took Alfred Wilson's horse, Champ, out of his stall and out to the riding ring where all three girls climbed up on his back. They continued to ride the big horse bareback until the yellow glare of an approaching car's headlights streamed across the ring. The girls slid off the horse and tried to rush him back into the stable. Tossing his head, Champ thumped around and bumped his leg as the girls struggled to pull the animal into his stall.

Thelma was at the switchboard the next morning when the stablemaster called to ask whether Barbara was up yet. "Champ has a lame leg," he explained hurriedly, "and I wonder if any of the young people have been riding him."

Thelma buzzed Barbara's room. Frightened when the telephone operator told her that Champ had been lamed, Barbara admitted that she and her friends had ridden the horse. And now that the veterinarian would have to be called to care for Champ's injury, the girl was doubly fearful. Even if the horse was no longer lame when the Wilsons returned home, the veterinarian's bill would be looked over carefully at the end of the month, and Alfred Wilson would want to know how and why the horse had been injured.

Sympathetic with Barbara's plight, Thelma and the stablemaster mapped out a plan to help the girl. The vet had to be called anyway for a mare in foal. If Champ's injury wasn't too serious, perhaps the veterinarian would put the entire charge on the mare's bill. But if the leg was seriously injured, there was no alternative but to record the injury, and Barbara would have to face the consequences. Fortunately, Champ's injury turned out to be a minor one that could be alleviated by exercising and rubbing with liniment.

With the ending of the war in 1945, Matilda hired a crew of workers and decorators from New York to renovate the west wing of Meadow Brook Hall for its reopening. While the work went on for more than a year, Matilda began to sort and file the mass of memorabilia she had collected over the years. Nothing was to be thrown out—only classified and filed.

Matilda's compulsion for saving and filing memorabilia was matched only by her obsession for charitable work in the years since her son Daniel's death. In gratitude for her twenty-eight years of service with the Salvation Army Women's Auxiliary, national officials of the Salvation Army presented Matilda with the Distinguished Auxiliary Service Cross in 1947. With the sale of the Wilson Theater in the late forties, the last vestiges of Matilda's big-business image had faded, yielding to the philanthropic image she was now acquiring.

In another type of show business, though, Matilda Wilson exhibited considerable competence, as her six-horse team of Belgian draft horses won the 1946 world championship; Dodge Stables' King Commando won the world championship in the pony competition; Meadow Brook's prize bull was a runner-up for the world's championship in that same year.

Since Jimmy Johnson's release from the Army Air Corps after the war, Frances and Jimmy had moved back and forth from Rochester to Frances' winter stables at Aiken, South Carolina. But Frances had recently purchased a historic estate, Castleton Farms at Lexington, Kentucky, where she was assembling one of the most outstanding stables in the country, buying the finest and most expensive harness horses.

The year 1947 was another outstanding one for both the Castleton Farms' harness horses and the Rochester Dodge Stables' show ponies. Frances, riding in the National Horse Show, won the three-gaited championship stake with By Appointment, and Showboat of Dodge Stables won the five-gaited championship stake. Frances' stallion, Victory Song, set a world record for stallions at Springfield, Illinois, in August when he covered the mile in 1:57 3/5, then was named "Harness Horse of the Year." And Frances had even greater hopes for Hoot Mon, the $50,000 colt that won the Hambletonian in 1947 by running the mile in two minutes, finishing the year with earnings of $56,810.

But when Frances and Jimmy went on to the Chicago Horse Show in October, their stables' blue ribbons rated less newspaper space than did Jimmy Johnson's brawl with another horseman. After competing in the $2,000 hackney-pony event, Jimmy went into the owners' lounge, where the winner of the event ridiculed Jimmy's ability as a horseman. Jimmy swung at the other man, and they scuffled. Bystanders ran into the lounge to find Johnson lying on the floor, his face cut and bruised.

Matilda was tight-lipped about the brawl when the story appeared in the newspapers, but she was far more upset the following January when it became public knowledge that Frances was filing suit for divorce from her husband, charging extreme cruelty and desertion. Her husband, Frances stated in her petition, had told her the previous March that their marriage was a mistake. He had been sullen for weeks at a time and had been absent from their home for extended periods without telling his wife where he was going, she claimed.

Although Johnson prepared to contest the divorce, he withdrew his objections and his claims to the custody of the couple's seven-year-old daughter Judith before the hearing was held in April. Blonde hair framing her tanned face, Frances nervously fingered her belted polo coat as she testified with trembling voice in the almost empty courtroom. Since a private agreement on a property settlement had been arranged, the judge granted Frances an uncontested divorce, and Johnson was given the usual rights to visit his daughter.

Matilda's turmoil over the whole affair was heightened by rumors that Frances already had plans to marry again and that her new husband would be a divorced man. After all the years of aloofness from "the other side of the family and all their terrible divorces," it was insupportable to Matilda that the same scandal was to be attached, now, to her own daughter.

When Frances came to the farm, her mother lashed out at her in a fury. "Get your things off the farm!" she ordered, blocking from her mind the realization that when Frances left, her little daughter Judy would go with her.

15

Ignoring Matilda's ultimatum to get her things off the farm, Frances came to Meadow Brook anyway, hoping her mother would gradually alter her opposition to the remarriage in spite of her demonstrated capacity to hold long-term grudges. Frances' fiance, Frederick Van Lennep, was not so sure that Matilda would relent. The man had everything to recommend him—distinguished good looks, impeccable manners, a Dutch family ancestry embellished with a coat-of-arms, an educational background that included prep school training at Phillips Exeter Academy followed by Princeton University, and the professional standing of a Philadelphia advertising executive. But he was a divorced man and the father of a son.

When Frances became Mrs. Van Lennep in January 1949, Matilda and Alfred were wintering in Arizona where they had bought a ranch-style home high on a mountain overlooking Paradise Valley. The Van Lenneps were married in a quiet ceremony in the drawing room of Frances' Castleton Farm manor—a Greek revival mansion built in 1806 and surrounded by hundreds of acres of rolling Kentucky bluegrass. Not grand in the style of Meadow Brook, the Castleton place was a comfortable and gracious kind of home that could be maintained by four or five people instead of requiring a retinue of servants. The house suited Frances' shy, retiring personality, as did her unpretentious home on the Florida oceanside.

Shortly after their marriage, the Van Lenneps made a half-million dollar purchase of mares and yearlings to expand their breeding and racing stock. And honors continued to compile at Castleton as Frances entered a series of competitions—riding her five-gaited champion stallion, Wing Commander; winning a harness championship stake with her bay stallion, Cupid's Beau; winning the three-gaited stake with Meadow Princess and the junior five-gaited stake with Socco. Her reputation as a horsewoman spiraled. By the time the 1952 International Livestock Show was held in Chicago, Frances accumulated an unprecedented sixteen firsts and seventeen seconds in that exhibition.

Frances' riding was curtailed for much of 1951 and 1952 though; the Van Lenneps' first child, Fredericka, was born in 1952, and their second child—a son named John Francis for his grandfather, John Francis Dodge—was born the following year. In this same year of John Francis' birth, the Van Lenneps decided to go into racetrack ownership, buying the tangible assets of the Wolverine Raceway in suburban Detroit plus 22 percent of the stock of the Michigan Racing Association for $888,000 cash.

Their purchase of the two-year-old raceway gave Frances and her husband control over a track boasting more horsemen facilities and customer comforts than any other track in the country—an 8,500 seating capacity, stable accommodations for 785 horses, parking for 10,000 automobiles, an outside mile track for thoroughbreds and an inside oval ½-mile track for harness horses. Van Lennep took personal charge of the night harness races, leasing the facilities to the thoroughbred association for its racing season.

In 1950, Frances' half-sister, Isabel Dodge Sloane, paralleled Frances' successes. Isabel's Brookmeade Stable became the top money-winning stable that year, a repeat of its 1934 accomplishment, as Eddie Arcaro rode Brookmeade's three-year-old Greek Ship to victory in Jamaica, winning the Empire City Gold Cup. And in 1951, the Thoroughbred Club of America paid tribute to Isabel as "the first lady of racing" at a dinner given in her honor.

Greek Ship brought another triumph to Isabel in January 1952 in a setting of lush tropical foliage and pink flamingoes at Hialeah. A crowd of 30,000 jammed the clubhouse overlooking the emerald-green turf as Isabel, accompanied by her sister Winifred, basked in the glory of another Greek Ship victory.

Lavish clubhouse parties and house party celebrations followed each of Isabel's victories. Her horses—First Aid, Capeador, Sailor— won the Bahamas Handicap, the Letellier Handicap, the Gulfstream and Campbell Handicaps, and Isabel's house in Palm Beach continued to be a mecca for houseguests. A Cleveland Amory column told of Isabel being taken to the hospital for an operation while her houseguests remained in the Palm Beach house, using her car and servants, her swimming pool, and even her personal manicurist. When Isabel returned home, she discovered her guests had not known that she had been in the hospital.

The childless Isabel, who had never remarried, lavished affection on her horses and on the several dogs she kept in the house for companionship. Throughout the years, the closeness with her sister

Winifred Seyburn had intensified. The two fashionable women were together frequently—at race tracks, in Palm Beach, and for their annual visit to the plush Main Chance resort in New England. At Christmastime, Isabel liked to come to the Seyburns' Detroit home to share in the family festivities as Winifred's four daughters, their husbands and children, came home for the holidays.

For the rest of the year, Winifred hostessed and attended dinner parties, traveled in various parts of the world, summered at her Manchester-by-the-Sea residence in the East and attained a social stature envied by others and unimagined by her parents—John Dodge and his first wife, Ivy. Caught up in their synthetic world, Winifred and Isabel were not entirely isolated from the more sordid side of life, however. Their brother, John Duval, had been dead now for some years, but the shadow of his ill-fated life reappeared in 1950. In June of that year, his widow Dora crashed her car through a lowered railroad crossing gate in Florida and onto the tracks directly in front of an oncoming train. On the day of the collision, her car had been parked near the tracks five minutes before the railroad warning lights had begun flashing, and as the car moved onto the tracks in front of the approaching train, an unidentified man had been observed running from the scene. An ambulance removed the critically injured woman from the smashed car to a hospital where an operation failed to save her life.

John Duval's only child, his daughter by his first wife, had been married three years previously. But the daughter's ties with her father's sisters, Isabel and Winifred, were almost nonexistent. The daughter and her mother had continued to live quietly in Detroit, removed from the flamboyant lives of the rest of the family.

Matilda Dodge Wilson too would have liked nothing better than to remain aloof from such flamboyancies. She ignored the publicity over Dora Dodge's death and concentrated, instead, on planning her adopted daughter's debut in mid-June 1950, after Barbara graduated from Miss Gill's School in New Jersey. Debut invitations were mailed, including one addressed to Matilda's long-ignored sister, Mrs. John Cline of Rochester. After some deliberation, Amelia's name had been included on the guest list because of Matilda's predilection for observing the socially correct response. After all, she rationalized, Amelia had done the correct thing in coming to offer her condolences at the time of Daniel's death.

But on receiving the invitation, Amelia considered it an offer of reconciliation. Happily, she prepared for the affair and then drove into the line of cars clogging Meadow Brook's circular driveway for the early evening reception. As her car was numbered and whisked away by a hired driver into the meadow where seventeen private detectives guarded the automobiles, Amelia went on into the Great Hall. There, other private detectives watched for party crashers as guests went through the receiving line and out into the garden where a platform had been erected for dancing to the music of Dick Jurgens' orchestra.

"We won't be giving many more affairs like this, so we want this to be perfect," Matilda said as guests admired the hundreds of yellow orchids decorating the hall.

For Amelia Cline, the affair was less than perfect. The lovely blonde debutante, in frosty-white marquisette, was understandably vague in her acknowledgment of the aunt who had appeared out of nowhere. And Amelia was greeted perfunctorily by Matilda, then left alone to wander through the clusters of people, few of whom she recognized.

Long before Barbara had changed into a buttercup-yellow net dress for dancing, Amelia had returned to her home in Rochester. Things had not changed, she reflected sadly. Her sister had not—would not—forgive nor forget.

In spite of her regret over the estrangement from her sister, Amelia had lived a pleasantly relaxed life since her marriage to John Cline when both were in their mid-forties. Amelia had her small inheritance from John Dodge and her savings. Cline had his savings from his twenty-one years of work and management at Meadow Brook farm. It was no longer necessary for him to work, so the pair had traveled companionably by automobile to every part of the country in their years together. When they were at home in Rochester, Amelia passed much of her time in clipping and collecting newspaper items publicizing the life of Matilda and her family.

The pleasure Matilda had taken in Barbara's debut was soon overshadowed by her agitation over her son, Richard. In recent years, as the genial fun-loving Richard had begun college, he had also attained favorite-son status in the family circle. Matilda had reopened Daniel's room and given it to Richard for his use. She also gave him Daniel's last car, a 1937 Studebaker. But now, with only one more year of college ahead of him before graduation from Michigan State University, Richard wanted to get married. Matilda and Alfred looked on the whole affair as a betrayal of their basic philosophy on the part of their son because the girl of his choice was a Catholic. To complicate things further, Richard was planning to be married in the Catholic Church—to become a Catholic convert.

When Richard Wilson and Elinor Baldwin were married in December 1950, none of the Wilson family was present at the Catholic Church in suburban Detroit to see the bride walk down the aisle. Richard had gone into the marriage in full knowledge that the ceremony would sever his relationship with his parents. He had recently seen evidence of Matilda's implacable attitude toward her only sister who had married in opposition to Matilda's will. Yet, he determined, he would live his own life as he chose, even though the doors of Meadow Brook would be closed to his wife and himself.

The newlyweds settled in Lansing until Richard won his degree in business administration in May of 1951, then moved into a new home near Rochester—a home financed with the $25,000 inheritance Richard had received from Daniel's will and with $6,000 borrowed at interest from Frances, to be repaid in monthly installments. During his early teen years, Richard had become good friends with Frances, whose circle of intimates had always been limited. The two younger adopted children, Richard and Barbara, were close because of their childhood ties, but between Frances and the teenaged, pretty Barbara, there was a wariness that precluded close friendship.

Barbara entered Garland Junior College in Boston the September after her debut, majoring in homemaking. To Matilda, who still personally supervised the housekeeping operations at Meadow Brook Hall, homemaking skills were essential for all women.

For Richard, life was real, life was earnest, as he worked at the Ford Motor Company. Soon, Elinor was expecting a child, and there were all the expenses incurred by a young married couple accustomed to a comfortable life.

Although Matilda and Alfred expressed no further interest in their adopted son, Richard began visiting Meadow Brook on weekends. He was ignored, at first, by Matilda, but not actually repulsed, so he continued his visits, hoping Matilda might relent slightly as she had eventually relented with Frances. In spite of the fact that there were no concerned questions from his mother about his family, Richard spoke casually of his children to his parents as his family expanded until he was the father of one son and three daughters. Gradually, the relationship between Richard and his parents regained at least a part of its former closeness, although Richard's wife never was invited to Meadow Brook Hall. Later, when he began taking the children, uninvited, with him on occasional visits, Matilda did not reject their overtures. She never asked them to come to lunch or dinner, however, nor did she ever remember them at Christmastime with gifts in spite of the importance she always placed on the rituals of the holiday season.

Still, when Richard mentioned casually that he and his family had outgrown their original home and were looking for a larger one, his parents suggested they might lend him the money needed for a larger house on the condition that they could see the house first and approve it. He took them over to the house and Matilda, approving the choice as a good and not especially extravagant one, offered to lend him $10,000, without interest.

The Van Lenneps had bought a home in Detroit's old Indian Village where they came annually in time for the late summer opening of their Wolverine Raceway, but Castleton Farm at Lexington still was home to them. They continued to sweep horse-show competitions in both harness and saddle horses. Frances' Wing Commander became the most famous and successful of all American saddlebreds, winning the Louisville championship for seven consecutive years and the international stallion title at Chicago for nine years.

Moneyed Texans, California movie tycoons, Oklahoma oil men, eastern millionaires, and midwestern horsemen made regular treks to Castleton to have their mares bred with champion stallions—Wing Commander, Speedy Scot, Bret Hanover, and others—and Castleton-bred yearlings brought top prices at auction sales.

Some time after the Van Lenneps had bought the Wolverine Raceway in suburban Detroit, Richard went to work for Frances and her husband, becoming general manager, and later, general manager and vice-president of that raceway. When the Van Lenneps built their Pompano Park raceway in Florida, Richard spent his winters there, working at the new track.

Since 1949, Matilda and Alfred had been spending their winters in their Arizona home in Scottsdale. In their late sixties now, both the Wilsons were active people. Alfred, tall and spare as ever, had become professorial-looking in the style of Woodrow Wilson, with a long, gaunt face and white hair. Honors came his way too. Presented with the Silver Keystone Award by the Boys Club of America, he was then asked to state his religious precepts as a part of a Detroit newspaper's "What My Religion Means to Me" series. Alfred responded promptly:

> Someone has aptly said, "Service is the rent you pay for the space you occupy in the world" and I feel the service is often better by reason of a religious base. . . . I do believe in a hereafter and immortality, but goodness has its own reward. I like to feel that my religious experience and practice in this life are going to be continued and fortified in a triumphant life hereafter and that death is not a tragedy.

Matilda was quoted also in the newspapers on the occasion of the dedicating of the Dodge Memorial Hall of Industry at the Detroit Historical Museum in October 1952. The 150-by-44-foot memorial hall had been built with a $135,000 gift to the museum's building program by both Dodge families for the establishment of a continuing display of all types of Detroit industry, with an "Automotive Hall of Fame" as a permanent feature. The senior Horace E. Dodge's personal 1919 coupe had been placed on display, and although the names of Anna and her son Major Horace Dodge, along with Matilda Dodge Wilson and her daughter Frances, were listed on the memorial programs, only Matilda was present from the family to speak on behalf of the donors at the dedication ceremony.

"I believe in tradition so long as it means progress and advancement," Matilda told the assemblage. "I believe in history if knowledge of the past helps face the challenge of the future."

Two months later, the newspapers carried another announcement from the Wilsons—an announcement of the engagement of their daughter Barbara to Thomas Eccles of New York, Since this was the first engagement within the family of which Matilda had approved in a number of years, elaborate plans were made for the wedding, which was to be held in Meadow Brook Hall's drawing room the following year. Matilda's sister, Amelia Cline, received an invitation as she had to Barbara's debut. But the cool reception Matilda had given her at the debut was still fresh in her mind. Amelia was not present that June evening to see the pretty blue-eyed bride, in ivory Duchesse satin and imported French Alencon lace, sweep down Meadow Brook's great staircase on the arm of her father. But Amelia collected all the published accounts of the wedding and added them to her collection.

When the newlyweds left for a Hawaiian honeymoon, Alfred and Matilda were alone at Meadow Brook Hall. Although the young people had been away at schools and camps for much of their lives, this was the first time that the hall had not been the home of one or more of the Dodge or Wilson children.

At Michigan State University's ninety-seventh commencement exercises in 1955, the seventy-year-old Matilda Wilson was awarded an honorary Doctor of Laws degree. As the prestigious award was made, there were few, if any, people in the auditorium who realized that this small and lively woman's formal education had ended with eighth-grade graduation. Matilda, who had calmly presided at meetings of Michigan political dignitaries and corporations' boards of directors and who had delivered speeches to the State Board of Agriculture, was now far removed from her early life as the shy and moody young daughter of a saloonkeeper.

Because of the recipient's known penchant for philanthropic endowment grants, there were those who looked askance at the conferring of the degree. But the facts were irrefutable. This was a poised and capable woman—a self-made woman, aided and spurred on by the John Dodge millions . . . a woman whose business-school training after the eighth grade had been only the miniscule beginnings of a self-education plan followed throughout her life. She had taken private lessons for a rudimentary understanding of music, and she had read and studied foreign languages, history, geography, architecture, and a wide variety of other subjects. And she had stacked the shelves of Meadow Brook's library with practical books chosen for content rather than priceless volumes chosen to impress visitors.

Still, in spite of Matilda's air of self-possession, she had never managed to rid herself of her early sensitivities and fears of rejection. Wary of people prying into her background, she consistently referred to herself as the daughter of a "merchant," informing those who asked about her schooling that she had been "privately tutored."

By the time the last of the children had married, Matilda decided to build a smaller, modern home on her Meadow Brook estate and to use Meadow Brook Hall only for her more lavish entertaining. The new home, named Sunset Terrace, was a contemporary pink brick home built in a circular style so that each room had rounded corners. Opposite the living room fireplace of Tennessee marble, deep rose draperies framed a semicircular windowed wall with a sweeping view of the horses grazing in the pastures.

From Sunset Terrace, the Wilsons made frequent business trips to various localities, went out to Bar Harbor, Maine, in the summer, and to their Arizona home in the winter—keeping two pilots on the payroll for their trips on the blue Super 18 Beechcraft plane Matilda had bought.

The Wilsons were still at Meadow Brook, however, on a sunny December day in 1956 when Durward Varner of Michigan State University visited their home by invitation. For some time, Matilda had been considering the disposition of her Meadow Brook estate, evaluating various plans for its conversion now that she and Alfred were in their seventies. When it was pointed out to her that Oakland County was the largest county in Michigan without an institution of higher learning, Matilda began thinking of donating Meadow Brook to Michigan State University for a college campus. Because of her years of association with the university while she had served on the State Board of Agriculture and because Meadow Brook itself was a farm, Matilda deemed the liaison with the university, which had specialized in agricultural courses, a most appropriate one.

Holding two dozen chrysanthemums of dinner-plate size, grown in the Wilson greenhouse, Varner left Meadow Brook Hall with a sense of amazement at the Wilsons' casual offer of 1,400 acres for the college, plus $2 million for the building program. The Wilsons had stipulated only that they would retain the title to Meadow Brook Hall, Sunset Terrace, and 127 acres of the estate until their deaths, when everything would go to the university.

With this gift of the estate to the university, the Wilsons moved their farming operations to a large farm in Fowlerville, Michigan. Matilda's hefty Belgian draft horses were moved into gleaming white horse barns on the new farm while the harnesses for the Belgians, valued at more than $1,000 each, were stored in heated and air-conditioned glass cases for protection of the chrome, brass, and leather fittings.

On a pleasantly warm afternoon in May 1958, the diminutive Matilda pushed a silver shovel into the earth in a ground-breaking ceremony for Michigan State University's first building in Oakland County. "This meadow is close to our hearts," Matilda said, going on to tell of the pride she and Mr. Wilson had taken in their farm products and stock. But now Matilda and Alfred would be content to watch the university grow up around them.

That fall—a year before undergraduate classes began at Oakland University—Matilda's interest in the fledgling school was so keen she enrolled in the first adult evening course, an efficient-reading class conducted in one of Meadow Brook's converted chicken houses. Honors continued to come to Matilda as she became the first woman to be elected elder to serve on the Session of the First Presbyterian Church in January 1959 and then became the president of the Women's National Farm and Garden Association that spring. In March, she was named Detroit's "Volunteer of the Year" and commended especially for her work with the Salvation Army. "The Army's work has never been glorified," Matilda said in reply. "It approaches areas other organizations never touch and deals with broken minds and broken people to help them find themselves."

In mid-June, though, Matilda took time from her philanthropic work to plan a debut for her granddaughter Judy Johnson—Frances' daughter of her first marriage—as the Van Lenneps came with Judy to Meadow Brook. More than one-thousand guests came to Meadow

Brook Hall on the day of the debut for afternoon and evening receptions, where they were greeted by Matilda, Frances, and Judy—the latter in a pale silvery-blue gown that blended with the sterling silver rose theme.

Judy, who had completed her first year at Transylvania College in Kentucky, had been Matilda's favorite grandchild ever since the girl had lived at Meadow Brook farm with her mother while her father had been in the air force. To Matilda, it was important that Judy should have the same kind of lavish debut party at Meadow Brook Hall that Barbara had had, even though Judy's mother and stepfather were planning a debut party of their own for their daughter at Christmastime.

But mingled with the more enjoyable segments of day-to-day life—the parties, the honors, the travels—were the inexorable reminders of changes that continued to come to the family as the years took their toll of their lives. Winifred Dodge Seyburn's husband, Wesson, died in 1961. And the year previous to that, John Cline—Amelia's husband—had died. Amelia was entirely alone now. At the time of her marriage to Cline and the estrangement from her sister, Amelia had withdrawn from most of the social life in Rochester, feeling that this withdrawal would free her Rochester friends from the embarrassment of making a choice between the wealthy, socially prominent Matilda Wilson and her younger sister. In the years that followed, Amelia retained very few friends in Rochester—she and her husband traveled to all parts of the country.

Now that Amelia was widowed, those few friends saw no reason why the two sisters should not be reconciled. But Amelia had already been rebuffed several times by her sister. It was up to Matilda, now, Amelia felt, to make any peace overtures.

With some behind-the-scenes maneuvering by Amelia's friends, the two sisters finally reconciled in 1961, thirty years after the estrangement. The reconciliation meant a great deal to Amelia as, once again, she was permitted to live on the fringes of her sister's eventful life . . . on hand to see Matilda open Meadow Brook Hall for a benefit ball for scholarship funds for the university . . . watching as Matilda took part in ground-breaking ceremonies for the university's first dormitory.

Meadow Brook Hall usually was the scene of the family's Christmas reunion. But when, in 1961, the Van Lenneps did not come north for the holidays, Christmas dinner was served at Sunset Terrace with the Wilsons' daughter, Barbara Eccles, her husband, and children as guests. The Eccleses and their five youngsters were now living in suburban Detroit while Barbara's husband worked for Kelsey Hayes.

In her preoccupation with each day's activities, Matilda evidenced no desire to reactivate any of the relationships reaching back to earlier days, about which her younger sister Amelia liked to reminisce. On one of Richard's visits to Meadow Brook, he was surprised when his mother asked him to drive her to Woodlawn Cemetery. As Richard parked the car on the curving road fronted by the stone sphinxes that guarded the mausoleum, the two got out of the car, walked up the steps, and Matilda unlocked the heavy door. Inside, light from a stained-glass window outlined the shadowy form of a box set on the shelf below the window. Matilda walked over to the window and stared at the slightly damaged cardboard mailing box, then reached out for it. Ashes dribbled out of one corner of the container.

Instantly suspicious, Matilda went over to the cemetery office and queried officials about the box. They knew nothing about it, they insisted. Matilda was quite sure, now, whose ashes they were. Della Dodge Eschbach, who had died out in California, had joined her brothers, John and Horace, in death. And there was no doubt in Matilda's mind as to who had placed the ashes there. Anna had the other key to the mausoleum and, for this time, Matilda's sister-in-law had prevailed.

But Matilda did not forget Anna's deception. Even after reading newspaper accounts of the ninety-year-old Anna Dodge having fallen and broken her hip, Matilda did not go to see Anna—nor did she make any mention of Anna's injury to her sister Amelia.

Inevitably, however, there were developments that demanded a response from Matilda. In March 1962, Isabel Dodge Sloane died in Good Samaritan Hospital at Palm Beach. Winifred Seyburn wanted her sister's body placed with her father and mother, John and Ivy Dodge, in the family mausoleum. Informed of Winifred's wishes, Matilda gave her consent, reasoning that, after all, Isabel had lived an unscandalous though lonely life in the midst of all the partying, the golfing, the grouse shooting. . .

Less than three years previously, Brookmeade's Sword Dance had been named horse of the year, and the following year Isabel's filly, Bowl of Flowers, had been named three-year-old filly of the year. Now, at Isabel's death at age sixty-four, it was suggested to track officials at Gulfstream Park that it might be fitting to drop the infield flags to half-mast to commemorate Isabel Sloane's passing. But a spokesman for the track shook his head. "The brass vetoed it," he said. "Said nobody'd know who she was."

Within days of Isabel's death, Alfred Wilson suffered a heart attack at the Wilsons' home in Arizona. When Alfred appeared to be recovering, Matilda flew home to Rochester to get the forty-four room Sunset Terrace ready for her husband's return, only to be called back to Arizona because his condition was worsening.

Alfred died on April 6 at age 79. His funeral services were held in the First Presbyterian Church in Detroit, where Alfred and Matilda had met almost forty years previously. Proper mourning attire had always been a matter of consequence to the Rausch sisters. The younger sister, newly reconciled with the older, was anxious that she should give Matilda no cause for offense. Should she buy new black clothing to wear to her brother-in-law's funeral, she worried, or would it be properly respectful if she wore the coat she already had? She finally risked not buying a new coat and noted, with some relief, that Matilda did not indicate any displeasure with her choice of apparel.

Amelia took her place with the family at the church and then in the funeral procession as it moved on to Woodlawn Cemetery where Alfred's body was placed in the smaller, pink stone Wilson mausoleum Matilda had had constructed next to the huge Dodge edifice.

16

Matilda had loved Alfred very much, but she faced her bereavement as bravely as she had faced the losses of her first husband and two children. Alfred had left small bequests to employees, to his favorite charities, and to Matilda's daughter Frances and granddaughter Judy Johnson. He had willed $10,000 to his son Richard, and $15,000 plus some $40,000 of insurance to his daughter Barbara. But most of his $571,000 estate went to his widow and to the Matilda R. Wilson Fund—the foundation set up by Matilda in the 1940s for charitable purposes.

Matilda, 78, and Amelia, 75, who saw each other more frequently after Alfred's death, looked more alike in their late years than they had in earlier years. Both were small women—Matilda still a bit taller and heavier. Both had sharp brown eyes and alert minds, and each tiny woman moved with the quick steps of an active and vigorous person.

When Matilda wanted to make a visit to Niles to see her first husband's birthplace, Amelia accompanied her. Hoping to find traces of the Dodge family, the sisters were disappointed to discover that the town had managed to lose or forget anything that might have given the Dodges a measure of immortality. In the cemetery record books, the name of Maria Casto Dodge, mother of the brothers, was followed by empty blanks some caretaker had neglected to fill. The Historical Museum had not a single item in its files under *Dodge*. The town newspaper had only one photograph of a modern Dodge car filed away under the family name—nothing else, although *Niles Star* early stories about the Dodges made up collections in Detroit. Old-timers in town were eager to talk of their famous favorite sons—Ring Lardner, Montgomery Ward, and a remarkably successful eye doctor named Bonine. But Dodge was a family about which no one knew anything. And while Henry Ford had built his "village" in Dearborn to immortalize his memory in his hometown, the only monument to the Dodge

194

brothers in Niles was the standpipe, to which anyone inquiring about the Dodges would be directed with a vague, "they lived somewhere in that direction."

In the October following Alfred's death, Matilda was invited to have lunch at the Oakland University cafeteria. She was pleasantly surprised when the room divider was drawn back to reveal a large birthday cake and the presence of the university students, who sang "Happy Birthday" to their energetic seventy-nine-year-old benefactress.

She was honored again in January at the clubhouse of the Federation of Women's Clubs of Metropolitan Detroit as she was presented with the Rosalind award. Named "Mrs. Federation," Matilda was cited as "a woman of intelligence, wit and enterprise . . . education, philanthropy, social welfare, culture, and Christian religion have prospered and been served by her blessings."

At the time the first group of seniors graduated from Oakland University, Matilda, who was an honorary charter member of the class, feted the graduates with a dinner-dance at Meadow Brook Hall. Although there were more than one-hundred graduates in the class, Matilda greeted each one by name and presented each graduate with a gift—a diamond-studded class ring or pin. She fondly referred to the students as her "family", although she was indignant when some of the students climbed the iron fence separating the acreage she had reserved for her personal use from the university grounds. Trespassers were warned they faced expulsion from the university. Matilda lived, now, back at the manor house into which she had moved from Sunset Terrace following Alfred's death.

Still preferring to spend much of the winter in Arizona, Matilda began urging her sister Amelia to move out to Sun City, Arizona, and to buy a home there. Since her husband's death, Amelia had sold her home and moved into an apartment in Rochester. "The Sun City climate will be healthy for you Melie," Matilda persisted. Assuming that her older sister wanted her companionship in Arizona, Amelia still hesitated to make the move. She enjoyed living in Rochester but finally agreed to go out to Sun City rather than risk her sister's displeasure. The two sisters flew out to Sun City in 1963, and Amelia settled into the home she had purchased there with $17,500 that Matilda loaned her—the debt to be paid at regular intervals.

Richard, who had agreed to drive Amelia's car out to Arizona for her, took his wife, Elinor, along for companionship. On their arrival in Arizona, they stayed at Matilda's home, then left with Matilda for the return trip to Detroit on her private plane. Matilda, who had completely ignored Elinor's presence in her home, now ignored her presence in the plane even though they sat directly opposite each other as the plane flew eastward.

Left alone in Sun City, Amelia was lonely. She continued to live a quiet existence, her loneliness broken only by summer trips to Meadow Brook and by what turned out to be very infrequent visits from her sister to Amelia's Sun City home, even when Matilda was staying in Arizona.

The Eccles family also had moved out to Arizona, where Barbara's husband had gone into the real estate business. But they had not lived in Arizona long when a family feud erupted over what Matilda believed to be her son-in-law's use of her reputation to enhance his own business dealings. The rift between Barbara and her mother was heightened when the Eccleses separated and Barbara went into a business of which Matilda thoroughly disapproved—the nightclub business. Quickly, another member of the family was alienated from the aging but no less adamant Matilda.

In the same year that Amelia moved to Sun City, the Van Lenneps came from Pompano Beach to Meadow Brook to spend Christmas with Matilda. They had had a good year—their three-year-old trotter, Speedy Scot, had won the harness horse of the year citation. The horse, running always with his tongue lolling from his mouth, had won the Triple Crown of the Yonkers Futurity, the Hambletonian, and the Kentucky Futurity, finishing the year of 1963 with earnings of $244,252. He had clocked 1.56 4/5 for the mile—a record time for a three-year-old colt.

Matilda, now eighty years old, still drove her show ponies on occasions such as the ground-breaking ceremonies for a new building at the Michigan State Fairgrounds in February 1964. For the ceremony, Matilda had sent her two champion Belgian plow horses—some 5,000 pounds of horseflesh—to put on an exhibition. Seven grooms and a trainer accompanied the two horse vans that brought the Belgians and Matilda's prize-winning hackney pony, Starlight, to the fairgrounds. Mane bright with red ribbons and tail arched high and wrapped in white curler papers, Starlight was led down the ramp, and Matilda was helped into the buggy. Slipping on her yellow riding gloves and picking up her whip, she whisked around the arena several times to the tune of "Happy Days are Here Again" blasted by a Dixie band.

Matilda shared her love of horses with Frances' eldest daughter, Judy Johnson. Judy, who had not been living at her mother's home in recent months, began living with her grandmother not long after Alfred's death. It was exhilarating to Matilda to watch Judy canter across Meadow Brook's pastures on one of the eight thoroughbreds Matilda had bought for her granddaughter. Deciding that Ju' needed a track where she could train her thoroughbreds, Matilda ordered a racetrack constructed at the north edge of her property.

The university continued to grow up around Meadow Brook Hall with the October 1965 dedication of a classroom-office four-storied building with an adjoining lecture hall and an art gallery. Later that month, Matilda applied the first trowel of mortar to the Matilda R. Wilson Hall that was under construction. By this time, there were 1,974 students enrolled in nearly one-hundred courses at Oakland University. Amelia came to spend some time at Meadow Brook Hall in the summer of 1966, happy to get away from Sun City now that she realized her sister was so totally involved with student activities at Oakland that she had neither time nor inclination for other things. During this visit, she was asked by Matilda to accompany her to the Dodge mausoleum at Woodlawn Cemetery. The two sisters were the only observers that summer day as workmen removed the coffins of Matilda's two children—Anna Margaret and Daniel—from the Dodge edifice and interred them in the nearby Wilson mausoleum with Alfred, where there were niches for only four coffins. Matilda had decided that she would be the fourth occupant. She felt she belonged with Alfred, she confided to her sister, because she had lived with him longer.

Amelia was troubled by this decision. John Dodge had fathered Matilda's three children. His millions had brought to his widow the status and life that she relished. Yet Amelia knew that Matilda had loved Alfred Wilson . . .

Matilda also loved her granddaughter Judy Johnson. But the grandmother was concerned about Judy's interest in a veterinarian who was several years older than she. Much more upsetting, in Matilda's opinion—the veterinarian was a divorced man. But her warnings to Judy went unheeded. One day in early August, Judy simply walked out of Meadow Brook Hall and married the veterinarian.

Immediately, Matilda ordered work stopped on the race track construction at Meadow Brook. With intentions of completely severing her relationship with her granddaughter, Matilda signed over to Judy the eight thoroughbred horses the girl had ridden and canceled a $17,000 debt Judy owed her. This was to be the end of the relationship as far as Matilda was concerned.

She refused to change her mind—even after the passing of time when Judy had a baby and wanted to bring the baby to her grandmother's home. Matilda was curt to other members of the family who tried to effect a reconciliation between grandmother and grand-daughter. She would not see Judy or the child, Matilda insisted.

But there was little time in her busy life for brooding over es-trangements. She was pleased when, in the fall of 1966, the first Matilda R. Wilson Honor Scholarship was set up by Friends of Oakland. With a vitality unusual for an eighty-three-year-old woman, she drove her own car out to Arizona that winter, accompanied by her secretary. Her arrival in Arizona meant very little to Amelia, however, because Matilda spent only a half-day with her sister in Sun City that season.

In the spring, Matilda served as honorary chairman of the $1.8 million building-fund campaign for the Salvation Army, climaxing more than fifty years of service to that organization. In July, she was presented with the Distinguished Citizen Award from the City of Detroit as she opened Meadow Brook Hall to more than 300 members of the Detroit Historical Society. Forty hostesses, personally in-structed by Matilda in the history and architecture of the huge estate, guided visitors on a tour of the manor and its grounds. "I have taken great pride in telling that this home is an American product," Matilda emphasized. Although the home was built in the style of an English castle, with many rooms that were replicas of rooms in Kensington Palace, the materials and workmanship were American. This was in sharp contrast, Matilda felt, with Anna Dodge's Rose Terrace—French in design and built by foreign workmen with imported materials.

When Matilda left Meadow Brook Hall in September 1967 for a trip to Europe, Oakland University was a thriving campus of 3,800 students. Among its new buildings were the Kresge Library, the Ket-tering Magnetics Laboratory, the Matilda R. Wilson Hall, and the Dodge Hall of Engineering.

Accompanied by her Fowlerville farm manager and his wife, Matilda planned to go to Belgium to look over Belgian draft horses to stock her farm. But they had been in Brussels only five days when Matilda was taken to the hospital with complaints of an upset stomach. The upset stomach turned out to be a serious heart attack. At two o'clock the next morning—September 18—Matilda died in the Brussels hospital.

On news of the death, three Oakland University students were dis-patched from Detroit's Metropolitan Airport to accompany the body back to Detroit where the family was assembling at Meadow Brook Hall. Orders were issued that campus flags should fly at half-mast un-til October 17—the date that would have been the eighty-fourth birthday of the university's benefactress. The Oakland University chorus prepared to sing at her funeral and at a campus memorial service, at which time the Detroit Symphony Orchestra also would perform in recognition of Matilda Wilson's support of the Meadow Brook Music Festival held each summer.

Funeral services for Matilda Rausch Dodge Wilson were held at the First Presbyterian Church of Detroit. As the mourners filed out of the church, the funeral procession rolled out Woodward Avenue to Woodlawn Cemetery where the coffin was placed in the fourth, and last, niche in the pink stone mausoleum, beside the bodies of Alfred Wilson and Anna Margaret and Daniel Dodge.

Following Matilda's death in 1967, newspapers paid tribute to the woman and her accomplishments and to her many acts of philanthropy. The bulk of her estate, with its assets of $20 million, was to go to the Matilda R. Wilson Fund. Her Meadow Brook Hall was now to be turned over to Oakland University with whatever furnishings seemed appropriate for the hall's use "as a cultural center," although no funds had been provided for the manor's upkeep.

Frances was allowed to take certain items from the house—some clothing, family portraits, the jewelry her father, John Dodge, had purchased, and personal things which had been hers while she had lived at Meadow Brook. But as Matilda had indicated during her lifetime, very little of her fortune was allotted to family members who had been unresponsive to her management. To Frances' eldest daughter, Judy, the grandmother left nothing at all. So this omission would not be overlooked, Matilda specifically made known her disapproval of her granddaughter in her will.

Richard and Barbara each were left $10,000 and small debts owing to Matilda were canceled. However, Matilda established generous trust funds for their nine children that would see them through college. And to her eighty-year-old sister Amelia, Matilda left only $7,500, plus cancellation of the $7,500 still owing on Amelia's Sun City home.

Although three veteran employees, in their seventies and eighties, were given incomes of $100 to $150 a month, and various friends and employees received amounts averaging several hundred dollars each, only a small percentage of Matilda's estate went to family and friends acquired in eighty-three years of living.

Amelia, who was still living in Arizona at the time of her sister's sudden death, had read the news of the fatal heart attack in her

Arizona newspapers. Distraught over the loss of her only close relative, she had phoned Barbara's Arizona home only to learn that Barbara had already left on a flight to Detroit for the funeral.

Amelia flew to Detroit with Matilda's Arizona housekeeper as a companion, joining Frances, Barbara, and Richard at Meadow Brook Hall. Although her nieces and nephews, grandnieces and grandnephews, were considerate of her, Amelia realized that these younger relatives of Matilda—arbitrarily separated from Amelia by the decades of estrangement—had no real ties with her.

Returning to Arizona the day after the funeral, Amelia picked up a Detroit newspaper to read the harsh facts of Matilda's will. Amelia had not anticipated becoming a wealthy woman by terms of her sister's will. But she had expected that her older sister would not leave her unprovided for in the event that she might become ill . . . bedridden . . . hospitalized. There was no family to aid; few close friends to feel much concern. And Amelia had always reassured herself, even during the years of estrangement from her sister, that Matilda would always provide for her when and if she needed help. Now she faced the reality of being eighty years old and confronting the specter of declining health and the infirmities of old age with little security.

Her worries were justified, she found, as she opened a letter from the administrators of her sister's estate, which confirmed the amount of her inheritance, already reported in the newspaper account. To Amelia, the letter was more than a confirmation of the sense of financial insecurity that she now felt so keenly. It confirmed Amelia's dawning realization that she had given up many things that were important to her in life in the childish hope of "pleasing" her sister, only to find herself isolated in her late years of life.

Almost a year after the filing of Matilda's will, Frances, Richard, and Barbara began a desultory challenge to the will, asking that the Wilson fund be dissolved and the money divided among them. Six months later, the court ruled that the will showed "an unusual indication of clear intent by the testatrix of how she wanted to distribute her properties."

There was little left to do, then, but dispose of the estate's assets according to Matilda's directions. First on the auction block was the collection of old master paintings she had acquired in the 1930s. Fifteen paintings were to be sold, including those of Van Dyke, Joshua Reynolds, and Corots, and a magnificent Rembrandt valued at a half-million dollars. But when the Rembrandt did not sell because the bidders did not meet the reserve price, the painting was donated, along with $80,000 from the Matilda R. Wilson Fund, to establish a Wilson Memorial gallery at the Detroit Institute of Arts.

The executors now began the business of sorting out the seventy years of savings preserved by Matilda at Meadow Brook. Fifty-year-old grocery bills and Christmas cards were dumped and burned. Objets d'art were sorted out, and those judged inappropriate for use by the university were tagged to be sold at auction.

Oakland University, which would later become an independent institution, began to wrestle with the problem of how best to use the mansion and finance its upkeep. University planners felt that the estate should become a national resource so its art treasures, its history, its beautiful gardens and woods, and the mansion itself would be a retreat available to the public and an attraction for tourists. The university opened the mansion as a conference and educational center in September 1971, but because the manor was not to be used in a degree-granting program, tax funds could not be used to support it. The estate, which cost $150 a day just to stand idle, would have to become self-sufficient.

A guild of Detroit-area women, including wives of top automotive executives, gave the manor its support as the 275-woman group planned tours and activities—gourmet parties, garden tours, tours of Frances' playhouse, art shows, symphony programs, fashion shows, and a Christmas Walk at Meadow Brook Hall that attracted 10,000 people to the manor in a single week and raised $40,000. The women of the guild continued to inventory the contents of the house, polish the silver, mend the linens, and dust the bric-a-brac—housekeeping chores many of them delegated to household help in their own homes—to save the salaries of the twenty-five employees that customarily staffed the estate.

On January 24, 1971, three years after Matilda's death, Frances became very ill in Boca Raton, Florida, immediately after the Van Lenneps celebrated their twenty-second wedding anniversary. Only a few hours after being admitted to a local hospital, Frances died, at fifty-six years of age, of an acute diffuse hemorrhagic disorder.

Frances' triumphs were detailed in *The Horseman,* in which she was extolled as one of the finest horsemen or horsewomen who had ever lived. Her establishment of a two-sport dynasty at Castleton Farms had never been equaled, the magazine claimed. In July of the year of her death, Frances was elected to the Hall of Fame of the Trotter.

A second triumph for the shy, insecure Frances was revealed when her will was probated. The money, always a barometer of approval or disapproval, indicated that she had found fulfillment in her marriage to Van Lennep. After certain deductions, she willed him half her estate and named him trustee along with the bank for the remaining half of the estate, which was to go to their two children.

Frances' daughter Judy, child of her first marriage, was left nothing in the will, but the will indicated that Frances had set up a trust fund at the time of her divorce from Johnson that designated her first husband a life beneficiary of the trust that would revert to Judith on her father's death. And, of course, John Dodge's own provisions ascertained that Judy would inherit, along with her half-brother and half-sister, Frances' undistributed share of John's fortune after the death of all his children.

With Frances' death, there was only John Dodge's eldest daughter, by his first wife, still alive. And the family of this daughter, Winifred Dodge Seyburn, had recently been shocked and saddened by the death of one of Winifred's grandsons in the war in Vietnam. There had been a flash of the old John-and-Horace Dodge type of generosity in the will written by this young soldier who had left several thousand dollars to two of his army buddies who had shared his Vietnam ordeal.

In early January 1980, Winifred Dodge Seyburn died, at age eighty-five, thereby terminating the $44-million John Dodge trust fund. Since the Dodge will specified that the trust should, finally, be divided among his children's "heirs," an important legal question arose. Was it John Dodge's intention that his money should go to his grandchildren, or was it his intention that any and all legal heirs of his children should share in the money?

As expected, the seven children of Winifred and Frances filed claims for shares of the Dodge trust. So, too, did an eighth grandchild—the daughter of the formerly disinherited John Duval Dodge. In a less expected move, lawyers representing the Matilda R. Wilson Fund claimed that since Matilda was her deceased son Daniel's legal heir when he died, that her own trust fund should benefit from the division of the John Dodge money. Another attorney filed a claim for Frances' husband. Matilda's two adopted children (Wilsons) also filed for a share of the money. And the widow of Daniel Dodge, dead since 1938 after a thirteen-day marriage, filed still another claim to a part of the fortune. The judge's decision awarded the bulk of the money to the eight grandchildren and to the deceased Frances' husband.

Even though all of Meadow Brook and the great "Wilson" fortune had been produced by John F. Dodge, Matilda had chosen to give her philanthropic foundation the name she had taken in her second marriage. One of the earlier Matilda R. Wilson Fund donations was a gift of $1.5 million for the building of a new aviary at the Detroit Zoo so that birds could be released from cages to fly free and unfettered. Such freedom was denied to Matilda's sister Amelia, however. In her eighties, she had become a kind of prisoner in her rented apartment. Alone in the apartment, she continued to hold to her savings in fear of an emergency situation. Longing to hire a car and a driver to take her on outings, she denied herself these pleasures because of her fears of spending her savings.

Matilda, perhaps, had not envisioned this paradox. Nor had she envisioned the thousands of visitors who came to Meadow Brook Hall with eager questions about the Dodge family. Guides, who had absorbed the life history of the Wilsons to dramatize the tour through the manor for visitors, found the curiosity of visitors contagious. They too were gripped with an eagerness to find out more about the flamboyant, yet strangely elusive, history of the Dodges.

On the campus of Oakland University, parts of sculptured columns and cornices from the old, never-completed John F. Dodge mansion in Grosse Pointe are now being used as giant flower pots and benches to embellish the landscape. The sculptured stonework had been moved, on Matilda's orders, out to Meadow Brook, where she had planned to use it as a part of her new home, just as she had used other architectural details of the old mansion for the new manor.

Inside the Meadow Brook manor itself, the large mahogany desk—at which John Dodge sat and directed the affairs of Dodge Brothers' plant—has been carted down from the third floor storage room and is ensconced in Alfred Wilson's study. The portrait of the blue-eyed, square-faced John Dodge continues to dominate the manor's red-carpeted drawing room. And the memory of the strong and powerful John Francis Dodge seems to have emanated from the shades of the dead to take possession of beautiful Meadow Brook Hall as if the huge mansion has become, at last, the completed showplace that he had once planned.

Part III
ANNA

17

In the months following Horace Elgin Dodge's death in December 1920, his widow, Anna, spent little time at Rose Terrace where every room seemed alive with memories of her husband and of earlier, happier days. Delphine Ione and James H. R. were living in an apartment in Philadelphia, and there was only the twenty-year-old Horace Jr. at home now to console his mother.

Horace Jr. was not always a consolation, however, because of his penchant for making newspaper headlines. Within a month after his father's death, he was arrested twice on charges of speeding—the second time for swerving dangerously close to people dismounting from Jefferson Avenue streetcars. Flaunting the gold deputy's badge that had been his father's, Horace threatened to arrest the policeman for interfering with county business. As Horace reached into his pocket for a gun to reinforce his threat, the policeman grabbed for the gun and a bullet hit the ground. Taken to the police station, the badge-sporting Horace was soon released by Sheriff Coffin who termed the affair a "misunderstanding."

Fleeing the loneliness of Rose Terrace, Anna left for Florida the first of February with Delphine Ione and her husband, Jimmy Cromwell. In the midst of Palm Beach social life, Anna, in mourning, remained secluded with plenty of time to worry about young Horace, who was mixing with a hard-drinking young set. If only her husband had lived long enough to guide their son and to get him established in the plant—this was Anna's lament. When the Albert Knowlson family came from Detroit to Florida for a brief visit, Anna was pleased to have Lois Knowlson, Horace's fiancee, stay on with them at Palm Beach. Lois' presence and influence could keep the good-natured and exuberant Horace away from too much night life, Anna hoped.

Anna and Horace Jr. returned to Detroit in early April for a christening ceremony for the large yacht, *Delphine II*—the ship planned and dreamed of by Horace Sr. who had had the ship's keel laid on the day of his daughter's wedding. On the morning of the ceremony, spectators began coming through the gates of the Great Lakes Engineering Works in River Rouge until some one-thousand people lined the sides of the slip into which the yacht would plunge.

Looking up at the white-hulled, five-deck ship with its bright yellow smoke stack, the spectators talked among themselves of the cost of the boat—a reported $1.5 million—and of the vessel's magnificent fittings and interior . . . a mahogany stateroom for the owners, a walnut music room with fireplace, and a $60,000 pipe organ. Equipped with eight small boats, two power launches, a service launch and an express launch with a speed of forty mph, the gray superstructure loomed high above the people who waited. Although Horace Dodge had wanted his yacht to be even larger, the designer had limited its size so that the *Delphine II*'s length of 257 feet, 8 inches, and its beam of 35 feet, 3 inches, could be accommodated by the Welland Canal's length-limitation of 260 feet.

Just before noon, Anna Dodge arrived at the shipyards, a mourning veil partly obscuring her face. Accompanied by Horace Jr., Delphine, and James H. R., the Stotesburys, her sister-in-law Matilda, and the ship's designer, Anna mounted the christening platform below the ship's prow. Delphine, her svelte figure hidden in the depths of a warm coat, stood near the towering bow, a beribboned bottle of champagne in her hand. As workmen knocked away the props from beneath the hull and ran for shelter, Delphine Ione leaned forward and smashed the bottle across the bow. Tugboats and freighters blew their whistles and band music blared as the new ship slid down and struck the river in cascades of water. The *Delphine II* listed heavily, river water rushing over its decks, then came upright, listed again, then righted itself, riding free in the swell of the water and in the wreckage of its props.

Still disconsolate over the loss of her husband, Anna had no plans as yet for cruising on the yacht that was to have been Horace's pride. And there were plans to be made—plans for the June wedding of Horace Jr. to Lois Knowlson. Anna anticipated the wedding with mixed feelings of regret and happiness. Regret that she would be entirely alone after her son's marriage. Happiness that her son was marrying a beautiful girl of good breeding. Lois, who had been educated at Miss Baldwin's School at Bryn Mawr, surely would be able to help Horace settle into a quieter and more stable life, Anna was certain.

Because Horace Dodge Sr. had died only six months previously, Horace Jr. and Lois were married quietly on June 1, 1921, at the Jefferson Avenue home of the bride's parents. The Stotesburys had come from Philadelphia for the wedding, but only a few other guests were present. Following the ceremony, the newlyweds boarded a train to New York whence they would leave on a European trip.

Before the end of July, Anna sailed to Paris for a meeting with Horace and Lois and a tour of the continent. On their return from Europe, Horace immediately went into the Dodge plant "to learn the work from the ground up," he told a newspaper reporter who interviewed the Dodge heir as he worked at a whining ripsaw in the wood and metal pattern department. He had wanted to start work here a couple of years previously, Horace confessed to the reporter, but his parents had wanted him to go to college.

"I guess I must have inherited a mechanical turn of mind," he said, grinning in the direction of the department supervisor, who was having difficulties restraining his trainee's impatience to try out various machines. The big ripsaw could sever a man's finger as neatly as a sharp knife could slice a wedge of cheese. And so far, Horace hadn't touched the planer, which was even more dangerous.

Foremen and supervisors found it nerve-wracking to have the high-spirited Dodge heir poking into the workings of the machinery. Their nervousness was justified when, before his first week of training was ended, Horace was burned when he edged in too close to a cupola being dumped in the foundry. Yet most of the employees felt a kind of kinship to this unpretentious young man with the friendly manner.

"My principal duty and my hardest is rolling out of bed at 6 A.M.," Horace cheerfully admitted. "It takes a fight sometimes, but I manage to get here."

There were times, though, in succeeding months, that Horace did not manage to get to the plant in spite of his good intentions . . . mornings after all-night drinking parties when he simply lost the fight to pull himself out of bed; periods when Anna wanted her son and his wife with her in Palm Beach. Still shocked by her husband's death, Anna had been saddened further in October 1921 by the death of her eldest sister, Catherine.

Because of her sister's death, Anna could not attend the October reception given by Lucretia Stotesbury in the ballroom of her home. The reception served a dual purpose—to introduce Delphine Dodge Cromwell to Philadelphia society and to mark the opening of the Stotesburys' new Chestnut Hill mansion . . . a $2-million structure of six stories, 45 bathrooms and 100 additional rooms, a swimming pool designed like a Roman bath, squash and indoor-tennis courts, and a large gymnasium. But Anna sent her Catherine the Great pearls to Delphine Ione to wear for the occasion.

The royal pearls had the effect Anna desired. Newspaper accounts of the formal opening of the Stotesburys' Whitemarsh Hall made repeated references to the $1.5 million royal pearls worn by Delphine Dodge Cromwell. Less than two months later, *New York Times* headlines proved doubly embarrassing to Anna.

$825,000 Necklace Sale Ends in Court
Importer Charges That Cartier Got 1 1/2 Million Dollars
for Rope Made of 389 Pearls

Cartiers, the *Times* article explained, had reported the sale amount for the pearls as $825,000. But the importers of the royal necklace, who were supposed to have a split of the profits from the sale with Cartiers, had seen the $1.5-million figure quoted repeatedly in newspapers and wanted their share of this larger figure. Government agents were questioning whether the purchasers had paid sufficient duty on the necklace. But the court suit was withdrawn as it became public knowledge that Anna's royal pearls had cost only slightly more than half the original reported price.

By this time, Anna was in Philadelphia as a guest of the Stotesburys before going on to Florida with them. She found solace in their friendship as she was confronted with various poignant reminders of her late husband. One of these reminders was the arrival of French war hero Marshal Ferdinand Foch, who visited the Dodge Brothers plant to pay tribute to the brothers for their assistance to the Allies during the war. Another poignant incident involved the composer, Victor Herbert, who wrote a musical composition shortly after Horace Dodge's death and entitled it "Dodge Brothers March." The composition was dedicated to Horace E. Dodge "in respectful appreciation of his efforts toward the advancement of American Music." The automobile company arranged for the recording of the march and for distribution of 100,000 records. The reverse side of each record carried a tribute to the unusually close bond of affection between the brothers, Horace and John.

When Anna and the Stotesburys left for Palm Beach, the young Cromwells were making plans to move into the Stotesburys' former Chestnut Hill home, Graystone. In February, Delphine Ione and James H. R. joined their parents in Palm Beach for the wedding of Lucretia Stotesbury's eldest daughter, the recently divorced Louise Cromwell Brooks. The daughter was now marrying Brigadier General Douglas MacArthur in a ceremony at the Stotesburys' Spanish mansion, El Mirasol. James H. R., handsome in his captain's uniform, was to serve as best man for the uniformed and bemedaled brigadier general.

At a time when middle-class Americans looked on divorcees as "fallen women," only families with the status of the Stotesburys could gracefully encompass the unpleasant notoriety surrounding a divorce and eclipse it with an impressive remarriage. Although middle-class young women were flaunting their independence by bobbing their hair, the Burlington Railway had recently issued rules that its female employees could not wear rolled hose, must keep knees covered, could not rouge their cheeks, and could use face powder "only in moderation." In Michigan, a bill had been introduced into the House of Representatives proposing that women found smoking in public places should be fined.

In March, Anna and her niece, divorcee Winifred Dodge Gray, boarded a ship for a Mediterranean trip. If, as had been claimed, one's social standing in Grosse Pointe was measured by the time a resident did not spend there, Anna's status was rising rapidly. She was still aboard ship when she was notified that her son, Horace, and his wife had become parents of a baby girl born the last day of March and named Delphine for Horace's sister.

Anna's travels continued that summer when she discovered the luxurious new *Delphine II* was an ideal setting for entertaining. With eighteen guests aboard, the yacht cruised up to Quebec, on up the Labrador Coast, and back home, via Newport and the Great Lakes. Delphine Ione and Jimmy Cromwell had been traveling too. But they returned to Philadelphia in time for Delphine to rest for a couple of months before the birth of a daughter, Christine, in early September.

Early September marked the beginning of a perpetual attempt by Horace Jr. to make a name for himself in boat racing as he entered the Mayor Couzens Detroit Trophy race with a twenty-foot, single-engined hydroplane. While 10,000 spectators turned out in the rain to watch the race on the Detroit River, Horace's *Baby Holo* roared into the first lap ahead of its only opponent, continuing to race along at top speed until the fourth lap when the boat nosed into a heavy swell. As cold water hit the hot exhausts, vapors enveloped the boat and the spectators thought there had been an explosion. A disgruntled Horace watched pensively as a patrol launch towed his disabled *Baby Holo* into a slip before it sank.

Two weeks later, Horace entered *Baby Holo* in the twenty-mile Niagara River race. This time the *Baby Holo* was the winner, setting a new world's record speed of 62.45 miles an hour for hydroplanes of the 2200 class.

Anna had no objections to her son following his father's interest in speedboats, but she was concerned that young Horace was not suf-

ficiently interested in working into the management of Dodge
Brothers. She decided that the Horace Elgin Dodge millions, left in
her control, could be her means of influencing young Horace to carry
on the Dodge business and tradition.

A 1923 inventory of the Horace E. Dodge estate valued the
holdings at nearly $37 million, the bulk of it in Dodge Brothers stock,
the remainder in Victory and Liberty bonds. Although $13 million of
the estate were held in a trust fund, the residuum was Anna's, to control as she wished as long as she lived. With both her son and
daughter dependent on her largesse for funds, Anna sent Delphine
Ione a monthly allowance and provided Horace Jr. with a regular al-
lotment that she considered commensurate with his requirements as a
husband and now a father.

When the Grosse Pointe Country Club members decided to sell
their clubhouse and lakefront property adjoining the Dodges' Rose
Terrace on the east, Anna Dodge bought the property with a top bid
of $625,000. Soon afterwards she provided a twenty-eight-room stone
house on the west side of Rose Terrace for Horace and his family—a
home promptly named "Gray House." By having Horace living in
the shadows of Rose Terrace and dependent on her for finances, Anna
hoped to continue her control over her son—to restrain his drinking
excesses with threats and promises. Delphine Ione, although removed
from her mother's immediate surveillance, was also a source of worry
to Anna, who was aware of the rumors that her daughter was drinking
too much and that there was friction between the young Cromwells.

Uneasy over her son's and daughter's inability to handle large
sums of money, Anna determined to see to it that her husband's fortune was not dissipated now—not even by her own children. The income from the principal amount was enough to assure a lavish life for
herself and the children. And the income also assured the continua-
tion of their constant travels. When Anna's sister-in-law, Della
Eschbach, came from California to visit in January, the two women
sailed on the *Mauretania* for Seville and Granada while the young
Cromwells wintered in Palm Beach, as did Horace and Lois. Anna
and Della's return to Detroit in August of 1923 coincided with the
birth of a son, named Horace III, to Horace and Lois. But long before
her return to Detroit, Anna had learned from her children's letters
and from newspaper reports that the dignified Stotesburys were no
more immune from unpleasant notoriety than were the Dodges.

The case of "The Broken Butterfly" burst into headlines on
March 15, 1923, when Ziegfeld Follies chorus girl, Dot King, was
found murdered in her New York apartment just a few hours after a

Stotesbury son-in-law had visited her. The case was headlined for months in the papers, as tales of intrigue and blackmail unfolded for public reading. Although the case remained unsolved, new developments kept bringing the murder back into the limelight for months to come. More than thirty years later, the case was to be included in a summary of outstanding events of the "lawless" 1920s.

Anna took no satisfaction in the public embarrassment of the Stotesburys, knowing that Lucretia Stotesbury was a very private person who, although she enjoyed entertaining in her palatial Palm Beach home, was rarely seen in public. The wiry, white-haired Ned Stotesbury was a more outgoing and lively individual, who sparked many of the activities of Palm Beach socialites, however. But both Stotesburys had been protective of Anna in her early months of widowhood, and she was grateful to them.

Now, more than ever, Anna was thankful for the strength of her friendship with Lucretia Stotesbury in their mutual concern for the stability of the Cromwell marriage—Anna's daughter, Lucretia's son. After the birth of Delphine's first child, Christine, Anna had been hopeful that the arrival of the baby would be a stabilizing influence on her daughter and son-in-law. She had to admit, though, that becoming a parent had failed to lift the playboy image from her son, Horace. Horace's training program at the Dodge plant was petering out as other interests intruded into his schedule—house parties and motorboat racing, weekend trips and motorboat racing, Florida vacations and motorboat racing . . .

Dodge factory employees saw the young Horace Dodge only rarely, for he entered his boats in one regatta after another, thrilling to the excitement of the race and the pounding of the waves against the shuddering speedboat. Reconciling herself to her son's obsession with boats, Anna decided it was best to be practical and to listen when Horace talked of setting up his own boatworks. If he was not going to apply himself to an apprenticeship that would lead to management of the Dodge plant, perhaps he could be a success as a boat manufacturer. Anna agreed, then, to finance the Horace E. Dodge Boat Works and to pay for the hiring of a prominent naval architect, George Crouch, to design the "Speed Runabouts" Horace wanted to produce—reasonably priced motorboats with comfortable lounges that would seat several people.

By July 1923, Horace had fifty men employed at the boatworks. Publicly, he insisted that his mother was the owner of the company—that he, himself, did not even draw a salary because if he did, he could get barred, as a professional, from competing in motorboat races.

Besides, he told reporters, he was still reporting for duty in the automobile plant.

Reporters, familiar with Horace's activities, doubted that his self-professed work schedule had any appreciable effect on the enlargement of the Dodge factory in 1923, with 20,000 men assembling one-thousand cars per day and the demand for cars still exceeding production. When the millionth car came off the Dodge assembly line on December 13, 1923, a record was set for number of cars produced by a company in the nine years and eleven days of its existence. The record was embellished by the fact that 90 percent of the first million Dodges manufactured were still in service at the end of 1923.

At the New York Automobile Show in January 1924, the Dodge Special Series was introduced—the roadster, the Type-A sedan, and the four-passenger victoria coupe, each with a nickeled radiator shell and automatic windshield wipers. As the automobile show was followed by the National Boat Show in Grand Central Palace, Horace's new production boat, the Dodge Water Car, made its debut. In a fake Florida setting where fashion models displayed the latest knitted one-piece bathing suits and crepe-de-chine beach pajamas, the self-styled Captain Horace E. Dodge stood near his water flivver, its African mahogany finish gleaming beneath gay pennants. With a speed of twenty miles an hour and selling at $2,500, his Dodge Water Car would revolutionize the boating industry, the Captain claimed. It would put working-class families on water as the Dodge Brothers had helped put them on wheels.

To bring more publicity to the boat show and to his Water Car, Captain Dodge offered to give a $10,000 trophy—a silver ship—as a prize for motorboat racing. The trophy, to be named in honor of his father, would be formally presented on the senior Horace's birthday anniversary, May 17.

Now that the Dodge Water Car was on the market, Horace abandoned any further pretense of interest in the automobile factory. Life for Horace now encompassed Water Car promotion, speedboat competitions, and partying, as he began to build a reputation for hosting the most lavish houseparties ever given in Detroit. He and Lois took over the grounds of Rose Terrace on July 4, 1924, when they hosted a $50,000 costume party in a "Night in Venice" setting. Guests gathered around street-cafe tables clustered near a simulated St. Mark's Square fitted with pillars flaunting the Dodges' winged-lion banners. At the water front, the *Delphine*, strung with lanterns, floated at anchor while aerial bombs and fireworks were launched from her deck.

The brunette Lois Knowlson Dodge, wearing a red ballet costume, smiled as she greeted debutante Muriel Sisman, dressed as a Tiger baseball player. Neither woman, nor any of the 500 guests, suspected that Lois and Muriel would be rivals for Horace's affections in less than a year's time.

A Mephistopheles in red satin knee-breeches and a scarlet cap with tiny horns, Horace raced back and forth from the *Delphine II*, where he exuberantly set off fireworks, to the lawn pavilion, where he danced with the young and animated Muriel.

Delphine Ione, who had visited in Detroit only a week earlier, was back again for the party—minus James H. R.—in a figure-flattering ballet costume. With Anna responsible for Delphine Ione's finances in her marriage, the young Cromwells had been spending money lavishly. They had recently made two major purchases of property— ocean-front property at Palm Beach adjoining El Mirasol and an estate on Manursing Island, Long Island Sound, known as "the old Cromwell place." The fifty-acre estate had been the birthplace of James H. R.'s ancestors, but the property had been lost to the family for a number of years.

In her eagerness to have both her son and son-in-law become successful, Anna willingly provided funds for business enterprises that seemed promising. In 1924, many automobile companies were adopting credit arrangements under which financing corporations extended credit to automobile dealers. Jimmy Cromwell convinced his mother-in-law that investing in a corporation for the financing of dealers in Dodge cars would be a sound business proposition. Within the same year, the Cromwell-Dodge Company, Inc.—with James H. R. as president and Horace as vice-president—opened for business on New York's 42nd Street with a capital of $200,000 and a surplus of $50,000.

To help promote the young Cromwells in both their business and social connections, Anna hostessed a party for the couple in the ballroom of Detroit's Book Cadillac Hotel when it opened in December 1924. No less extravagant than her son Horace when giving a party, Anna hired Sara Burnham to help with the planning of the affair. The two women spent $20,000 just on lighting effects and decorations for a setting where swans swam in fountains, canaries fluttered in cages, and oranges could be picked from real orange trees. To Anna, the expenditure was justified when the party attracted 800 guests who fawned over the handsome Cromwell and his sparkling Delphine Ione. Anna chose to ignore the snide comments about her party's guests of honor when the comments were published in a Washington

magazine's gossip column. "The tabbies say the couple is not so popular in Rye, New York, and in Philadelphia, where they have palatial
residences in both cities. However, Detroit likes Delphine if easterners
do not, in spite of the lack of blue-blooded ancestors."

Newspaper reporters had continued to find Delphine Ione's
brother Horace equally good copy while he followed the boat regattas
from one place to another throughout the summer of 1924. In Detroit,
he entered three of his Water Cars in the first day's Junior Gold Cup
race, divided into three heats of thirty miles each. Piloting *Watercar I*,
Horace gripped the wheel as his speedboat's sharp nose broke waves
and water into yards of spray through the first heat. But before his
boat had thundered very far along the course in the second heat, the
motor began missing as a cylinder-head blew.

As Horace's boat jounced into the pit at the Detroit Yacht Club
while the race continued, someone on the dock cupped his hands to
his mouth and shouted a question. What was the trouble? the spec-
tator wanted to know.

"Rotten motor!" Horace yelled back, frowning fiercely. "What's
it to you?" he demanded, raging like a wounded bull. "They gave me
a rotten motor, that's all!"

His frustration worsened as *Watercar II* also developed motor trouble, and the third Dodge entry was not fast enough to meet the competition. Where his father had reveled in the mechanical intricacies of
a malfunctioning engine, Horace could only fume and curse and call
for a mechanic.

Regardless of frustrations, Horace's attention was scarcely
diverted from his boats throughout the incorporation of the Cromwell-
Dodge Company nor during the sale of Dodge Brothers plant and
business in March 1925, when Anna bought 60,000 shares of the new
Dodge company stock for herself. By this time, two new speedboats
were under construction in Horace's boatworks at the river's edge.
The boats were intended for entering the late summer Gold Cup races
at Port Washington, New York. One speedboat was for Horace; the
other, named *Nuisance*, was Delphine Ione's. The restless spirit of
adventure was as strong in Delphine as in her brother Horace. Her
name brightened sports pages when she announced her intention of
becoming the first woman to compete in the grueling 90-mile Gold
Cup races.

"I'm going to be in that race," Delphine insisted when it was
pointed out to her that the course had perilous one-stake turns with
plenty of wash to overturn a boat even when the bay was calm. "Not
even the ship's irons can keep me out," she added dramatically.

Agitated race officials offered alternatives. She could ride in the mechanic's seat for the first heat while *Nuisance* was piloted by a professional driver. Perhaps she could take the wheel in the second heat. Delphine was unaccommodating. It was obvious to her that officials thought she would be ready to surrender her place in the boat after a first-heat experience in the throbbing, leaping racer.

Race day, the last Saturday of August, dawned clear and sunny, with some 1,500 pleasure boats, from small power cruisers to steamers almost as large as the Dodge yacht, floating in the Bay area. The calm bay waters sparkled under the sun's rays and the yachts, sporting colorful pennants, were crowded with spectators, field glasses strung around their necks.

As the motors of the nine competing speedboats reverberated while the drivers awaited the starting signal, spectators focused their field glasses on the four Dodge entries, trying to distinguish the slight, feminine figure of Delphine at the wheel of a powerboat. But Delphine had been advised by her physician not to compete in the race, they learned. The spectators were disappointed, but no more disappointed than the Dodges as each of their craft limped away from the course before the race ended—one going out with a broken rudder, another with a damaged propeller, a third with a smashed connecting rod, and the fourth with motor trouble.

Determined not to be sidetracked a second time from her ambition to drive a speedboat in competition, Delphine Ione got into the lineup for Detroit's ninth annual powerboat regatta on the Detroit River on Labor Day weekend. Hardly recognizable in her padded lifejacket, helmet, and goggles, Delphine bent over the wheel of *Nuisance* as ten boats leaped away from the starting line on signal. For 102 miles, Delphine's slim hands retained their grip on the wheel of the bobbing racer until, as the boat's propeller snapped, the *Nuisance* had to be towed from the course. Still, Delphine had been the first woman to drive in the marathon event. Next year, she vowed, she would prove that a woman could stay in the race—and finish.

During Delphine Ione's preparations for the races, her husband had been absorbed in business affairs. Before the end of 1925, his year-old Cromwell-Dodge Company, on the brink of failure, was absorbed by industrial bankers. But James H. R. already had plans for a new and bigger project. His plans were inspired by the Palm Beach land boom of the past two years.

Via the land boom, South Palm Beach lots were now selling for five times their 1918 value, as socialites vied with each other in building elaborate mansions for winter occupancy. Three mansions, each costing over $1 million, were constructed on the Palm Beach ocean front in 1923—the most magnificent of which was the palatial home of J. S. Cosden, New York oil man. The Cosden home was the $2-million creation of Addison Mizner, self-taught architect whose services were eagerly sought by the wealthy. When the new Mizner-built mansions threatened to match the Stotesburys' El Mirasol in size and magnificence, E. T. Stotesbury drew up plans for a $200,000 addition to his home.

Jimmy Cromwell's new plans were for the formation of a syndicate of investors and the building of a luxury winter resort—a Floridian resort for international society figures that would surpass in elegance any resort in the country. Everything pointed to success in any area of Florida land development. The first highway ever built over the shifting muck of the Everglades now connected Tampa with Palm Beach. Northerners were pouring into Miami by train and boat, and as incoming boats dropped anchor in Biscayne Bay, real estate salesmen waited on the pier. The Dixie Highway was filled with automobiles of people driving south past roadside signs advertising choice properties for sale.

Both Anna Dodge and the Stotesburys invested in Cromwell's latest business venture, named the American British Improvement Company. Using snob appeal as a sales technique, the company, with James H. R. as president, proclaimed its 3,600-acre development as "a winter resort for American and British society." The development, located at Fort Lauderdale and named Floranada, was to include a new Plaza Hotel of 900 rooms that would cost an estimated $6 million without furnishings, and was to have Venetian canals, lakes, lagoons, golf links, a bathing casino, and yachting and motorboat-racing facilities.

From London, the Earl and Countess of Lauderdale lent their names and prestige to the Floranada project. "I want to make the place popular with English society," the Countess said. "Biarritz is ideal in the summer, but there is no winter bathing, and English travelers will find plenty of bathing all winter at the Florida resort." The royalty appeal to moneyed Americans was heightened by advertisements carrying the name of ex-King George of Greece as one of the backers of the Floranada Club.

While the project's backers were stimulated by the quick appearance of workmen and building materials, shovels, and trucks on the Fort Lauderdale site, Anna Dodge had distractions to mar her pleasure in her son-in-law's quickly mushrooming development. Horace had gone to Europe in early winter, and there were persistent rumors that he had gone there in pursuit of young Muriel Sisman, last year's debutante and the daughter of a Detroit builder and contractor.

Upset over these rumors, Anna was even more distressed when her attention was called to the gossipy barbs printed by a Washington paper:

> Evidently the nouveau riche climbing mother of Grosse Pointe who took her beautiful and sophisticated daughter to foreign shores to escape the male wiles and likeable ways of young Horace Dodge did not succeed in keeping the Lothario and builder of speedboats away from the child of her bosom.
>
> The day before the maid's departure, at a tete-a-tete luncheon in a secluded corner of a popular hotel, Horace and the maid planned a hectic rendezvous in a country of wine, women, and easy divorces.

In a burst of indignation, Anna demanded that Horace come home—immediately. Horace complied reluctantly. He was still en route in December when he was given the news that Lois, involved in an automobile crash near West Palm Beach, was in Good Samaritan Hospital—the institution endowed by Horace Dodge Sr.

It was not a happy Christmas for the Horace Dodge family. But Anna hoped the shock of the accident, in which one of Lois' friends had been fatally injured, would bring Horace and Lois closer together. There was every reason for them to be happy—their two healthy children, financial security, an accepted place among the elite of Detroit and Palm Beach. Surely things would work out if Horace would make an earnest attempt to keep his family together, Anna reasoned. She determined to do everything possible to ascertain that Horace *did* make the attempt.

18

After her recovery from the automobile accident, Lois showed an interest in her husband's motorboat business that winter by opening a Dodge Watercar sales office in Palm Beach. Anna was heartened by this. Too much leisure time was not good for either partner in a marriage, she felt. Young energetic women could not completely fill their time with parties and benefit teas and Fannie Ward beauty treatments at a thousand-dollars a head.

By early spring, Lois' business venture had ended and divorce rumors were spreading when she left for Europe and moved into a Paris apartment. With Lois away, Anna moved into Horace's Palm Beach home to be with her grandchildren, little Delphine and Horace III. But this arrangement was only temporary. Anna was already planning the purchase of the Mizner-designed palace originally built for oil tycoon J. S. Cosden at the edge of the blue Atlantic. In an era when there were some 500 millionaires in the country, Mizner had made the comment that he designed homes only for "people who couldn't stand the sight of anything that didn't cost a great deal of money."

Anna's expenditure for Playa Riente ("Laughing Sands") was quoted by some sources as $3 million; by others as $4 million. The discrepancy may have been accounted for by the generous commission rumored to have been paid the agent who managed the purchase for Anna. This agent was the personable and affable Hugh Dillman, former actor turned real-estate agent and arts-society manager.

When Anna left Palm Beach for New York by private plane at the end of April, she was accompanied by her two grandchildren and her realtor, Hugh Dillman. A week later, newspapers were given the announcement of the wedding of Anna and Dillman, scheduled for the following noon—May 8, 1926.

220

The remarriage of the wealthy widow activated reporters. They searched their files and telephoned correspondents in Ohio for background on Hugh Dillman. Reports came in fast. Dillman was one of four children of a Columbus tailor named McGaughey. A former actor in various stock companies, young McGaughey had taken the professional name of Dillman, then married the successful actress Marjorie Rambeau in 1919. But the marriage soured as Hugh and his wife were frequently apart because of career demands. In November 1923, the beautiful Marjorie had sued for divorce, claiming desertion.

With the announcement of the Dodge-Dillman plans, the glamorous, but untrue, account of the couple's first meeting was detailed in a story that was to be resurrected and polished at frequent intervals in the coming years. This meeting, in Venice, supposedly involved the collision of the gondola in which Anna was riding with another gondola. In the resulting argument between gondoliers who brandished stilletos, a masterful American man was supposed to have ordered the gondoliers, in Italian, to put away their weapons and go back to their work. The man, of course, was Hugh Dillman.

Although Hugh had had some experience in being the target of such exaggerated stories during his marriage to an actress, the earlier experiences were miniscule in contrast with the dramatic publicity he was to encounter as a Dodge appendage. Hugh had visited England in 1923, as manager of the Fisk Jubilee Singers, but had not gone to Italy. In his late thirties, with his handsome face beginning to flesh out and his waistline to thicken, Hugh was no longer in the competition to fill the young-lover leads on the stage. With the tour to England, he had found a career that suited him—the managing of a concert and-arts series for the enrichment and entertainment of Palm Beach socialites.

Although Dillman had little more than a high school education, he had a natural appreciation for aesthetic values combined with a magnetic personality and an attractive appearance. As he moved easily into the inner preserves of Palm Beach, he had met the widowed and art-conscious Anna Dodge.

On the Dodge-Dillman marriage application, the age difference of six years did not seem great. Born in 1885, Dillman actually was two years younger than the forty-three years he listed, however. Anna's exact age was fifty-four, rather than the forty-nine years she listed. But Dillman was unaware that Anna was thirteen years older than he.

On Saturday, Anna and Hugh were married at 12:30 P.M. in the fern-banked sunroom of Horace's house adjoining Rose Terrace.

Wearing a beige and coral lace dress and a lace picture hat over her short marcelled dark hair, Anna looked not much younger than her fifty-four years. Her only jewels were gifts of the groom—a platinum pin and an inch-wide bracelet sparkling with diamonds, a necklace and wedding ring ablaze with sapphires and diamonds. Each piece had been designed by Dillman.

Anna's single attendant was Dillman's younger sister, Mary McGaughey. Dillman, slightly taller than his bride, smiled his slow, pleasant smile as the newlyweds received the good wishes of family members and the few guests invited to attend, including the Stotesburys. Matilda and Alfred Wilson were also there to see the couple start off for New York in Anna's chauffeur-driven automobile.

Tuesday morning, the Dillmans arrived at the New York pier to board the *Berengaria*, sailing for England. Their return was scheduled for August—in time to see the young people compete in the powerboat races off Long Island.

The Dillmans left the country just in time to avoid a May 31st *New York Times* front-page story headed:

> *Floranada Club Fails with $8,581,576 Debts*
> *Prominent Persons Listed among Founders*

Floranada President Jimmy Cromwell was questioned at his Park Avenue home in New York. "The trouble was," he said, "we came too late when there were no more buyers." With sales negligible, he continued explaining, the company could go no further with its plans until it got hold of more capital funds, which were not forthcoming. "There was no alternative to bankruptcy," he added.

James H. R. had other reasons for the failure too. He insisted that lavish advertising had given prospective buyers an "absurd" idea of the project. "The exclusiveness of our project was emphasized beyond all reason and probably frightened away many more buyers than it could ever attract," he said.

Reporters persisted, asking if the names of the Countess of Lauderdale, ex-King George II of Greece, John S. Pillsbury, the Stotesburys, Dodges, and others had not been useful in making sales.

"More people of prominence were interested in it than in any large development in the state," Cromwell agreed. "But we had ten thousand lots to sell, and under such conditions how could we be 'exclusive?' "

The Floranada fiasco continued to rate embarrassing publicity for the Cromwell-Stotesbury-Dodge families throughout the summer, as creditors charged that corporation people had dumped papers and documents into a Fort Lauderdale canal. Although the wealthy, the prominent, the pacesetters had to learn to live with constant public exposure as part of the price extracted for the privileges they enjoyed, Hugh Dillman plunged into the role of interceptor, trying to protect his wife from unpleasant publicity. For the first time in years, Anna felt sheltered even while accounts of her own loss—reported to total $4 million—continued in the news as the Dillmans honeymooned in Europe.

By the middle of August, both Delphine Ione and Horace were getting ready for the Manhasset Bay Gold Cup races. Visiting in Detroit on a Sunday afternoon, Delphine inspected one of the Dodge boats anchored in a boatwell on the Detroit River. As she stepped back from the boat onto the dock, her gold mesh bag dropped out of her hand and splashed into ten feet of murky water. While divers tried to recover the bag, Delphine bemoaned the loss of $40,000 worth of jewelry inside the bag. Only two days previously, she had notified her insurance company that she had lost $13,200 worth of jewelry at Detroit's Book Cadillac Hotel. The police were still unsuccessfully investigating that loss.

Now, as Delphine Ione resigned herself to notifying her insurance company of the second loss of valuables, one of the divers emerged from the slimy, black water in the boatwell. Delphine gingerly took the dripping bag from his extended hand. "I never dreamed anyone could see in that dirty, oily water," she marvelled, thanking him but turning away with no mention of a reward.

In preparation for the races at Long Island, Horace sent three of his speedboats from Detroit by rail express. Next he sent the yacht, *Delphine*, carrying 1,500 gallons of hi-test gasoline for the race, up the St. Lawrence River to New York. Then Delphine Ione joined her brother in chartering a special train to transport two more of their boats and thirty people, including mechanics, ignition experts, and pilots, from Detroit to Long Island.

Under the command of Captain Jarvis, the *Delphine*, with her cargo of gasoline, was moving slowly through the Welland Canal when there was a grinding, wrenching noise as the big yacht scraped through the locks where the water was at low level. On arrival at Long Island, the Captain advised Horace that the yacht should go into dry dock for repairs.

But the Dillmans had returned from Europe as planned, and Horace wanted to anchor the yacht along the speedboat course during the races. This would allow the Dillman party to watch the competition from the luxurious *Delphine*, even though the pumps would have to operate to keep the yacht afloat. In spite of dull, lowering weather and biting wind on the day of the race, hundreds of boats floated at anchor between the *Delphine* and the judges' barges. The fifteen competing boats were almost ready to begin the race when Delphine Cromwell, sporty in white sweater and cap, slid into the cockpit of *Nuisance*, adjusted her goggles and lifejacket, and became the first woman to compete in the Gold Cup races.

Last to cross the starting line, Delphine Ione determinedly clung to the wheel and veered to avoid hitting a driver who had been catapulted into the water from the cockpit of a preceding boat. Maneuvering around the sharp turns at either end of the course, she stayed in the race, never posing a threat to the winner but working up to a respectable sixth place in the third heat. Although none of the five Dodge boats was a winner, Delphine Ione had proved that a woman could handle a boat throughout tough competition.

After the races, the Dillmans returned to Detroit on their yacht, planning to have the yacht repaired there. Delphine Ione and Jimmy Cromwell left New York on their houseboat to arrive in Detroit in time for the 150-mile sweepstakes race on Labor Day.

On the day of the sweepstakes, the riverside was fringed black with people and automobiles as Horace, Delphine Ione, James H. R., and the other pilots got into their boats. A $60,000 all-metal speedboat, *Cigarette*, shot out in front of the others at the start, leaping through the waves as a stiff northwest wind whipped the rolling surface of the river into whitecaps. Cromwell had gone only 150 yards when his *Watercar Detroit*, caught in the swells and wash of other boats, turned over. Cromwell surfaced and got free, but his mechanic remained under the overturned boat, his lifejacket snagged in the cockpit. When the boat finally rolled upright, the man was rescued, suffering water in his lungs, a broken right hand, and wrenched shoulder, but still alive.

Shocked at seeing her husband's boat capsize in front of her, Delphine Ione headed *Nuisance* toward the pits and gave up the competition. Horace, in *Miss Syndicate*, pursued the lead boat to the first turn in the tenth circuit when he opened the throttle and daringly shot *Miss Syndicate* around and past the *Cigarette*. For eighteen laps, the two boats jockeyed for first position. On the eighteenth homestretch, Dodge veered to the inside of the course and roared past the other boat, just shaving the first turning buoy. The *Cigarette* began to fall behind until, on the thirtieth lap, she was still second, but trailing by a half mile. Then *Cigarette* was out of the race as her gas tank came loose and the fuel ran into the bottom of the boat.

With two-thirds of the race completed, Dodge's nearest challenger, the *Rowdy*, was twelve miles behind as *Miss Syndicate* swept past the judge's barge. But near the Belle Isle bridge, *Miss Syndicate* began slowing . . . then stopped. The *Rowdy* passed the judge's barge once, and then a second time before a furiously cursing Horace and his mechanic got *Miss Syndicate's* motor restarted. But when the motor continued to jerk, Dodge drove the boat to the pits for what he hoped would be a quick repair. The automatic gasoline feed had snapped, the mechanics discovered as they worked feverishly to repair it. By the time *Miss Syndicate* was out on the course again, the *Rowdy* led by two laps. Dodge's mechanic was manually pumping the gas now, his hands blistering as he worked to keep the boat operating. But the race was lost for the Dodges.

Repairs on the scraped *Delphine* were completed in mid-September. Then Hugh Dillman's sister Mary and several other friends accompanied Anna and Hugh on a cruise up the Hudson River. On the evening of September 21, the Dillmans and their friends went ashore to a dinner in New York City and to a performance of La Traviata. In their absence a crewman smelled smoke, then saw flames shooting out of a locker room. Smoke billowed from the boat by the time a fireboat and police launch cut through the dark waters to the *Delphine*. The rescuers ran lines to the blazing yacht and poured torrents of water into the boat. Then, towing the still-burning *Delphine*, the fireboat moved toward the foot of 95th Street, calling for fire apparatus to be ready at the pier. Before the listing yacht reached the pier, the fifty-four crew members left the *Delphine* in lifeboats. Less than ten yards from the pier, the yacht suddenly lurched to the side and sank. Only the bow of the luxury yacht protruded from the water.

When the Dillmans returned to the dock around 1:30 A.M., Captain Jarvis was waiting to tell them about the fire. Upset at the thought of Horace E. Dodge's dream-yacht resting at the bottom of the Hudson River, Anna relied on Hugh to make arrangements for everyone to stay at the Hotel Ambassador. Then Hugh checked to find out what, if anything, had been salvaged.

A maid had saved Anna's personal jewelry valued at a quarter of a million dollars. But everything else had been lost, including Anna's complete wardrobe purchased in Paris during the honeymoon.

In their Hotel Ambassador suite, Anna and Hugh talked over the fire and the loss of the yacht. Recalling that he had turned on the

Delphine's organ the morning of the fire and received a shock, Hugh mentioned this to Anna. Convinced, then, that the fire had started from a short in the organ wiring, Anna reproved Hugh for not having said something about it immediately. To her grandchildren many years later, Anna was to persist in saying the fire had been Hugh's fault.

While the *Delphine* was being raised and refitted, Hugh and Anna went down to Columbus to visit Hugh's mother and the McGaughey family. Influenza confined Anna to a Columbus hospital, and continued cold weather lengthened her stay there. The Dillmans decided not to open their Palm Beach home that winter but to buy a house in Columbus and remain there while Anna, who also suffered from low blood pressure, recuperated from her illness.

Horace came to visit briefly in Columbus. He left for Detroit with a check from Anna in his pocket. As Dillman drove his stepson back to the depot, Horace confessed cheerfully that he had not expected to get $35,000—that he usually asked for more than he expected to get, since his mother customarily gave him less than he requested.

Anna's children and grandchildren came to Columbus for Christmas, and for the Dodges it was a return to the simpler pleasures of earlier Christmases almost forgotten. For the McGaugheys, it was a revelation to observe the gift-giving by the Dodges. Valuable pieces of jewelry were exchanged . . . even a house. Anna's gifts of houses, though, were always safeguarded by titles retained in her own name.

The twelve adult Dodges and McGaugheys at the Christmas dinner table were drawn with the children into a treasure hunt planned by Dillman, whom the children called "Uncle Hugh." No one was more excited than Delphine Ione Cromwell, who dashed around the house and yard, followed by little Christine, in her determined search for the next clue. With delight, Delphine finally unearthed the prize— a gold coin placed inside a baby pot and buried in the vegetable garden. Triumphantly she held the gold-painted pot in her hands as though, in the simple game, she had discovered a treasure more valuable than the jewels she had carried in her gold mesh bag.

The quiet gathering for a family Christmas in Columbus turned out to be only a lull in a procession of difficulties for Anna. Still upset over the Floranada bankruptcy and its attendant publicity, Anna was forced to abandon any pretense of hope for a Horace-Lois reconciliation in the early weeks of 1927. Horace moved into a Whittier Hotel apartment. Lois, who had returned to the young Dodges' Gray House, sued for divorce in January. Immediately, then, Horace was

off to Europe, leaving the Dillmans to confer with Lois and with attorneys. When Anna and Hugh returned to Columbus in early
February to attend the wedding of Hugh's sister Mary, they took with
them the two young children of Horace and Lois. Then they took the
children with them by train to California so that Lois, unnerved by
the divorce, could have a rest and a trip to Honolulu.

Horace, in Cannes, found that determined reporters followed him
to the gambling tables. Was he going to marry Muriel Sisman, they
asked. "I'm not divorced yet," Horace answered, grinning at the
blonde Muriel who sat beside him.

His romantic interlude with Muriel ended, though, at the Dillmans' insistence. Lois, they told him, was in poor health. They stern-
ly demanded that Horace return from Europe and go to Hawaii to be
with her. Under pressure, Horace left Cannes and made a cross-
country trip to California. Then he boarded a ship to Hawaii where
Lois was recovering from a nervous collapse.

By late May, however, Lois was in Circuit Court in Detroit to
testify in her divorce suit. Her husband's interest in speedboats kept
him away from home and made her unhappy, she charged. He had
violent temper spells—would go away and stay away for weeks at a
time, she added.

Although the couple had agreed privately to divide custody of their
two children over six-months' periods, the final divorce decree
remained unsigned for a time. The delay was occasioned by a provision, engineered by Anna, that neither party should marry for two
years. Anna also guaranteed a generous financial settlement for Lois,
rumored to be somewhere between $600,000 and $1 million. But the
divorce decree continued to remain unsigned until the striking out of
the provision against either party remarrying for two years.

Horace was still in Detroit awaiting the running of the Labor Day
Sweepstakes race when reporters converged on Gray House. Would
he make a statement, they asked, about his reactions to Lois Dodge's
sudden marriage to a Lieutenant Manning in Hawaii? Horace's jaw
slackened. "I've never heard of Lieutenant Manning!" he said, running a sun-bronzed hand through his curly reddish-brown hair.

He would go to Honolulu and see for himself if everything was all
right with Lois and his two children, he decided—but only after the
Sweepstakes had been run. He spent the last few days of August revv-
ing up his twelve-cylinder boat, *Sister Syndicate*, and his rebuilt *Miss
Syndicate* on the Detroit River. Determined to take the "world's speedboat king" title away from Gar Wood, Horace bragged of his own

prowess after a test run in *Miss Syndicate*. "Gar doesn't know how to build a boat," he boasted. "He may be able to drive and he may know motors, but he can't put speed into a hull."

Gar Wood, thrown from his boat four days before the race, did not compete in the Labor Day race. Instead, he sent two drivers to pilot his boats. Riding the wave crests at an average speed of 47.4789 miles an hour for the 150 miles of the course, Horace drove his boat to victory. He was jubilant over his win, but disappointed that he had not defeated Gar Wood personally.

As much as he wanted to go on to Washington for the President's Cup Regatta in the flush of his Sweepstakes victory, Horace left instead for Honolulu to arrange for his six months of child custody. His sister, Delphine Ione, was to enter the race in his place. For the past six months, Delphine Ione had been having serious marital problems that could not be concealed from Anna. The financially pressed James H. R. was forced to sell his Manursing Island estate for $750,000— just a year after he had repurchased the Cromwell-family property.

But as Delphine Ione slipped into her lifejacket on the day of the President's Cup Regatta, she was happily flushed with excitement. With her delicate, heart-shaped face obscured by goggles and helmet, she gripped the wheel of *Miss Syndicate* as President Coolidge watched the race from his yacht, the *Mayflower*. While navy planes zoomed and looped overhead and an army blimp hovered in the sky, Delphine Ione gunned her sleek black boat over the foaming waters. Spectators cheered the petite young woman as she led the competing boats at an average speed of 52.170 miles per hour in the first heat and 51.255 miles in the final heat.

In Honolulu, Horace read with pride of his sister's accomplishment as he amiably golfed with Lois' second husband and prepared to collect his children. Delphine's triumph brought a final bright touch to Anna's year in November. At that time, Delphine Ione was presented with the President's Cup by Calvin Coolidge in a ceremony on the White House lawn as she became the first woman speedboat driver in the country to receive the trophy.

With the year 1927 closing, Anna was not sorry to see it end and to hope that the new year would be a less disruptive one for her family. Horace's divorce was irrevocable, but Anna was still optimistic that the Cromwell marriage would survive in spite of its difficulties.

1928. Mary Pickford appearing in Kathleen Norris' "My Best Friend" at Detroit's United Artists Theatre. Bicycle racing attracting crowds to Olympia stadium. Detroit-born "Lucky Lindy" already a millionaire in the wake of his nonstop solo flight to Paris the previous year. Americans across the country weeping as they wind up their victrolas and spin their recordings of "Poor Little Marion Parker," while William Edward Hickman, slayer of the twelve-year-old Marion, appeals his sentence of death on the gallows.

And in Palm Beach, the private cars of the Vanderbilts, the Stotesburys, the Phipps family, Anna Dodge Dillman, and other socialites bring the wealthy occupants to their winter homes. The winter of early 1928 was the first season Anna and Hugh Dillman spent in the Spanish castle, Playa Riente, its foundation rising out of the waters of the Atlantic.

The rambling, sandstone Playa Riente was an ideal setting for the gregarious Hugh and the socially aspiring Anna to entertain guests. Hundreds could commingle in the great ballroom or in the vaulted-ceilinged dining room illuminated by fifty-seven four-foot-tall candles.

The Dillmans were making plans to entertain forty guests with a string quartet brought from New York in mid-January, when Delphine Ione arrived suddenly at her mother's Palm Beach home. Anna was immediately suspicious. Where, she demanded, was Jimmy? Delphine admitted that he had gone to his mother's home, El Mirasol.

Delphine Ione was not unprepared when Anna's disappointment over Horace's divorce proliferated into a protracted agitation over her daughter's separation from James H. R. Delphine had been aware, since childhood, that Horace was his mother's favorite. She knew that, even in adult life, Anna demanded of her daughter a conformity to the mother's will that was never required of Horace. True, Horace was complaining that his mother had cut his monthly allowance to $20,000 and had demanded the deed to Gray House returned to her because of his divorce. But Delphine expected that her brother would soon charm his way back into his mother's good graces.

The Cromwell-Dodge separation immediately became the subject of journalistic satire. An *American Weekly* article pointed out that Delphine and James H. R. "had similar tastes in amusement, which was fortunate in a pair of lives devoted to nothing else." Both young people, the article stated, "were so popular with everyone else among the elite of New York, Philadelphia, and Florida, that it seemed impossible that they could become unpopular with each other, but they managed it somehow."

The young Cromwells' financial problems vied with their marital problems for press coverage. Faced with a court order to settle a

$20,000 note for an apartment building he had leased on New York's Park Avenue, Cromwell brought a countersuit for $232,000. Charging fraudulent representation, he claimed he had been duped into leasing the building, then into subleasing on unfavorable terms. He sought to have all the tenants' leases canceled, including that of his wife who occupied the building's top three floors.

Nineteen-twenty-eight had already turned into a year of embarrassment for Anna. From March through July, the embarrassments proliferated as Horace filed suit against a syndicate in which he had invested heavily for purchase and improvement of 1,060 acres of land in Michigan's Oakland County. Dodge had been influenced "by high powered sales talk" into giving syndicate organizer Milton Truss $120,000 in notes, his attorney claimed. The notes, he added, had been used by Truss to take care of personal debts. "Am I to believe," the judge demanded of Horace's attorney, "that this man was sane and sober when he gave away all this money without getting a receipt?"

The attorney nodded assent. The press picked up the attorney's statement that Dodge "was the goose that laid the golden egg." Truss filed a countersuit for $750,000, claiming breach of contract and false and malicious charges.

On the witness stand, Truss was unflappable. Dodge had not only been eager to invest in the land-development syndicate, he said, but he also had asked Truss to help him refinance the insolvent Horace E. Dodge Boat Works, Inc. Truss recalled the projects being discussed thoroughly with Horace's mother at her Palm Beach home, where Horace had begged for financial backing. He needed the money, he had told his mother, because he "never before put money into anything that turned out well."

Before the suits were settled, Horace left for England, taking his two children with him. In London, his plans for marriage to Muriel Sisman were made public as he filed a declaration of intention to marry, required by English law.

The Dillmans sailed for England on the *Aquitania* on May 9. Eight days later, they attended the wedding ceremony as Muriel became Horace's wife in the Presbyterian Church at Westbourne Grove Terrace. They watched as Horace's children—four-year-old Horace Elgin III, ring-bearer, and six-year-old Delphine, flower-girl—came down the aisle. Then everyone's attention turned to the bride, in white satin, her blonde hair partly hidden under a veil and her eyes sparkling under thinly arched eyebrows. The notoriety that had surrounded Horace's unsuccessful business ventures did not prohibit the papers from embellishing accounts of the wedding with comments that

"Dodge added millions to the family fortune by the manufacture of motor boats."

Accepting her son's remarriage gracefully now, Anna circulated among the 250 guests at the reception in the Mayfair apartment leased by Muriel's father. But Anna was still angry at Delphine Ione, who had not come to England for her brother's wedding. Anna suspected that Delphine was already on her way to Reno to file for divorce.

In July, while still in England where he and Muriel planned to make their permanent home, Horace agreed to an out-of-court settlement of his land-investment suit against Truss. The settlement provided for the return of the larger part of the canceled notes. Anna and the Stotesburys would have liked to have had the Floranada Club suits settled as quietly, but the Floranada affair threatened to be a headliner for months to come. Jimmy Cromwell was already in New York, where he had been summoned to testify in bankruptcy proceedings for the Floranada corporation.

When a builder, filing a damage suit, brought the names of Major General Douglas MacArthur and other prominent people into the proceedings, the publicity escalated. Cromwell had listed MacArthur's name on Floranada brochures even though MacArthur never bought any stock in the corporation. Another builder charged that the corporation had represented itself as having sufficient capital to carry out an elaborate $11.5 million program of development, whereas there was less than $100,000 available for this purpose. He was misled into advancing money for building, the contractor claimed, when the promoters published drawings of a home that the king of Greece would build and occupy. But it was known by the promoters, he added, that the king did not intend to build on the property.

The Dillmans' return from England with Horace's two children faced Anna with several unpleasant issues apart from that of the Floranada publicity. She expected that Delphine Ione's divorce suit would soon flare into prominence. She was unhappy at having to deliver her grandchildren into the custody of their mother Lois. And Anna was indignant over Horace's insistence on remaining in England and leaving the responsibility for the financially unsound boatworks with Hugh and herself.

A few days after her return to Detroit, Anna issued an ultimatum that ricocheted into the newspapers. *Mrs. Dillman Closes Dodge Boat Works. Son's Plant Where Famous Speeders Were Built Shut Down— Employees Dismissed.*

Quick to anger and equally quick to relent where her son was concerned, Anna softened her stand after a series of cablegrams from Horace. A second statement was given to the newspapers. Mrs. Dillman had *not* closed the plant, they said. The plant was closed only for the weekend and Labor Day. The cutback in employees was a seasonal procedure.

Horace and Anna had agreed on another matter—that it was not a good thing to have little Delphine and Horace III passed back and forth between sets of parents. Even if Muriel would consent to have Horace keep his children with them permanently, it was not likely that Lois would give permission for the children to live in England. Nor could Anna conceive of letting the custody of the children pass from the Dodges to the children's natural mother and a stepfather. After all, Horace Elgin III was the bearer of the family name and tradition. Anna was prepared to spend any amount of money to get the children and rear them as Dodges within the family circle.

Anna and Hugh talked with Lois, pointing out the advantages if the children were placed in their grandmother's custody. Lois finally signed her consent to the arrangement, and the custody of little Delphine and Horace III was given to their grandmother, Anna Dodge Dillman.

The two children were now privileged to enjoy all the advantages of great wealth—spacious bedrooms and playrooms presided over by a series of nurses and governesses, meals served to them in luxurious isolation, playmates coming in only by special invitation, private boarding schools, and occasional visits from a grandmother, who preferred to be called "Mammá," in between her trips to Palm Beach, New York, Europe, and other faraway places. There were even fewer visits from their globe-trotting father.

While the negotiations about Horace's children had gone on, Anna had been troubled with Delphine Ione's problems. In late September, the fragile-looking Delphine Ione had appeared in a Reno courtroom to charge that from the time of her marriage in 1920 until her separation from Cromwell, she had never received any money from her husband. She had been dependent on an allowance from her mother—the size of which angered Cromwell into being abusive of Mrs. Dillman, often in the presence of other people.

"On one occasion," the bill of complaint read, "through persistent urgings, the plaintiff was prevailed upon to write a letter to her mother containing statements of an unkind nature, which resulted in a brief estrangement. The plaintiff suffered great mental distress and unhappiness."

An agreement concerning the custody of their daughter, Christine, had already been reached, and a property settlement arranged to both parties' satisfaction, Delphine assured the judge. She left the courtroom, giddy with the thought of being a free woman once more. But already there was gossip that Delphine would not be known as the ex-Mrs. Cromwell for long.

During her stay in Reno, Delphine had been seen frequently with bank president Raymond T. Baker, a former director of the U.S. Mint. Immediately following Delphine's divorce, Baker was divorced by his wife, the former widow of Alfred Vanderbilt.

Anna had ambivalent feelings about Delphine's new marriage plans. Her daughter's first marriage had been an impulsive one. She didn't want the girl to make another mistake. But from everything she had heard about Baker, he appeared to be a mature, settled man whose stability might provide a balance for Delphine's impetuous nature. He was not a drinker, so that too might sustain Delphine and keep her away from drinking, Anna hoped.

The Dillmans had already gone to Palm Beach for the winter when Delphine Ione planned a December fourth wedding to Ray Baker. Anna made a brief trip to New York for the quiet wedding, which took place in her Ambassador Hotel apartment. Horace and Muriel arrived from England in time to see Delphine exchange vows with Baker, while a harpist and violinist provided a musical background.

Immediately following the wedding, the family members went their separate ways—the newlyweds heading for Palm Beach before settling into a Washington, D.C., home. Horace and Muriel planned to sail for Honolulu, then to leave on a six-months' trip around the world. Anna returned to Playa Riente, where she and Hugh would remain until spring. In the spring they planned to board the *Delphine*, now frozen into Lake St. Clair, and to join Horace and Muriel in Europe. For now, Anna hoped that she and Hugh could enjoy a pleasurable winter in Palm Beach, free of family problems.

19

Although Horace and Muriel had continued to make their home in London, Anna encouraged her son to return to the United States. She would, she promised, back him with millions of dollars to satisfy his ambitions in the powerboat-production field. In the boom year of 1929, mother and son formed the Horace E. Dodge Boat and Plane Corporation. Horace was named president, and all the stock was held by the Dodge family.

Anna purchased one-hundred acres of land in Newport News, Virginia, for the construction of facilities for the manufacture of boats and of planes—sea and amphibian. The corporation was planned to become the world's largest pleasure-boat factory. Construction of the landing field, hangar, dock, and boathouses began in September 1929. On completion of the facilities, Horace would return to oversee nearly 2,000 workers.

At the time construction of the new plant was begun, Anna left with Hugh for a trip around the world. The trip was to be a leisurely one so that the Dillmans could collect art objects and furnishings. These would be used to decorate the new French chateau they anticipated building on the grounds of Rose Terrace. Anna decided that the new chateau was to be more magnificent than the original Rose Terrace . . . more grandiose than Matilda's Meadow Brook Hall . . . and she was willing to spend any amount of money to achieve her objective.

The Newport News plant was partly constructed by October 29, 1929, when the New York stock exchange collapsed. With the crash, Horace's plans to capitalize on the yearnings of the common man for recreation were strangled. Pleasure boats lost their appeal to middle-class people, who could no longer afford, or who were too cautious to buy, anything but the necessities of life.

Regardless of the depression that settled over the country and the world, the Dillmans continued on their tour. Anna was not at all reluctant to spend her money. She was introduced by Hugh to Lord Joseph Duveen, world-renowned art connoisseur. Duveen left London to travel with the Dillmans as an adviser in the purchase of *objets d'art* that would make their new home a repository of treasures.

They were still traveling when, in April 1930, Horace and Muriel had their first child. The boy, born in London, was named David Elgin.

In early May 1930, the Dillmans moved on to Seoul, Korea, and then to Peking. Fascinated by oriental silks and brocades, jardinieres, jade pieces, and curios, they bought jewelry, bolts of exotic materials, jars and vases, and a dozen five-foot-high Chinese statues. When they finally settled back at Rose Terrace late that summer, the Dillmans' attention was diverted to little Christine Cromwell, the daughter of Delphine Ione and James H. R. After his summer months of custody of Christine, Cromwell was not willing to surrender the child to her mother in September 1930. When a bitter custody fight threatened, both Anna and Lucretia Stotesbury joined forces again to prevent a court battle. Anna was determined to settle the matter privately, no matter what the expense might be. She would not have the delicate balance of her daughter's life upset when Delphine Ione was trying so very hard to make a success of her marriage to Ray Baker. Delphine was also trying to launch a new musical career for herself. Any emotional entanglement, Anna feared, might defeat Delphine's will to wean herself from her dependence on alcohol. Delphine applied herself to hours of piano practice daily to regain power and dexterity in her slender hands. Now, as Anna and Lucretia Stotesbury conferred, they arranged for a sudden out-of-court settlement providing for custody of Christine by her mother.

Before leaving for Palm Beach for the winter season, Anna and Hugh drew up plans for their new chateau, then entertained Della Eschbach, who had come to visit them from California. When the Dillmans went to Palm Beach, they divided their time between Playa Riente and Hugh's lakefront Sandy Loam Farm, just outside of Palm Beach. Anna had no objections to the time and money Hugh put into the development of his farm. She took a vicarious pleasure in his enthusiasm for constructing new outbuildings, furnishing his log house with choice antiques, and hiring the best of gardeners and florists to grow the finest and rarest of fruits, vegetables, and flowers. But Anna *did* object to Hugh's friendly approach to his farm employees. To Anna, there was loss of respect in speaking to an employee in anything less than a master-servant inflection. It infuriated her that Hugh refused to change his casual management tactics, even though she recognized that it was Hugh's unchanging amiability and outgoing personality that had opened the way to closer attachments with the society people in whose company Anna was happiest.

In the Palm Beach social life within the restricted confines of the Everglades Club, Hugh Dillman was a pivotal figure. The club had been failing financially when Hugh was elected its president, even though such personages as Florenz Ziegfeld, Virginia Thaw, Prince Christian of Hesse, and Mrs. William Randolph Hearst had graced the portals of the club at various times.

Almost immediately, the energetic new president began pumping a new vitality into the stodgy membership. Wealthy widows, bored divorcees, and lonesome matrons swarmed around the personable Hugh, enraging Anna to the point where it became difficult for her to trust Hugh. Even though she could see that men liked Dillman almost as much as did women, Anna could not be objective about the youthful Hugh's relationship with other people. And the women of Palm Beach had more idle time in which to seek out Hugh . . . more problems . . . more need to be included in the magic circle of Dillman's friends who were invigorating the club.

When the Dillmans dined at the Everglades Club, Anna's lips tightened each time a waiter approached to summon Hugh to the telephone. She was suspicious that one of the women was trying to ensnare Hugh . . . that there might be arrangements for a clandestine meeting. Although Anna had undergone a face lift, the operation had not given her the magical lasting effects she desired, nor the assurance that she could hold Hugh. She tried to convince herself that he had not married her for her money, but the idea nagged at her. Nor did Hugh's reassurances of faithfulness and circumspect behavior satisfy Anna, particularly after Dillman learned of her true age.

The secret was divulged when Hugh's sister Mary visited his farm, and Anna's sister May had been invited over for lunch. With May was her houseguest, Isabelle Smith—the woman whom John Dodge had divorced in 1907 so he could marry Matilda. Isabelle had managed to retain her friendly ties with the Thomsons without intruding, at any time, into the John Dodge side of the family. Now, as the Dillmans and their guests sat at the luncheon table, Isabelle made a casual reference to the birth date that she and Anna shared—August 7, 1871. Hugh's face registered amazement. Anna was not eight years older than he, as she had told him, but thirteen years older! He decided to overlook the deceit, understanding Anna's sensitivity about her age. Nevertheless, Anna's pride was injured, and this heightened her jealousies of the younger Hugh.

Anna remained friends with Isabelle. She knew the age disclosure had been made innocently. She found it puzzling, though, how the John Dodge family had been able to keep all mention of John's second marriage to Isabelle out of the newspapers. They had even kept knowledge of it from some members of the immediate family through the years. Yet every triviality on the Horace Dodge side found its way into print.

The many lawsuits, major and minor, filed against the Dodges had heightened Anna's insecurities too. Was everyone interested only in her money, she wondered. Did her friends really feel any warmth toward her—or was it the golden touch of money that attracted companions?

In February, Anna and Hugh returned to Grosse Pointe by plane to select the spot on which their chateau should be built while the original Rose Terrace was torn down and its rich paneling, chandeliers, and imported tile flooring were put up for sale. While the new home was under construction, the Dillmans planned to live on the *Delphine* for the summer months.

The site chosen by Anna for the new house was a symbolic one. The chateau would rise on the adjoining property she had purchased some years ago from the Grosse Pointe Country Club—on the exact spot where the old clubhouse had stood, denoting Horace Elgin Dodge's victory over Grosse Pointe's bluebloods.

Delphine and her husband, Ray Baker, also were planning building a $348,000 limestone home on Foxhall Road in Washington, D.C. Delphine Ione was back in her mother's good graces now. Anna was delighted that her party-loving daughter had rededicated herself to her musical career since her marriage to Baker. In December 1931 Delphine debuted as a concert pianist in Washington, then gave her first performance in her home state of Michigan at Ypsilanti State Normal College with the school's little symphony. Friends and employees of the Dodges sat in the darkened auditorium on the spring evening of the concert as Delphine Ione, spotlighted at the piano, ventured hesitantly into the opening passages of Grieg's Concerto in A Minor. But within moments, her hands swept with assurance over the piano keys through the first dreamy movement and on to a brilliant, brittle allegro. Because of this brittleness and lack of sensitivity in Delphine's technically fine performance, Conductor Gabrilowitsch denied Anna's request to have Delphine solo with the Detroit Symphony. His decision was not a practical one because Anna immediately withdrew her generous financial support of the orchestra.

When, in the late 1930s, the orchestra was not able to pay its rent for Orchestra Hall, Anna remained unmoved. Hadn't the orchestra's rejection of Delphine helped undermine her daughter's musical ambitions? Not a penny of her millions would go for the support of the Detroit Symphony, Anna determined. Not even at her death.

After the Detroit orchestra's refusal to have Delphine perform, there were only one or two other concerts in the United States for Delphine before she went to England. She stayed in London for periods of months at a time during the next few years, studying music. Not only were Horace and Muriel frequently separated by the Atlantic Ocean, but now Delphine and Baker were often separated by the same stretch of water.

Anna too was frequently away from Hugh as he became more deeply involved with his Palm Beach farm and the Everglades Club. He worked at beautifying his farm with a bird sanctuary, where quail, ringed doves, and colorful pheasants strutted around a goldfish pool rimmed with rare orchids. His flowers won prizes at garden shows, and he sold them to local shops as a business venture.

In the summers, the Dillmans spent more time together, frequently entertaining friends on the *Delphine*. Anna's grandchildren sometimes stayed on the yacht with them. It was to "Uncle Hugh" that little Delphine, Horace's daughter, confided her childish ambition to get married and have lots of children. Her children were not going to be sent to private schools or boarding schools, she insisted. They were not going to have governesses, and they would eat in the dining room with their parents. It was clear to Hugh that young Delphine yearned for a different kind of family life than that provided by the continent-hopping Dodges.

Horace made only periodic appearances at the Newport News boat and plane factory where work was stalemated because of the continuing economic depression. But the depression did not dampen Horace's enthusiasm for racing his boats. In August 1932, he piloted his *Delphine V* in the Gold Cup races on Montauk Bay but had to be towed off the course when his boat developed engine trouble in the first heat. He stood and cheered, then, as his pilot, young Bill Horn, drove another Dodge boat, the *Delphine IV*, to victory in the sixty-mile-an-hour record-shattering race. Horace, regretful only that he had not personally been at the wheel of the winning speedboat, was feted a couple of weeks later at the Detroit Boat Club and presented with the

Gold Cup. In 1933, for the first time in ten years, the Gold Cup race would be held on the Detroit River, with Dodge retaining the winner's trophy in Detroit until then.

In the same year the Dodge boat won the Gold Cup, Horace and Muriel became the parents of a second child, a girl named Diana. Delphine Ione was also expecting a second child, her first by Baker. In February 1933, the Bakers' daughter, Yvonne (named Anna Ray Baker, but always knows as *Yvonne*), was born. Although the passage of the Lindbergh Act in 1932 had made kidnapping a federal offense, wealthy families of the thirties were preyed upon by kidnappers. After receiving kidnapping threats, the Dodges hired eighteen private guards to watch over their homes when Horace returned from England with three-year-old David and one-year-old Diana.

With the Gold Cup race slated for Detroit in 1933, Horace planned to enter five of his *Delphine* speedboats in an attempt to keep the trophy. His sister Delphine arrived in Detroit from her music studies in England a few days before the race. Slim and girlish in a short skirt and leather jacket, she came down to the boat wells to see the glistening new *Delphine VII* docked there. "I'll not open it up," she said as she stepped into the cockpit. "There's such a thing, you know, as wearing out a motor." But within minutes, the white and mahogany hydroplane was roaring down the river, throttle opened wide.

In spite of the months of preparation spent in readying five boats for Detroit's Aquafest Week, when the Gold Cup, the Dodge Trophy, and the Harmsworth Races would be run, the week was not a success for the Dodges. One of the boats—all named *Delphine*—was not ready in time. Another of them, built at a cost of $70,000, lagged sluggishly in the Gold Cup race. Delphine Ione could not push her boat to pass the two lead boats in any of the three heats. Each time, she placed third. Bill Horn, driving the *Delphine IV*, was the only serious competition for the winning *El Lagarto*. Before starting the race, *El Lagarto's* driver had determined that he had to "get out in front or break my neck" because if he started behind, he knew he'd never get his battered-looking craft through the maze of glittering *Delphines*. With each starting signal, *El Lagarto* jumped into the lead and won the trophy.

With the Dodge Trophy race the next to be run, Horace protested that the *El Lagarto* failed to meet the requirements for this race. The irate owner of *El Lagarto* had his mechanics tear down his boat to prove it met the requirements.

With the *El Lagarto* lying in Motorboat Lane, its engine parts strewn all over the shop, there was only one remaining threat to

Horace in the Dodge Trophy competition. But the other boat was running with a new piston, so there was little chance the Dodges would not win their own trophy. Wrapping his life jacket around his white serge racing suit, Horace stepped into one of his Delphines and drove it to victory. Another of his boats had stayed in a challenging position throughout the race, however, so that Bill Horn could take over the lead for his boss if trouble developed with Horace's boat.

Horace had another boat, the *Delphine V*, ready for the big Harmsworth race, brought to Detroit by Gar Wood who had won the trophy the previous year. One-half hour before the start of the race, flames leaped up suddenly from the *Delphine V*, and the boat caught fire and burned, leaving Gar Wood to win the Harmsworth again in his *Miss America*.

Horace's expenditures for the Aquafest Week amounted to $58,000 that year, including $25,000 as fire loss, $3,000 for boat repairs, and $20,000 for the cost of having twenty men bring two of the Delphines from the Atlantic coast to Detroit.

Still, Horace had bigger and better plans for the following year. Attending the American Power Boat Association's annual meeting in November, Horace advocated a proposal he had been pushing for several years. He wanted the Gold Cup boats equipped with superchargers. Infuriated when the proposal was voted down by the other members, Horace threatened withdrawal from the association. He would not compete in next March's international races, he irately announced. He was going to beach the largest fleet of Gold-Cup class boats ever raced by an individual.

The frequent separations between Horace and Muriel turned into a permanent separation in August 1933—a month made doubly frustrating to Horace by the disappointing results of the Aquafest competitions. He decided to return to England, however, and to take the two children of his first marriage with him because of kidnap threats. Anna had recently acquired an English estate, St. Leonard's Castle, which overlooked the British royal family's Windsor Castle. Horace was to stay there with the children for a while, his mother ordered. Then Anna herself would come to the castle to be with the children.

Horace's younger two children were with Muriel, as was agreed when the parents separated. And there were rumors that Horace was already planning a third marriage to blonde showgirl Mickey Devine. To inquisitive newsmen, Horace denied the rumors. When asked about his decision to get out of racing, Horace now gave a different reason for giving up powerboat competition. The cost, he claimed, was prohibitive.

Once again, he had reasons for worrying about expenses. Disturbed over the dissolving of her son's second marriage, Anna was, once more, restricting her handouts to him. She was disturbed too by her daughter's separation from Ray Baker, in whose steadying influence Anna had placed so much hope. While Delphine Ione was living in London, Baker was back in Reno. Reno, he insisted, was his legal and voting residence. His presence there had nothing to do with divorcing his wife.

The tangled marital relationships of the Dodges and their spouses were thrust back into headlines with the thirty-eight-year-old James H. R. Cromwell's *coup de grace* in February 1935—his marriage to twenty-two-year-old Doris Duke, known as the "wealthiest girl in the world." Cromwell listed his business on the marriage license as advertising, even though he had recently aspired to the profession of author.

In *The Voice of Young America*, published by Charles Scribner's Sons in 1933, Cromwell was critical of tax-exempt securities bought by the "parasitic" wealthy. He advocated limitations restricting the amount of money that could be left to heirs by an individual. He went on to advocate birth control, and sterilization and segregation of the insane and criminal. He decried large families among the poor, the payment of veterans' benefits, public-works programs for indigents, the victimizing of husbands by the alimony racket, and the conducting of dishonest and misleading deals by businessmen.

With marriage to Doris Duke, Cromwell set off on a second around-the-world honeymoon. In India, the newlyweds sat on the floor of a tiny room to meet the wizened Mahatma Gandhi, clad in his white wrapper. Doris Duke Cromwell came away from the meeting with the feeling that she had "talked to a Messiah comparable to Confucius, Buddha, Christ, or Mohammed." She immediately commissioned a Delhi architect to draw up plans for the rebuilding of a wing of her Florida mansion in the style of the Taj Mahal, with Indian marble and with mosaic-adorned windows and doors.

While Delphine Ione's first husband honeymooned with Doris Duke, Delphine remained in London with her two-year-old daughter Yvonne. She was still in London when Ray Baker died of a coronary thrombosis in Reno in late April 1935. The fifty-six-year-old Baker left an estate valued at only $65,000.

Money continued to be a major problem in Horace Dodge's life as Muriel, now in New York, filed three suits against him, involving some one-half-million dollars in property and the custody of David and Diana. Horace, who moved back and forth regularly between the United States and England, sailed back to England again in June 1935. This time he came to serve as best man at his recently widowed sister's marriage to import agent, Timothy Godde.

Anna left St. Leonard's Castle just before Horace's arrival. She wanted no part of the wedding in her distress over an alienation of affections suit filed against Delphine Ione by Godde's first wife. The suit was withdrawn only after the Dodges reportedly made a settlement of a quarter-million dollars.

The August 21st wedding took place in a registry office, after which Delphine Ione returned with her new husband to St. Leonard's Castle for a brief reception. Then the newlyweds departed by airplane for Paris, Vienna, Budapest, and Berlin.

Pursued by process servers working on behalf of his estranged wife Muriel, Horace made frequent moves to avoid the men who hounded him. His pride took a battering each time he was forced to beg Anna for money. And the money was never enough to cover the next debt, the next lawsuit, the next of the many problems that dogged him. Each time he received another handout from his mother, he was asked to sign a note for the amount. This, in Anna's opinion, made him more responsible for his actions and more accountable for his spending sprees. The unpaid notes mounted, and Horace's carefree, bubbly, friendly manner became a facade that endured only as long as he was insulated from reality by an alcoholic haze.

After she had returned from England shortly before Delphine's marriage, Anna planned to give some time to the three grandchildren now staying in Detroit—Delphine Ione's daughter, Christine Cromwell, and Horace's two older children. The two girl cousins were boarding at Kingswood School in suburban Detroit. The grandson, Horace III, was at neighboring Cranbrook. When Anna remembered the children's needs, she would plan an elaborate affair, such as a supper party at the Grosse Point Club. But Anna was seen more often at the symphony concerts that season—impressive in satin gown under a long ermine coat with sable collar, sitting beside Hugh Dillman in their box within the glittering golden horseshoe rimming Orchestra Hall. While she would no longer support the orchestra financially as she had in earlier years, she did not deprive herself of the pleasure of its concerts.

In January 1936, the Dillmans hosted a reception for Delphine Ione and Timothy Godde at the new Rose Terrace. By this time, Anna had adjusted to her daughter's new marriage. Elegant in wine-colored matelasse shot with silver threads, Anna stood next to Hugh in the fruitwood library to greet the guests entering the French eighteenth-century home through the grand entrance hall, rising two stories. Delphine Ione, in sapphire velvet and purple orchids, stood next to Godde, a pleasant-faced man of medium height who had a receding hairline. Guests coming into the library saw, above their smiling hostess, a large new portrait of Anna, posing as a French court lady, painted by Gerald Kelly of London. The visitors moved on from the exquisite collection of Chinese porcelains and Kang Hsi-period lamps in the library to one room after another decorated with French inlaid furniture, Claude Michel and Goutier statues, Royal Bouvais tapestries, antique pieces of crystal, gold, silver, and jade. They walked on blue-bordered carpets that were reproductions from fragments of carpets at Versailles palace, and rewoven on French looms.

Anna reigned proudly over her chateau as touring guests admired the mellow sheen of the oak-paneled dining room. This was the room the Dillmans considered a master tribute to the quality of their tastes. During their world tour, Anna and Hugh had marveled over the wood texture of barns they saw in Greece. They had bought nine-hundred of the barns and had them torn down and the wood grains matched. Then they had ordered the wood shipped to France for shaping and carving by French artisans for the paneling of their dining room. In France, where the couple had been equally charmed by an antique village inn, they had bought the entire inn and shipped it back to Detroit for use as a barroom at Rose Terrace. Guests at the party could see that the inn's flooring was dented with the imprints of horses' hooves supposed to be those of Napoleon's mount.

The barroom was a popular place at the party. Guests gathered there to a background of orchestra music alternating with organ selections from Horace Dodge Sr.'s great instrument, reassembled in the chateau, its three floors of pipes concealed by Flemish tapestries. The melody of "I'm in Heaven" drifted through the house as guests walked through the drawing room, with its piano that had been used by King Louis XV, and into the white and gold music room . . . the games room . . . the breakfast room.

Pleased with the sensation she had scored with her party in ornate Rose Terrace, Anna opened Playa Riente for the first time in a few seasons when she and Hugh returned to Florida. Here on platinum sands lapped by the ocean, they sunbathed and planned some of the elegant soirees they wanted to host in Playa Riente's huge downstairs ballroom. They planned too the gatherings they would have in the formal drawing room with its rare Ming vases, Venetian antiques, and its $50,000 rug that had originally been cross-stitched by nuns for a palace in Spain.

Having Hugh back at her side after a number of lengthy separations, Anna was confident that he could help her in successfully competing with the Stotesburys' extravaganzas at El Mirasol. Anna had recently employed a new social secretary whose expertise would make everything run smoothly. Even guided by the debonair Hugh, whose double chin and slightly bulging midriff scarcely detracted from his handsome appearance, Anna was nervous about making a grammatical error or a *faux pas*.

Still, many people thought Anna had an overbearing manner, particularly to servants. There were only a few close friends to know that Anna's snobbishness was the defense of an introvert . . . an introvert who feared her servants might not give her proper deference. The closest of these friends was a woman much younger than Anna—Florence Sisman. Florence had been, first, a friend of Horace's, then had married a brother of Muriel Sisman. When her husband died and left her a youngish widow, Florence had gone into the shipping and crating business, working herself up to complete ownership. She had also become a confidante of Anna Dodge. Noting that Anna sometimes passed people she knew without speaking to them, the outspoken Florence called these omissions to Anna's attention. "I wish I could be friendly like you," Anna told her wistfully. "The next time you see me passing up someone I should speak to, give my arm a hard squeeze."

In January 1936, Horace had returned to New York for the boat show. Although he had been replaced as president of the Dodge Boat and Plane Corporation, he came each day to the show where a twenty-six-foot Dodge cruiser, newest addition to the Dodge line, was on display.

At the close of the winter season in Palm Beach, Hugh remained to supervise the remodeling of the Everglades Club. Anna, however, had plans to return to Detroit and then to go abroad. In a democratic gesture, she decided to send her grandson, Horace III, to a northern Michigan camp that summer with the son of one of her employees. Her granddaughter, Delphine, was to be sent to a girls' camp near Traverse City.

Registered to stay at the camp for two months, Horace III found himself in a normal situation with boys of his own age for the first time in his life. As he happily threw himself into camp life, he made new friends to whom the name *Dodge* meant nothing. When, after a month, his grandmother changed her mind and decided that the grandchildren should be brought home to accompany her to England, young Horace protested strongly. But protests were useless, and in July, the two children and their grandmother arrived in England.

Anna visited Delphine Ione and Godde in London, then went on a trip to Vienna and Paris with her son. After she had returned to Detroit, she received word of the death of Della Dodge Eschbach, sister of John and Horace, in Santa Monica. Della's remains were cremated as she had requested, and shortly afterwards, Anna received a mailing box containing the ashes. It seemed only fitting to Anna that Della and John and Horace, who had been so very close in life, should be together also in death. But Anna knew of Matilda's dislike of Della. She knew that Matilda would not approve of placing Della's ashes in the jointly owned Dodge mausoleum. Anna stared at the small nondescript mailing box and wondered. Then she made up her mind to use her key to the crypt and to place the box in it unobtrusively.

20

Again in 1937, Anna spent the summer in England with Horace's two young teenagers—Delphine and Horace III. On their return from England, Anna discovered that a $2-million suit was being filed against her daughter, Delphine Dodge Godde. Filed by screen actress Judith Allen, the lawsuit charged Delphine Ione with alienation of the affections of the actress' husband, Jack Doyle, in London. Although Miss Allen was in the process of divorcing the handsome, curly-headed Doyle, the divorce had not yet been finalized. The actress claimed that Delphine Ione had enticed Doyle, a boxer, away from a reconciliation with his wife with promises of several hundred-thousand dollars.

To Anna's dismay, Delphine Ione had been staying in Reno since the middle of July, establishing residence so she could divorce Godde. By September, she and Doyle were flitting back and forth between Hollywood and Reno, publicly announcing their plans to marry as soon as possible.

Resplendent in a flowered green robe and red muffler, Doyle puffed slowly at his pipe when reporters were admitted to his hotel suite. The lawsuit would make no difference to his and Delphine's plans, he informed them. "Delphine is wealthy, of course," he admitted. "Sometimes I wish she were not," he added, going on to inform them he was giving up boxing to go on the London stage, after which he would study voice in Italy.

A newspaper photograph of Anna's daughter and Doyle in twin beds with a row of champagne glasses on the headboards was the catalyst that brought Hugh Dillman on a flight westward to demand that Delphine Ione leave Doyle and come back at once to the Dillmans' home. If she did not comply with the ultimatum, Delphine Ione was to have her allowance and future support cut off immediately.

Registering for airline passage under an assumed name, Dillman brought the disheveled and distraught Delphine Ione back to Detroit. Still dressed in yellow silk pajamas that almost matched her hair— dyed a brassy yellow from its natural chestnut, and worn page-boy style—Delphine Ione was driven quickly from the airport to Rose Terrace and installed in an upstairs bedroom for the night. In the morning, Anna stalked into the bedroom to deliver to her errant daughter an accusing diatribe that left the already shattered Delphine crying copiously.

Although Doyle had been removed from Delphine Ione's life, the alienations-of-affections suit continued to get newspaper coverage until it was thrown out of court. Shortly before Christmas, Timothy Godde finally came from London to Palm Beach. He and Delphine Ione then embarked on a fishing trip while the Dillmans issued a terse seven-word statement to the press: "Mr. and Mrs. Godde have become reconciled."

Anna was not destined for any respite from her children's problems, however. In mid-April, Horace filed suit for divorce from his estranged wife, Muriel, charging cruelty. His wife, he said, had made humiliating comments about him in other people's presence.

Within months, the suit became a bitter battle of charges and countercharges. Her husband, Muriel claimed, regularly and continuously spent time in Florida and England with "a woman whose name had been connected with his for a number of years." This roused Horace to point out that nearly a year-and-a-half before he married Muriel and while he was still married to his first wife, both Muriel and her mother went to Europe and toured the continent at Horace's expense.

Anna was distracted temporarily from her own family problems by the sudden death in May 1938 of Edward Stotesbury. For some time previous to his death, Stotesbury had spent money lavishly, dipping freely into a principal already drastically diminished by the depression years. Within two years of his death, Lucretia Stotesbury would quietly place her valuable jewelry on sale at a New York jeweler's and would put the Philadelphia and Bar Harbor estates up for sale at prices far below the costs of the properties. Even the fabulous El Mirasol would be placed on the market to languish for want of a buyer.

James H. R. Cromwell had brought his wife, the former Doris Duke, to attend his stepfather's funeral. Not being included in the Stotesbury will hardly impoverished James H. R., whose wife had received her second payment of more than $10 million inheritance on her twenty-fifth birthday the previous November.

Although the John Dodge and Horace Dodge widows rarely associated with each other by the mid-thirties, Anna attended Frances Dodge's wedding in July 1938. When, in August, she heard news of the tragic death of young Daniel Dodge in Lake Huron's waters, she ordered her chauffeur to drive her out to Meadow Brook Hall. To Anna, her sister-in-law's loss of an only son was terrifying with its reminder of how quickly death could snatch an adored son from his mother. She could remember so clearly too the bereavements she and Matilda had shared in 1920 with the deaths of their husbands. Yet her natural sympathy for Matilda was dulled by her awareness of the indignities that her own two children had brought to the Dodge name with their problems—and of Matilda's reaction to the unfavorable publicity. Matilda's complete withdrawal had been another blow to Anna's pride.

But now, as the chauffeur pulled the big Chrysler to a stop in the circular-driveway approach to the Wilsons' English Tudor home, Anna stepped regally from her automobile. Perhaps her children's entanglements had been embarrassing, but to Anna it was ironic that Matilda chose to make such judgments. Matilda was ignoring the fact that she too had married a divorced man—John Dodge—in an earlier and more puritanical era when divorce was a scandalous affair. But *that* divorce had been kept a secret. Anna held her head high in the knowledge that she had not stooped to disclose Matilda's secret, and entered the manor house.

Inside the great hall, Anna was greeted by the newly married Frances, who had rushed back from New York to be with her mother. Ill at ease but hoping to find the right words to express her sympathy, Anna offered her condolences to Frances, who left the room to get her mother. As the daughter was returning with Matilda, Anna asked quickly, "Did they find the boy yet, Matilda?" The loud question, rising out of Anna's own anxieties, sounded offensive and insensitive to Frances and her mother. Although Anna had come to observe the amenities, the breach immediately widened between the two sisters-in-law.

Anna put in an appearance at Daniel's funeral and then abandoned any lingering thoughts of a closer relationship with Matilda. She left, with her social secretary, for Palm Beach in time to reopen Playa Riente for the Christmas holidays that year. Horace also spent much of the winter in Palm Beach, where he escorted showgirl Mickey Devine about town.

Anna resigned herself, now, to more embarrassment because of Mickey's penchant for attracting the attention of newsmen to herself. Grim-faced, Anna read a newspaper item that reached from a Paris nightclub across the Atlantic. The exuberant Mickey, meeting the world's champion boxer Primo Carnera in the nightclub, had offered him a few pointers on how he could have made his last fight a better one. As the blonde with the cupid's-bow lips demonstrated how she would have thrown a left-handed punch, the hulking Carnera bent his scarred face down so he could hear the instructions above the noise of the crowd and the orchestra. At that moment, Mickey's dainty fist collided with his lantern jaw, her diamond ring gashing his chin. Blood dripped from the champion's face, the gendarmes were called, and reporters snapped pictures.

Near the end of May, Anna boarded the *Queen Mary* for a trip to England with Horace's young daughter Delphine. For the celebrity-conscious Anna, the trip was an exciting one because Jessica Tandy, Beatrice Lilly, Lauritz Melchior, and Douglas Fairbanks were aboard. On their arrival in Berkshire, Anna and her granddaughter had their first view of the newly renovated St. Leonard's Castle. Anna, who had read extensively of the Yorks, the Tudors, Stuarts, and Hanovers in her fascination with English history and royalty, loved the 400-year-old castle and the way its yellowish-stone turrets overlooked Windsor Park.

At the end of October, Horace and Muriel finally were divorced, with a settlement of $2,500 monthly for Muriel plus $500 monthly for the support of David and Diana. This year, Anna planned to celebrate the Christmas holidays at Rose Terrace, combining a family houseparty with the debut of Horace's daughter, Delphine. Now that Delphine had graduated from Fermata in South Carolina and was ready to go to Bryn Mawr, it was time for her to move into the young social set in Grosse Pointe. She had only a few friends in Grosse Pointe, however, because she had lived there only at brief intervals.

Anna's social secretary vigorously pursued her job of inviting and inveigling the necessary number of Grosse Pointe boys to attend young Delphine's party in numbers matching those of the girls. On the day after Christmas, the blonde, blue-eyed debutante, shining long hair gently curling to her shoulders, greeted her guests at Rose Terrace. The chateau looked its loveliest in its glittering holiday decorations with ice-carved swans, holding caviar, on the tables.

With the holidays and Delphine's reception behind them, the Dillmans returned to Palm Beach, leaving orders that their yacht should be readied for them on their return in late spring. Now that World

War II had begun in Europe with the invasion of Poland by Germany, Anna and Hugh planned to spend the summer on the *Delphine* instead of making a trip to England. Several weeks before the Dillmans' return to Grosse Pointe, thirty-five men began working on the *Delphine*, painting, scraping, polishing, and glazing the ship's hull.

Just as Anna and Hugh left Palm Beach to return home, the forty-year-old Horace married twenty-seven-year-old Mickey Devine in Baltimore, Maryland. On the previous Saturday, Horace's ex-wife, Muriel, also had remarried.

While the Dillmans enjoyed the luxury of their floating palace during the summer of 1940, they entertained a number of guests aboard their yacht. They had guests aboard for a fishing trip in early August when Captain Knight headed the boat north into Lake Huron. In the thick fog of the third day of the cruise, the *Delphine* approached South Baymouth at the tip of Manitoulin Island—the beautiful island that Daniel Dodge had loved and where his young life had ended. There was a sudden jar as the *Delphine*, shrouded in fog, shuddered and ran aground on a reef. For two days the passengers and the 52-man crew remained aboard ship as the fog gradually lifted. But the bulky *Delphine* resisted all the efforts of the three tugs and a ferryboat to dislodge the yacht. Only when a more powerful tugboat arrived from Sault Ste. Marie was the *Delphine* finally pulled back into open water.

As soon as the Dillmans returned to Rose Terrace on the *Delphine*, it was time for Anna to arrange for the debut of her second granddaughter, Christine Cromwell. Christine had spent the summer in her typical transient fashion, first with her mother, Delphine Ione, in the Goddes' home in Rye, New York, then with her maternal grandmother, Lucretia Stotesbury, in Philadelphia.

On the late afternoon of the September debut at Rose Terrace, Christine greeted hundreds of guests in the music room. Her cousins, young Delphine and Horace III, were on hand to round out the picture of family unity. And Christine's Uncle Horace had arrived with his new wife, Mickey, who was stunning in a Grecian gold-lamé dress with pleated skirt and jade-and gold beaded trimming.

Although Anna was attracted by her new daughter-in-law's infectious charm and bubbling personality, Mickey was jittery as she changed into her evening gown of black velvet and white satin for the supper party and dancing at the lakeside terrace. As the dancing began and Mickey still had not made her appearance on the terrace, Horace went upstairs to their suite. His wife was not there. When one of the Dodges' trusted employees found Mickey hiding in a small office room crying nervously, Mickey poured out her problems to the sympathetic woman who had found her sanctuary. The Grosse Pointers who were arriving for the supper party had known Horace in earlier years . . . had known his previous wives and would be resentful of an outsider, Mickey feared.

"Here, fix your face," the woman consoled Mickey, offering her a handkerchief. "Forget about being nervous. There've been plenty of scandals in the lives of the people who will be guests here tonight."

When Mickey edged out to the terrace, one male partner after another gravitated toward her, whirling her around the dance floor built in the middle of three terraces leading down to the lake. Covered with a striped marquee, the dance pavilion overlooked a display of fountains, tinted with colored lights, that streamed from the breakwater and formed a background for geysers of glycerine bubbles floating up from tanks of hydrogen sunk into the lawn.

Partygoers were willing to overlook their usual criteria for the privilege of being included at this, and future, Dodge extravaganzas. It was not too difficult to trade one's restrictive judgments for the pleasure of dancing to the music of Emil Petti and his orchestra, flown in from New York for a few hours between performances at the Savoy-Plaza roof gardens. And the guest of honor, seventeen-year-old Christine—her dark hair and flashing eyes contrasting with the delicate blondness of her cousin Delphine—danced happily until the party ended at dawn. Then, as she finally went up to her room to rest after all the excitement, she took with her the bouquet her father, Jimmy Cromwell, had sent.

Cromwell was involved in politics now. After appointment as U.S. minister to Canada, he'd been criticized for attacking American isolationists. Now, he was campaigning in New Jersey as the Democratic candidate for the U.S. Senate.

Although Franklin D. Roosevelt won a third presidential term in the November election, Cromwell became one of the few unsuccessful Democratic candidates that year. Three days after the election, he admitted that he had been estranged from Doris Duke for the past five months.

With his mother, James H. R. went down to Palm Beach for the winter season while his daughter, Christine, divided her time in Palm Beach between the homes of Mammá—Anna Dodge Dillman—and her other grandmother, Lucretia Stotesbury. By the middle of April, the Palm Beach season was usually winding down. But the news of the arrival, on April 18, of the Duke and Duchess of Windsor from the

Bahamas for a three-day visit in Palm Beach, set off a scramble among the resort people to entertain the former king of England who had abdicated his throne only a few years previously.

Anna's niece, Winifred Seyburn, executed a coup by arranging for a dinner party for the Duke and Duchess on the patio of the Seyburns' home, Casa Giravento. Because the royal couple had specified there should be no formal entertainment because of the war, the Seyburns' party was limited to twenty-four guests.

The Duke and Duchess had elected to stay at the Everglades Club. When Anna heard that the Duke's old friend, Captain Alistair MacIntosh, was planning to entertain the royal couple at a soiree at his supper club, The Alibi, she thought she saw an opportunity for a coup of her own. Since MacIntosh, known as "Ali" to his friends, was one of Hugh Dillman's close friends, perhaps Hugh could persuade him to see things her way.

"There's really no need to hold the reception in a saloon," she told Hugh. "We have all the room we need here at Playa Riente—and all the accommodations."

When Hugh convinced MacIntosh that it would be better to have the reception at Playa Riente, Anna hurriedly informed her staff to plan a cocktail party for fifty people and to get a guest list together. The cocktail-party plans were being hastily assembled when MacIntosh and Hugh told Anna they would like to have more people attend the affair. Working frantically against a new deadline for a luncheon for 350 people, Anna's social secretary was revising the plans and the guest list when Anna told her to concentrate solely on the details of the luncheon itself. "Mr. Dillman and his friend said they would take care of the guest list by getting the names from the Everglades Club," Anna added.

The luncheon hour approached with everything proceeding as smoothly as if the plans had been in the making for weeks—tables set up on the patio, food and drinks prepared, the Dodge private guards in their usual unobtrusive stations, and the servants carefully instructed.

James—the second footman and silver man—was ordered to stand in his usual place at ground level between the two great staircases, one curving up to the left, the other to the right. Posted between the staircases because of his graceful bow, with which he could direct guests out to the patio by a masterful sweep of his arm, James performed in his customary majestic style as guests arrived. It was important that all the guests should be assembled out on the patio before the arrival of the Duke and Duchess, since protocol demanded that royalty should arrive last. Suddenly, however, it became apparent to both

Anna and her social secretary that something had gone terribly wrong. Guests were strolling aimlessly and wandering toward the staircases. James was missing from his post—something that had never before happened.

Another servant was quickly sent to replace the missing second footman during the search for James. The footman was finally located, sulking in a secluded corner because, he said indignantly, he had found himself bowing to the barkeep who ordinarily served him his drinks on Saturday nights when he stopped in at a local bar. Among the invited guests, Anna soon discovered, were many of MacIntosh's associates in the liquor business. Others were flower-shop owners to whom Hugh sold the flowers he raised at Sandy Loam. Anna was dismayed but not unduly surprised. It was typical of both men that they did not distinguish among friends according to the caste system. But when it seemed that "David and Wally" were oblivious to the fact that many of the people presented to them were not of social-register quality, Anna decided to overlook the whole thing.

The Dillmans' usual preoccupation with early summer plans for travel or for cruising was disrupted the second week of May when Anna's granddaughter, eighteen-year-old Christine Cromwell, eloped with Frederick Putnam White, son of the prominent Loring Quincy Whites of Cohasset, Massachusetts. Upset over the elopement, Anna telephoned her daughter Delphine Godde in Rye, New York. But Delphine Ione knew little more about the young couple than did Anna. Christine had been a guest of the White family for the weekend while she attended a houseparty at Brown University where Frederick was a freshman. Then Christine and young White had disappeared, only to turn up in Elkton, Maryland, where they were married.

Public interest in the romance of a debutante—even a debutante as wealthy and attractive as Christine—was fleeting now that there were more important, frightening things that demanded public concern. Hitler's troops massed near the Soviet border that spring, and it became more apparent that the United States would be drawn into the conflict.

On the morning of December 7, 1941, Japanese planes bombed the U.S. Pacific fleet at Pearl Harbor. The United States was at war with Japan, and within days, with the other Axis powers.

When the Philippines were captured by the Japanese in 1942, Americans began to experience the more severe penalties of war. Nor were wealthy Americans immune to the sacrifices demanded by a wartime government. Anna Dodge Dillman was in Washington visiting her daughter, Delphine Ione, when the captain of her yacht telephoned to inform her the navy was taking over the *Delphine* for war service. By the time Anna returned to Detroit, the pipe organ had been ripped out of the music room, and the boat had been stripped of its expensive furnishings.

The production of war materials was priority work now for private industry, including the Horace E. Dodge Boat & Plane Corporation's Newport News plant, which began to manufacture rescue boats for the navy. Before the end of July, Horace E. Dodge II, aged 42, was commissioned a major in the army.

Within a week of the announcement of the commission, Michigan's Senator Brown received so many letters protesting the appointment that the War Department was asked for an explanation. Horace, sporting gold oak leaves on a major's uniform, went to live in Washington's swank Warman Park Hotel with his civilian-aide bodyguard, whose duties were varied. When the two made their regular stop at the Mayflower's cocktail lounge crowded with military men, the bodyguard sampled his employer's drinks to ascertain whether they were of the proper mixture. The aide also commuted to New York or Detroit at Dodge's side, just as he had in civilian life— ready to telephone Anna's business manager in Detroit if assistance was needed to get Horace out of one of his numerous scrapes. Anna's business manager was under orders to drop whatever he was doing at any hour to go anywhere as a troubleshooter for Horace. On her adviser's return, Anna would place her hands over her ears if he tried to give her an accounting of what had happened. "I don't want to hear," she would say.

But Anna could not close her ears and eyes to the repercussions from her son's appointment. Still, she felt better about the publicity when there was a public announcement from the secretary of war stating that "Mr. Dodge was recommended for appointment by the commanding general of the Army Air Forces on July 22, after a board of officers had passed upon his qualifications and found him to possess qualifications as a well-known expert and exponent of speedy small craft used extensively by the Army in landing and other coastwise operations, which make his services desirable."

The war had effected the return to the United States of many people formerly living or vacationing in Europe. Horace's two children of his second marriage—David and Diana—had been brought back to New York from England by their mother previous to the war, however, when David was old enough to begin school in 1935. Young David had begun his boarding-school life at an early age, moving on from one private school to another, as did Diana. The brother and sister were sent to spend summers with their father, which meant they usually spent the summer months at Rose Terrace in the care of governesses. And when the children were at their mother's home, they saw Muriel only in hurried bits and snatches—usually when they were brought by their English Nanny into their mother's presence for a goodnight kiss, if she happened to be at home at that hour.

Muriel led an eventful life in these years, divorcing a second husband and marrying a third. The lonely little David liked to sit down at the small melodian his father had given him, and to pick out melodies on its keys. When he discovered that one of his "nannies" could play the piano, he asked the woman whether she would give him piano lessons. He would have to ask his mother, the nursemaid told him. After Muriel forbade the lessons, the boy's disappointment turned to grief when the melodian disappeared from his mother's home. And he was openly envious when his Aunt Delphine Ione decided it was time her younger daughter Yvonne Baker should begin to study piano—studies which Yvonne found distasteful within a brief time.

To the lonely David and Diana, it was inconceivable that anyone should not love their Aunt Delphine, whose affection warmed the children's lives. The brother and sister had been especially devoted to their aunt since an earlier summer, when they were being taken to Europe on one of their several trips across the Atlantic. Clinging to their nursemaid in the midst of the bustle of passengers and visitors enjoying bon-voyage parties, the children had excitedly hopped up and down when their Aunt Delphine came to their stateroom to give them a bulky package. "Now you mustn't open it until tomorrow," she warned gaily, as she swept them into her scented embrace and kissed them goodbye. Inside the outer package, the children found individual packages containing a different present for each day of the trip—a thin balsa-wood airplane with a rubber-band launcher, a blow-tube that ejected a parachute . . . inexpensive gifts treasured by the children because of the personal attention behind them.

There were few other pleasurable moments in the children's lives. One of the joyful times, though, was the Christmas they spent at Playa Riente in Palm Beach when Hugh Dillman, dressed in a Santa Claus suit, flew in an airplane over Playa Riente's lawn. As he dropped Christmas presents from the airplane, the children shrieked and ran to retrieve the packages, some of which fell into the ocean.

Life for the children was much more formal with Mammá at Rose Terrace, where the youngsters were reminded by their grandmother to stand tall . . . to sit at the table without slouching . . . to speak precisely . . . to mind their manners . . . to come down the great marble staircase single file so they could walk on the borders of the lush blue Savonny carpeting and not wear out the center section. Nor did Mammá give them lavish allowances. It was clear that Anna thought the lives of her own two children might have been very different if Delphine Ione and Horace had not been smothered in luxury.

For David, day-to-day life at boarding school was tolerable because his alternative was so much worse. Enrolled in Allen-Stevenson School in New York for the primary grades, David sang in the school choir in spite of his mother's protests to school directors. Choir singing was a requirement at the school, the directors pointed out firmly. But when Muriel also protested her son's participation in ballroom dancing, David became the only Stevenson student not to attend the dancing classes.

Muriel had other ideas for her son—he should train to become a boxer and wrestler, she insisted. Baseball and football were the things that should interest him, she told the boy. To placate his mother, David played football for one semester, then gave up the sport as "an insane game."

David then went on to Harvey, a pre-prep boarding school, and finally to Hotchkiss. At his eastern school, the boy felt very much alone during the war years. His father was in the military, and his mother was living at the other end of the country, in California, where she had placed Diana in a west-coast boarding school. On the one Sunday of the month the boys were permitted to leave their school to visit someone, Uncle Tim—Delphine Ione's husband—drove over to get David and take him back to the Goddes' home in Stamford, Connecticut. For the affection-starved boy, Godde became a father-figure, who took the time to make the trip to the school with rationed gasoline. And David liked staying with the Goddes, where he observed, with approval, his Uncle Tim's devotion to his Aunt Delphine Ione.

Delphine had stopped drinking and had settled down to a good marriage with Timothy Godde, but alcohol had already done its damage. By June 1943, Delphine Ione was hospitalized in New York City. Anna came to New York to be with her daughter, but even as she worried over Delphine's weakened condition, she fretted also over letters and telephone calls she received from Dayton, Ohio, where Horace was stationed at Fairfield Depot. Anna left her daughter's bedside to go to Ohio because of the difficulties Horace was having with his superiors. Perhaps she could convince Horace to stay sober, she hoped.

Like his father and uncle, Horace had a rapport with the men who worked for him. But neither army officials nor civilian aides were able to keep Horace sober enough to make use of his abilities to keep the civilian workers on the job. Workers were scarce, and absenteeism was the greatest deterrent to peak production, but Horace was unable to separate his drinking from his work obligations.

Anna was still in Dayton with her son when, in late afternoon on June 18, Delphine Ione died of pneumonia at the age of forty-four, with her husband and her physician at her bedside. Immediately, Anna and Horace left for New York to accompany the body back to Detroit. The servants at Rose Terrace, notified of the death, talked in awed voices as they prepared the house for the funeral. They watched in silence as the casket was carried into Rose Terrace and as Anna, leaning on the arm of Major Horace Dodge, returned home. At the end of the line of people accompanying the casket to Rose Terrace, the bewildered ten-year-old Yvonne Baker—Delphine Ione's younger daughter—trailed the others. The chauffeur's wife observed the desolate child. Having experienced what it was like to be an orphan, the chauffeur's wife went over to the child and made the little girl her special protegee. In Agnes Swan, Yvonne had found her parent-figure.

21

A newspaper photo of Delphine Ione, captioned "The Golden Girl is Gone," headed a story reconstructing the more flamboyant events in her life. But Detroiters were distracted from accounts of Delphine Dodge Godde's life and death by a race riot that broke out in the city on the night of June 20. By Tuesday, the day of Delphine Ione's funeral, army troops had moved into Detroit, walking down Woodward Avenue with fixed bayonets after the killing of eleven people and injuring of 500 in the rioting.

The Dodges lived out their own death drama in the midst of the greater drama around them. As the lengthy funeral cortege followed the hearse to Woodlawn Cemetery, Matilda and Alfred Wilson, Winifred Dodge Seyburn and her sister Isabel Dodge Sloane, represented the John Dodge side of the family at the cemetery. Delphine Ione's casket was placed next to those of her father and of her Uncle John and his first wife, Ivy, and of her cousins John Duval, Anna Margaret and Daniel.

Delphine Ione had stipulated in her will that her former husband, James H.R. Cromwell, should not become a trustee of the trusts she had created for her two daughters, Christine Cromwell White and Yvonne Baker. Because Delphine had not outlived her mother, however, the trusts for the two girls and for Timothy Godde were invalidated.

Anna's grief over the loss of her daughter grew sharper when Horace entered an army hospital after his sister's funeral. He was still hospitalized a month later when his wife Mickey filed suit for separation, asking $60,000 a year alimony. Dodge, she claimed, had consorted with other women and engaged in drunken brawls in public places. She had been under a doctor's care for a cerebral hemorrhage as a result of Horace knocking her down on one occasion, she added,

258

classifying her husband as "a positive detriment to the war effort." "My husband has no more to do with the military effort than before he put on his uniform," she informed the court. "He has been drunk practically from the day of his induction until the present time."

Within days of the publication of Mickey's accusations, an army medical board announced that Major Dodge was not physically capable of field duty. He was to be placed on inactive duty.

Regardless of the misfortunes within the family, the grandchildren had their own lives to live. Horace's daughter Delphine, of his first marriage to Lois Knowlson, was planning to marry. Delphine's fiance was now taking courses at Rhode Island State College under the army's specialized training program.

Anna resigned herself to her eldest granddaughter becoming a Catholic on her marriage to Private Robert Petz. She knew that her granddaughter's sweet and amiable personality did not prevent her from having strong views, and Anna respected this strength of character. Although she had recently been ill in Palm Beach, Anna traveled to White Plains, New York, in February 1944 to see her son Horace walk down the aisle of St. Bernard's Roman Catholic Church with his daughter. There were only two days for the newlyweds to be together before Private Petz returned to college. Delphine remained in White Plains with her mother Lois, who had been married and divorced twice since her divorce from Horace.

When Delphine's younger brother, twenty-one-year-old Horace III, decided to marry in October of the same year, his father objected vehemently. "I'm not going to have my son make a damn fool of himself. I've done enough of that sort of thing myself, " Major Dodge spouted, although his own divorce the previous July and the awarding of three-quarter million dollars of Anna's money to Mickey had not prevented the elder Horace from jumping into another liaison. This new romantic attachment was to the WAC nurse who had taken care of him in the hospital.

But after telephoning his son, the senior Horace had one of his mercurial changes of mood. Horace III and his bride-to-be agreed to postpone their wedding from Tuesday to Thursday to await the senior Horace's arrival in Colorado, where the son was an army corporal at Lowry Field.

When his father did not arrive for the wedding on Thursday, young Horace was not surprised. His father had managed to be late for most things as far back as the children could remember. The bride and groom went ahead with the wedding without a single relative present.

The youthful Mrs. Horace Dodge III, a sculptress and industrial artist, exuded confidence as reporters asked about future plans. "We want four little boys, and they'll probably be redheads too," Margery said. They would not allow money to be a problem, she explained, because the couple was going to live on Horace III's salary as a corporal.

The philosophies expressed by her grandson's bride pleased Anna, who had determined, in her respect for the work ethic, that each of her grandchildren should earn his or her way in the workaday world in early life. Although she had set up a million-dollar trust fund for each grandchild, none of the grandchildren could collect even the interest on the trust until he or she had reached the age of thirty-five. Her hopes for her own children had not been realized, but she anticipated more productive lives for these grandchildren. She had been gratified when Horace III had studied electrical engineering at Union College in Schenectady until he had gone into the army.

Divorces matched the number of weddings within the Dodge family in the mid-forties. By January of 1945, granddaughter Christine was suing for divorce from Frederick White, now on duty with the navy. Christine's divorce was uncontested, but her two children remained in the custody of their father. When Christine came to stay at the Dillmans' Palm Beach home, it seemed to Anna that unhappy marital tangles were to be the destiny of the grandchildren just as they had been the destiny of her own two children. Christine's marriage had lasted only three and one-half years. Several weeks after her divorce, she married paratrooper Edward L. Williams.

Surrounded by such rapidly changing family alliances, the younger Dodges clung to the few relationships that remained firm. Even after Delphine Ione's death, Timothy Godde continued to have David stay with him on short visits from boarding school. And at Christmas time, Godde brought David with him to Rose Terrace for the holidays. David was a prep-school student now in Connecticut. His mother Muriel was in the process of divorcing her third husband; his father Horace in the process of marrying his fourth wife. No longer spending any time with his mother in California, fifteen-year-old David got permission from his father to begin taking piano lessons after years of composing music without ever learning piano techniques.

Both Horace and Anna worried at this time about the well being of David's sister Diana, who was still living in California. On holidays and vacations from boarding school, Diana returned to her mother's home, where she was alone much of the time. She could come to her Grandmother Dodge's home only for a few weeks in the summertime, according to the divorce agreement. For those few weeks, Diana and David were happy just to be together.

In her attempt to influence her grandchildren's lives, Anna promised David, Diana, and their cousin Yvonne—just as she had promised the other grandchildren earlier—that each of them would be given "something very nice if you don't drink or smoke until you are twenty-one." David was determined to get the promised reward. He and his sister had seen so much of the excesses of their parents that the two children disdained this kind of behavior. To them, it seemed no hardship to abstain from tobacco and alcohol.

Horace's concerns for David and Diana did not interfere with his plans to go to England soon after the war ended. In late spring, he arrived in Windsor to marry army nurse Lieutenant Clara Mae Tinsley, a full-faced young woman with heavy dark eyebrows and short dark fluffy hair. This time Anna would not be reconciled to her son's marriage. She remained adamant in her refusal to recognize her new daughter-in-law, embittered by reports brought to her of the couple's drinking excesses. The one kind of influence her son did not need, Anna felt, was a permissive attitude on the part of his partner toward his predilection for alcohol.

Anna had tried, and exhausted, many tactics to distract Horace from the bottle. She had found that having him aboard the *Delphine* on a cruise was one of the more effective ways of keeping him nearly sober when she was there to ration his drinks and to keep the servants from bringing any extra liquor onto the boat.

The teenaged David Dodge had his first ride on the *Delphine* when he returned to Detroit with his grandmother on the yacht after the government released the boat at the war's end. So huge that it had to move diagonally through one lock of the Welland Canal, the *Delphine* took two weeks to get them home, with frequent stops for breakdowns.

Anna was willing to spend money freely to restore the yacht to its former luxury after its use as a floating headquarters and flagship for Admiral Ernest J. King, chief of naval operations. She commissioned a quarter-million-dollar renovation job in 1947, then registered the yacht in her son's name. New employees, coming aboard the renovated *Delphine*, were awed by the luxurious furnishings, paintings, and the thick Persian rugs that were quickly rolled up from the decks whenever a gale threatened.

In view of such opulence, employees were astonished by Anna's careful economies in mundane matters. On weekdays, Anna's standing orders to the cook were that only hard-boiled eggs should be served, so the leftover eggs could be eaten at another meal. Fried eggs were a breakfast treat reserved for Sundays. If there were strawberries for dessert and a few were left, Anna's next day's menu would include the notation *seven strawberries* as she gave the order to the butler each morning. She was equally exacting in noting if any of the furniture had been moved a few inches from its position and would chastize servants who cleaned beneath furniture and failed to replace it. But her employees were well paid for their services, and Anna did not find it difficult to keep her workers.

By the time David and Diana's mother had remarried for the fourth time in 1946, there had been so many marriages and divorces within the family that even the youngest of the children had become accustomed to them. But when, in May 1947, Anna appeared in court to divorce Hugh Dillman, there were many people, even within the family, who did not understand why the divorce had been filed.

Whatever Dillman's motives had been in marrying Anna, he had made an effort to help his wife with her family responsibilities. Serving many times as rescuer, advisor, and father-confessor to Anna's children and grandchildren, "Uncle Hugh" was remembered with affection by the younger Dodges. And while other widows of wealth had to entice escorts to attend them, the handsome Hugh had been available to Anna, opening new social vistas for her and bolstering her insecurities in awkward situations.

Yet the seventy-five-year-old Anna was finally overwhelmed by doubts when rumors drifted about that Hugh was fond of entertaining Hollywood starlets at his Palm Beach home. Over and above all, though, was the doubt that burdened Anna in the same way it burdened many other people of wealth. Was it only the money that made her desirable?

Among Grosse Pointe people and Palm Beach residents, there was talk that Anna was making a private settlement of $1 million to Hugh Dillman. Publicly, Anna asked the court for permission to take back her former name as the widow of Horace Elgin Dodge, and the permission was granted.

Life changed rapidly for Anna after that. She no longer had a husband, her daughter Delphine was dead, and her last sister May

McNutt died in Palm Beach in 1948. Anna herself was alone in the world except for her son Horace and the grandchildren.

With Horace married to a fourth wife, Anna saw her son less frequently, as he and Clara moved about from his Palm Beach home to homes in Connecticut and Louisville as well as to St. Leonard's Castle. But at Rose Terrace, Clara was not welcome. She came to Rose Terrace with Horace only when Anna was out of town.

After the end of the war and the expiration of defense contracts, the Newport News business had faltered and lost money in 1946. The Virginia plant was dismantled then, and the remnants of the Dodge Boat and Plane Works were moved back to Detroit, where Horace's personal boats were produced, stored, and repaired.

Despite her seventy-seven years, Anna would not permit her new sense of mortality and loneliness to commit her to brooding over the past. In earlier years she had bought homes for her two sisters, made it possible for her parents and sisters to winter in Florida, financed college educations for the nieces and nephews who wished to go to college, and built a mausoleum for the Thomsons where her mother, father, and two sisters, plus her sister May's husband, were interred. She had taken care of her family responsibilities, and there was no compulsion to look back—only to go determinedly into the future, busying herself with the symphony, with parties, with travels.

Whenever Anna was at Rose Terrace coinciding with any of her grandchildren's between-semester visits, she had always taken a personal interest in the children—proud of David's skill at the piano, concerned over Christine's and Yvonne's tendency toward plumpness despite her prodding them to diet, stern with their infractions of her rules, determined that their schooling should be the finest.

But often, Anna had not been at home to see that her orders were followed. Discipline was relaxed during her absences. One of Anna's standing rules was that the children must not fraternize with the servants. For Delphine Ione's daughter Yvonne, this rule was another barrier to normal communications with the people around her. In her loneliness, Yvonne often walked down the wide tree-lined drive leading from Rose Terrace to Anna's chauffeur's two-floor apartment adjoining the garages. There, Yvonne visited with Norval Swan's wife, the Scotch-born woman who had befriended the girl on her arrival at Rose Terrace at the time of her mother's death.

Many Grosse Pointers had sought out European immigrants for personal employees in their search for the style of European nobility. Because of her Scotch ancestry, Anna Dodge liked having Scotch employees, trained in the particularities of formal living. Although most of her employees addressed Anna as *madame*, the chauffeur always addressed her as *milady*, or referred to her, in conversation with others, as *the lady*. In the intimacy of Yvonne's relationship with the Swans, there was no such formality. The child called the chauffeur *Pappy*, his wife *Boots*.

Boarding schools were a problem both to Yvonne, who was consistently unhappy at school, and to Anna and some of her administrative employees, who had to shift the girl from one school to another. Anna finally sent Yvonne to an Episcopalian convent in Illinois where she hoped the nuns would help her granddaughter to adjust to convent-school life. Yvonne ran away after only three months.

In her shifting from school to school, Yvonne was registered for a while at Kingswood, north of Detroit. She had been there only a brief time when she telephoned Rose Terrace, saying she needed clothing. Thinking this a strange request, three of Anna's trusted employees drove out to the school. They found that Yvonne, in her attempt to win friends, had given her clothes to schoolmates.

Later, while attending Grosse Pointe's Sacred Heart Academy, Yvonne found a close friend. When the schoolmate's father died and her family was pressed for tuition money, Anna paid the fees so Yvonne could keep her friend near her. The close relationship was valued so highly by the loyal and generous Yvonne that when her friend became critically ill some years later, Yvonne underwrote some of the hospital expenses.

Anna too clung to some friendships she valued. In spite of her daughter Delphine's troubles with her first husband Jimmy Cromwell, Anna had retained his friendship through the years.

The one love affair to which Horace had clung throughout the years was his infatuation with powerboats. After carrying out his threat to withdraw from speedboat racing in the early 1930s, Horace had finally realized that his departure from racing was more painful to himself than to officials of the powerboat association. But then had come the war years. . . his fourth marriage. . . money problems.

Although his muscular stockiness had long since slackened into paunchiness, the forty-nine-year-old Horace was afire with boyish eagerness in the spring of 1949 as he watched his boatworks' employees putting the finishing touches on a sleek new craft. The boat, *Delphine X*, was the one he envisioned piloting to a glorious finish in that year's Gold Cup race. He also had another racer, named the *Lotus* after the Dodge brothers' early boat, under construction for the Harmsworth contest. But before the Gold Cup race began, Horace's *Delphine X* cracked up in a trial run.

When the Gold Cup contenders roared into the first heat, a disgruntled Horace, cursing his bad luck, sat among 200,000 spectators. His eyes followed the progress of driver Guy Lombardo as Lombardo piloted his own boat, but was having trouble with the steering. A shiny red boat driven by Wild Bill Cantrell, Kentucky-born daredevil who also raced cars at Indianapolis, had zoomed into the lead early in the race. Horace's eyes now fastened enviously on the flashy red *My Sweetie* as driver Cantrell zipped along the smooth and sunny Detroit River and claimed the Gold Cup with a new record speed of 78.645 mph for a single heat.

Horace's hopes for a triumph in the Harmsworth Race were dashed when the *Lotus* developed mechanical difficulties that could not be corrected easily. As usual when he was depressed or perplexed, Horace appealed to his and Anna's confidante, Florence Sisman.

"My back is to the wall, Florence," he complained, his face sagging with disappointment. "I haven't got a boat, and I want to get in that race."

The small, blonde Florence was quite accustomed to bailing others out of trouble particularly her good friend Horace. Whether the situation required bullying or blarney, bitching or cajoling, Florence managed to get people moving in the direction she thought best. Now, as Horace despaired over his lack of a boat for the Harmsworth, Florence had a suggestion. Why didn't he buy *My Sweetie* from its Detroit owners?

Horace had wanted to build a boat that he could drive to victory, but he was willing to compromise and buy a boat that he could pilot to a win. Right now, he lusted for the *My Sweetie* as much as he had lusted for any woman. But he needed money, and there was only one way to get it. Would Florence intercede with his mother, he asked, to try to get the purchase money?

The role of mediator between Horace and the mother he called "the queen" was a familiar one for Florence. She pondered the request, knowing that Mother Dodge would scold and harangue but would eventually write out a check and have Horace sign another note for the money.

This time, Anna wrote a check for $25,000, making it possible for Horace to clamber into *My Sweetie*'s single cockpit and enter the qualifying trials for the Harmsworth. As he circled back after finishing his trial runs, his friends clustered around him, congratulating him on a great performance.

Although Horace had qualified for third place on the United States' team of three defending boats, the other two qualifying boats had averaged 97.44 and 94.296 in contrast with Horace's 87.561 mph. "We are far from satisfied with Dodge's performance; we hope that Dodge will step down and allow Bill Cantrell to take over the pilot's seat," the chairman of the Harmsworth selection committee told reporters who crowded around him for his announcement of qualifying boats. Enraged by the official's statement to the press, Horace thundered his defiance when he was told that race officials might vote to replace him as pilot of his own boat. *My Sweetie* would be withdrawn from the race then, he insisted.

On the Saturday of the race, Horace was in *My Sweetie's* cockpit, accelerating his boat through the waters and maneuvering the turns, trying desperately to gun the boat at top speed and to retain control, but never catching up with the other two American boats. The United States, however, retained the trophy against a Canadian contender. The winning boat averaged 94.285 mph, breaking the previous record. Horace's speed was 81.672.

After that, Horace permitted Cantrell to drive *My Sweetie* in the big races. Cantrell chalked up a number of impressive victories winning the National Sweepstakes title at Red Banks, the Silver Cup at Detroit, and winning the first fifteen-mile heat on the roughened, choppy Potomac River for the President's Cup in September when the next two heats were canceled because of a stiff wind. Horace and Anna and Cantrell were then received at the White House for presentation of the President's Cup by President Truman. Later, the American Power Boat Association ruled the race "no contest" because only one heat had been run, and ordered the return of the cup to Washington.

Already having problems in his fourth marriage, Horace tried to forget his difficulties with Clara Mae by entering *My Sweetie* in another series of races in the summer of 1950. In the Detroit Memorial race, *My Sweetie* zoomed ahead of the other contenders, a rooster tail of spray fanning out from the speeding boat as its driver swooped gracefully around the turn stakes. Horace watched the craft with a pride that changed to concern when the boat sprang a leak in the second heat. At the end of the third heat, *My Sweetie* zeroed into the pits, her bilge heavy with water but still the winner.

Horace yearned to share more completely in *My Sweetie's* successes by driving the boat to victory himself. But the lameness that had plagued him for many years had now progressed to a pronounced stumble. A driver had to be in peak physical condition, he was reminded by his friends and his pilots. Still, when Horace went out to Las Vegas in November, he was determined to drive his own boat in the Lake Mead sixty-mile race. Splitting the driving with Bill Cantrell during the four heats, he won the $2,500 APBA trophy with only token opposition from two 225-class hydroplanes.

Anna considered her investment in her son's boats worthwhile if Horace would expend his enthusiasm on the boats instead of on women. Repercussions from his second marriage had brought Horace into a federal courtroom early in 1950 for a pretrial settlement of his differences with Muriel over alimony payments. And this was only the first of a number of legal problems between family members in that same year.

The marital affairs of Anna's granddaughter Christine flashed back into the newspapers when the young woman filed suit for divorce from her second husband. "Christine," her husband complained, "was always dashing around the country and expecting me to follow her." He didn't want her money, he added. He only wanted a wife like "other fellows have." The husband withdrew his opposition, however, when Christine set up a $400,000 trust fund for their small son, with the child's father given the right to administer the fund and share custody of the boy. Within months of the divorce, Christine married a third time at St. Thomas, Virgin Islands.

Two weeks after this third marriage, Christine filed suit in Federal Court to establish her claim to one-fourth of her grandfather's estate, valued now at approximately $57 million. According to her grandfather's will, the estate would be divided, on Anna's death, in halves. One half was to be split between his daughter Delphine Ione's two children, Christine and Yvonne. The other half was to be shared among his son Horace's children.

Christine's lawyers described the suit as a routine move to prove their client's vested interest. Intimates of Christine knew, however, that the granddaughter's lavish expenditures were based on expectations of the inheritance she would receive at Anna's death. At the very least, Christine needed proof of this expected inheritance to enable her to continue with her life of luxury.

Court suits continued to compile when Timothy Godde filed suit in July 1950. After the death of his wife, Delphine Ione, he asserted, he had waived rights to his wife's estate with Anna's promise to pay him $48,000 a year for his lifetime. The payments, Godde insisted, were more than $130,000 in arrears. Anna settled her son-in-law's complaint out of court.

At the end of what had been a decidedly unpleasant year, Anna turned her attention to her two youngest granddaughters—Yvonne and Diana. The girls were of debutante age now, and since Rose Terrace had been the site of the coming-out parties for the other Dodge grandchildren, Anna wanted to launch Delphine's daughter Yvonne and Horace's daughter Diana from the same setting. The debut party was held between Christmas and New Year's Day, but it was not as lavish as those of earlier times.

With her obligations to her granddaughters discharged, Anna returned with Horace to Palm Beach for the winter season. But the social whirl of the early 1951 season was disrupted when Horace collapsed and had to be rushed to Good Samaritan Hospital. Anna, who had lost so many of her family, was frightened at the thought of losing her son also. She was even more terrified when his collapse was diagnosed as a coronary thrombosis. But by early February, Horace's condition had improved enough for him to be released from the hospital.

Under doctor's orders to restrict his activities and his drinking carefully, Horace pleased Anna by being the dutiful son for a while. He accompanied his mother to musicales, parties, and even to a fashion show—this last an event that changed his life. As the mother and son sat in the select Palm Beach audience and watched the show put on by a New York Fifth Avenue couturier, Horace was entranced by a stunning platinum-blonde model who strolled down the ramp. When the girl returned to her dressing room, boxes of furs and dresses—reported to be worth $59,000—were stacked in the room, gifts of Horace E. Dodge II. The girl was Gregg Sherwood, nee Dora Mae Fjelstad of Beloit, Wisconsin.

Pretty little Dora Mae, stepdaughter of a Norwegian janitor for a public school, had always been ambitious to get ahead in the world. Beauty contests were the first step—she was crowned Miss Wisconsin, then placed fifth in the Miss America contest. An early marriage to a ticket agent for the New York Yankees ended after the ticket taker confessed to appropriating nearly $45,000 from Yankee funds to buy gifts for his wife.

When modeling jobs for John Robert Powers were frequent enough to give her only a taste of the lush, successful life she wanted, Dora Mae—now known by the more glamorous name of Gregg

Sherwood—went to Hollywood. Here she played roles in five movies, including one with a fledgling actor named Rock Hudson. But her career was mainly occupied with modeling, and her classic features appeared on the covers of 144 magazines.

By June 1951, there was talk that Gregg would be the next Mrs. Horace Dodge. "I think Miss Sherwood is just trying to get more free publicity," Horace said, ungallantly denying the rumors.

Whether Horace's ungentlemanly remark was a result of a tiff with Gregg or whether he was being protective of himself as a still-married man, the couple's close relationship continued on through the late summer and fall. By this time Horace had a new blue speedboat named the *Hornet* for the other of the Dodge brothers' original boats. When he sent the *Hornet* out to Seattle for the Gold Cup competition, the boat came in second.

In September, Anna and her friend Florence Sisman flew to Washington for the President's Cup race, Anna proudly wearing the diamond pin that Horace had given her, with *My Sweetie* spelled out in jewels. They were at Horace's side when Guy Lombardo, driving *My Sweetie* for the Dodges, spun out in the last heat when the motor quit. And Cantrell had to take the *Hornet* out of the race when the boat's gear box shook loose.

Anna sympathized with her son in his disappointment over the loss of the race. But the same month brought Anna a keen personal disappointment when her young granddaughter, Yvonne, impulsively married a news reporter for a radio station in St. Thomas, Virgin Islands. Because Yvonne was an orphan, Anna had always felt more responsibility for the girl. She was angry and hurt now that the eighteen-year-old girl had acted so irresponsibly. And it was impossible not to be concerned that the youthful Yvonne was following her half-sister Christine's pattern of careless and rash behavior. In her discouragement, Anna refused to acknowledge the girl's marriage.

22

Anna's loyalty to her family had remained unshaken through the years. Two months after Yvonne's wedding, Anna relented and sent the newlyweds a wedding present as a mark of reconciliation. There were other demands on Anna's loyalty at this time, though, as Christine continued her efforts to get control of a share of the Dodge trust fund. And by January 1952, Christine's latest marriage was fragmenting. While the divorce was pending, she took a ten-year-lease on the Maurice Petit botanical gardens in the Virgin Islands, including a bar and night club and fifteen acres of orchids and tropical flora.

Anna had no such problems with her grandson David and his sister Diana. Not only had David claimed his reward for abstaining from liquor and cigarettes until the age of twenty-one, but he also had studied at Oberlin for two years, then applied for, and received, a Taliesin scholarship, becoming an apprentice at the Frank Lloyd Wright studio-workshop in Arizona in the fall of 1951. At the same time, Diana entered college. Her mother Muriel, who had controlled the daughter's life up until this time, wanted Diana to go to California's Stanford University, so application was made there. But when Diana was asked on the questionnaire why she wanted to go to Stanford, she replied that she did *not* want to attend the university but that her mother was forcing her. When she was not accepted at Stanford, her brother rejoiced that "Diana finally escaped from Mummy," as the girl went East and enrolled in Smith College, majoring in mathematics.

Despite Horace's previous denial of plans to marry Gregg Sherwood, he was at the dock for farewells to Gregg and her mother when they left for Europe. Then he surprised them by flying to Cherbourg and greeting them when the boat landed there. From that point, Horace was an attentive escort in his usual lavish and good-humored style, and Gregg and her mother became his houseguests at St. Leonard's Castle and he became their guide on tours of the continent.

In June, Horace staged a party in Cannes, at which he presented Gregg with a $100,000 diamond ring. Florence Sisman hostessed the party around a horseshoe table on the Casino terrace, blanketed with more than 1,500 dozen roses and hundreds of $15 orchids flown in from Paris. A magnificent ice-carved eagle, holding sixty pounds of caviar and costing $4,800, formed a centerpiece.

In his eagerness to match Gregg's glowing vitality, Horace led the slim model out on the dance floor several times, but his stumbling gait marred the couple's attempts to match the rhythm of the orchestra. A broken leg suffered from a fall on the tennis courts had added to Horace's increasing disabilities. The disabilities did not hamper his travels, however, although he was usually accompanied by an entourage—a physician, an attorney, two secretaries, and a bodyguard—just as he was, at this time, at Cannes. The engagement party ended with a brilliant display of fireworks designed by Horace, who had always been fascinated with pyrotechnics. Women guests left the terrace with large jars of perfume, and men carried away gold cigarette lighters.

"I hope it was an engagement party," Horace told inquiring reporters. "But who knows whether she is going to like me within a week?"

Horace had reason to wonder about Gregg's changes of mood. She had abruptly left him on the Riviera after a quarrel and flounced up to her hotel room. Experienced in ways of winning reluctant ladies with generous gestures, Horace dispatched an entire night-club orchestra up to Gregg's door to play "Unforgettable."

Sometimes, though, he found it expedient to use tactics that were less than generous. When Gregg visited his Grosse Pointe home and left in a huff after another argument, Horace telephoned police to report that Miss Sherwood had taken some gold cigarette lighters from his home. Intercepted by police, Gregg was taken to the police station where Horace quickly appeared to explain it was all a joke—a ruse to keep Miss Sherwood from leaving town.

Three months after the party in Cannes, Clara Mae Dodge filed suit for divorce. Anna's granddaughter, Christine, was also still busy with court actions. In September, it was disclosed that Christine had borrowed $1,345,000 against the millions she expected to receive at her grandmother's death. Through the court actions, various amounts of her anticipated assets were assigned to her creditors.

Anna's concerns over court actions were minimized, though, by worries over her own health when her doctor informed her that she should be hospitalized for surgery. At eighty-one, she underwent an operation for the removal of an abdominal tumor. Still recovering when the Dodge Memorial Hall of Industry was dedicated at the Detroit Historical Museum in October of 1952, Anna could not attend this tribute to her husband.

As Anna slowly regained her strength, she became a great-grandmother again when Yvonne had her first baby in November. In the following spring, Christine married for the fourth time at the Palm Beach home of her mother's husband, Timothy Godde. Although Godde had remarried, Delphine Ione's two daughters continued to visit him, as did David. And despite his recent lawsuit against Anna, Godde remained friendly with his former mother-in-law, sharing her interest in psychic phenomena.

Over the years, Anna had arrived at the same conclusions of most of the super-wealthy—that their money was fair game for all contenders while the possessors of the fortunes were entitled, in defense, to protect their holdings with every possible maneuver. Along with many of her wealthy friends, Anna had learned to separate her personal attachments from these financial and legal skirmishes. She forced herself to overlook Godde's, Christine's, and others' attacks on her fortune and continued her relationships with them. But in self-protection, she followed a policy of keeping gifts in her own name and of not paying bills or obligations incurred by her free-spending family until pressed by court action.

Christine's latest bit of free-spending was the building of a new home on an 1,800-foot elevation overlooking St. Thomas Island and the harbor—to be called Estate Christine. Within months of her latest marriage, Christine was borrowing heavily again against the inheritance she would receive at Anna's death.

Even before Christine's springtime wedding had taken place, Horace and Gregg Sherwood were married in Palm Beach. The patio of Anna's Playa Riente had been the scene of the wedding of Anna's only son, in gray cutaway and striped pants, to the slim model from Beloit. Wearing a ballerina-skirted powder-blue dress and with a small blue hat on her shining platinum hair, Gregg entered the patio on the arm of her stepfather. A gold necklace set with diamonds encircled her graceful neck; a matching bracelet and ring—gift of the groom—sparkled on her wrist and hand.

After a wedding dinner at the Everglades Club, the newlyweds boarded a plane for Havana and a honeymoon at the Hotel Nacional

Gregg's parents would join them there, and later Anna and Florence Sisman would meet them in a chartered yacht off the Florida keys. Near the end of May, the newly married Dodges sailed from New York to see the coronation of Queen Elizabeth II.

Although Anna had been unhappy over the idea of a fifth wife for Horace, unless that fifth wife could have been Florence Sisman, the Dodge matriarch eventually had been captivated by Gregg. She was charmed by the lovely blonde's good looks, warmth, and cleverness. She admired Gregg's openness and her closeness with her parents. And Gregg was attentive to her mother-in-law. Anna, who had become very susceptible to flattery with the passing years, basked in this attentiveness. A couple of months after the marriage, Anna loaned her son $155,000 for the purchase of a chateau in Cannes. Built at the foot of the Maritime Alps, the chateau had fifteen bedrooms and a swimming pool.

In November of that first year of marriage, the couple's first separation occurred when Gregg walked out of the Palm Beach penthouse with her maid, suitcases, and her two dogs. The quarrels between the impulsive, quick-tempered Dodges rarely remained private. The thirty-year-old Gregg talked freely with reporters, telling them she had no intention of returning to Horace from Beloit "unless my husband sobers up." She was not contemplating any legal action but just wanted a "happy marriage," she insisted. But it was difficult to find happiness when Horace "threw dishes out the window, locked up my clothes and the car keys, and annoyed my pet dogs," she explained.

One of the stipulations accompanying the million-dollar trust fund set up by Horace for Gregg at the time of their marriage was that the fund was void if she filed for divorce. Extracting a promise from Horace that he would stop drinking, Gregg, now six months pregnant, returned to their elegant penthouse at the Colony Hotel in time to trim the Christmas tree. Gregg's parents also came to winter in Florida—in a home Gregg bought for them in Miami.

In March, Gregg gave birth to an eight-pound son in the Anna Dodge Maternity wing of Good Samaritan Hospital. Horace proudly announced that the boy would be named "John Francis Dodge. . . after my uncle, the late John F. Dodge."

Anna's pleasure over the new grandson was offset by the renewed suits against the estate begun by Christine the previous summer. Claiming that the estate's trustees had invested the money at low interest rates instead of in common stocks, Christine also requested surcharging the trustees for $16,800,000 because the purchasing power of the trust had been reduced by inflation. In response, the trustees defended their investment of the money in tax-exempt municipal bonds and U. S. government bonds as a sound policy during a wide span of economic problems.

More than a year elapsed before an official hearing took place. In September 1954, Judge O'Brien moved his court to the Jefferson Avenue home of Anna's son Horace in deference to what was referred to as Mrs. Dodge's eighty-six years of age. Anna was now permitting herself to be publicized as more than three years older than her actual age, even though she had claimed to be eight years younger at the time of her marriage to Dillman.

As the judge and six lawyers—four of them representing Christine—came into Horace's home, Anna, gray hair piled high on her head and pearls at the neckline of her blue dress, seated herself in a high-backed chair in the sitting room. Above the chair, an indirectly lighted oil portrait of Horace Sr. looked calmly on the scene of the bitter family feud over the fortune he had amassed.

Anna plucked nervously at her pearls as the judge presided at a marble-topped table and the lawyers argued their cases. In answer to cross-examination, Anna insisted she had followed her husband's instructions in the investing of the fortune. She became unnerved only once. "Must you ask the same question over and over?" she complained.

"We're questioning the propriety of a large number of investments, resulting in Mrs. Dodge receiving a tax-free income at the present time of over $1 million annually, with no diversification of holdings," Christine's lawyer argued. "We maintain she kept the money invested in tax-free holdings to insure her personal income, despite many warnings that we were in an inflationary period and the only safe thing to do was to invest a portion of the estate in high-grade stocks."

Another year passed before the legal battle ended, with Christine's claims denied. The resulting rift between Christine and herself was troubling to Anna. But there was a greater misfortune within the family that year when a great grandchild—the three-year-old son of Horace III—died of a brain tumor in November 1954. The child's body was brought from Albany, where young Horace was now working for the General Electric Company, to Detroit and placed temporarily in the Dodge mausoleum.

In the summer preceding his grandson's death, Horace II had gone back into speedboat racing after a lapse during his courtship of Gregg. In the fall of 1953, while in a wheelchair after an operation on his leg, the excitement of racing had become a fever within him again. He ordered his boatworks' employees to get three boats ready for the 1954 competition—*My Sweetie, My Sweetie Dora*, and *John Francis II.*

Anna and Gregg were at Horace's side in September when the three boats competed with seven other racers in the Silver Cup race. Although the *John Francis II* broke down in the final heat, the *My Sweetie* and *My Sweetie Dora* finished first and second. This was the first time Horace had seen two of his boats finish in the two lead positions. An exultant smile spread across his face when a committee spokesman acknowledged: "He built this victory . . . he didn't buy it." Then the three Dodges posed for pictures with the Silver Cup. The balding Horace, puffy-faced and unsteady of gait, stood between the statuesque blonde Gregg and his aging mother, her thinning hair cut short and curled, ringlet style, close to her head.

After that victory, whether Horace was in the country or at his chateau on the French Riviera or at St. Leonard's Castle, he had his drivers enter powerboat competitions whenever Dodge boats were in shape to run. But in a practice heat just before the July International Trophy race in 1955, *My Sweetie Dora* sheared away its cavitation plate and sank with a hole in its bottom. This was the beginning of a streak of bad luck for the Dodge boats.

My Sweetie, entered in the 1956 Silver Cup race, bucked and threw its driver before sinking into the Detroit River. When the repaired *My Sweetie Dora* was squeezed out of the Gold Cup competition during the elimination trials by another boat that had qualified after the deadline for entries had passed, Horace sued the APBA, seeking 6¢ damages. The suit was dismissed two months later.

Although the lure of racing was still strong for Horace, the many disappointments, money problems, and his own physical disabilities weakened his competitive aspirations. Other powerboat pilots occasionally observed Horace being lifted bodily by a number of his workmen into one of his racing boats so that he could steer the boat out into the river for a short spin before surrendering the wheel to an aide.

For Anna too, these years were a time of change; she returned to her Palm Beach maisonette at the Everglades Club in the early winter of 1956-57. Within the past year, she had had word of the death of her divorced husband, Hugh Dillman, in his hometown in Ohio. Coinciding with Dillman's death, Anna reluctantly ordered the razing of Playa Riente. Her taxes on the Spanish palace amounted to some $50,000 a year—more than the annual taxes paid by the big hotels. A plan to convert the estate into a school or a private club had failed approval by the Palm Beach council. Anna felt the council's negative decision was because of the influence of Joseph P. Kennedy, who objected to zoning changes and to what he referred to as "bailing Anna Dodge out of her difficulties."

Before the furnishings of Playa Riente were sold at auction, the mansion was opened for visitors, with proceeds from the $1 ticket sales donated to charity. None of the family was present to watch the thousands of people filtering into the home, climbing the tiers of stone steps, walking the miles of tiled floors, and looking through plate-glass windows that rolled down to disclose Spanish archways vaulted with filigree. On Sunday, an hour after the last paying customer left the mansion, Anna, in black chiffon, waited to receive more than 100 guests for a final supper party before the bang of the auctioneer's hammer the following day. In that hour before the guests' arrival, a fleet of chefs, servants, and decorators had moved in with their equipment. Tall thick candles, at $100 each, were lighted on the patio, red and white spring flowers and tropical plants were set out, rare oriental rugs were unrolled on the floors. And the usual Dodge centerpiece—the ice swan filled with caviar—was placed on the buffet table. Musicians had been ordered to play only lilting, happy music so the haunting memories of former parties in the downstairs ballroom where such celebrities as Lily Pons and Gladys Swarthout had appeared, would not dampen the gaity of the evening.

After the last of the guests departed, Florence Sisman was at Anna's side, jollying the aging woman so there would be no tears as they got into the waiting car. As the automobile moved down the driveway, lights blinked off in one after the other of the mansion's windows. Playa Riente gleamed silver in the light of the moon and then disappeared from the view of the automobile's occupants as the car accelerated toward the Everglades Club and Anna's apartment.

Before the auction opened for the sale of Playa Riente's furnishings, Anna unexpectedly encountered her estranged granddaughter, Christine, in a Palm Beach nightclub. Unlike her sister-in-law Matilda, Anna could not retain grudges against any blood relative. The grandmother and granddaughter were reconciled that evening, although Anna continued to be disturbed over Christine's leap-frog marital entanglements.

In her admiration for people with a healthy respect for work ethics, Anna found comfort in the promising lives of Horace's four adult children. Delphine Petz, his eldest daughter, was observing her youthful pledge to have a lot of children and to take personal care of her family in her Grosse Pointe home. Her brother, Horace III, and his wife, who were still adjusting to the death of their young son, had three other small children to fill their lives. Horace III continued to work for General Electric.

Anna had high hopes that the two children of Horace's second marriage were going to be equally responsible adults. David was happy in Arizona, working under Frank Lloyd Wright. Anna liked nothing better than to have David visit Rose Terrace, where he would sit at the five-keyboard organ to play some of the music Anna loved. Sometimes she imagined it was Horace Sr. sitting there because this grandson had inherited his grandfather's musical sensitivities as well as his red hair. Anna was proud too that David's sister Diana, who had done very well with her studies at Smith College, was now working with computers for General Electric.

She worried, though, about Delphine Ione's two daughters. Yvonne, the mother of a girl and a boy born of her first marriage, had been dirorced and recently had married a second time. Despite Yvonne's and Christine's marital ventures, though, there was a softness about each of the half-sisters and a generosity of spirit. There was, above all, a basic insecurity that spurred both girls to reach out for a shield against a buffeting world.

Now, as Anna reconciled with Christine, the auctioning of Playa Riente's furnishings continued. Some of the bidders swelling the auction crowds walked off with the bargains they had hoped to find—a set of Crown Derby service plates banded in ruby and gold and selling for less than a hundred dollars. Others walked away just as happily after paying inflated prices for mediocre items—three glass novelty lemon trees worth no more than $25 each, selling for $300. Anna had specified, though, that the eight Jose Sert *Sinbad the Sailor* murals that had graced Playa Riente with a quarter-million-dollars' worth of art should not be sold. Instead, she presented the murals, originally ordered from the artist by King Alfonse of Spain, to the Detroit Institute of Arts.

Settled into her luxurious Everglades Club apartment with her servants and her miniature poodle Blackie, Anna relied on Florence Sisman to take her down to the weekly tambola luncheon-fashion shows and to escort her to the canasta sessions she enjoyed at the homes of friends. Christine had returned to the Virgin Islands and, before the end of the year, was divorced for the fourth time, only to remarry two months later. Christine continued to operate her Virgin Islands night spot, the Mahogany Club. When financing was tight, she borrowed still more on her inheritance.

Anna was eighty-six years old when the *New York Times* in October 1957 ran a list of the seventy-six richest Americans reported by Fortune magazine. Mrs. Horace E. Dodge Sr. was listed along with

Henry Ford II and his two brothers as possessors of fortunes estimated to range between $75 million and $100 million.

The $150,000 allowance given annually to Horace by his mother was not enough to sustain the junior Dodges' style of living, however. Anna might have been more liberal if her enchantment with her beautiful daughter-in-law, Gregg, had not changed to disenchantment as the name of Gregg Dodge enlivened a number of headlines. A punch delivered to Gregg's dainty nose by a musician in a nightclub. Gregg heaving an ashtray at a roulette wheel in Cannes. A fight with policemen in her hometown of Beloit. Then, while living in the Bel-Air section of Los Angeles and attempting an acting career, Gregg was brought into court to face drunk and battery charges. Relieved to escape a jail sentence on these charges, a chastened Gregg concentrated on acting in scenes for the movie *The Indian*, playing opposite Michael Ansara of television's *Cochise* fame.

While her problems with authorities gradually faded out of the news, her problems with finances became the subject of gossip. Gregg, who was rumored to have used gold safety pins from Tiffany's for her baby's diapers, was now reported to be running up bills in Detroit, New York, Los Angeles.

A national women's magazine published an article in 1958 naming women with the country's most prized jewel collections. Mrs. Horace Dodge, Sr., and Mrs. Horace Dodge, Jr., were listed as owners of collections said to be worth at least $1 million. The prestige of this inclusion was marred by a number of claims for nonpayment of Gregg's bills filed by various jewelers, including one in Paris.

To add to the younger Dodges' financial problems, their huge Palm Beach home, Seaspray, was heavily mortgaged. Floridian creditors' liens on the home had been taken over by Anna, who was now angrily threatening foreclosure.

Anna was disturbed too by financial problems enmeshing another of the grandchildren, since Yvonne was following Christine's lead. She assigned the remains of her one-quarter interest in her grandfather's undistributed estate to a California bank as collateral security to repay loans already assumed and to take care of advances for the future.

At eighty-seven, Anna left on another trip around the world, visiting Ceylon for the first time and returning in the spring for a quiet summer at Rose Terrace. For the most part, she was content with a slower pace of life—going out to dinner occasionally, attending concerts with her friend Florence Sisman, and visiting regularly at the home of her granddaughter, Delphine Petz, and with the Petz children.

Winters at Palm Beach were times for canasta sessions with other wealthy widows and for dinners, concerts, and parties for which a retinue of younger male escorts was available to the aging widows for generous gratuities. Anna had always been happiest in the company of men and, even in her late eighties, enjoyed having a male companion at her side. The men were also available for card playing at high stakes, with the widows usually the losers but content to pay for the entertainment and the attention in their late and lonely years.

In spite of the publicity that Gregg had attracted earlier, she had little difficulty in luring any numbers of Floridian socialites to parties at her Palm Beach home. But even this acceptance by people of wealth was not enough for the ambitious Gregg, who seemed to feel challenged to strive for an improved public image. By February 1960, her name brightened society headlines with her plan for a ball to benefit her new project, Girls' Town. Enlisting the support of Eleanor Roosevelt as national chairman, Gregg envisioned enlarging her plan into a design for establishing a Girls' Town in every state in the union. But it would all begin on 250 acres of land just north of Orlando— land that Gregg wanted donated for the construction of a southern-plantation-type home for underprivileged girls.

Newspeople admitted to the Horace Dodges' four-acre Seaspray estate were given a personal explanation by Gregg of the upcoming benefit ball for Girls' Town. Meeting reporters at her poolside cabana, Gregg briefed them on her plans for the Fontainebleau Hotel ball—Frank Sinatra headlining the entertainment, Elsa Maxwell hostessing, and 2,200 guests paying $100 each.

Although Gregg had never learned to swim and might have drowned had she fallen into the pool waters sparkling under a bright sun, she was the perfect prototype of a Palm Beach mistress of the manor. Her soft brown eyes contrasted with her short bleached-blonde hair. Her skin was tanned, and the curves of her slim figure were molded by a lavender cotton dress embroidered in white.

Asked by reporters about her personal life with Horace, she extolled her husband's marvelous sense of humor. "We are very compatible," she explained. "But when we even raise our voices in a restaurant, it makes the papers."

Gregg's declarations of compatibility proved inaccurate in August 1961, when Horace filed suit for divorce. His wife ignored him, he charged, and preferred the company of other people. She remained away from their Grosse Pointe home and lived in other states and other countries and returned home only to badger him for more money. Her temper was so volatile, he alleged, that he feared for his safety.

The ninety-year-old Anna retained a dignified silence in regard to her son's divorce suit and her granddaughter Yvonne's marital problems. Marrying for the third time in 1961, Yvonne now became Mrs. James Ranger. Anna retained her zest for life, as well—even after falling and breaking her hip at Palm Beach in November. In spite of her age, she made a good recovery in Good Samaritan Hospital, taking several steps in her hospital room before the end of January. Arrangements were made, then, for the *S. S. Caronia* to turn off its course and pick up Anna Dodge at Fort Lauderdale.

Horace's pending divorce suit did not prevent him from making frequent attempts to reconcile his differences with his wife that winter. In May, he met with Gregg in his mother's apartment in New York's Waldorf Astoria. Their reconciliation, during which Gregg acquired a new summer wardrobe, was only temporary.

As predivorce hearings were arranged, Gregg promptly denied Horace's allegations. "Horace must have been drinking when he signed the papers," she commented. "From October to June, I'm at our Palm Beach home," she defended herself. "I'm with our son who goes to school in Florida. When Horace is drinking," she continued, "he goes back to Detroit. I don't want him drinking in front of John. This is the arrangement we have." She hadn't been to Europe in two years, she added, and, as far as her extravagance was concerned, "I've had a good teacher," she finished.

An entranced American public followed accounts of the hearings, which centered around Horace's request that Gregg be restrained from making charges on his credit, pending the divorce trial. He had been forced to borrow money, he claimed, far in excess of his income by reason of his wife's "inordinate appetite for waste and extravagance." Moreover, his wife insisted on his affection being "predicated upon an appointment in advance based at her convenience," he added.

Cane at his side, Horace slumped in his chair and listened as his lawyer enumerated Gregg's bills in a droning monotone—$8,000 worth of gold dishes, a $3,500 grand piano sent to Gregg's mother in Florida, a $21,500 platinum pin, bills for designer clothes and airline tickets for Gregg and her friends . . . more than $300,000 worth of bills.

"I can't afford her," Horace said, regret tinging his gravelly voice as the day's session ended.

When Horace failed to appear at scheduled hearings, his lawyer produced a letter from his client's doctor. Dodge, the letter stated, suffered chronic heart disease and a "markedly irregular pulse . . .

brought on by stress and worry." Two days later, the physician testified that his patient was complaining of chest pains. Dodge's health would be jeopardized if he attended the hearings, he said.

When the judge ruled that a heart specialist should examine Dodge to rule on his ability to appear in court, the day's session moved on with Horace's secretary testifying on her employer's finances. In addition to his $150,000 annual allowance, Mr. Dodge borrowed more than $4,000 monthly from his mother, giving her a $25,000 promissory note every six months, the secretary stated. He also borrowed an extra $850,000 from his mother in the past two years, she added. And he owed more than $22,000 in back taxes on the Dodge Boat and Plane Corporation.

After the heart specialist ruled that Dodge was well enough to appear in court, Horace returned to acknowledge the accuracy of his secretary's report on money borrowed from his mother. He'd had to claim his wife's debts as his own, he said, because his mother would not give him money to settle Gregg's debts.

Gregg's lawyer pointed out that the question of whether his client's spending was excessive had to be considered in relation to her husband's resources and the couple's previous standard of living.

When the couple returned to the courtroom after a week's recess, Horace shifted in his chair and tapped his cane nervously. The judge read the decree finally agreed to by both parties, limiting Gregg's spending to $6,250 a month and prohibiting her from using her husband's charge accounts. But Horace was obliged to settle more than $300,000 worth of bills already accumulated.

Still, Horace saw Gregg regularly in Palm Beach again that winter. In March, they gave a dinner party at the Colony Restaurant in New York. Heads close together, the Dodges romanced like honeymooners; Horace told his friends that he had Gregg on probation. "We're not living together," he added. "I can't afford her."

The next week, Horace joined Gregg in Palm Beach for the ninth birthday celebration of their handsome son John. Then Horace had plans for a trip to England. Somewhere along the travels, he found the opportunity for a stopover at the East Coast dock where the *Delphine*'s captain had moored the huge yacht. The yacht had been listed, recently, in Lloyd's *Register of American Yachts* as the largest American craft. World wide, there were seven yachts larger than the *Delphine*, including the Queen of England's *Britannia*, Aristotle Onassis' *Christine*, and the King of Norway's *Norge*. Although Anna had transferred the ownership of her yacht to her son some years previously, the ship had not left the private dock at Rose Terrace from 1955 until 1962. Then it had been towed to a nearby shipyard for repairs and sent on to the East Coast port. Now, as the *Delphine* loomed high out of the waters of her solitary mooring, Horace looked up sadly at her white bow. "There she is," he murmured, "in an old shipyard by herself, and it looks like she is going to die."

Anna, in a wheelchair a great deal of the time now, had gone down to her large Florida apartment in the Palm Beach Tower before Thanksgiving. An ailing Horace remained at his Grosse Pointe home, planning to go to Palm Beach for the Christmas holidays. Gregg too was back in Palm Beach, where young John Francis was attending school.

Two weeks before Christmas, Horace's condition worsened, and he was taken to Jennings Memorial Hospital. Anna was notified but not told of the seriousness of her son's condition. She called the hospital from Florida several times daily, checking his progress. Horace's children, David and Diana, had arrived in Palm Beach by this time, and they and their grandmother were anticipating Horace's recovery in time for him to be with them for Christmas. When it became apparent that Horace was not going to get out of the hospital for the holidays, Anna tried to reserve space on various Detroit-bound flights. But holiday travel was heavy, and all space had been sold in advance. Then came the ominous news that could no longer be kept from Anna—her son's condition was critical. The airlines provided emergency space for Anna and her two grandchildren, and they left Palm Beach on Sunday, December 22, for the flight north.

Four of the people closest to Horace were at his bedside that Sunday afternoon as the plane continued on its journey to Detroit. His eldest daughter, Delphine Petz, was there, as were Florence Sisman, his personal secretary, and his lawyer. The sixty-three-year-old dying man murmured, "Where's Mother?"—his last words before he slipped into a coma as his life ebbed away. He died shortly before 7 p.m. of acute hepatic encephalopathy resulting from cirrhosis of the liver, complicated by heart disease.

When the plane landed at Metropolitan Airport, Anna and the two children got into grandmother's waiting limousine. A police escort cleared the freeway for a fast trip to the hospital, where Anna was helped into a wheelchair and wheeled toward her son's room. Her physician met her there. Her shoulders sagged as she was told, gently, that her only son had died.

Although her world had shattered, the ninety-two-year-old Anna did not shrink from the decisions that had to be made. She wanted her son's casket to be an exact duplicate of the coffin in which his sister

Delphine Ione had been interred twenty years previously. The funeral would be held in the Jefferson Avenue Presbyterian Church, where the organ had been donated by Horace and Delphine Ione and where Delphine had been married to James H. R. Cromwell in a blaze of glory.

Gregg Sherwood Dodge and her son, John Francis, also arrived by plane at Metropolitan Airport, and Gregg stayed at Horace's Gray House, adjoining Rose Terrace. With a black mourning veil obscuring her blondeness, Gregg arrived early at the church for the funeral the day after Christmas, her son at her side. A towering Christmas tree and wreaths were mute reminders of the holiday season, while organ elegies were played softly in the background. As Anna Dodge was assisted from her black Chrysler into a wheelchair at the west entrance of the church, family members and friends gathered around to shelter the mink-clad, bereaved mother from curious stares. But the protective cordon was unnecessary. There were no crowds at the church.

Inside, Gregg and her son sat apart from the rest of the Dodge family during the service, then remained within the church after the heavy bronze casket was lifted from its red velvet bier and taken to the hearse, followed by Horace's mother, his four adult children, and other relatives and friends. James H. R. Cromwell was among the friends who had arrived from out of town and who helped make up the funeral cortege that moved out Woodward Avenue to Woodlawn Cemetery.

Tall and erect in her black cloth coat with black mink collar, Gregg emerged from the church several minutes after the rest of the mourners had joined the funeral procession. She and her son walked over to her car to be driven by her private chauffeur out to the cemetery.

At the cemetery, again, Gregg and John remained after the brief ceremony ended and all the others had departed. Then Gregg asked to have the mausoleum opened so that she and her son might see Horace's resting place. The woman and the boy stood inside for a moment. Then the son pulled at his mother's hand and led her away from the stained-glass window and out of the mausoleum, down the steps and back to the warm, comfortable interior of the car. The tires of the sleek automobile crunched over the drive as the car rolled away from the stone mausoleum and back to the world of the living.

23

A lonely Anna Dodge shrank visibly into the debilities of old age after her son's death. Immediately, a furor erupted over Horace's estate—eleven wills were filed. All of them had been written by Horace during the last thirteen years, when he had not anticipated being outlived by his aged mother, nor remaining dependent on her for allowances and loans for his lifetime. As lawyers for various hopeful beneficiaries prepared to argue their clients' contentions, an avalanche of claims against the estate threatened to wipe out the assets, estimated, at first, to approximate $2 million.

Horace's fourth wife, Clara Tinsley, filed a one-half-million-dollar claim for the balance of the divorce settlement owing her. And each day brought a pile of new creditors' claims—$3,000 for a house call made by a New York doctor to Detroit, $1,000 worth of toys bought for John Francis on a single shopping trip, back wages for servants, interior decorators' and florists' bills, hotel bills, lawyers' fees, mortgage notes.

Before the end of February, Anna Dodge filed a $10.4 million claim for loans she had made to Horace. With this amount swallowing up the entire estate, the probate judge admitted it had been "a long time since I have seen such a complicated and mixed-up family affair." When the judge gave his opinion that approved claims would be paid off on a pro rata basis, the lawyers for Gregg Dodge reversed their tactics. Now Gregg filed an $11 million suit against her mother-in-law, charging the ninety-two-year-old Anna with alienation of affections. She asked an additional $1 million judgment, maintaining that her mother-in-law had guaranteed to pay off the prenuptial agreement between Horace and herself.

By the end of April, Horace's first two wives also had filed suits for settlements. At the same time, Gregg's two lawsuits against her mother-in-law were officially dropped, and Anna Dodge suddenly settled Gregg's claims out of court for a reported $9 million.

Anna Dodge and her lawyers refused to verify the amount of the private settlement, but Gregg spoke freely at a press conference at the Statler Hilton Hotel. "The amount is $9 million, free and clear," she said forthrightly. "You see, what most people never knew is that Horace and I never intended to be divorced," she confided to reporters. "I have a paper he gave me saying he would never consent to go through with the proceedings. . . Horace and I were never really separated. . . I was with him in Grosse Pointe last November, shortly before he became ill and went into the hospital."

Reporters' questions about another marriage in her future were promptly denied. But in April 1965, one year later, Gregg walked down the aisle of St. Patrick's Cathedral Chapel in New York to marry twenty-nine-year-old Daniel Moran, a former plainclothesman with the New York police force. The darkly handsome Moran and his blonde bride, who had given her age as forty-one, had been the subject of rumors for a couple of years previous to their marriage. Horace, it was whispered, had hired the plainclothesman to shadow the beautiful blonde, and Moran had fallen in love with the woman he had been hired to follow. Gregg gave a different version of her acquaintance with Moran. Horace and Dan had become friends first, she insisted. Then Horace had asked his Irish friend to escort the young Mrs. Dodge to various functions in New York when she was in that city without her husband.

Just a month before the widowed Gregg finally had received her settlement from Anna Dodge, Moran left the police force and relocated in Palm Beach, where he went into the real-estate business. The Morans had been married only a short time when the athletic Moran was seen often with young John Francis at his side as the two swam together, water-skied, and played tennis. To friends, Gregg confided that her son was developing an interest in studying law because of his fascination with Dan Moran's stories of his police work in New York.

With marriage to the very Irish Dan Moran, Gregg became friends with Bishop Carroll of Palm Beach. This resulted in a merging of her grandiose plans for Girls' Town with the more practical plans the diocese was forming for a home for underprivileged girls.

In 1968, Dan and Gregg moved from their white stone villa to a more lavish Palm Beach estate—the former home of dime-store heiress Jessie Woolworth Donohue. Now Gregg delighted in remodeling the palatial home while the Morans lived in a glass-walled poolside home that would later become a guest house. A major part of the renovation job on the Donohue palace was the conversion of the marble-floored living room into a master bedroom, plus construction of a 120-foot-long louvered closet for Gregg's clothes.

While the main house was being remodeled, the Morans did not suspend their entertaining. Their 1969 St. Patrick's Day bash was a poolside affair, with Florida's Governor Kirk and his wife as honored guests. A television crew, filming an "Inside Palm Beach" special, focused cameras on the 160 socialites attending the party. Without obvious effort, the pretty, outspoken blonde from Wisconsin had moved into an upper strata of society that had eluded Anna Dodge in her early years of striving for acceptance. Gregg shed all the unpleasant notoriety she had generated as freely as a dandelion releases its cotton puffs into the summer air. Even the will litigations that dragged on after Horace's death had been skirted by Gregg as the private settlement from Anna had been quickly made.

But the private settlement that Gregg bragged of receiving in 1964 had removed only one contestant from the continuing will litigations, which established during court testimony that Horace had not filed an income-tax return for the last ten years. He had not earned more than $600 in any of those years but had lived on a trust fund. This was support for Dodge lawyers' claim that more than $500,000 of Chrysler stock registered in the son's name actually belonged to the mother— assigned to her in 1943 and the dividends turned over to her since that time. The ownership of Gray House, adjoining Rose Terrace, also was in question, since the deed had been switched back and forth between mother and son so many times.

Three years passed before the tangled estate was finally settled at less than four cents on the dollar. Only $718,278 remained in the estate at the time of settlement, and this amount had been paid by Anna for various properties of her son's. Anna bought back the *Delphine* "for sentimental reasons," and she purchased Horace's estate in Cannes, plus his stock in the Dodge Boat and Plane Corporation.

While the litigations were still in progress, Anna's granddaughter, Yvonne Ranger, received court permission to live in Gray House. Shortly afterwards, Yvonne borrowed against her inheritance from her grandmother, buying Gray House for a permanent residence for her family when they were in Detroit.

To Anna, it was comforting to have Yvonne, her husband Jim, and Yvonne's three children living next door. She particularly liked Jim Ranger—an outgoing, pleasant-mannered man who had been employed on Yvonne's ranch outside Alamos, California, where he worked with her Arabian horses. Ranger, who made a dignified and handsome appearance in well-tailored clothes at social functions with

Yvonne, was a free-spirited man who provided the pliant Yvonne with the strength she needed. Anna was pleased too when Ranger legally adopted Yvonne's young son and two daughters, and it began to appear that Yvonne's third marriage could be a solid one.

Sitting up to watch television in her canopied twin bed, Anna liked to turn toward her second-floor west-end window and catch sight of Jim Ranger's lithe figure striding across the expanse of lawn connecting the Gray House with Rose Terrace. His visits brightened her day. He had taken up speedboat racing since his marriage, and his accounts of the boats and the practice runs revitalized Anna's memories of Horace and the powerboats.

On occasional visits to Detroit, Guy Lombardo was another of Anna's visitors with recollections of Horace and the races in which they had competed. But Anna's own recollections of early days, even when shared with her close friend, Florence Sisman, were colored by a protective veil. When she spoke of "Dad"—Horace Sr.—she would admit only that he liked "a little pony of beer."

Anna herself enjoyed a before-dinner cocktail—bourbon on the rocks—each evening. Since she expected Florence to come for dinner every night, she also wanted Florence to join her for a dinner drink. Florence, who did not like drinking before dinner, regularly made an excuse to go into the marble bathroom where she proceeded to pour her Scotch down the drain and refill the glass with water.

Florence had bought the old Dodge boatworks from Anna. She put in a full and active workday at the crating plant, either at her desk or roaring around the grounds in a red golf cart, checking on any snags, chewing out laggards, and snapping orders that commanded instant responses. But while she relished the operating of her flourishing crating and shipping company, Florence was never too busy to rush out of her office and over to Rose Terrace when a call came from Anna Dodge.

Ties between the two women became so strong that Anna called her lawyer and told him she wanted to adopt the younger woman. Florence was firm in her "no" to this plan. Knowing that Anna was extremely possessive, Florence confided to close friends that she valued her independence and freedom of choice and was not willing to abandon either. But she would call Anna *Mother*, she promised in an attempt to mollify the aged widow.

Yvonne and Jim Ranger continued to divide their time between the California ranch and Gray House in Grosse Pointe. To Yvonne, Gray House was a memorial of her Uncle Horace, one of the few people who had been kind to her in her childhood years. And the sentimental Yvonne, having only faint memories of her mother Delphine Ione, also wanted to have something of her mother's—especially the Catherine of Russia pearls. Once again, she importuned her grandmother. Could she have another advance on her inheritance to purchase the pearls her mother had worn on so many special occasions?

The five-strand, lustrous set of 389 pearls was removed from its bank vault and brought, by guards, to the bank office where the official transfer of the jewels took place. Once the necklace was in Yvonne's hands, the job of the security guards was done. Yvonne dropped the necklace into the depths of her purse as if it were a dime-store purchase and walked out of the bank.

At the time Anna had learned of her former daughter-in-law Gregg's marriage to an ex-policeman, she was in poor health after suffering a stroke that paralyzed her lower limbs. But within the stiffened body, Anna's strong will fought to prevail. There were decisions that must be made. . . projects to arrange.

Desiring to have a riverfront powerboat marina and memorial built that would carry her son's name, she donated $150,000 for that purpose. And she had been pondering what was to be done with the *Delphine*, still idling away the years at its East Coast berth. Anna knew now that she would never again board the beautiful yacht that epitomized her husband's dream. As various purchase offers and conversion plans failed or were rejected by Anna, she feared that her husband's prized ship might possibly end its days ignominiously as a banana boat. She decided then to donate the yacht to Project Hope. But later the boat was sold to the Seafarers International Union and assigned to the union's maritime school, where it was to be used in training men for jobs on the high seas.

But while Anna entertained no plans for her personal use of the *Delphine*, she did not yet visualize herself as permanently housebound. She decided to order a new car—a Chrysler because she had always been loyal to the company that had purchased Dodge Brothers. Since Chrysler had no limousine, she bought a Chrysler Imperial and had it shipped to the Ghia factory in Italy. There the car was cut in half, lengthened to limousine size, and equipped with air-conditioning, mohair upholstery, and pink plush carpeting—bringing the car's total cost up to $18,500. But Anna Dodge was not destined to ride in the car . . . would never even view it.

Although Anna spent much of the day in bed in her last years of life, her nurse and maid lifted her from bed to wheelchair for her meals. Her faithful chauffeur, Swan, often pushed his "lady" in her wheelchair into the glass-fronted elevator with its embroidered Chinese panels and wheeled her down to the main floor. There she liked to sit in the white-and-gold music salon or in the gold-draped breakfast room overlooking the lawn and the lake.

After Anna suffered the stroke that worsened her condition, Hugh Dillman's sister Mary came to visit at Rose Terrace. Anna's niece Ella was also staying with her at that time. Ella had an invalid daughter of her own in Arizona, but now that her Aunt Anna needed her, Ella had responded quickly because the ties between aunt and niece had always been strong. To both women, who could recall the plushness of Rose Terrace at its zenith, it was depressing to see some of the antiques and furnishings under dust covers. They deplored the absence of many of the beautiful accessories and pieces of jade and ivory that had dressed up the home and warmed its hugeness. The valuable pieces had been put away because of the flow of people moving in and out of the house in visits up to the ailing Anna's second-floor suite.

The grandchildren—including Delphine Petz's nine youngsters—came to visit, of course. Doctors and nurses went in and out. Old friends stopped by, none more welcome than Jimmy Cromwell at whose presence Anna twittered as happily as a girl. And always there was the companion-friend, Florence Sisman, who alternately prodded, wheedled, flattered, and bullied Anna into following doctors' orders on the increasingly frequent occasions when the dowager Dodge widow became stubborn and resistant.

The days when Anna was wheeled down to the south-end sitting room of her suite to play solitaire or to talk with friends became more infrequent as the widow weakened. But even as her vitality ebbed, there was little fading of her interest in the changes taking place within the family—whether for better or worse. She grieved when her poodle—her constant companion and a gift from her son Horace—died. There was greater sorrow when her great-grandson Edward, one of Christine's five children, an offspring of her second marriage, was killed in an automobile accident in 1966. But there were happy events too. Her great-granddaughter Delphine IV—eldest daughter of Horace III—was married in the same year that her grandson David left for Switzerland to continue working with the Frank Lloyd Wright Foundation. In Switzerland, David met the girl who was to become his wife. Before marrying Anneliese, who worked as a governess, David brought his bride-to-be to Rose Terrace for introductions to his grandmother.

Although Anna was now being given twenty-four-hour-a-day nursing care, she consented to talk with a reporter in the summer of 1967. When she spoke of the possibility of a birthday party in August, the reporter asked her age. "Sixty-five, maybe," she replied. "Maybe one-hundred-five. I haven't decided yet."

Officially, Anna would have been ninety-six that August. But her age had been obscured so often that even some of her grandchildren were uninformed as to her true age. Anna was content now to listen while someone read aloud to her—a mystery story, a newspaper article, or passages from the Bible. Although she tired of watching television for long periods, she rarely missed her two favorite programs— Bonanza and a locally produced travel show that brought back memories of her world travels.

As Anna continued to weaken physically, new instructions were issued. The traffic through the house was to be shut off. Guests, including the many family members, would be admitted only by arrangement so that the patient would not become unduly excited or have her rest disturbed. When Anna became intractable, there was one person with the ability to manage things. That person was Florence Sisman, and she was frequently called to Anna's bedside at odd hours of the day or night. Aware of her grandmother's dependence on her close friend, Yvonne invited Florence to live at Gray House. Florence was agreeable to this, although she had refused Anna's invitation to live permanently at Rose Terrace as an adopted daughter.

Summoned by telephone on one occasion by the nurse at Rose Terrace, Florence ran out to her car in the darkness of the early-morning hours. She accelerated the automobile across the adjoining lawns of Gray House and Rose Terrace, forgetting there was a case of liquor in the back seat until a bottle flew up and hit her in the head as the car bounced over the grass. After she had calmed Anna, Florence tried to amuse her with the account of the bottle and her bruised head. But Anna refused to be amused. Instead, she scolded Florence for driving across the lawns rather than coming via the driveways.

Although visitors to Anna's suite were limited, her chauffeur Swan stopped in to see her each day. "Where's my Swan?" she demanded on the first day he did not appear. When she learned he was ill, she dispatched one of her nurses to look after the chauffeur—an assignment that continued until the man's death. Then Anna ordered that the chauffeur's widow should be permitted to stay in the garage-apartment in which the Swans had lived for so many years.

Anna's concern for the widowed Mrs. Swan was appreciated particularly by Yvonne, who had been so close to the Swans since childhood. In her own concern for her friend, Yvonne ordered an escalator installed from the apartment's first-floor living room to the second-floor bedroom, since the chauffeur's widow suffered from arthritis.

Because of Anna's increasing infirmities, her canopied bed had been replaced with a hospital bed. This made it easier for her nurse and her maid to get her out of bed and into her wheelchair, since Anna was a dead weight of some 150 pounds. Despite the presence of the hospital bed, an aura of luxury still prevailed over the sickroom with its rich Aubusson carpet, its chaise lounge, the Louis XVI furnishings, and the delicate pieces of porcelain and jade that had been left in Anna's suite.

By this time, the great-grandchildren were seen only rarely at Rose Terrace, the grandchildren not much oftener, and the niece Ella had returned to her Arizona home, and Anna was separated from her family in the isolation of approaching death. Still, her hairdresser came regularly to cut and set the short white hair into curls, doctors visited daily, and nurses were always at hand to follow the orders given by the doctors and by Florence Sisman as they offered sedation and provided an oxygen tent at intervals.

Anna Dodge continued her tenuous grasp on life, watching eagerly for her doctors' visits and, nightly, for Florence's arrival for dinner. The predinner cocktail continued to be a ritual when the doctor said there was no harm in it. But the lavish dinners served in Rose Terrace's richly paneled dining room had changed now to simple fare— Anna enjoyed macaroni and cheese casserole with ice cream for dessert—served at the bedside and with Florence usually there to check on the household staff for Anna.

Impatiently brushing aside complaints from within and without the immediate household in regard to her taking over the management of Rose Terrace and Gray House and Anna, Florence devoted herself to the fragile, wealthy woman who wanted to adopt her. The doors of Rose Terrace were open too to Jimmy Cromwell, who came frequently. Anna was always pleased when Jimmy and Florence sat at either side of her bed and gave her the attention she craved. Whether Florence called her "Mother" or "my little rosebud" made no difference to Anna as long as the attentive younger woman was nearby. But when Anna dozed against her pillow and wakened to find Florence and Jimmy gone, she would ask plaintively, over and over, where they were and when they were coming back. Told that they were "down at the pool," she would watch the door until they returned or until her watery eyes closed and she fell asleep—disappointed.

In the late spring of 1970, Anna's minister, Reverend Zaun, visited her frequently. On the visit that was to be his last to the second-floor suite at Rose Terrace, the minister and Anna sang together several of her favorite hymns—"What a Friend We Have in Jesus," "The Old Rugged Cross," "Jesus, Lover of My Soul." A few days later, Anna Thomson Dodge died quietly at night in her silk-walled bedroom. The date was June 2, 1970; Anna Dodge was 98 years old. Even in death, however, the Dodge matriarch's age was exaggerated, with newspapers quoting her age as 103.

Immediately, family members converged on Rose Terrace. Gregg dropped her business dealings for the purchase of the huge Southampton estate of the late Victor Galluci and came, with her husband and son, to Grosse Pointe. They stayed with the agreeable Yvonne at Gregg's former home, Gray House. David and his Anneliese flew back from Switzerland. Christine, Horace III—all came quickly to Detroit.

For two days, Anna lay in state in her gold and white music room while the seldom-used iron gates at the main entrance were opened to the public. Visitors by the hundreds walked up the circular driveway, through the great doors of Rose Terrace and between the velvet guide ropes to view the wealthy widow. Her $35,000 cast-bronze casket was surrounded by arrangements of orchids, sweetheart roses, gardenias, and a twenty-foot-long rope of mixed flowers fashioned by Yvonne Ranger as "the last thing I can do for Grandma." Professional florists remained in the background to keep the flower arrangements fresh and lovely. They immediately removed wilting blooms, particularly the fragile gardenias, and replaced them with fresh blossoms. Their bill was $5,000.

Early on Saturday morning, June 6, the one-ton casket, covered in white orchids, was lifted from the hearse and wheeled into the Jefferson Avenue Presbyterian Church. By eleven o'clock, the seven grandchildren—Christine and Yvonne, Delphine Petz, Horace III, David, Diana, and young John Francis Dodge—were seated in the front pews. Several hundred people listened to the minister speak of Anna Dodge being the "calming and strengthening center about which the lives of many devoted persons gathered . . . a queen mother, royal in dignity." Her death, he continued, marked the "passing of an era."

But there were flashes of the opulent past as sixteen black limousines rolled up to the curb to pick up assigned groups of mourners as they left the church. Anna's grandchildren, Delphine Petz and her brother Horace III—oldest children of Horace II—stepped into the lead car, Anna's glistening Chrysler with its made-to-order Italian body. Three of the great-grandchildren rode with them.

Five-times divorced Christine Cromwell, long curly hair parted in the middle and hanging loosely around her plump face, was escorted into the second automobile by her fiance. The burly ex-boxer's well-groomed hair and custom-made suit did not quite succeed in making him look like anything but a bodyguard. With the couple were Christine's daughter and the daughter's husband.

David Dodge and his German-born wife carefully shepherded his grandmother's eighty-one-year-old niece Ella, as they took their places in the funeral procession. David's sister Diana—unmarried at thirty-eight and more interested in the several Arabian horses she owned than in male friends—walked with the brother who was the only person to share the lonely childhood memories locked inside her.

Dark glasses concealed Yvonne Ranger's red-rimmed eyes as her husband helped her out from the car and into the shelter of the weatherbeaten funeral tent at Woodlawn Cemetery. The plump and blonde Yvonne was flanked by those closest to her—her husband, her daughter, and the widowed Agnes Swan, the chauffeur's wife.

At this funeral, Gregg Sherwood Moran was included among the family mourners, and she and Daniel Moran accompanied the youngest Dodge grandchild—handsome sixteen-year-old son of Horace II and Gregg—in the procession. Behind young John Francis and the Morans came the great grandchildren; the aging Winifred Seyburn—the only representative of the John Dodge side of the family—in her Rolls Royce; Jimmy Cromwell and his grandson—Christine's first child of her first marriage; Lois Knowlson and Mickey Devine—two of Horace II's former wives; Hugh Dillman's sister Mary; friends and employees.

The death of Anna Dodge had brought the family members together in a final observance of family unity and respect to the matriarch whose loyalty to them had never wavered. The family stood, heads bowed, for the cemetery service. Then they walked back to their cars and moved out into Woodward Avenue's afternoon traffic as the coffin was placed inside the mausoleum. At last Anna rested near her husband, son and daughter . . . near, too, the remains of John Dodge and Ivy and two of their children, John Duval and Isabel.

Not far behind the sphinx-fronted Dodge mausoleum, Thomson family members rested in the smaller stone structure built for them by Anna. And right next to the Dodge edifice, the pink marble Wilson mausoleum sheltered Matilda and Alfred, Anna Margaret and Daniel.

With the death of Anna Dodge, the bond that had held the family members together began to crumble. And yet there was to be one more strong testimony to Anna's devotion and loyalty to her playboy son, Horace, in the reading of a part of the documents of her will. "If any member of my family or otherwise, shall institute or lend support to any act or proceedings directed against my son, Horace E. Dodge Jr., for the appointment of a guardian or to restrain his freedom or to impose a status of incompetency upon him, or any other effort to abridge, limit or interfere with his sole control and distribution of his property, every such party shall not thereafter be entitled to receive any of the benefits provided for such party under this will and testament . . ."

This last protective tribute of loyalty to her son had been written prior to Horace's death. Things had changed—Horace had died long before his mother's death. At last the multimillions that Mammá had controlled were to be distributed, and already some of the heirs were threatening to contest the will.

24

Within two hours of Anna's death, a tight network of security was thrown around Rose Terrace. Cars leaving the estate were searched and women's handbags, which might conceal a bagatelle worth thousands of dollars, were inspected. Twenty-five persons, mostly servants and gardeners, were issued permits to enter Rose Terrace. The grounds were patrolled around the clock by guards and watchdogs, and a new electronic alarm system was ordered by the executors of the Dodge will. A wire fence was installed to prevent access from Lake St. Clair and from neighboring Gray House.

With the filing of Anna's will for probate the day after the funeral, the major provisions of the document were made public. The bulk of her personal estate, estimated at $20 million, was left in trust to the oldest four of her son Horace's five children. To the fifth child—John Francis, son of Gregg—Anna had designated $25,000 and "no more." The two children of her daughter Delphine—Christine and Yvonne— were also excluded from the trusts. Christine and Yvonne, of course, would have larger shares of their grandfather's estate than the rest of their cousins. Their omission now from Anna's will would narrow the differences among the various grandchildren's inheritances.

And now, with Anna's death, Horace Sr.'s $48 million were to be divided into two equal parts for the heirs of the deceased daughter Delphine and son Horace. Delphine's $24 million share would go to her two daughters, Christine and Yvonne. Horace Jr.'s $24 million would be split five ways.

Anna's will donated Rose Terrace's music room, with its valuable art collection, to the Detroit Institute of Arts. An additional $1 million cash bequest provided for the care and housing of the music room, left as a memorial to Horace Sr. and herself. Another million-dollar bequest was made to Detroit's Children's Hospital for the construction and operation of a proposed new hospital with one floor to be known

as the Anna and Horace E. Dodge floor. A $2 million bequest was to
go to the City of Detroit for the construction of a fountain—the
Horace E. Dodge and Son Fountain—at the riverfront.

Anna left a total of $378,000 to employees, relatives, and friends,
including Delphine's former husband—James H. R. Cromwell;
Horace's former wives—Lois Knowlson and Mickey Devine; and Jim
Ranger and Robert Petz, husbands of two granddaughters.
Remembering her niece Ella, just as she had during her lifetime,
Anna provided an income for both Ella and the niece's invalid
daughter. To other grandnieces and grandnephews, as well as sons
and daughters of friends, Anna left varying amounts "for college expenses."

In addition, Anna's long-time friend and companion, Florence
Sisman, was remembered with $50,000, plus an annuity of $12,000
and the French chateau on the Riviera; while Florence's sister was
also given $12,000 a year for life.

Churches, hospitals, and Manlius Institute were remembered with
bequests in Anna's will, but the disposition of Rose Terrace and its art
treasures was not mentioned. Before her death, Anna had tried to
donate the estate and its contents to the City of Detroit, but was rebuffed when she would not set aside $10 million as an endowment for its
upkeep. After watching the demolition of her beloved Playa Riente in
Florida, the doughty Anna had no taste for solving the problem of
Rose Terrace. She simply avoided the question of what was to become
of the mansion and its vast treasury: the vaults of lace, jade, silver, and
jewels; furniture constructed by craftsmen who made the finest objects in Western civilization's history; the expanses of Beauvais
tapestry; of Gainsborough, Joshua Reynolds, and Fragonard
paintings; the wide sweep of Aubusson carpets. She had tried to escape her fears of the wrecker's ball turning into rubble her dreams of
royal grandeur, tinged with ghosts of Catherine of Russia, Marie
Antoinette, Madame de Pompadour, Tallyrand, and King George III.

Anna had realized, long before her death, that none of the Dodge
grandchildren could afford to keep up her Rose Terrace. She had
known that her manner of life had become obsolescent—very wealthy
people were electing widely different lives from that demanded by
Rose Terrace, its current value fixed at $6.5 million for insurance pur-
poses and its contents at another $6 million. Taxes, utilities, and in-
surance totaled $100,000 a year, and the expenses of staffing the estate
were astronomical. In the single month before her death, Anna had
paid $1,624 in nursery and landscaping bills plus an additional $812
for lawn cutting. And the *Detroit News* had complained of "shock" at
seeing signs of "seediness" at Rose Terrace at that same time.

With no disposition of the estate provided for in Anna's will, Rose Terrace became part of her personal estate to be managed by its trustees. David Dodge, who had witnessed the demolition of Playa Riente with his grandmother, was emotionally and artistically appalled at the thought of Rose Terrace coming to a similar end.

But the problems of settling the Dodge estates were only beginning. Within two months after Anna's death the legal battle lines were drawn for courtroom contests as two sets of contestants filed suits. According to Yvonne's and Christine's lawyers, Anna's will had come as a great shock to their two clients. The half-sisters insisted their grandmother had expected all her grandchildren to share in her *personal* estate. During one of the hearings, it was disclosed that both Christine and Yvonne had managed to borrow so heavily against their expected legacies that some 750 creditors, together with 150 lawyers, were claiming the larger part, if not all, of the anticipated inheritances.

From the time she had been old enough to sign a legal contract in 1944, Christine had been accumulating creditors. After her unsuccessful suit in 1955 against her grandmother's administration of her grandfather's estate, Christine had continued with her borrowing to subsidize her high standard of living, sometimes realizing as little as thirty cents on a borrowed dollar after paying finance charges for the loans. Some of these loans were sold, subsequently, to other creditors who accepted "shares" in her estate as collateral.

When Christine and her grandmother were reconciled in 1957, Christine also began receiving the income from the $1 million trust Anna had set up for her and for each of the grandchildren, designed to begin payment on their thirty-fifth birthdays. This was not enough for Christine who was again borrowing from other creditors. To prevent her granddaughter from seeking further expensive loans, Anna advanced her money to be paid back from Horace's estate . . . loans amounting to more than $1 million at Anna's death. But Anna's plan had not stopped Christine's borrowing, although the younger woman had attempted, some years previously, to set aside $9 million of her future inheritance in trust for herself and her children.

When Yvonne followed Christine's pattern, Anna acknowledged defeat. She loaned the younger woman pearls and Gray House—all of which were to be charged against Yvonne's legacy from her grandfather's estate. Still, Yvonne visited the banks for additional loans. The summer after Anna's death, Yvonne's creditors came forward too. Estate administrators reported that Yvonne had borrowed some $6.5 million from her grandmother and $1.3 million from Detroit Bank and Trust Company for loans dating back to 1954, plus other assorted loans.

When the executors of the estate found that Christine's list of creditors filled seventy-four pages, they requested a decision from the court. Was fraud or coercion present in any of the loans? Were many of the loans usurious and therefore illegal? Or had she intentionally set up the loans in this fashion to avoid eventual payment? The court was asked to rule on the legality of the $9 million trust that Christine had set up for herself and her children. If the fund was legal, only a small part of her inherited millions would be available to settle the millions claimed in debts.

Christine's lawyer, trying to establish the legality of the trust fund, insisted that his client had arranged for the fund before most of the loans had been made. Her creditors, he added, knew of the trust and understood that the sum involved could not be claimed by them. But with the diminishing of their expectations of receiving fortunes from their grandfather's estate, Christine and Yvonne focused their hopes on their grandmother's personal fortune, trying to break her will. They were joined by Gregg Dodge Moran, who sued also on behalf of her son John.

Suits also were filed in behalf of two long-time employees of the Dodges who had given the family a total of seventy years of service. Horace Jr. had left bequests to these employees in his will, but the bequests had not been honored because his estate had no funds to cover them. Although Anna, in her will, had ordered her family to see that all her bequests were paid even if money had to be taken from their grandfather's estate, she had not honored her son's bequests during her lifetime nor in her will.

The will contestants based their claims on their assertions that Anna, who was ninety-one to ninety-five years old during the years her will was written, "lacked mental competency or capacity." And while neither Horace's nor Anna's estates could be distributed until the hundreds of suits were settled, the court gave permission to the estate to pay debts it considered legitimate and to distribute the bequests Anna had made to the city.

The executors then initiated plans to sell Anna's personal property, choosing Christie's of London as an auction house. The most important pieces of Anna's collection would be sent by air freight to London, while objects of less value would be auctioned from the Grosse Pointe estate.

In December, Christie's closed up shop in London and brought its staff to Rose Terrace to appraise Anna's belongings. Nothing escaped the auctioneer's label. The rare jewel cabinet made by eighteenth-century craftsman Martin Carlin for Maria, Empress of Russia. The table of Catherine II of Russia. Marie Antoinette's monumental candelabra from the Palace at Versailles. The two enormous paintings Madame du Pompadour had commissioned for her King Louis' birthday. The priceless, gloriously colored porcelains, laid over rare wood, ornamented with ormolu and bronze and fired with a layer of gold at the edges.

The relentlessly efficient staff of Christie's listed "a gentleman's gold wrist watch (winding button missing) engraved *Horace December 25, 1937.*" A set of paper wastebaskets was assessed, hopefully, for $20.

When the appraising was done, Rose Terrace's music room furnishings were moved to the Detroit Institute of Arts. Some 700 pieces of furnishings and art objects were packed and shipped to London to be auctioned in late June 1972 in a $5 million sale.

The Dodge auction prices provoked a national controversy led by a surly *Time* magazine essay. The essay focused on the purchase, by Iranian oilman Henri Sabat, of the companion piece of the Martin Carlin cabinet now owned by the Detroit Institute of Arts—a Louis XVI tulipwood table embellished by Sevre porcelain plaques. The purchase price was $415,800. *Time* referred to the "spindly, exquisite and useless object" as the most expensive piece of furniture in history. The price of the table, the magazine pointed out, would support 1,260,000 Iranian families for a year.

The backlash of the sale was felt also in Detroit where Detroit Institute of Arts' officials were criticized for spending a sizable portion of Anna's $1 million cash bequest on more of Dodge treasures at the London auction. The Institute's art curator, outbid for the Carlin table he had wanted, purchased, instead, $336,000 worth of other Dodge baubles at the auction—two Louis XVI torchieres and two terra cotta sculptures. The Mr. and Mrs. Horace E. Dodge Gallery was opened to the public at the Detroit Institute of Arts that autumn.

At Rose Terrace, preparations had continued for the auction, in September 1972, of the last of Anna's personal belongings. The auction would be preceded by a four-day preview of the mansion and of the articles to be sold. On the day for the first public preview, people began lining up, four abreast, outside the great iron gates emblazoned with the Dodge coat of arms.

One of the auctioneers, with many European and English castle sales behind him, declared he had seen nothing to compare with the crowds at Rose Terrace for the preview. "It's what would happen if a free tour of Buckingham Palace were offered in London," he marveled. But this tour was not free. And yet thousands came, paying their few dollars admission, simply to stand for a few minutes in the footprints of the Dodges.

The spirit of Anna still hovered about the mansion, even though the rooms were filled with glass cases crowded with rows of jade, porcelain, and jewelry. People upended Anna's chairs, peered through her crystal, ran their hands over her gold plates—all tagged with the auctioneer's lot numbers. Romantics among the visitors were perturbed to discover that Dillman's suite was entirely separate from Anna's. They were mollified to find that Anna's suite contained an elaborate bed, however, with headboards carved with rosettes and scrolling foliage and upholstered in pale blue silk damask. Overall, rose silk damask curtains were draped regally. The curtains were fringed and tasseled, lined and interlined, and were suspended from a giltwood crown.

Visitors, for an instant, were imaginary queens, luxuriating in the sign of Anna's bath—carved from a single piece of rose Carrerra marble and large enough to bathe a Volkswagen. Even her commode chair was elaborate, carved and cane-paneled of Louis XV design.

With the end of the four days of preview, Christie's staff stripped Rose Terrace's rooms and moved everything portable to the tent and grounds in readiness for the auction. Admission to the sale was by catalog only—the catalog priced at $8 and admitting two people.

A thousand wooden folding chairs had been piled underneath the huge auction tent. Sound systems and telephone lines had been installed, and a television connection had been made between the tent and the city auditorium. Bowing to prospective buyers' more fundamental needs, sale officials had placed a pair of bright blue Porta-Johns between the house and the tent. Visitors arrived from Rome, London, Hong Kong, and various cities. One California businessman had spent $74 acquiring his catalog—having had a Western Union messenger pick up the book in Detroit, take it by taxi to Metropolitan Airport, and put it on a flight to San Jose.

Auction day dawned, bleak and sunless. A damp chill penetrated the lakeside area. A gray funereal shroud of fog rose from the lake and wrapped itself over the Rose Terrace estate as the boats passed ghostlike at the foot of the mist-veiled terraces. Their mournful dirges echoed into the fog.

The exclusivity and elegance that had marked every affair at Rose Terrace were ignominiously routed this morning as hordes of determined-looking matrons squashed through the mud to scramble for front seats in the tent. Fastidious lawyers in toe-rubbers guided eager clients around puddles. Tire-kicking car buffs swarmed over the collection of Dodge automobiles, while art dealers, museum directors, and private collectors greeted acquaintances with wary cordiality.

As the 1,000 seats were filled, auctioneers began their work in crisp and polished British accents. "I have $500 offered. Will someone improve on that? . . . The bid is against you, sir. . . . Sorry madam, the bid is in $50 increments."

One of the first items auctioned, the Goutier statue of Venus and Cupid appraised at $2,500, set the pattern for the bidding, bringing in $11,000. Twelve eighteenth-century chairs sold for $16,000. A battered dollhouse, valued at $100, sold for four times that much. Bidding continued to be good-natured but excited as prices escalated. Texan Lamar Hunt casually strode into the tent, bid $3,200 for a marble table, told Christie's to "ship it," and strode back out. Climaxing the Dodge mania, a desperate Bloomfield Hills woman bid $70 for a wastebasket set.

For three days, the auctioneer orchestrated the sale, using a long red baton to direct the cadence of the bidding. And while the bidding rose and fell inside the tent, Gustave—Anna's oldest employee—watched over the dissolution of all he had spent a lifetime nurturing. He circled the tent repeatedly, stumbling over wires from national television cameras as he walked, keeping his anxious vigil over the death throes of the Rose Terrace he had helped construct forty-one years earlier.

After the last sale was gaveled, a Christie's representative marveled that he had "never had a sale before in which every lot was sold." Spectators lingered to arrange for the transportation of their Dodge memorabilia. When they finally turned to leave, their departure was accompanied by the lugubrious, grinding cacophony of the overloaded Porta-Johns' contents being pumped out into disposal tanks.

Although the auction at Rose Terrace had concluded with a flourish, it appeared that the $2 million bequest for construction of a Dodge fountain in Detroit threatened to become a courtroom issue. The fountain plan had been initiated some years previously when the mayor of Detroit and the editor of the *Detroit News* had decided that a focal point was needed for the new riverfront development that was in the planning. They wanted something as distinctive as New York's Empire State Building, St. Louis' Arch, or Chicago's Calder sculpture. When they took their idea for a fountain to Anna Dodge, she had been convinced by their arguments that the fountain would stand out as the centerpiece in the whole waterfront renaissance.

The fountain plans began to take shape soon after Anna's death, along with the new waterfront project—Renaissance Center—that was to bring a rebirth to the city. David Dodge was fired with enthusiasm at the thought of a Dodge fountain for Detroit. As an

architect, he devoted months of his time to the preparation of a fountain design that he thought of as both outstandingly beautiful and
practical. Since David also served on the mayor's committee that was
to oversee the project until its completion, he was disappointed when
he discovered the city had decided to give the fountain contract to
architect Isamu Noguchi before David had had an opportunity to present his own plans. He was even more disappointed when he discovered that the fountain site had been set up some thirty feet from the
foot of Woodward, thereby removing the memorial from the focal
point agreed upon and stipulated in Anna's will.

When an attempt to work things out privately with city officials
failed, the disagreement was thoroughly aired in the newspapers. The
generous $2 million gift, given at the request of the city, was made to
appear as an attempt to turn the riverfront plaza into an outsized
memorial to the Dodge family.

The legal hassle over the distribution of the Dodge fortune still
continued. It promised to stretch on indefinitely as lawyers and judges
tried to work out the financial tangles complicating the dividing of Anna's millions. But the division of Horace Sr.'s remaining millions
would guarantee a legacy for the youngest grandchild of them all—
John Francis, son of Gregg and Horace Jr. The money apparently assured the young man, now a student at the University of Arizona, his
place among the young set of Beautiful People. For John's nineteenth-
birthday celebration, Caroline Kennedy and her cousin, Sydney Law-
ford, were among the twenty dinner guests at the Morans' Palm
Beach home. There was no foreshadowing, at that time, of the financial difficulties that would finally involve Daniel and Gregg Moran, in
1978, in a charge of procuring a loan from a bank under false
pretenses . . . a charge that Moran found so depressing that he would
shoot himself.

Delphine Petz and her brother Horace III had remained un-
touched by the legal maneuverings; they continued to live the quiet,
productive, family-centered existences they had established early in
their lives. Their half-brother David had settled, with his wife and
baby son, into a modest home in Switzerland, the entire cost of which
was less than the amount his grandmother had spent for a year's taxes
on her Palm Beach mansion. The sandy-haired David of polished
speech and manner had the rich man's hearty respect for the fortune
that Horace Sr. left him. But he was able to consider the wealth with
the perspective of a man who had found security in the love of a wife
and a child and in the enjoyment of his architectural work. The
trauma of an unhappy childhood had left its mark on his sister Diana.
She was wary of human relationships and satisfied to expend her af-

fection on her Arabian horses and thoroughbreds. After inheriting her money, she gave up her computer work and expended her energies in building her stables and in fox-hunting across the Virginia countryside.

The affection in which the grandchildren held Anna's memory refuted the gossip projecting the grandmother as unloving, stingy, tyrannical. And each of the grandchildren had always known that no matter how outrageous the behavior might be of anyone of her family, Anna Dodge never abandoned anyone she loved.

The grandchildren who had found ways to get their money in spite of Anna's protective withholding were disadvantaged by their own efforts. Christine, pursuing her claim to her protected trust fund through the courts, lost the first round when Detroit Judge Kaufman concluded, "It would be a fraud any way you look at it, if you set up a trust, and people buy an interest and can't get their money." Christine did not accept this verdict. Her lawyers promptly planned appeal strategies, suggesting that each of the 700 stockholders, some of whom had died since lending the money, might have to prove each case on an individual basis. Since these tactics would stretch the proceedings out for years, the entire inheritance continued to be held by the estate administrators. The desperate idea that Christine and Yvonne had fastened on in boarding school—if they distributed enough money, somehow it would buy them affection—had shadowed the sisters into adulthood. Now, more than thirty years later, an overweight, fiftyish Christine was still looking for love . . . and still a victim of tragedy. In 1974, her teenaged son John drowned while sailing alone in a small boat.

Her younger, gentle half-sister Yvonne had about her too the scent of the victim. Prodded by debtors and those who hoped to enrich themselves at her expense, Yvonne pursued her suit against her cousins through the courts.

Although newspaper stories persevered in portraying Yvonne locked in combat with the rest of the grandchildren over Anna's legacy, her cousins retained the same kind of objective attitude that Anna had evidenced during previous lawsuits. David smiled indulgently and said that because his cousin Yvonne used money at such a terrible rate, she really needed it more than he. While the court hearings went on, David continued to value his friendship with Yvonne, whom he considered a sister. The only one closer to him, apart from his wife and baby, was Diana. Opposing lawyers, afraid their cases might be upset, were amazed at the warm friendship among their clients. "It's only money," David told them with a shrug of his shoulders, "and I don't care that much about it."

He cared very much, though, about the disposition of beautiful Rose Terrace. The Detroit Boat Club considered purchasing the mansion, but their plans dissolved when Grosse Pointe Farms officials refused to change the zoning regulations. The great house stood, stripped and barren, with only a few servants remaining to provide a minimum of upkeep. Representatives from Paramount Pictures made a request of the Dodge estate administrators for permission to rent Rose Terrace to film a remake of "The Great Gatsby," but permission was refused, and the great halls of the Versailles-like palace echoed nothing but emptiness. In despair, David Dodge envisioned Rose Terrace being razed. "I know the labor and love that have gone into this house. . . . It just can't be crashed and crunched up," he protested. "It's not just Mammá's history, but a treasure in itself . . . a fine example of Louis architecture, built to last." His mild blue eyes sparked with indignation. "Grosse Pointe will be punished if it allows Rose Terrace's destruction," he insisted.

For a time, it seemed there was hope for Rose Terrace. City officials gave permission for a zoning change that would permit alteration of the huge chateau into luxury condominium apartments, with additional condominiums to be built on the grounds—9.17 acres of the most valuable land in the city.

For two years, the condominium apartments remained only in the planning stage as the land-developing company failed to exercise its option. Then, the plans were scrapped as being impractical for the changing market in real estate.

In 1976, Rose Terrace was partly dismantled just before the wrecker's ball smashed the empty mansion into a pile of litter and debris. Ironically, the demolishing of the beautiful home and Detroit landmark occurred in the bicentennial year when the preservation of historical buildings was being promoted. With the wrecking of the mansion, nothing remained on the shores of Lake St. Clair of Horace and Anna Dodge's dream of regal splendor.

Books

Anderson, Rudolph E., *The Story of the American Automobile*. Public Affairs Press, 1950

Automobile Manufacturers Association, Inc., *Automobiles of America*. Wayne State University Press, 1970

Ballard, Ralph, *Tales of Early Niles*. Fort St. Joseph History Association.

Bernard, Harry. *Independent Man: The Life of Senator James Couzens*. Scribner's Sons, 1958.

Beasley, Norman, & Stark, George, *Made in Detroit*. Putnam's Sons, 1957.

Bingay, Malcolm. W., *Detroit Is My Home Town*. Bobbs Merrill, 1946.

Cleveland, Reginald M., and Williams, S. T., *The Road Is Yours*. Greystone Press, 1951.

Chrysler, Walter P., *Life of an American Workman*, Curtis, 1938.

Cromwell, James H. R., *The Voice of Young America*. Scribner's Sons, 1933.

Detroit Public Library, *Detroit In Its World Setting*. 1953.

Donovan, Frank, *Wheels For A Nation*. Thomas Y. Crowell, 1965.

Glazer, Sidney, *Detroit, A Study in Urban Development*. Bookmen Associates, 1965.

Hill, Frank Ernest, *The Automobile: How It Came, Grew and Has Changed Our Lives*. Dodd, Mead & Company, 1967.

A History of Berrien and Van Buren Counties, Michigan. D. W. Ensign & Co., publishers, n.d.

Leland, Mrs. Wilfred C., *Master of Precision: Henry M. Leland*. Wayne State University Press, 1966.

Lewis, Eugene, *Motor Memories*. Alved Publishers, 1947.

Lodge, John, *I Remember Detroit*. Wayne University Press, 1949.

MacManus, Theodore F., *Men, Money, Motors*. Harpers, 1929.

Miller, James Martin, *Amazing Story of Henry Ford*. 1922.

Musselman, M. M., *Get A Horse*. Lippincott, 1950.

Nevins, Allen, *Ford: The Times, The Man, The Company*. Scribner's Sons, 1954.

Niemeyer, Glenn A., *The Automotive Career of Ransom E. Olds*. Michigan State University, 1963.

Pound, Arthur, *Detroit, Dynamic City*. Appleton-Century, 1940.

Quaife, M. M., *This Is Detroit*. Wayne University Press, 1951.

Rae, John B., *The American Automobile: A Brief History*. University of Chicago Press, 1965.

Rae, John B., *American Automobile Manufacturers*. Chilton Company, 1959.

Richards, H. F., *The Last Billionaire*. Scribners, 1948.

Sann, Paul, *The Lawless Decade*. Bonanza Books, 1957.

Sinsabaugh, Christopher G., *Who Me?* Arnold-Powers, Inc., 1940.

Sloan, Alfred P. Sloan, Jr., *Adventures of a White-Collar Man*. Doubleday, 1940.

Smith, Philip Hillyer, *Wheels Within Wheels*. Funk and Wagnalls, 1968.

Stark, George W., *In Old Detroit*. Arnold-Powers, 1939.

Sward, Keith, *Legend of Henry Ford*. Russell and Russell, 1948.

Periodicals

American Weekly, January 13, 1926.

Antique Automobile, Vol. 28-29.

The Automobile, December 23, 1915.

Automobile Topics, December 18, 1920, and others.

Automotive Industries, January 21, 1926.

The Club-Fellow, December 16, 1925, Cline Collection.

The Club Woman, March, 1925 and others (Magazine of Detroit Federated Women's Clubs).

Country Life Magazine, November, 1917, Cline Collection.

DAC News (Detroit Athletic Club) Cline Collection and Burton Historical Collection, Detroit Public Library.

Detroit Boat Club News, 1928.

Detroit Historical Society Bulletin, Fall, 1968 and others.

Detroit Saturday Night, Detroit society magazine, March 20, 1915 and others. Cline Collection and Burton Historical Collection.

Estep, H. Cole, "How The Dodge Plant Was Reorganized," *Iron Trade Review*.

The Horseman, February 16, 1972.

Impressario Magazine, October, 1965 and others.

The Literary Digest, April 25, 1925.

Michigan Manufacturer and Financial Record, December 18, 1920 and others.

Motor Age, April, 1916 Chrysler Archives.

Newsweek, June 11, 1973.

Pacific Motor Boat Magazine, Cline Collection.

The Valve World, Cline Collection.

"Who Needs Masterpieces at Those Prices," *Time*, July 19, 1971 and April 3, 1972.

Newspapers

Chicago Herald Examiner, December 6, 1935.

Detroit Evening News, October 4, 1901, and others.

Detroit Evening Times, October 10, 1935, and others.

Detroit Free Press, 1901 to present.

Detroit News, 1901 to present.

Detroit Times, 1903-60.

Niles Daily Star, March 24, 1936, and others.

New York Tribune, January 7, 1917.

Oakland Observer, October 22, 1967, and all.

Orion Review, May 12, 1933 and others.

Pontiac Press, December 21, 1926, and others.

Rochester Clarion, July 1, 1953, and others.

Rochester Era, Cline Collection.

Royal Oak Tribune, September 21, 1967, and others.

Walkerton Herald Times, August 18, 1938 (Cline Collection).

Public Records and Collections

Anna Thomson Dodge Will and Estate Papers, Wayne County Probate Court, Detroit. File 605, 322.

Matilda R. Wilson Will and Estate Papers, Oakland County Probate Court, Pontiac. File 94, 140.

Alfred Wilson Will and Estate Papers, Oakland County.

Frances Dodge Van Lennep Will and Estate Papers, Wayne County Circuit Court, File 612, 953.

Silver Brook Cemetery, Niles, Michigan Records.

Woodlawn Cemetery Records, Detroit.

Niles, Michigan School Records.

Detroit, Michigan School Records.

Niles Public Library files on *Dodge*.

Niles Historical Museum.

Burton Historical Genealogical Records.

Oakland University, Kresge Library.

King Collection, Beecroft Papers, Detroit Public Library.

Automotive Collection, Detroit Public Library.

Census records, Van Buren County, City of Port Huron, Michigan.

National Archives, military service and pension records.

Birth, death, marriage and divorce records in Scotland, Ontario, California, Michigan, Kentucky, Florida.

"Echoes of Splendor," TV special on Rose Terrace.

Meadow Brook Hall TV special.

Interviews

Brandt, John. Employee in the Dodge Brothers' shop during early years of Dodge car production

Brooks, Marilyn. Head of volunteers at Meadow Brook Hall

Bunnell, John, E. Head of Corporate Identity, Chrysler Corp.

Cline, Amelia Rausch. A series of more than twenty-five extensive interviews took place with the sister of Matilda Dodge Rausch Wilson in preparation for this book. Employed by Dodge Brothers in the firm's early days with Ford, she has memories of their associations and has shared all her personal recollections, papers, family portraits, and other memorabilia with the writers. She was part of the company during the time the Dodge car was developed. She lived with John and Matilda most of their married life, so was a witness to their personal life also.

Dodge, David. Anna Dodge's grandson and family spokesman. The second son of Horace Jr.

Du Mouchelle, Ernest. Owner of one of Detroit's finest galleries of art objects. Matilda Dodge was a life-long customer; he was familiar with her collection and buying habits. He ultimately auctioned off much of her personal belongings.

Donlin, Vera. Secretary to the Wilsons and daughter Frances Dodge Van Lennep for thirty years.

Ecklund, Lowell. Dean, Oakland University. Worked with Matilda Dodge Wilson in founding the university on her estate. Presently manages Meadow Brook Hall estate for the university.

Fox, Mary. Anna Dodge's nurse in later years.

Gensler, Marvin. Employee of the Gregory Boat Works that serviced the Dodge yachts and boats.

Gregory, Ed. Owner of the Gregory Boat Works.

Henkle, Lou. Watchman at Rose Terrace, Anna Dodge's estate.

Kerbrat, Frank. For many years, has worked as superintendent of Rose Terrace.

Knapp, Joseph. Former Director University Relations, Oakland University. Also former Chrysler Corporation employee.

Leland, Mrs. Wilfred. Wife of Wilfred and daughter-in-law of Henry Leland, associates of the Dodges and manufacturers of the Lincoln and the Cadillac.

Love, Mary (Mrs. John G.) Anna's sister-in-law. The sister of Anna's second husband, Hugh Dillman.

McKinven, Robert. Grandson of Anna Dodge's sister, Catherine.

Milligan, Thelma Banta. Worked for Frances Dodge in her stables; later for Matilda Dodge Wilson at Meadow Brook Hall switchboard.

Nilson, Anne Marie. Social acquaintance of Matilda Dodge Wilson.

Schearer, Donald. Archivist, Chrysler Corporation

Sisman, Florence. Related by marriage to the Dodges. Closest confidante of Anna Dodge in later years.

Smith, Marion Gray. Richard and Barbara Wilson's tutor and governess at Meadow Brook Hall.

Standish, Marion Coburn. Personal secretary to Anna Dodge for 30 years.

Upton, Mrs. Frank. Wife of accountant for Dodge Brothers' Corporation. Also took charge of the personal business for both brothers, and later for Anna and Matilda.

Van Lennep, Frederick. Husband of Frances Dodge, John Dodge's daughter. Delegated his secretary to provide information.

Von Buelow, Ella. Anna Dodge's niece. Daughter of Anna's sister, May McNutt.

Whittaker, Beatrice. Matilda's personal maid.

Wilson, Richard. Son of Matilda Dodge Wilson and Alfred Wilson.

Zoll, Catherine McKinven. Granddaughter of Anna's sister, Catherine.

Booklets and Pamphlets

Rose Terrace Auction Catalogue, Christie, Manson and Woods with McNierney, Stalker and Boos, Inc.

Matilda Dodge Wilson Estate Auction Booklet. Du Mouchelle Art Galleries, December 9, 1971.

Dau's Blue Book. Detroit Society Blue Book, 1904 and on. Burton Historical Collection, Detroit Public Library.

Brochure announcing Dodgeson Car, January, 1926. Automotive History Collection, Detroit Public Library.

Smith and Mobleys Second Book of Valuable Information for Automobilists. Automotive History Collection, July, 1903.

Detroit Street Traffic Ordinances, 1917

Rules of the Road. Automotive History Collection, Detroit Public Library. 1906.

A History of Dodge 1914—1964. Chrysler Corporation, May, 1972.

A Pictorial History of Chrysler Corporation Cars. Chrysler Corporation, Engineering Office, Technical Information. 1968.

The Chrysler Corporation Story. Community Affairs Department, Chrysler Corporation.

Restorers Guide. Historical Collection Department, Chrysler Corporation, 1973.

Also many pamphlets and brochures published by Dodge Brothers which are in the private collections of Amelia Rausch Cline and in the collections of Matilda Dodge Wilson at Meadow Brook Hall.

Minutes of the Ford Motor Company Board of Directors' meetings, October 13, 1903, and others. Ford Motor Company archives.

Annual Reports, Ford Motor Company, 1904 and others. Ford Motor Company Archives

Fairlane Papers, Box 116, Ford Motor Company Archives.

General References

Marquis, Albert Nelson, *The Book of Detroiters*, 1908.

Burton, *City of Detroit*.

The Complete Encyclopedia of Motor Cars 1885—1968. Edited by B. N. Georgano, E. P. Dutton and Co., 1968.

Cowles, B., *Berrien County Directory and History*, 1871, Niles, Michigan.

Detroit City Directories, 1870 to present.

Groves, W. W., *An Atlas of Berrien County from Surveys and County Records*. Rand McNally, 1877.

Luedders' City Directory. Niles, Michigan.

The National Cyclopaedia of American Biography. J. T. White, 1937.

New York Times Obituary Index.

Private Collections and Documents

Chrysler Archives.

Detroit News Archives.

Meadow Brook Hall—Matilda Dodge Wilson's estate and most of its contents were given to Oakland University. The writers had access to Matilda's collection of sixty years: recipes, family photos, diaries, letters, journals, company papers, mechanical drawings, books, bills, school papers, newspaper clippings, etc.

Amelia Rausch Cline—the sister of Matilda Dodge Wilson worked in the office of Dodge Brothers during its first fifteen years. She has saved a vast collection of memorabilia, from her first report cards to newspapers and magazines carrying mention of the Dodge name. She has shared this collection, plus her memories of the Dodge family, with the writers.

Index

HORACE ELGIN DODGE

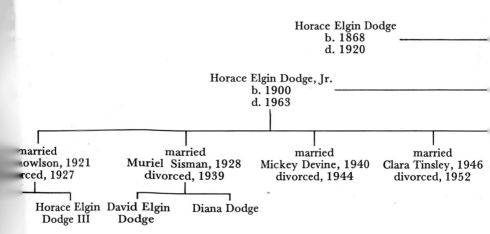

Horace Elgin Dodge
b. 1868
d. 1920 ——————————

Horace Elgin Dodge, Jr.
b. 1900
d. 1963 ——————————

married
owlson, 1921
ced, 1927

married
Muriel Sisman, 1928
divorced, 1939

married
Mickey Devine, 1940
divorced, 1944

married
Clara Tinsley, 1946
divorced, 1952

Horace Elgin
Dodge III

David Elgin
Dodge

Diana Dodge

Lois K
div

Delphine
Dodge